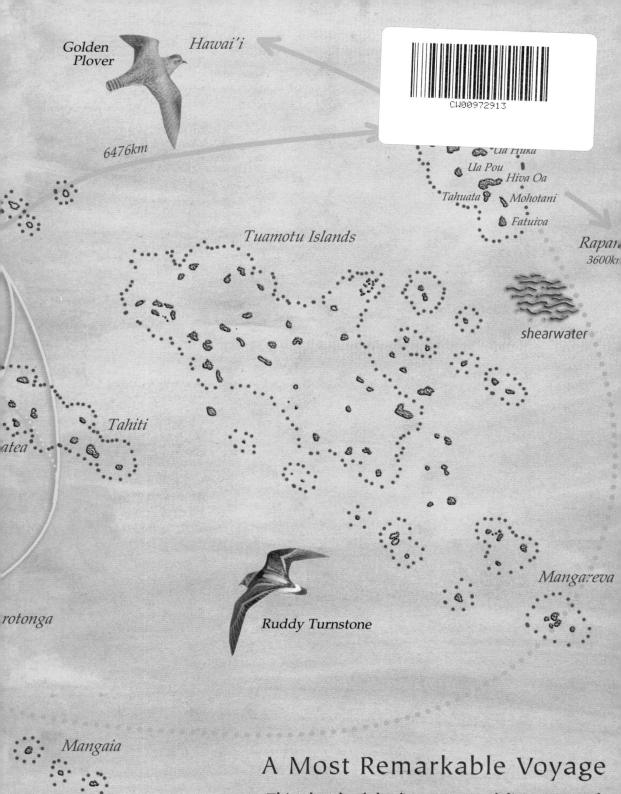

Golden
Plover

Hawai'i

6476km

Tuamotu Islands

Ua Huka

Ua Pou

Hiva Oa

Tahuata

Mohotani

Fatuiva

Rapa

3600km

shearwater

atea

Tahiti

Ruddy Turnstone

Mangareva

rotonga

Mangaia

A Most Remarkable Voyage

This sketch of the first voyage of discovery and
settlement of Fenua'enata (The Marquesas) from
Hava'iki (Homeland) two thousand years ago was
created by Emily Brissenden.

Rapa

The Miegunyah Press

This is number fifty-three in the
second numbered series of the
Miegunyah Volumes
made possible by the
Miegunyah Fund
established by bequests
under the wills of
Sir Russell and Lady Grimwade.

'Miegunyah' was the home of
Mab and Russell Grimwade
from 1911 to 1955.

REVIEW COPY:
Beach Crossings
Voyaging across times, culture and self
Greg Dening

Hardback $49.95, July 2004
THE MIEGUNYAH PRESS

For further details contact:
Susan Hornbeck, Publicist
Melbourne University Publishing
Tel: 03 9342 0319
Email: hornbeck@unimelb.edu.au

www.mup.com.au

BEACH CROSSINGS

Voyaging across times,
cultures and self

GREG DENING

THE MIEGUNYAH PRESS

THE MIEGUNYAH PRESS
An imprint of Melbourne University Publishing Ltd (MUP Ltd)
PO Box 1167, Carlton, Victoria 3053, Australia
mup-info@unimelb.edu.au
www.mup.com.au

First published 2004
Text © Greg Dening 2004
Design and typography © Melbourne University Publishing Ltd 2004

National Library of Australia Cataloguing-in-Publication entry

Dening, Greg, 1931– .

 Beach crossings: voyaging across times, cultures and self.

 Bibliography.
 Includes index.
 ISBN 0 522 84886 9.

 1. Navigation, Primitive—Oceania. 2. Indigenous peoples—
Oceania. 3. Oceania—Discovery and exploration. 4. Oceania—
Description and travel. 5. Oceania—History. I. Title.

910.9164

For our son
Jonathan
A Memorial
He never knew us
His crossing was too brief

Contents

Illustrations

Prologue
A Most Remarkable Voyage

About two thousand years ago—perhaps three hundred years more or three hundred years less—there occurred the most remarkable voyage of discovery and settlement in all human history. A va'a tauna, a double-hulled canoe, leaves a cluster of islands in the western Pacific. Later descendants of this settlement voyage would call those islands Hava'iki, Homeland. They were the islands of Samoa, Tonga and Fiji. The va'a tauna sails on a northeast tack across open sea. This takes it to the north and beyond the many islands of the central Pacific as yet uninhabited but which we know as Tahiti and the stretch of seventy atolls of the Tuamotu that spread umbrella-like across the eastern entry of the Pacific. After 4000 miles they land and make their home on islands which the Spaniards in 1595 will call The Marquesas. The descendants of these first settlers call their islands Fenua'enata, The Land of the People.

Let me tell the story of this first beach crossing in the Land of the People. I tell the story with the certainty of my factual knowledge, the probabilities of my understanding and the possibilities of my interpretations. The story needs to be told. It belongs rightly to a people's identity and pride.

THE PLEIADES HAVE RISEN. The Mataiki—'Little Eyes'—are into the second of their four-month stay in the sky. The season of plenty is in harvest. The west winds are reaching further into the east against the prevailing north- and southeasterlies. The voyaging time has begun. They are well ready.

One hundred and fifty generations ready. Three millennia ready. For three thousand years this sea people has lived on the eastern edge of a forty millennia movement of people from the west down a corridor of islands

1

into the ocean they call Moana, the Great Ocean. For three thousand years this sea people has made a sea of islands their own. Samoa, Tonga and Fiji enclose that sea. The sea people sail the 1000-mile circuit of the sea and its 300-mile ocean stages with confidence. They trade. They raid. They adventure. They are blue-water sailors. Their bodies have responded to the sea's demand on them. They are the largest humans on earth. They are survivors in wet and cold. They are at home on the sea, day and night and in all seasons. They have learned that with the horizon all around them and a vessel in motion, the old land order no longer prevails. Night and day there must be someone responsible for all the tasks necessary to keep the vessel on its course. All the activities of living—sleeping, eating, working, playing— are on a different cycle at sea.

Above all, the millennia have given this sea people an artefact of cultural genius, their *va'a,* their canoe. Their *va'a* is a thing imprinted with millennia of experience as generations find the woods, the fibres, the resins that pull and strain, resist work fatigue and rotting, seal. Their *va'a* is a thing of very precise design—of curves that give strength, of asymmetric shapes that play wind and water against one another, of structured balances that avoid congestion of strain, of aerodynamics that free it to fly along the wind.

It is the way of such artefacts of cultural genius that the real genius lies in simplicity. For the *va'a* three things made it unique in the inventiveness of humankind in mastering the sea environment. A lug. A triangular sail. An outrigger. The lug, a projection on the inside of the hull, perforated so that cordage could be pulled through, makes it possible to compress all parts of the *va'a* together. The triangular sail, without masts or stay, pivoting on its head, held high by a prop, creates a self-steering vessel without need of rudder or pulleys. These days we see the windsurfers exploit its simplicity and speed. The outrigger on the windward side, fitted to the hull by means of the lug, gives stability and manoevrability. The double *va'a,* the *va'a tauna,* removed the need of the outrigger and by means of a platform over the two hulls, perhaps 12 feet wide and 40 feet long, allows the vessel to carry fifty to eighty people, a shelter, a sand fire-pit and cargo of up to 65,000 pounds.

With Mataiki's rising comes also Na Kao (Orion's brightest star) and 'Ana-Muri (The Follower of Pleiades). All these stars beckon to the northeast. In the west on the opposite horizon Metau-o Maui (Scorpius) and Maitiki (Sagittarius) are setting. So there is an arc of light over the corridor of warm waters to the northeast. The sea experts among them know every step and stage of that arc, especially the stars that stand in zenith over their Homeland. The zenith stars would be like beacons beckoning them back.

Through the millennia they had sailed eastward on exploring voyages for days, perhaps weeks, at a time, confident that the wind would bring them home. The southerly tack takes them to cooler waters, the northerly to warmer waters. The risks are less in the warm waters. When they make the decision to seek new lands to settle, they know that they will have to go farther than they had ever gone. That there is land out there to the east they are sure. Its signs are in the flotsam that comes to their shores. They are always confident that that they will make a landfall on that land to the east. The land-nesting birds and the myriad other birds will guide them, as will the phosphorescence beneath the surface in the lee of islands. Lagoon reflections in the clouds, shadows of islands in the ocean swells—there is land to the east and they are confident that one day they will reach it. They know the annual monsoonal cycles that drive the west winds. There are other cycles, also, every four or seven years. The temperature of the sea drops. Fish change their habits. Birds change their migratory lines. In these cycles the west winds win out more easily over the east winds. We call these seasons El Niño.

The *va'a tauna* for this voyage of discovery and settlement has a name. We don't know it. Let us call it *Vav'au* for its island of origin. It is to the island Vav'au in the Tongan group of islands that the people of the Land will want to return in the millennia to come. But this *va'a tauna* has got not just one name. It has many names, a name for each of the vessel's parts. 'That's my head', someone of power and wealth would have said of the bows, the sterns, the hulls and side planks of the two *va'a* that make their platform vessel. 'That part is sacred to me—*tapu*—and has my name.'

Those parts reside in the houses of those whose names they proclaim. The *va'a tauna* becomes a living whole when all its parts are assembled. And at that moment it becomes an icon of something else, of the group whose heads had come together in this founder's vessel. And in these heads is imprinted a genealogical past which reaches back to another founder.

Vav'au itself reaches back several generations. The living *temanu* trees (*Calophyllum inophylis*) from which the hulls and other parts of *Vav'au* is constructed had been dedicated and shaped by the fathers' fathers of those who sail it. As was the *mio* (*Thespesia populnea*) from which the forked sterns and bows and the stays and supports come. The *temanu*, sometimes 10 feet in diameter, gives *Vav'au* strength and size. The tensile properties of a tree under the stress and strains of weather for decades, even centuries, were a perfect preparation for whatever stresses the waves would put on it. Bark would be stripped in a long line on the weather side of the tree to make a scar whose knots would eventually strengthen the hulls. The *mio*, the sea people had long learned, is resistant to the rot of seawater and the creatures in it. *Toa*, ironwood, has the strength for masting; *purau* and bamboo, the lightness and flexibility for spars. Pandanus gives matting for sails. Hibiscus gives bark for lashing and the coconut sennit for lines. Their fibres are durable in seawater. They fill out when wet in the caulking. The breadfruit provides the gum for sealing.

Vav'au not only transports the founders of a new settlement. *Vav'au* is a founder in itself. Very few of the woods that made it could survive a sea crossing by themselves to the far eastern edges of Moana. So *Vav'au* carries the nuts, the seeds, the cuttings from which would eventually come all the voyaging canoes of Oceania.

There are two names from *Vav'au* that Enata remembered, Taipi and Teii, two brothers, probably two younger, later-born brothers. Perhaps they are the names of the two hulls of *Vav'au*.

We cannot say whether *Vav'au* was assembled and launched in haste in answer to some natural or social crisis, or whether there was calm, deliberate preparation for a new settlement. Archaeologists are doubtful that it is overpopulation that triggers the movement eastward. But they say as well that those three thousand years of the sea people in and on the edge of Hava'iki were characterised by a vigorous population growth. Therefore, a vigorous development of cultural roles and systems. Therefore, a vigorous exploitation of land and sea resources. Therefore, the likelihood of tensions among those whose birth order excluded them from access to all that a firstborn would inherit. Therefore, the gamble of adventure-voyaging to new lands was potentially more rewarding than staying home.

Let us say—because *Vav'au*'s cargo is so complete—that the voyage is begun less in crisis than with determined and planned intention. The motivations are not necessarily different whether there is a crisis or not. The sea people's histories, once they were established through Oceania, Near and Remote, are full of tensions created by a birth order that pushes younger sons into roles other than chieftainship which was the firstborn's right. The brothers Taipi and Teii are likely to have been younger sons. They will become chiefly by right of being founders. Then they will compete with one another.

We must make some presumptions about the crew of *Vav'au* and their number in our story. Let us say that there are four families and two male servants—ten adults and three or four children. One of the males is a *tuhuna pu'e*, a sea expert. One is a *toa*, warrior. One or more is a fisherman. They know that they will only survive in their new land on fish till their crops take hold. On a trip so dangerous, all the males have the skills and capacity to work the *va'a* in company—steering, paddling, sailing, repairing, bailing. The women bring their craft skills with them—bark-cloth making, weaving, food gathering and producing.

From the time its woods are dedicated, and its trees felled by fire, *Vav'au* is imprinted with memory and knowledge. The sea people manage every stage of its building—its first hollowing on the site of its years of growth, its cartage to the boat-building hangar, the carving of its keel and its asymmetric sides that gave it bite in the water against the wind, its polishing with sharkskin, its assembly and launching—with song, ceremony and exchange. The *atua*, the heroes of older voyaging times, were ever present in its making. Boat-builders, like farmers, are highly conservative in their problem resolution. Once a problem of speed into the wind is solved with sail or tampered hull; once a problem of stress and strain is solved with compressed and flexible parts; once a problem of preservation is solved with choices of wood and cordage—the solutions are passed on from generation to generation, from master to apprentice. The value of that knowledge is in its precision—it is learned with careful and long schooling—and in its secrecy—it belongs to the specialists who exchange it only in conditions of sacredness *(tapu)*. The mysteriousness of the knowledge that made the *va'a*, the exchange in *tapu* that bonded the *va'a*'s makers and the group who used it, made the *va'a* larger than itself.

The capital of cultural knowledge for generations to come is in the heads of these ten adults. No doubt they keep it alive with songs and recitals, with genealogical chants, with calls to their *atua* (gods) for assistance. We have to wonder how they coped with deaths and even newborn lives on the way.

Vav'au has a crew of ten and some children who will need to be cared for and protected. They must cater for a voyage of three or four weeks. They must have food and water for these weeks, some extra materials—lashing, matting, stays for replacement, and the tools to manage breakages. They must have bailers and paddles. They must have their domestic utensils of wood, stone and shell for the trip itself and then for their settlement. They will want to bring what is precious for them—their ornaments, their sacred things, their *tiki*, maybe even their houseposts. They will need all the roots, seeds, cuttings for their new island home— *tiare* slips, gourd seeds, bamboo shoots, *aue* roots, *aute* twigs, *temanu* nuts and many other green shoots and tubers.

We have a relic of this first voyage, found on the earliest site in The Land. It is perhaps the most remarkable archaeological find of the whole Pacific. It is a shard of reddish earthenware with characteristic geometric or dentate (toothed) design stamped into the wet clay before firing. Lapita, the pottery is called. Lapita pottery was an item of eager deep-sea trade in the Homeland. It was a luxury trade in its early years, then a more ordinary, everyday trade. We know it was a deep-sea trade because minerals specific to particular islands—such as obsidian on the Lo islands of the Fijis—are to be found in pottery in Samoa and Tonga, as were other geological items— chert and metavolcanic stone. There is Fijian obsidian to be found in this shard of Lapita pottery discovered where it was brought by *Vav'au* to Fenua'enata. That shard is surely an icon of Pacific seafaring. It is a symbol of the sea people's mastery of their environment. They travelled large distances to trade. They travelled vast distances to discover and settle.

Mei, the month of *Vav'au*'s departure on the west winds, is the month of abundance, the fruiting and harvesting season of the breadfruit tree. The sea people had learned a lesson they would take with them to the far east of their ocean. They could bank, in a season of plenty, on the abundance of their breadfruit against seasons of paucity. They could preserve their breadfruit as *ma*, a fermented paste. It would last for decades in pits in the ground, for months in cakes. They collect those cakes with their supplies for their voyage. They could dry and salt fish. They could keep octopus alive. They could catch flying fish attracted to their candlenut torches at night. They could keep a fire going in a sandbox. They could hold their water in bamboo containers and catch the rain with their matting. There would be a shelter that they would erect on their platform. There was room in the hulls of their two *va'a* to stash their cargo.

So some night in the month of Mei, when Mataiki, Nao Kao and 'Ana-Muri were rising, and Metau-o Maui and Maitiki were setting, when the west winds gave signs that they would last, *Vav'au* with its settlers and their cargo move beyond the reef into the open sea. It is an embarrassment for me, the storyteller, that I cannot say with certainty that the beach of *Vav'au*'s launching was in Samoa or Tonga. The island of Vav'au in the

Tongan group would be my choice. It further embarrasses me that I cannot say with certainty whether the direction of *Vav'au's* sailing is northeasterly or southeasterly. I say northeasterly more in hunch than in certainty. And I say it with some impatience. I know that in some future from now—what would it be? ten years?, twenty years?, thirty years?—archaeology might give me the answer. I cannot wait that long.

My story of *Vav'au* takes their settlement voyage on a northern loop to Fenua'enata, around the great island screen of the Tuamotu, and the central Tahitian islands that they screen. *Vava'u's* northerly voyage is 4000 miles. *Vav'au's* voyage in a southerly loop would be just as dramatic and just as long. My reason for choosing a northeasterly direction for *Vava'u's* voyage is that I am more comfortable with the proposition that *Vava'u's* voyage was preceded by exploratory voyaging in the warm northern waters than in the cool southeasterly waters.

As they set out, the crew of *Vav'au* must provide for the possibility that they will be thirty, maybe forty, nights at sea. Experience would have told them that the west winds aren't constant. Wind direction will fluctuate in a day's sailing. Inevitably for most of the time they will be sailing into or across the wind. They will be wet nearly all the time. They would have known that survival will mean maintaining their body heat, especially the women. Their body size will be their living capital. They will need daily to consume one-fiftieth of their weight to maintain their body heat.

If they set their course on the rising of Na Kao (Betelgeuse in Orion), 'Ana-Muri (Aldebran) and Mataiki (Pleiades), they move to the northeast. That will be the star setting for travel from Samoa to Pukapuka for the next two millennia. As they tack across the northeasterly trade wind that constantly returns, they inevitably move east-northeast. They are on a course that curves them to Fenua'enata. They get some small lift to the east on the equatorial counter-current. Their sea expert is on watch at dawn to see in the water shadows the overriding swell of the southern massive counter-clockwise circle of winds and currents that shapes the world's weather. Then they catch the breaks in the swell made by a chain of islands they will come to call Fenua'enata.

The *tuhuna* will be watching the sun coming north from its southern solstice, and nearing its zenith overhead in the weeks of their sailing. They will come to know the seasonal changes that the zenith brings with it, and the west winds that will drive them further in the season of the zenith in the last stages of their journey to their landing.

They land on the lee side of an island they will come to call Ua Huka. No doubt the myriad of seabirds on the islet near their landing finally attracts them there. It is a dry landscape that they see, but there is a stream and a beach to land on behind the rocky headlands. There is no reef. That will be their first surprise. They must become fishers in ways they had never been before. Perhaps some go looking for a better place to settle on an island they can see to the west. They will call it Nukuhiva. Perhaps this is the division that their later legends will tell them of—between Taipi and Teii.

The narrow valley behind the beach leads back to the heights of the island. In time they will fill the valley with their houses. But not now. Now they must stay near the beaches and the sea. Shellfish and seagreens are there in abundance. They can wade the waters of the bay and cast their nets. They have lines and hooks for fishing off the rocks. In these first days— months? years?—they are a gathering people over again. They will have disassembled *Vav'au*. Their *va'a tauna* is their lifeline, in their minds a means of escape, if their island proves more dangerous than it seems on their arrival. The island must have seemed barren. The basic foliage and undergrowth would have been familiar. Sea, wind and birds had brought most of it from further west than they had come. Already through the millennia these plant and insect voyagers had begun to fill all the niches in the environment in new ways and to make new island species. The settlers must have looked closely at it to make their old life out of new things. Women looked for their oils and seeds and resins and barks that would heal, comfort, ornament and clothe themselves and their children. The *tuhuna*, the experts, among them would have scavenged the vegetation for the materials of their crafts. No doubt, in the way of every migrant that ever was, their images of Hava'iki, their Homeland, grew greener and richer.

They build shelters, of course, round houses in imitation of what they had known at home. Their more squarish houses on stone floors, then stone platforms, would come later. They set the treasures they had brought with them in stores on the floors, walls and joists of their houses. Maybe the precious, prestigious Lapita pottery that had come so far was a shard already. It would stay where they put it for two thousand years, a sort of foundation stone for their new life.

There must have been some anxiety to see if the seedlings and cuttings they had brought with them would strike. Their taro they plant in the wetlands by the stream, the yams on the drier slopes. It would be many years before they turn to their pigs, dogs and fowl for subsistence.

The marvel of this first voyage is that the men and women who came on it had millennia of culture in their heads and in the small cargo of their *va'a tauna*, and they seed the millennia of culture to come, not just for Fenua'enata but for Hawai'i, Tahiti and Aotearoa (New Zealand) as well. That is the miracle of *Vav'au's* voyage. We are watching a cultural embryonic stem cell at work. In the minds and bodies of its ten adult crew is the cultural DNA of two millennia through all the Pacific.

So this most remarkable voyage of discovery and settlement is done. It humbles me as a storyteller that so much of its detail must be conditioned by my uncertainties. That must not force me into fiction. Fiction is too disrespectful of what these first people in the Land have achieved. Fiction is too disrespectful of the generations of archaeologists, anthropologists, linguists, historians and scholars of all descriptions who have helped us know what we know. Fiction is too disrespectul to the thousands of descendants of these first voyagers to the Land who by song, dance and story have clung to the historical truth that two thousand years ago, a hundred generations ago, their ancestors seeded Fenua'enata with a living spirit that they had brought across two thousand miles of sea. Besides such blue-water seamanship, the rest of the world are coasters.

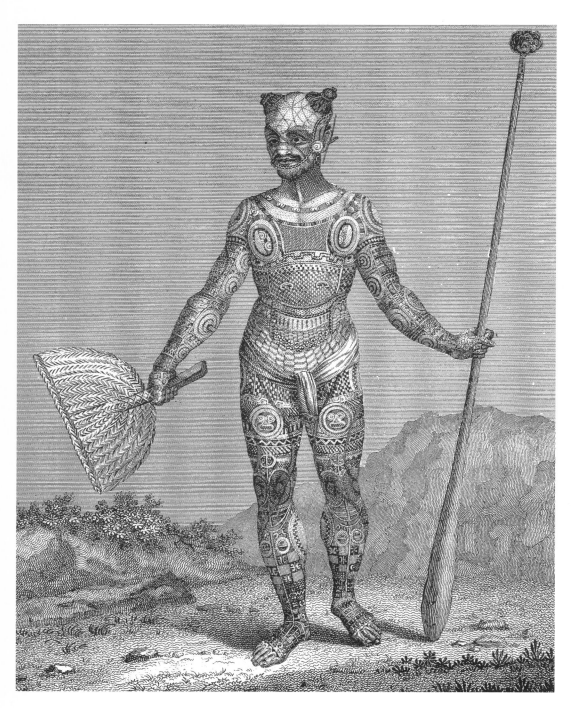

Pahutiki—'*Wrapped in Images*'

Beginning

All voyages, all stories of voyages, have a beginning. This is mine. Sometimes, for dramatic effect, stories of voyages begin at the end. Mine begins in-between. If I had a personal global positioning system, it would always place me there. In-between.

I AM AT THAT STAGE in life when the years to come seem too tidily numerable and the years that have gone too full of memories to let go. That is no excuse for a book, of course, but it may be an explanation for this one.

I have many stories to tell. Of myself and others. Of others, the stories are sad and awful, triumphant and celebratory. They span thousands of years broadly and a few short years, 1796–1814, intensely. Of myself, the stories are mostly happy, of wonderment and excitement at my privilege at being engaged in a life of learning. They span my last fifty years in this life of learning. It might seem self-indulgent to bind these stories of self and others together. It probably is. But all writing—and reading for that matter—is self-indulgent. There is more to it than that. Let me tell my first story to show it.

Some years ago, a friend called me excitedly from South Africa. Around the South African National Gallery in Cape Town she had seen a huge banner quoting words of mine in great red letters. Here is what the banner said.

> There is now no Native past without the Stranger, no Stranger without the Native. No one can hope to be mediator or interlocutor in that opposition of Native and Stranger, because no one is gazing at it untouched by the power that is in it. Nor can anyone speak just for the one, just for the other. There is no escape from the politics of our knowledge, but that politics is not in the past. That politics is in the present.

11

Fifty years ago I made a discovery that changed my life. I discovered that I wanted to write the history of the 'other side of the beach', of indigenous island peoples with whom I had no cultural bond, of Natives. And on 'this side of the beach', my side as an outsider, as Stranger, I wanted to write the history of people whom the world would esteem as 'little'. I wanted to write history from below. Not of kings and queens. Not of heroes. Not of writers of constitutions, saviours of nations. 'Little people'. Those on whom the forces of the world press most hardly. I wanted to celebrate their humanity, their freedoms, their creativity, the ways they crossed the boundaries around their lives, the ways they crossed their beaches. These peoples on both sides of the beach were to be my Natives, my Strangers.

Fifty years ago, it was not fashionable to have an interest either in the other, native, side of the beach or in the 'little people' on this side. When I told my professor that I needed to give myself the anthropological skills to read into this otherness of the Native and to hear the silences of the Stranger in this sort of history, he said: 'Dening, this is the end of your academic career'. It was impolitic for me, he was saying, to turn my interests to things on which society, culture and university put so little store.

It was impolitic. Sad to say, it is probably still impolitic fifty years on. Happily for me, I did not need to be politic. The course of my life was set. I belonged to a religious order of priests, the Society of Jesus—the Jesuits—who put a supreme value on learning for its own sake. I did not need an academic job or even scholarship support, although I had and was to have both. For twenty years the Jesuits gave me freedom to be engaged utterly and altruistically in learning. That is the true privilege in my life.

The four focused fields in the twenty years of my learning—philosophy, theology, history, anthropology—were all built on a common platform with two founding principles. The one was that there was no closure to learning or to the knowledge that was learned. Knowledge was imbedded always in a dialectic, an ongoing conversation.

The other founding principle was modernity. These four focused fields in my learning all embraced all the strategies of knowledge-advancement of modernity—perspective, exhaustive research, critical dialogue, disengagement as far as humanly possible from whatever filters that knowledge with prejudice and error. But there was a newness that flowed like a breeze through all these focused fields. I hope to describe it. I now have a name for that newness that I did not have long ago. It was a neomodernity—in history, philosophy, theology, anthropology. Not a postmodernity. The modernity in principles of knowledge-advancement can never be gone, be 'post-'. A neomodernity. A renewal of modernity in the light of all that we have learned of knowledge-making in the twentieth century. A modernity that is in touch at the same time with both the possibilities and limits of knowing, a modernity that is expressive of what is known and how brokenly it is known, a modernity that begins with the real and enlarges it with imagination is a neomodernity.

I suppose my discovery was that I wanted to practise my neomodernity on islands in Oceania. 'An island always pleases my imagination as a small continent and as an integral part of the globe', Henry David Thoreau once wrote. For fifty years I too have had my imagination filled with islands. And for much the same reason as Thoreau. Islands are 'small continents', manageable totalities in themselves. And 'integral parts of the globe'. Cut-off but playing variations on the same humankind themes.

Whatever else *Robinson Crusoe* and the *Swiss Family Robinson* sparked in our imagination, it was the ludic element of islands as 'small continents' that engaged us. The play lay in the remaking of a strange, even threatening environment of an island into a cultural order of some sort. Perhaps that is the Claude Lévi-Straussian element in our mythmaking. On islands there seems to be a magical inventiveness in making Culture, order, out of Nature, chaos. I can't tell you the hours I have spent in libraries and archives reading mission priests' diaries, beachcombers' word-lists, naval officers' botanical collections, just marvelling how islanders make the totality of their new world—its dyes, its medicines, its wealth, its taboos, its beauty, its decorations.

And islands have beaches. Beaches have to be crossed both by those who come first and those who come after. My stories to come are of all the crossings it takes to make islands and of the crossings it takes to tell the stories of their making. All are told in a neomodern way.

Fifty years ago, the past seemed to belong only to those who were prepared to acquire the skills to tell it. Fifty years on, I now know that not to be true. The past belongs to all those on whom it impinges. We are bound together by the encounters of Native and Strangers in our past. There is no 'other side of the beach', no 'this side of the beach' in a history of this all-impinging past. Such a history needs to be inclusive. Each side can only tell its own history by also telling the other's. That is its politics. Each side must disempower itself in some way. The beginning of such a voyage will always be a disempowerment of self. Let me begin that disempowerment by eschewing all closed models of knowledge and embracing some metaphors to voyage by.

Metaphors for Reflective Voyaging

Encompass

... to walk a boundary with a measured step; to circumnavigate; to envelop a space with knowledge, with the human spirit.

Every year in late September, if I am lucky, I can look down from the desk where I do much of my writing, across the tops of eucalyptus trees, over the beach and rocky coastline, and see for hours a long black procession of birds snaking its way south around the headlands and into bays.

'Kaoha!', I say to them. 'Welcome Home!'. They are the yolla—the shearwaters, the 'short-tailed shearwaters', 'slender billed puffins', *Puffinus tenuirostris*, 'moon-birds', 'mutton-birds'. They are on the last leg of their 19,000-mile circuit of the Pacific. Their line ripples and rolls as one living body. In their hundreds of thousands, they look to be in direct, determined and undistracted flight. They are flying home to nest where they nested last year, and who knows how many years before that.

I see hundreds of thousands of yolla in a stream maybe 30 feet deep and 150 feet wide. Matthew Flinders from the 33-foot longboat, *Norfolk*, in which he charted these waters in 1798, calculated that he saw 100 to 150 million of them in a stream 150 to 250 feet deep and 1000 feet or more wide. Civilisation hasn't been kind, at least in the last two hundred years of the perhaps two million years that the yolla have been making this journey. The birds sustained convict settlements in their starving needs, and were killed off in uncontrolled frenzy. They had sustained, in more controlled ways, the first people in Tasmania and along this Victorian coast where the yolla are my neighbours for perhaps forty thousand years.

James Cook saw these yolla in the cold waters of the Behring Sea in the northern summer, 1778. on the last voyage of his life. William Ellis, his artist, gives us our first images of these 'short-tailed', 'slender-billed' dark birds. We have Ellis' exquisite drawings of them in the British Museum of Natural History. Their stiff-winged shearing, arcing flight is the yolla's grace. Into the troughs of the sea and up the weather side of the waves, independent and intense in their search for food, they are as much part of the grey north seascape as foam and cloud is of a Turner painting. They are not really northerners, though, just visitors, restless visitors. As the summer warms the northern waters a little, they cluster at the cold upswells that bring to the surface the krill, crustaceans and small fish on which they feed.

Cook had first seen the yolla at the other ends of the earth, in the *Endeavour*, as she approached the coast of what Cook would call New South Wales. It was April 1770. The yolla were on the start of their voyage. The autumn southwest winds will drive them northeast above the north island of Aotearoa (New Zealand) for the first leg. There they will veer to the northwest between Fiji and the Solomons and drive north to the Japan Sea, curving east after that to the Behring Sea, as far north as 71 degrees. If all conditions are right, they will have flown six thousand miles in little over a month, almost two hundred miles a day. They will feed themselves as they fly, skimming, diving. The warm tropical water will be their greatest obstacle. It will force a fast on them. The return flight down the northwest coast of North America and across the vast Pacific east of the Tuamotu will be more life-threatening. In the years in which the cool waters of the Humboldt Current up the west coast of South America do not reach out into the Pacific—during El Niño—the yolla are likely to falter and die in huge numbers.

These remarkable birds soar and and scythe and knife their way over a vast space of sea and islands. They have time and space imprinted in their bodies. They have ways of interpreting signs that they have never seen before, in ways I cannot explain to you, nor science to us all.

I will call that vast space they circuit, Oceania. It has had other names these past four hundred years—'South Seas', 'Pacific', and currently 'Sea of Islands'. The peoples who lived on its islands for the two thousand years before that would call the great ocean in their different dialects 'Moana'.

I'll keep to the name Oceania. Oceania is a lived-in space as much as a natural vastness. It is a tracked-on space. The wakes of ships and canoes that have crossed it have left no permanent mark on its waters. But if we voyaged in a *New 20,000 Leagues Under the Sea*, looking up to the canopy of the sea's surface above us and had a sort of time-exposure vision, we would find the tracks a closely woven tapestry of lines. Very few of these lines would be random. They are all directed in some way by systems of knowledge—of stars, of time, of distance—and of purpose—of trade, of empire, of science, of way-finding. There are many other tracks, too, of whales in seasonal migration, of tuna, of birds. These too, more mysteriously, are directed by systems of knowledge.

I call this enveloping of space with knowledge, 'encompassing'. Encompassing is imprinting this island-seascape with spirit and life—human, animal, vegetable. For nearly a lifetime now, I have dreamt of encompassing Oceania. The flight of the yolla is my metaphor for encompassing Oceania. The yolla encompass Oceania every year in their twelve-year life span. I would like to do it just once in my mind.

Beaches

> . . . a double-edged space, in-between; an exit space that is also an entry space; a space where edginess rules.

My life with all its memories is filled with them. My books are all written beside a beach or overlooking one or within the sound of one's waves. As I write now, the combers on the beach below my window roll into a continuous rush of sound. It is the white noise that separates my mind from my body and lets me think to write.

There is hardly a week that I don't walk a beach. These days I can't walk their soft white sand. There is too much pain, too many reminders of mortality in that. A dune to cross to reach a beach drains energy and resolve. No! The beach I walk is the hard wet sand at the sea's edge. It is an edge that moves with the tide and each wave in the tide, of course. So, unless it is barefoot, the walk meanders just beyond the reach of the largest wave in a set—always the ninth, don't the fishermen say?

This glistening strand between high and low tide is my freedom trail. I lose myself as I walk. I write in my mind. The waves are my worry beads. It is an in-between space in an in-between space. The last reach of the sea soaks into the sand. On one side colonies of gulls and terns dry themselves on the white sand. On the other, the sea side, gannets dive into the troughs between breakers. Occasionally dolphins are to be seen surfing in the green transparencies of the waves. In the soak of the sea life stirs almost immediately as the crab holes bubble. Worms and burrowing molluscs wander just below the surface, sucking life from the brine seeping into their world. Sandpipers ballet after the retreating waves.

This wet stretch between land and sea is the true beach, the true in-between space. Among the peoples of Oceania about whom I write—the *maohi* of Tahiti, the *enata* of the Marquesas, the *kamaiana* of Hawai'i—it is a sacred, a *tapu* space, an unresolved space where things can happen, where things can be made to happen. It is a space of transformation. It is a space of crossings.

Yesterday, when I felt the need to reflect on what it meant to write that the beach is a 'space of transformation', 'a space of crossings', I went for a walk on my favourite beach. It was the first day of the southern hemisphere summer. The tide was low. The soak of the sea was a glistening twenty yards wide. The beach curves for five miles in the shelter of hills just a road-width back. There is a fishing harbour at one end behind a rock groyne. Squid boats shelter there. I see their lights at night like UFOs on the horizon of the sea. At the other end of the curve, the beach ends, as so many Australian beaches end, with a small stream riding against a rocky headland. That stream is always my walking goal.

This first day of summer was brilliant. Pale blue sky, deep blue sea. Miles of white, white foam. What is it that the oceanographers say? At any one time 2 per cent of the earth's surface is under sea foam? That is pretty in-between. The breeze beats against the green, green hills. The spring rains still hold their effect. It is a steady breeze, just right for the hang-gliders who float above my head. That is an in-between space that I haven't dared try.

I'm thinking beaches, of course, as I walk. And crossings. A very rewarding thing happened to me in this last year. Fenua'enata, The People of the Land, the Marquesans, through their Association Eo' Enata, published a French translation of *Islands and Beaches* in a splendid edition. It was a great honour for me. I was humbled to be giving these sad and silent islands a history that they could never before read.

Islands and Beaches (1980) was an important book for me. I had long wanted to write the history of Oceania in a double-visioned way. I wanted to write the history of Pacific islands from both sides of the beach. I began to read the voyagers—Cook, Bougainville, Bligh, Vancouver, La Pérouse— then the whalers' logs, missionary letters, beachcombers' journals, not so much to tell their stories as to see what their unseeing eyes were seeing, life on the other side of the beach as the islanders actually lived it, not as it was framed in the mind-galleries of outsiders. What attracted me most of all were the beachcombers, those who left their ships and 'went native', those who crossed beaches.

There were hundreds of beachcombers in the years I was interested in—the mutineers of the *Bounty* among them. They were a peculiar breed. They were as varied as humanity itself, and as good and as evil. They were always a scandal to the societies they left, deemed traitors to them. They took freedoms that other men (there were no women among them in these years) didn't dare or want to take. They soon found that their beaches were dangerous places. If they were wise, they did not bring any material goods with them. These would be taken from them, with their lives if they resisted. What they couldn't bring with them was all the cultural and social support, including language, that made them who they were. To survive, they had to enter into native society in some way, its language first of all. They had to bow to the realities of politics and social relationships. They had to be good mimics and actors. They had to be able to read gestures and understand the ways in which power and class and gender can be in a colour or a shape or a look.

So for me, who wanted to see across the beach, the beachcombers' eyes saw more than most. I began to 'see' The Land, Fenua, The Marquesas, through the eyes of a beachcomber, Edward Robarts, and a lone nineteen-year-old missionary-beachcomber, William Pascoe Crook. They both wrote long manuscripts of their experiences in The Land. *Islands and Beaches* grew out of that seeing.

Islands and Beaches freed me in many ways. It gave me courage to take risks in the theatre of cross-cultural writing. The metaphor 'beach' allowed me to escape the tunnel vision of an island topic and to discover the many ways in which there are liminal spaces in life. I experimented structurally in the book, balancing the two requirements of the historical endeavour, narrative and reflection, in a quite explicit way. I gained a freedom especially by giving back to Enata—The People—of Fenua—The Land—something of their own identity in how they named themselves and their islands. But more importantly, how they structured their identity in the opposition of native (*enata*) and stranger (*aoe*). It was a first and small step in inverting the priorities of our cross-cultural gaze.

'Life is a Beach', the T-shirts in every seaside resort proclaim. Yes, life *is* a beach, though the truth of that is not as hedonistic as the T-shirts are meant to imply. Life is the marginal space between two unknowables—its befores and its afters. All of living is a crossing. Living is all the crossings within one crossing.

It is the process in these crossings that intrigues me. The process, not so much the change. Not essences and polarities that never were, but the creative unfolding. How does one catch creative unfolding, movement, in words? Music might catch the flow of things, and so might painting. But there is stasis in a word that describes the world as *things*. 'To arrest the meaning of words, that is what the Terror wants', Jean-François Lyotard once wrote. The Terror: the terror of fundamentalism; the terror of auto-da-fé; the terror of science in service of power. And Herbert Marcuse put his slant on the idea: 'All reification is a process of forgetting. Art fights reification by making the petrified world speak, sing, perhaps dance.' I want to write history that avoids both the Terror and the forgetting. I want to write history with compassion.

Poetry might keep my words alive, make them dance. It wouldn't shame me to tell my stories in poetry, or at least to write my prose poetically. Let me be more ambitious than that, though. Let me represent all the crossings that are in even one beach crossing. They are all there—yours, mine—whether we know it or not, whether we like it or not.

All living is in flow, but our cultural living is sentenced, paragraphed, chaptered. In all the passage moments, in all the crossing moments, of our cultural life—in becoming adult, or married, or healthy, or educated—in all the specifying moments of roles—gender, age, status, kin—the normal times of living are interrupted by times of defining, moments of marking, occasions of abnormality. We sometimes call these marking and abnormal times ritual. They are always theatre: moments of in-between, moments of seeing, moments of reflection. Beaches. Let me be a storyteller of beach crossings of others and catch the flow of living and telling on the beaches of my own mind.

My own life-crossings have been very privileged ones. There is not a day but that global and local news remind me of that. The beach that is my life has had no pain or drama beyond the ordinary. Its blandness has little theatre. Its ordinariness has little spectacular. Maybe, in an era of the spectacular, that is its theatre. In any case, every difference has a sameness. Every smallness has a largeness. Every particularity has a generality. Every shape, every colour, every gesture has a theory. Think of my storytelling and my reflections on the stories as a dance on the beaches of my mind

There is no beach without sea, no sea without sky, no sky without the earth's curve. In the view from the beach, the forefront is all detail and movement, all history, one is tempted to say. But the ordered restlessness of the waves diffracts the gaze, dissolves attention into reflection. From a beach, things loom in the glim of the horizon and in the shimmer of the mind's eye. From a beach, it is possible to see beyond one's horizons. Beaches breed expansiveness. My beaches do, anyway.

19

Crossings

. . . sometimes made with delicate steps, sometimes with closed eyes;
moments of catharsis and transition; discoveries of self in the mirror of
otherness; a storyteller's soliloquies.

My study is an archive of my mind, an archaeological site of my spiritual
and intellectual voyaging. The books that surround me are those that have
taken me on my journey. They cluster in their spaces on the shelves in the
themes of my thinking—about sign and symbol, about theatre, about
narrative, about encounters, about boundaries, about sacrament and ritual.
Or they cluster as places to which I return again and again—The
Marquesas, Hawai'i, Tahiti. Or as subjects that will intrigue me forever—
ships and the sailing of them, the sky, oceans. Or topics that shame me for
my ignorance—language, genetics, geology; journeys I have gone so far on,
but never far enough. There are shelves of books written by my students
and my friends and colleagues. These are precious books, reminders that
writing is never a solo enterprise. These students and friends are in my
books. I am in theirs.

These books on their shelves are not just a library. They are me. An old
friend and mentor could not wait to be rid of his books once he was done
with them. I will never be done with them. When they are gone, I will have
gone before them. I look at them and see my mind evolving with the
influence of this or that scholar. I look at them and wish, and wish again,
that I had written this one or that. I look at them and see when I was in
touch, not just with the frontiers of my disciplines, but with the paradigms
and discourses that make us something new, year by year.

Then there are my files. There has never been a lecture that I have heard
or given, a book that I have read, or written, not an article or a chapter or a
document that has not its relic in these files. I suppose that if there was ever a
passion that absorbed me, it was the passion to be exhaustive in every inquiry
I make. I am driven to go not one, but many steps beyond what is thought to
be necessary. My notes in their superabundance are my steps beyond what is
necessary.

My study is at the bottom of my garden. I designed it myself to my
needs of light and working spaces. I walk down the garden each morning
from the kitchen door. It is a voyaging that begins my day, takes me to my
special place. I work at my writing each morning, early. I never have been a
night person. As often as not, I come from my sleep with sentences or

phrases needing to be put on paper. So I am at my desk, pen in hand, looking back up the garden when the birds possess the garden. I know their characteristics well, and the generations of them. They are hatched in the vines and shrubs that shelter my study. This is a special time for me, sometimes filled with my eagerness to fill a new page. More often it is going back to the last sentence of the day before and writing it over again with the hope that this time the mind will leap over the period at its end into the next thought easily, or at least quickly.

I am engulfed in my study by the materialised presence of all the spiritual and intellectual pleasures of my life. I have no sense of odyssey in these pleasures, but I have a sense of voyage. I would take you, reader, with me. Perhaps it will be to places you have never been, but I cannot promise you that. If you would like to celebrate the mysteriousness of a life of learning, I can promise you a celebration.

The past I visit—the 200-year past that I visit—is on paper. Mostly. Sometimes it is in things with human creativity encapsulated in them— ships, ornaments, art, buildings, landscape. A 200-year past is beyond experience and memory, though. And beyond the radar of our various electronic recording systems. There are no voices from two hundred years ago, no smells, no touches, no movement.

No, the 200-year past I visit is stilled on to paper, millions of pieces of paper. Written-on paper. One-off pieces of paper, mostly without copy. Not printed paper. Handwritten paper. Script. The first mark of my history is always a pen's or a pencil's. The first mark of my history, the first readings I make, are always shaped by the transience of the moment in which they were made. The hand that writes them is still trembling with anger or fear or sorrow. Or it is scribble in a hurry. Or it is flourished with power. It is stained or burnt on its edges, or blotted. It is corrected and erased. It belongs to times that are as long or short or broken or continuous as the human experience that sustains it.

To visit my 200-year past, I read and look. I read to write. No, actually, I read to live. Reading for me is life. I love the dance on the beaches of the mind that reading is. I read fast and slow. I love the slow reading of a poem. Better still, I love to hear the slow reading of a poem. I slow-read the sacred texts in my life. I soak up the timelessness of their words. These sacred texts look like they are bound to time but they are not. Their meaning stretches out to me beyond the meaning their writers ever had. I easily fly over their contradictions and errors and know what truth they hold for me.

I read fast most of the time. That is because reading books, as distinct from the written-on pages of my 200-year past—reading books is my conversation with the world. My eyes are ahead of my mind when I read fast. I gobble sentences, paragraphs, pages whole. There is a white noise in the back of my mind as I read. It is the babble of worldwide conversations that affect my thinking. I'm in conversation with novelists, philosophers, anthropologists, historians, critics in this sort of reading. It is full of erotic, ecstatic moments when I think that what they are saying is what I myself am just about to say. But I'm going to say it better!

Reading, in the view of Michel de Certeau, a French Jesuit polymath, is a creative act 'full of detours and drifts across the page, imaginary or meditative flights taking off from a few words, overlapping paragraph on paragraph, page on page, shortlived dances of the eye and mind'. Reading for me is also proactive, creative. It is in no way passive, a mirror to someone else's thoughts. My eyes might be attached to the page, but my mind is soaring.

That is reading books. When I read my one-off pieces of paper in script, it is somewhat different. I read to write. I write to give back to the past its own present moments. There is no better place to catch that tenuous, trembling moment than when the pen is first put to paper. Reading the written-down past is special. It is as creative as the ordinary reading of books, but there is something more. My eye must travel from the word on the page up the pen and hand and into the person of the writer. That word on the page has a past and a history. It is not just born there and then. But it doesn't yet have its future. I, the historian two hundred years on, might think that I know the future and consequences of that word. But the writer doesn't. The present moment for the writer is full of ambiguity. My stories to be true must catch that ambiguity.

All history, then, must begin where the past inscribes its own present on paper. Let us begin there.

1

Writing the Beach

The beach is Vaitahu. The Spaniards called it Madre de Dios in 1595. James Cook called it Resolution Bay in 1774. Vaitahu is on an island, Tahuata. The islanders who have lived on Tahuata for two thousand years call themselves Enata, The People, and their islands Fenua, The Land. Because those that 'discover' places are deemed to have naming rights, we, the Strangers, have called Fenua'enata, The Land of The People, The Marquesas Islands and the islanders, Marquesans.

In 1796–97 three Strangers crossed the beach at Vaitahu: Edward Robarts, Joseph Kabris, William Pascoe Crook. Because they found their experiences so extraordinary, they wrote them down. Their stories are the start of ours.

Fenua'enata (The Marquesas)

The ten islands of Fenua'enata (Marquesas) form a cluster by themselves 775 miles northeast of Tahiti, beyond the seventy atolls of the Tuamotu, near the doldrums of the equator where the southeast trade winds falter. The South American coast is 3400 miles to the east; Hawai'i, 2500 miles to the northwest. Fenua'enata is at the centre of the earth's greatest ocean. Look at a map. Fenua'enata seems to be at the crossroads of the sea between Canton and Cape Horn, between Panama and Sydney. But it has never been easy to reach. It lies off the Great Circle way of ships. It is tucked away in a backwater of the open sea. These days it is mostly the yachties who make Fenua'enata their first port-of-call in Polynesia from their North American marinas.

Fenua'enata forms two groups of islands that lie along the southeast–northwest line of the trades. The windward group of the southeast comprises the larger islands of Tahuata, Hiva Oa and Fatuiva, and the smaller islets of Motane, Fatu'uku and the rocky outcrop Thomasset. Alváro de Mendaña and his pilot Fernández Pedro de Quiros 'discovered' this southern group in 1595 and called them Las Marquesas de Mendoça for their patron, the Viceroy of Peru. The leeward, northern, group of Nukuhiva, Ua Huka and Ua Pou form a triangle within easy sight of one another. Beyond the horizon to the northwest are the uninhabited islands of Eiao, Hatutaa and Hatuiti. The northern group were not 'discovered' till 1791 when a series of French, British and American sea-captains gave them a profuse number of names in honour of their revolutions and patrons.

The French claimed ownership of *Les Iles Marquises* in a fit of empire in 1842. They have been a lonely and neglected part of French Polynesia ever since. Before the French, an American, Lieutenant David Porter USN, had established a prisoner-of-war camp for the four hundred British whalemen he had captured in the Pacific at the beginning of the Anglo-American War of 1814. Thinking he recognised among the natives a 'republican spirit' similar to his own, he also had a fit of empire, the first if not the last for the USA. President Madison, however, declared he had enough 'Indians' of his own already and declined Porter's claim of ownership. The British, in a peeve at what Porter had done to them, pulled down all his monuments and declared The Marquesas were theirs. But no one ever believed them.

Whalemen seeking refreshment and traders looking for sandalwood for the China trade were the most frequent visitors to Fenua'enata during the first half of the nineteenth century. Herman Melville deserted from his whaler on Nukuhiva in 1842 and wrote his novel *Typee* about his experiences. Paul Gauguin came to Tahiti in 1891 but went on to Hiva Oa in 1901 looking for the last savages. He died looking there in 1903.

Edward Robarts

Calcutta, 1811

In November 1797 I saild on board the ship Euphrates . . .

The rich travelled on the shoulders of the poor in Calcutta in 1811. Sir Thomas Stamford Raffles, in his palanquin, bobbed along above the heads of the coolies and beggars in Tank Square. He did not see the short man with a sailor's gait and a scarred, near-toothless face, but Edward Robarts saw him. Seeing Raffles gave Robarts hope. For ten months on this, the harshest of his beaches, Robarts had been on the slide. Calcutta was a company town, an East India Company town. A white man without Company connections, or without a trade that the Company valued, had nothing to sell but his poverty. In an Empire city where there was no space between the empowered rich and the disciplined native population who did their work for them, the relentless pressure on the poor white man was down. A man never went up in the rounds of begging a few rupees from vestrymen's wives and daughters. There was only the trading of one disrespectful gaze for another degrading judgement.

Just a year before, Robarts had reached the highest rung on his social ladder. But this had been in Penang. He had been butler and cook to Sir Thomas Raffles' sister there. There had been soirées and parties aplenty, enough anyway to delude his sense of social status. Death, however, rode the shoulders of rich and poor alike in the East. Raffles and his family fled Penang. Robarts had to find another beach in Calcutta.

Robarts came to Calcutta with what he thought of as his two greatest capitals in life—his 'royal bride' and his story of 'a long and singular career of an enterprizeing and unfortuneate life'. His wife was Enoaaoata, daughter of 'King' Kiatonui of Nukuhiva in The Marquesas. She came to Calcutta with their three children and pregnant with the fourth. Hers was the unfortunate life, we have to think. She had left her native islands with Robarts, first for Tahiti where she tried to hang herself as she faced Robarts' violence as he brewed rum for the convict colony at Botany Bay and succumbed to it as well. Whenever we meet her on all the beaches of her life, she is in tears. It is hard not to think that with a language none could speak, except her husband, and he haltingly, she was wrapped in a terrible silence. She lasted only a couple of years in the makeshift compounds behind the godowns of Taretta Bazaar where they lived. Her children lasted not much longer.

Robarts always saw himself as 'enterprizeing' in the face of harsh circumstances. 'Bumptious' would probably be the word others would have used. If only half the stories of how he rescued people and ships were true, he would have been a hard man to live with. But anyone who has a story that he believes others will want to read probably is to be seen as bumptious. Robarts had already begun to write his story when he went looking for Raffles.

He had no trouble discovering him. 'A Great man everyone knows, but a poor man sits in his corner unnoticed.' When he knocked on Raffles' door, it was opened by a Malay servant who recognised Robarts from Penang. He was taken immediately to Sir Thomas.

'Why, Robarts,' Raffles said. 'We've been looking for you.'

At Raffles' side was a bespectacled man with an air of great learning. It was 'that morning star of Literature, the Immortal' Dr John Caspar Leyden—linguist, theologian, poet, medical practictioner, Freemason, professor of Hindustani, Judge of the Twenty-Four Pergunnahs and Commissioner of the Court of Request. Leyden was a collector of stories and languages. He had acquired thirty-four of the latter and thought that through Robarts he might acquire another.

He asked Robarts what he had been doing in Calcutta.

'Looking for employment and writing my Narrative of what I had gone through since I left London.'

'What? You have turned author!'

'Yes, Sir! Anything to raise the wind for an honest morsel.'

'What? Raise the wind!' Leyden laughed at the sailor's metaphor.

'Yes, Sir! I have been lying becalmed these ten months, and if a breeze does not spring up, my unfortuneate Bark will founder on the rocks of adversity.'

'Is your wife from the islands with you? Bring her with you and let me see your narrative, and then I shall be better judge of your abilities.'

So Robarts returned in a few days, with a few pages of his 'Vocabalry of the Marqueasas Language', and Enoaaoata to pronounce the words. The rooms of Leyden's house were filled with Persian scholars transcribing texts. Leyden offered Robarts a desk and forty rupees a month to tell his story. Robarts only received that January's first month stipend. Leyden went off with Lord Minto and Raffles on their expedition

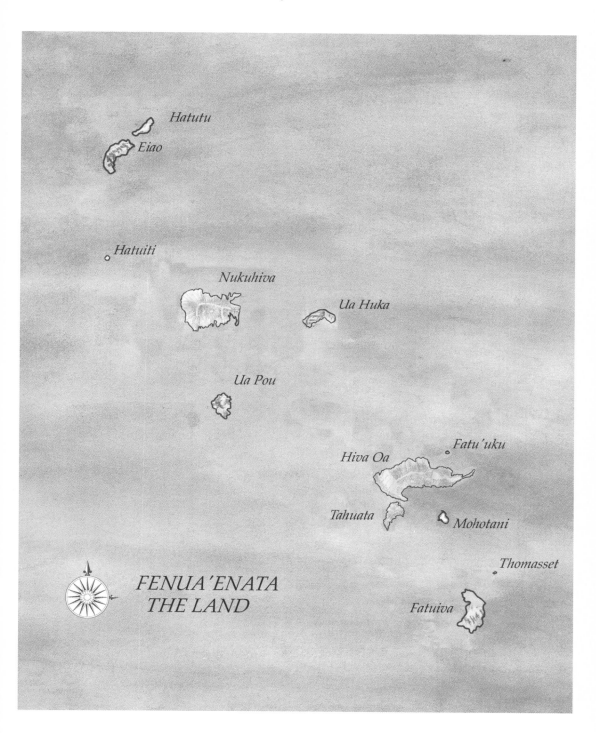

FENUA'ENATA
THE LAND

to annex Java. Searching an airless library in Batavia for manuscripts, it was said, he caught a fever and died, learned and young.

Robarts' story, written in a neat, small hand, breathlessly without stop, comma or paragraph for 171 pages, is not signed as completed until 24 July 1824. By then he has many, many more vicissitudes to tell of. But in January 1811, sharing a desk with a Persian scholar, he began:

'In November 1797 I saild from Blackwall on board the Ship Euphrates, bound round Cape Horn in search of sperm whales'.

Robarts is twenty-six years old, born near Barmouth in Wales. Already he has sailed the arctic waters to St Petersburg and the equatorial waters in the slave trade out of Jamaica and Santo Domingo. He has unsuccessfully wooed a Cheshire farmer's daughter, sister of his closest friend on the *Euphrates*. He is by his own estimation only a little man, and his journal is all that saves him from oblivion.

In May of 1824, he is finishing his story in Murshidebad, India. He has been fourteen years on his manuscript in the hardest, most disappointing part of his life. He has been cook, sailor, carpenter, builder, moonshiner, midwife, storekeeper, butler, overseer of the Calcutta Botanical Gardens, pearler, trader, deserter, slaver and Marquesan warrior in the years that we know of him. His beach in life is both ordinary and extraordinary. It is more put-upon than putting-on, always in-between.

He finishes his story as pennilessly poor as he started it—poorer because now he has lost his Fenua'enata wife and three children in a Calcutta cholera epidemic, and a second wife, seven months' pregnant, from the same disease. He has his second-born daughter, Ellen, still. Ellen is 'royal', he thinks. She is the grandniece of the 'King' of Taiohae. He thinks maybe she will be able to go to England and have her royalty recognised when he earns some money from his published manuscript. He is a small man much deluded by his dreams.

In the last sentences of the manuscript, he is musing on whether a trading venture would realise enough to save against a 'rainy day'.

And then I shall be able to judge what to do in the Evening of life, as I have had a long and singular career of an entreprizeing and unfortunate life up to the age of 53 years, and I thank my God that I am now as active as when I was 20 years of age, but I am not so strong. I hope I have not intruded too much on my readers time.

He writes that and is gone. Every year from 1822 to 1831 his name appears simply as a Police Constable in the *East India Register*. In 1832 there is nothing. In 1833, among the death notices there appears: 'August 22, 1833. Mrs E. Robarts'. Whether this is Ellen, or a third wife, or a misprint for himself, we do not know. He is unfortunate to the end.

I have a copy of his journal before me now as I write. I haven't looked at its 171 pages of small, neat handwriting for thirty-seven years. I feel nostalgic for the time I first saw it and began to transcribe it, giving it punctuation, paragraphs and chapters. Harry Maude, a mentor of mine, a genius in the discovery of historical records, an expert in beachcomber literature, a protagonist of the double-visioned history of the Pacific we were proclaiming, guided me to Edward Robarts' unpublished manuscript.

I had first met Edward Robarts on the pages of accounts by Adam J. Von Kruzenshtern and Georges H. Von Langsdorff of their visit to Taiohae on Nukuhiva in 1805. Kruzenshtern's ship *Nadezhda* had missed the narrow entry to Taiohae Bay when a canoe bearing a white flag hailed them. To their surprise, the 'naked' bronze-skinned, tattooed figure in the canoe turned out to be an Englishman, Robarts. Robarts presented them with letters of introduction from whaling captains and offered to be their pilot and interpreter. He warned them, though, against a Frenchman also in the bay, Jean Joseph Kabris. The Russians, commenting wryly on how endemic national rivalries were, would use both Robarts and Kabris as their eyes, ears and tongues in Taiohae.

Robarts would not see himself as the Russians saw him until the publication of their narrative in English in 1813. But he caught a glimpse of himself in an unlikely place, *Tilloch's Philosophical Magazine* 1805, volume 22. Kruzenshtern had anticipated his final publication with a letter from Japan. Someone of the Calcutta Orientalists, probably 'that morning star of Literature the Immortal Dr Leyden', must have pointed it out to him. Robarts wrote to a Dr James Hare telling his story. Hare passed on the letter to Kruzenshtern who made an appendix of it in his 1813 edition.

Harry Maude and I went looking for the papers of James Hare. He seemed a lead to Robarts. We found them in the National Library of Scotland, Edinburgh. When we asked the librarian did he know of the papers of Edward Robarts, he replied: 'We were wondering when someone would ask about them'.

I edited *The Marquesan Journal of Edward Robarts* in 1974. An editor, I suppose, needs a suspicious mind. Fraud is always a possibility, self-delusion inevitable in any personal story. Pursuing facts, places, names in someone else's presentation of them is altogether a different—and more difficult—historical task than collecting them to write one's own story of events. Interpretation is subordinated to verification. In editing one is snatching at detail in all directions rather than saturating oneself in reading an archive.

Identifying the watermarks on Robarts' manuscript gave me confidence. The first 160 pages were watermarked 'S and C Wise 1814' with the registered heart-shaped icon of the company. The last, larger, pages were marked similarly but dated 1821. The paper matched the times of his story-writing. The writing fills every space on the loose folio pages, much as a later Herman Melville filled his pages. It is fair copy with few corrections. It ends with a statement written in this same but larger hand. 'This Narrative is given to the Care of James Hare Esqre MD by me (Edward Robarts, the writer and true owner of the Acct of the ~~Acct of the~~ Marquesas Isles, Calcutta July 14th 1824)'

I can only smile as I see it again. This is Edward Robarts lifting himself into performance mode, making formalities of role and relationships. It is something he has done through all the preceding pages. He is self-defensive, of course. Self-defining. The numerous incidents with sea-captains who rob or trick him, or with Calcutta gentlemen who criticise him and deny him jobs are described in moralising terms which leave no doubt as to Robarts' high-mindedness, his undying gratitude, his sense of hurt pride. Being literary for him is a performance. His deeply emotional reactions to situations such as favours done for him, or misfortunes suffered, are described in clichéd terms. A dozen times a silent tear slips down his cheek, or a thousand tender ideas spring into his mind, or there is sparkling joy in his children's eyes, or he receives the uncharitableness of others with a sad smile. But these are not so much signs of hollowness in his character as evidence that, for him, being literary meant presenting a conventional persona, showing the mask more than the personality. His memory of his Fenua'enata days is highly romantic, not in what he did but how he did it. His gallantry to Fenua'enata women, his self-conscious role of protector of the weak, belong more to his literary medium than to himself. There are many places where he decides that a little style is called for by the drama of the moment. Moonlight on a reef, a drowning in a canoe, a sea-captain enduring slices being cut off his leg by cannibals, all stir some turgid prose. Being literary for Robarts strained his resources to their limit. But he did it. He had the advantage on all of us. He was there.

Beaches will push performances to extremes. There is an edginess in beaches that is foil to the edginess of self and the writing of self. Beaches are a mélange of order and disorder, of idealistic yet bloodied reality, of regressive and yet progressive ambitions. Beaches are *limen*, thresholds to some other place, some other time, some other condition. Writing a beach will always be a reflection on that edginess, a reflection *of* that edginess. Writing a beach will always be stories of defining moments. But writing beaches, too, will always be frozen moments of definition. On beaches there is contingency and universality, both; total particularity and system, both.

In editing Robarts' writing of his beach, I also had to write the beach. I had his stories of how Enata actually lived their lives. I also had his set descriptions of Enata rules and roles of living in their cultured lives. So long as I remembered that his—or anybody else's—set descriptions of the systems of cultural living do not have the rigidity of a model, only the fluidity of a metaphor, then I will write the beach somewhere near what it actually was.

Joseph Kabris

Valenciennes, 1822

Six months after the unfortunate Quiberon affair I boarded an English vessel leaving for a whaling expedition to the Pacific Ocean. . . .

It took a long hard day and a harder night till dawn for Joseph Kabris to die on his hospital bed at Valenciennes, 22–23 September 1822. His gangrene's poison took him slowly and painfully. There was no family beside him, save in his feverish mind as he mourned for his 'princess' wife and his daughters ten thousand miles away on Nukuhiva.

There was a stranger from Geneva there, though. He had come looking for Kabris, found him dying and stayed to the end. Not really a stranger. Ferdinand Denis was the publisher of a fourteen-page pamphlet, *A True and Accurate Account of the Residence of Joseph Kabris, native of Bordeaux, in the Islands of Mendoca, located in the Pacific Ocean at 10 degrees latitude and 240 degrees longitude.*

There was no great self-interestedness in Denis' visit and stay. He admired Kabris and he knew that the true pain in his dying was not the gangrene but the humiliations of his perceived freakishness. And there was another reason for his staying. In the corridors of the hospital lurked more than one purveyor of curiosities. They had half a hope that they might skin Kabris when he died. Joseph Kabris had his beach written on his skin in his tattoos.

'Imprinted with nobility', the English traveller Richard Ker Porter had written of Kabris and his tattoos. Porter had seen Kabris in Moscow at the court of Emperor Alexander I, soon after the Russian explorer, Adam von Kruzenshtern, had taken Kabris accidentally from The Marquesas Islands in 1804. It was an accident for which Kabris never forgave Kruzenshtern. He had lived his Marquesan life to its exuberant and bloody full and forever mourned his being snatched away from it.

In those first years of his return, the courts of Europe—at least those of Russia, France and Prussia—had wanted to see him. Porter thought that Kabris' tattoos were like a 'beautiful damask pattern', 'in forms not inferior to the finest Etruscan borders'. 'To me, there is something very admirable in the idea of a fine male figure without any other covering than these beautiful enamellings.' 'Like a savage god.' He reminded his readers that when the President of the British Royal Academy first saw the Apollo Belvedere in Rome, he had said: 'What a fine Mohawk warrior!'

There was something achingly beautiful in Kabris' ideal civilised body with its savage markings. Porter could hardly take his eyes off him as Kabris told how he had killed a cannibal 'with the horrid morsel still in his mouth'. Porter just knew that, if this naked hero in a savage uniform had only been allowed to stay, a 'rude civilisation' would have grown among the natives.

Ten years in Russia exploiting another savage skill he had learned in the islands—swimming—by teaching the Royal Marines at Cronstadt were enough for Kabris. After the chaos of Napoleon's Grande Armée defeat in 1812, Kabris joined the packs of escaping French prisoners and walked back to France.

Back in Bordeaux, he was no longer an 'ideal beauty'. A stint in a 'Cabinet des Illusion' exhibiting his 'enamellings' and performing savage dances and wild sacrificial rituals only ended in his own disillusion. He wandered the provincial fairs—Le Havre, Rouen, Grenoble, Orléans— making theatre of himself beside a 400-pound 'fat lady' and a three-headed cow. His moment of despair came in Orléans where posters of *Kabris Le*

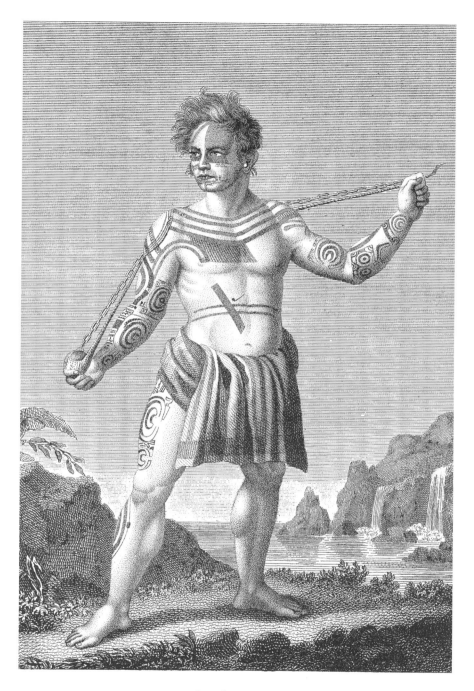

Joseph Kabris, Le Tatoué

Tatoué were pasted side by side with posters of *Munito Le Chien Savant*. Everything he thought himself to be because of his beach experiences was mocked in that. He came to Valenciennes to die.

Who knows whether he knew in those last moments what the skulkers in the hospital corridors were planning to do? Perhaps he asked a last charity of Ferdinand Denis to protect him. Anyway, Denis oversaw a burial that would destroy the tattoos forever. Corpses weren't scarce in the hospital at Valenciennes: Kabris was buried without a coffin between the bodies of two paupers. There may have been some recognition of where he lay, however. A *Promenade au Cimitière de Valenciennes* of the time describes a stroll past the graves of a 'goddess of reason', a Jesuit, an English colonel killed at Waterloo, a Freemason, a comic artiste—'et Kabris le Tatoué'.

Denis, looking down on these 'damask patterns' on the skin of the dead Kabris, could not have known what they meant or what story was written into them. Perhaps he recognised the clay pipe imprinted on Kabris' stomach. But he would not have known, any more than we do, whether this was some native tattooist's joke, or Kabris' signature of his difference on a native beach. He certainly could not have known that that diagonal line across Kabris' forehead was called *pi'e'e*, 'running shit', and that patch over his eye, *mata epo*, 'shitty eyes', that line across his mouth, *kutu epo*, 'shitty snout'. Those marks were probably his first tattooings, giving him his 'rubbish names', titles that showed him to be at the beginning of his initiations and at his most degraded point, the 'shit' of gods and chiefs. That chaos of calabash coils, crab eyes and turtle shells—the *pahutiki*, the 'wrapping in images'—on his skin, these would have been other signs, not of degradation but of triumph and honour for the occasions when he pulled himself out of the shit by killing a man, winning a battle, doing some famous deed. Kabris, we have to think, was reborn in a social sense with this new wrapping of his skin. It protected him as an armour. It clothed him with family and kin. It joined him to a mythic understanding of who he was. It gave narrative to his life.

Kabris had another narrative to his life. It was the small pamphlet which he sold at the entry to the theatre of his exhibitions and his dances. It was full of his conviction that the story told by his tattoos was true. Perhaps Denis picked it up from among the small collection of Kabris' things beside his bed and opened it. Perhaps he didn't. If he had, he would have read: 'Six months after the unfortunate Quiberon affair I boarded an English vessel leaving for a whaling expedition to the Pacific Ocean'.

34

The still wind in the lee of the ridges that surround the bay of Taiohae meant that sailing vessels had always to warp their way to anchorage, and out again. After ten days of refreshment at Taiohae, the Russian ship *Nadezhda*, now joined by the *Neva*, began to pull her way out of the bay against her kedge anchors. Edward Robarts said his farewells at the last minute. Kabris stayed on, the Russians thought to get some advantage over Robarts. As the *Nadezhda* reached the two island sentinels at the mouth of the bay, she was without way. At that moment she was hit by a strong southeast gust and was immediately driven towards the cliffs and the rocks beneath them that were being beaten by twenty-foot waves. A crowd of Enata quickly gathered, clearly in high excitement at the prospect of a wreck.

With some of the crew in boats and the rest adjusting sails, the Russians had not much thought other than for their survival. Certainly not for Kabris. When they were safe, the boats stowed and were some miles out to sea, Kabris asked if he could be taken back, or be given something, a plank, anything, and be allowed to swim back to his wife and family. The future Cronstadt Marine swimming instructor might have been confident of his reaching shore, but the Russians weren't. They would not let him go. Kabris was to be with them first to Hawai'i and then to Kamchatka. So he would write his beach on the decks of *Nadezhda*, in the palaces of Moscow and Paris, and on the stage in French country fairs. Kabris would write his beach by performing it.

The naturalists on the *Nadezhda*, Georges Langsdorff and Wilhelm Tilesius, were delighted to have for their inspections what they thought as near a native as a civilised man could be. They could copy the designs of his tattoos very particularly. He danced and sang to them and they notated his music. He played the sorcerer for them and found it did not work because there was no *tapu* place on the *Nadezhda* for him to bury the spittle or hair or rags that would catch the souls of his victims. He gave them Enata vocabulary, more than four hundred words and phrases. He acted out a warrior's attack and told them all they wanted to hear about cannibalism. No! He had not eaten men. He had killed three enemies, however, and swapped their bodies for pigs.

Language interested Langsdorff and Tilesius most. Kabris had forgotten his native French in his years in Fenua'enata. All he could say when he first met the Russians was: '*Oui moi beaucoup François, Americanish ship, ah dansons la Carmagnole*'. 'And then', the Russians remarked, 'he would laugh like a native of Nukahiva.' No doubt about it, Kabris' thespian skills were great. He had learned to lose his own otherness on the beach. He laughed like a native.

The Russians watched Kabris' memory come back, too—his own name, his parents' names, where he was born. He would sing patriotic revolutionary songs: the Carmagnole, the first identifying characteristic he displayed, was a revolutionary dance. We will see soon his involvement in the revolutionary wars. The Russians were interested especially in those memories of Kabris that seemed to flash spontaneously in his stream of consciousness. He would suddenly exclaim as if he had seen a vision: '*Beaucoup de chandeliers, beaucoup de violons, beaucoup de musique, les madames, les mademoiselles!*' He was remembering being in the theatre.

Indeed he was. He would write his beach in theatre. As he did his capers on the deck of *Nadezhda*, he was learning to fine-hone his beach experiences to those that would tease the prurience of an audience—war and violence, man-eating, survival tactics among savages, sex, and, of course, tattoos.

He learned something else when he went on stage in the country fairs. He needed a story. It wasn't enough for crowds to see his otherness, they needed to read it as well. So he tells it to a M. A. F. Dulys who writes a *Précis Historique*. It is this *True Account* that Kabris has printed, with minor adjustments, in Paris, Grenoble, Rouen, and Paris again. These are Kabris' pamphlet-tickets to his show. He tells how his tattoos were done, and all the tricks to avoid gangrene. He points out the moon-shaped design. *Meama* he says is its name, and it is. It is a sign that he had been made Chief Justice of the island. Well, perhaps!

Those writers who inscribed Kabris' story in his pamphlet clearly believed that some romance was needed to balance the savagery. So they have Kabris rescued from certain cannibal death by a 'princess', named 'Walmaiki', who saves him by becoming his bride. (Pocahontas has her beaches, too.) There are Crusoesque features as well, as Kabris is made to come ashore on a plank after the sinking of his whaler at sea in a storm. He is made to share that plank with the whaler's cook. Robarts would have been furious at being involved in Kabris' story in that way. Robarts knew that Kabris was only a 'runaway' like himself, no shipwrecked innocent.

Taking the savage to city stages and country fairs did not begin or end with Kabris. For a hundred years, for two hundred years if we include film, the 'civilised' have found catharsis in exhibitions of the 'savage'. The theatre of savagery has always made the 'civilised' comfortable in their superiority. Theatre is always unsettling, however. Like the beach, theatre is an insight into the relativity of things.

In the otherness of his beach and of his acting, Kabris had insight into the relativity of things. Writing his beach by performance, Kabris experienced the contingency of his otherness—his tattoos, his Enata ways—and the universality of his humanity—the affection for and generosity towards him by his Enata wife and family. He died in the hospital at Valenciennes mourning all that he had humanly lost.

I wonder if he was so immersed in his beach that he would have realised that the citizens of Valenciennes, had they flayed him for his tattoos, would really have given him back his Enata life. We will see how the flaying of the *pahutiki*, the 'wrap of images' was a way of resurrection for Enata.

William Pascoe Crook

Newport Pagnell, 1799

On the 6th of June the Duff arrived in Resolution Bay. . . .

The forty-mile carriage ride up the Great North Road from London to Newport Pagnell was hard and long. There were many stares at his sunburnt, weathered face which was almost as dark as the native boy's sitting beside him. His outdoor look did not fit the indoor appearance of his sombre, near-clerical clothing. His talk was pious and godly, but he did not have the posture or voice of a minister of the church. He looked different and out of place.

Different and out of place was how he felt, too. The stares would not have worried him. He was more frightened by the thought of the gaze he would be subject to at Newport Pagnell. He was the Mission Society's first failure, though there were others they did not yet know of. He was the first to come back those ten thousand miles from the Pacific mission to England. His conscience was clear. The fervour of his beliefs had not cooled, though his soul had been raked like no other man's. He had seen scenes too obscene to describe, too terrible to understand. There had not been a minute in all the death around him that he had not thought that he too would die—uselessly, mocked and taunted on his beach for his difference.

He knew that the Directors would have been disturbed by the only letter they had received from him before he turned up unannounced on the whaling ship *Butterworth*. 'I desire to blush and be confounded before the Lord forever', he had written in that letter. 'Temptation has been violent and of such strange sort that I persuaded it would be the greatest presumption in anyone knowing them to encounter.'

Now that he was approaching Newport Pagnell, he remembered his boldness in that letter. Who was he, nineteen years young, and without any other certainty than that God had called him, to tell these great men that they had got it wrong? The *Duff* had left him alone on the beach at Tahuata with a Bible, some seeds and tools, some paper and ink. The heathens had laughed at his poverty and ignorance. He reminded the Directors that he had attached himself wrongly to the opinion of 'some respectable members of your body' against the true founder of the Mission Society, Dr Thomas Haweis. Haweis had thought that there was only one way to convert the heathen, and that was by establishing a community of believers whose shining example of good living would give meaning to their words.

Dr Haweis was right, the young whitesmith-cum-missionary now knew, because language was such a barren thing in itself. 'God', 'sin', 'redemption', 'resurrection', 'eternity'—what use were words when there was no experience of what they meant? What story of salvation was there to tell, when the heathens mocked the weakness of a god who couldn't give his servant food or skills to obtain it. Language and its translation was the key. But there was not true translation without experience of a language's meaning.

So here he was with a native boy who had followed him all those miles. The boy was tattooed with a diagonal line from his left temple to his right cheek. He had been initiated into the band of dancers, *kai'oi*, whose moral deprivations were without end. That boy, attracting so much attention, was doomed. He was dying now of cold. How could he have eternal life, bewildered as he was? There would be not much time to extract all that there was in his mind. And he himself had a story no one else could tell. In this place where everybody looked at him with a knowing, cynical look, even his own story was disappearing from his mind. He needed the boy like a mirror to see himself in a different place.

The servants at Newport Pagnell took them through the mansion to a book-lined study. This was to be his new beach. He saw the books of the Pacific—Cook, Bligh, Bougainville, Hawkesworth, Forster—almost before he saw the sickly figure of the great Dr Samuel Greatheed on the couch beside them.

'Ah! Mr William Pascoe Crook, I am very glad to see you,' the good doctor said. 'And this is Temouteitei? Kaoha! Welcome.'

Dr Greatheed was the Sir Joseph Banks of the Mission Society, a great scavenger of knowledge and collector of stories. He had created a vocabulary and grammar of the Tahitian language out of the memories of the *Bounty* mutineers when they were dragged back for trial and execution. Out of secret manuscripts describing the mutineers' experiences at Tahiti, out of all the other published literature of the Pacific, out of interviews with captains of whaling and trading ships, he had formulated a description of Tahitian society. The missionaries on the *Duff* had it to learn on their way out and to help them in their strategies of conversion. Now he had the most exciting possibility of his intellectual life. The Pacific had come to him in the person of Temouteitei and of the young, intelligent, questioning Crook.

'Do you know,' Greatheed said to Crook, 'I persuaded the Directors that two guineas was not too much to spend to get you here. I know you are disappointed that you missed the *Duff* on her return voyage. But God works in strange ways. If you were with them, you would be now prisoner of the French. Work with me now on the language of the South Seas. It is in the cause of Christ.'

So they turned to conversations that lasted months over several visits. They culled the books on Greatheed's shelves, traced Temouteitei's network of kin, evoking stories from him as they went. With a frame of their physical, biological and botanical environment, a *dramatis personae* of individuals, a list of institutions, a day-by-day narrative of happenings, they wrung Crook's memory for details. In that way they wrote a 280-page 'Account of the Marquesas Islands' and 'An Essay toward a Dictionary and Grammar of the lesser-Australian language, According to the Dialect used in the Marquesas'.

That part which belongs to Crook's living narrative began: 'On the 6th June, 1797, the Duff arrived in Resolution Bay'.

The gaze—the perspective—of the 'Account of the Marquesas Islands' is Samuel Greatheed's. He shapes the 'Account', gives it order, sets the otherness of Fenua'enata into a discourse that he has already begun about the sort of knowledge missionaries will need to do God's work.

The narrative of the 'Account' is William Pascoe Crook's. It is his story. He has had an experience of otherness that very few have had. Much of his experience is indescribable—to himself and to an audience of pious faithful at home. He would never be thespian enough to lose himself in the parts he had to play. He held on too tightly to his own civilised self and Christian soul to let himself go. He never did get over the shock of entering another language that slid so easily into a sexually explicit domain. He never did really cope with apparently uncivilised raw emotions. In the same way he could not see the etiquette that controlled them. There was a carelessness for others seemingly unmoderated by a social contract that he had learned to presume in his own society. What he can describe and translate are all the superficialities—the land and its products, places with all their structures, people and all their roles. He puts time, space and particularity into a small slice of Enata living. It won't be enough for what we would like, but it will be something.

The 'Account' is different from all other documentation of the encounter of Euro-American strangers with Enata, and indeed of the encounter with all native peoples of Oceania. It is written with the aid of an informant, Timouteitei—Timotete to give his name in an orthography more sensitive to the Enata tongue. There had been other island visitors to Europe, most famously two Tahitians, Mai with Cook to England, Aotourou with Bougainville to France. These others, however, were more socialite phenomena among an elite class than transcribers of their own native ways. Timotete was something else. He is an ordinary player in the theatre of four generations of one family, in one valley, Vaitahu, on one island, Tahuata. He is joined by relationship, story and name to more than seventy individuals. The sixteen-year-old Timotete is a tiny pebble, but the ripples of his life are many.

Timotete had other names—Naonukuhiva ('Lost-in-Nukuhiva'), given to him on the death of his father in Nukuhiva, and John Butterworth, under which name he is buried, 2 December 1800, after the twenty cold months of his stay in England. He was the tenth and last child of his father Pahauhonu, who was in turn the brother of Honu, the *haka'iki* (chief) of Vaitahu when James Cook visited what he called Resolution Bay in 1774. Honu fathered Tainai, whom we are about to meet and who acted as protector of Crook during his stay at Tahuata.

Timotete's beach in England was hard, but not cruel, we have to think. Those responsible for him are careful of him. They move him from country to town as the weather changes. They inoculate him against smallpox. They leave him for only a short time in an institution with twenty-four similar waifs on an English beach from Sierra Leone. They remark—and it is a remark made often on other occasions and about other islanders—that his light brown skin seems to give him a sense of superiority over the black Africans. It seemed to vindicate something on their minds!

If the gaze—the hard looking of Greatheed and Crook at Timotete—was not cruel, it was discomforting nonetheless, and Timotete felt it. The older men have a near prurient interest in the violence of Enata society, and of course in its cannibalism. Timotete is defensive. 'Why are you always looking at my people?', he asks them. 'Why not look at our enemies?' 'How come some victims of "fishing" were eaten and others not?', he is asked. (*E ika*, 'fishing', was the Enata expression for catching victims.) 'Of course you wouldn't eat what belongs to the *atua* [gods]', he angrily responds. It does not shake their prejudice that all pagan religion is insincere, but it is a small window on the inner logic and consistency of others' beliefs.

Timotete is too ill most of the time to have the energy or attentiveness to learn what they want to teach him. He only learns English in mono-syllables. He readily learns the Lord's Prayer, which they translate for him into his own tongue. The phrases he learns are clearly those to do with politeness and etiquette—no doubt his 'thank-yous' and his 'how-do-you-dos'. He is remarkably astute in recognising facial and bodily characteristics. He is good at mimicking gestures and behaviour. Above all he catches the shapes of formal gestures in ritual—family devotions, church meetings. In that he is like all the other islanders in their encounter with the strangers. The body in its dances of prayer or of marching guards or of flag raising translates meaning more easily than words.

It is the paucity of Timotete's language that hinders his understanding larger religious thoughts such as the rewards and punishment in a future state, divine grace, vice and virtue. Or so they think. He is self-satisfied in his identity, too. That is a barrier. He knows he is correct in his beliefs, because he has heard his gods speak through crickets. He hasn't heard crickets in England. England has no gods, he says. He is patient with their ignorance. It is because of the paucity of their language, he suggests.

Timotete's short stay with the Mission Society shakes their confidence. They had gone on this first mission to Tahiti, Tonga and The Marquesas in the high hope that they only had to cross the beach with God's Word and it would be heard. 'Forgetful of our national pride and self love, we have fondly imagined that they needed only to see our manners in order to prefer them. But it is exactly the reverse. Although they call us *Atua*s [gods], they say we can do nothing so well as they can, who are only men.' The truth was that those who would missionise had not crossed a beach at all. They might have learned what *atua* really were if they had.

I remember well when I first read 'Account of the Marquesas Islands'. It was in the scorching January heat of 1964. I was researching in Canberra in a set of Nissen huts left over from the Second World War. They passed at the time for the National Library of Australia. They were set on the edge of a bulldozed wasteland that was to become Canberra's Lake Burley Griffin. The five-mile bicycle ride I had taken in the heat from another set of huts that served as the Research School of Pacific Studies at the Australian National University ensured that my hours of reading in the cool 'library' would be long.

The 'Account' I read was a transcription copied on the pink-inked, wafer-thin paper of the copying process of the day. 'Dittoing', I think the process was called. I dare say that you would find the same transcription now on much faded paper in all the great national and university libraries of the world. Certainly they have been wherever I have voyaged for knowledge of Fenua'enata. These transcriptions have had a longer life than that of the young scholar whose gift to scholarship these transcriptions have been. George M. Sheahan Jr was his name. I pay homage to him. His 'Marquesan Source Materials', prepared for a Harvard graduate degree he never successfully completed, made my steps on his same path much easier. Sheahan, in deep depression at his academic failures, killed himself.

I have my own failures in regard to the 'Account' of the Marquesas Islands to record. I, too, have transcribed every word of the 'Account' from the leather-bound quarto volume in the Mitchell Library, Sydney. And I have done the same for the 'Essay of the Lesser-Australian Languages' and a 'Marquesan-English Dictionary' in the London Missionary Society papers in the Library of the London School of Oriental and African Studies.

The Mitchell Library acquired the manuscript 'Account' from the Australian booksellers, Angus & Robertson. All three manuscripts are in Samuel Greatheed's handwriting. Presumably they came from Greatheed's papers, the bulk of which are still undiscovered. Crook himself had a copy of the manuscript. In his letters from Tahiti, to which he returned as a missionary in 1815, he referred to the manuscript as being in three volumes. He said that he had enlarged and corrected the 'Account' over the years, but that copy does not seem to have survived. We remain uncertain how the totality of the manuscript—the general description of the Marquesas, the particular description of individual islands with Crook's story, the linguistic essay and the dictionary—divide themselves into three volumes.

My failure is that I have completed the editing of this totality of manuscripts these past twenty years. For reasons outside my control they remain unpublished. They are here before me as I write. I can only hope that they will pass on to the same archives that George M. Sheahan Jr's had and will be of equal use to scholars as his have been.

While it is true that publication of the 'Account' has been out of my control, that is not the whole story. That years of word-for-word labour have gone unconsummated is painful for me, but I have crossed many beaches in these twenty years. One of those beaches has been the discovery that the display of encyclopaedic knowledge is more self-indulgent than useful. That knowledge more properly is put to use in telling true stories. Let me tell my true stories of writing beaches.

CROSSINGS

Voyaging into Deep Time

I break my narrative for a first Crossing. There will be seven Crossings to come to interrupt my storytelling. Think of them as soliloquies in my theatre. Soliloquies, Raymond Williams told us, are disturbing. 'Ontologically subversive' are his words. Soliloquies are not just stage devices to reveal an inner mind or resolve conflicts in the drama. Soliloquies also blur genres, disturb conventionality. These Crossings bring me, the storyteller, into my stories about beach crossings. That disturbs the conventionality that scholarly learning should be impersonal and that the storyteller should be distant from the story. My belief is to the contrary. A storyteller is always in the story, heart, mind and soul. Better to be occasionally seen than to hide. These crossings are not autobiography, but they are autobiographical. They focus not on my life-story, but on those moments in my life-story that I feel give me the authority to tell the story as I do.

These are moments of 'catharsis' and 'mythos', in Aristotle's words of the theatre. 'Catharsis': the moment of enlightenment when we see the plot. 'Mythos': the emplotting of deep-seated truths into story and drama. There have been moments of crisis and moments of reflection in my life when I have felt that I have seen the plot in this complex business of writing cross-cultural history. I tell of those moments in story.

The Crossings do not join one part of my narrative with another, but they join the whole together. I write in a time in which the writing of cross-cultural history has been reduced to ugly polarities. I cannot change the past but I can soften a hard present with the justness of my reading and the compassion of my understanding.

Deep Time

We all live in deep time. All of us alive are equally distant from our human beginnings through the generations, through the millennia, through the eons of evolution. But deep time impinges on us differently. The deep time reaching back two thousand years to Jesus Christ makes me, a Christian, differently from the way deep time reaching back to Muhammad makes a Muslim, or to Buddha a Buddhist. In a period of 'discovery', encounter, settlement, colony and post-colony, deep time impinges differently on those who come first and those who come later to a land.

These days we who voyage into deep time with our archaeology, our history or our anthropology have a protocol when we perform our learning. 'I honour the first people of this place where I stand to speak', we will say. We do that in Oceania, Australia, the Americas, wherever a people of more shallow time—say two or three hundred years—live in settlement beside a people whose presence in that place reaches back two, forty, sixty millennia. Our protocol is our way of acknowledging that we are conjoined to those with deep time imprinted on their memories, spirits, being and identity. There is no history in these places so modern and contemporary that deep time does not impinge upon it.

Such acknowledgement is 'politically correct' some will say. Yes, it is. It is politely correct as well, and morally correct. Such proprieties are always political. Words empower and disempower. There is a sort of cultural osmosis in such sensitivity. It grows until it is killed by formalism.

I have voyaged into deep time in scientific ways. My Crossing is about how I had to learn to voyage into deep time in other sorts of ways to learn how deep time impinges on the lives of others, and on myself.

F ORTY-TWO YEARS AGO I was privileged to participate in what I believe to be the founding moments of modern Australian archaeology. I was student labour on John Mulvaney's archaeological dig at Fromm's Landing on the Murray River, near Mannum, South Australia. I remember standing on the bottom of the ten-foot pit, the brown/black/red bands of stratified soil all around like a 4000-year history time chart. Mulvaney could hold in the cup of his hands the micro flake artefacts that had come from this pit. But the real knowledge that came from it were in the pollen, the seeds, the sands, the charcoal, the bones and shells that would picture the landscape and the lifestyles of those who lived in it through these four thousand years. I had seen the passion and commitment that had driven Mulvaney to that point. He has never been one for rhetoric and poetry in his words. Let me make the poetry for him. He was a searcher for time in a timeless land.

In Oceania—the Australasian–Pacific region Mulvaney was introducing us students to—the intellectual puzzle was how to describe a past when all of time was on the surface of things—in the typology of artefacts, in the glottochronology of language, in the genetics of blood groups, in the ethnobotany of plants. Time is the sections of a fish's earbone; time is the rings of growth on a tree; time is a pollen count; time is the character of sands on a dune.

Time on the surface of things is made up of a multiplicity of assumptions. Inquiry is inevitably a lateral pursuit as assumptions that give depth and time to any shape and design are tested and debated.

Knowledge of this sort is hard won, full of debates and counter claims, zigzagging through a dozen disciplines. It is never static. There are no short cuts. It is self-interested—in personal ambitions, in institutional rivalries, in the scramble for funded support. There are schemers and frauds and nastiness in such pursuits of knowledge. But altruism and ideals suffuse it too. There is a passion that such knowledge be public, that it be subject to critical appraisal, that it serve a good that is greater than an individual's fame, that it be not destructive of future inquiry.

Archaeology is a political sort of science. Digging up the past is different from writing and reading the past. In archaeology, something is always disturbed—someone's land, someone's bones, someone's property, someone's rights. In archaeology there is rarely going back. Sometimes something can be left to future technologies and future sophistication in research, but there is no undisturbing the disturbed.

So archaeology can never turn in on itself. It can never close its eyes and protest the purity of its ideals without acknowledging how that purity affects others. Archaeology has to negotiate the cultural realities.

History has to negotiate the cultural realities, too. And anthropology. That is Deep Time's beach crossing. To know Deep Time, we need to know more than the archaeologists can tell us. We need to enter into the ways that the first peoples experienced themselves and their timeless land. Any entry into such otherness requires some giving. We need to give the first peoples their language first of all, and with their language all the silences we can't translate. We need to listen. We need to look.

I moved away from archaeology when I began to focus on Pacific studies. I enjoyed the intellectual puzzle of archaeology, but there was not enough narrative, not enough person and passion in archaeology for me. I wanted to study where deep times encountered shallow times. 'Culture contact' I called it for a while. But cultures don't come in contact and 'contact' was too pretty a word to describe the awfulness of what happened. 'Prehistory', but that was to beg the question on how far back history can reach. 'Ethnohistory', yes, if what is meant is the different ways different peoples make sense of the past; no, if it means ethnohistory for native peoples, history for the intruding strangers. Let us not cross beaches on names just yet. History's grace is that it is both a humane science and a humane art.

There was an element of the bizarre and extravagant in Pacific studies that attracted and distracted us forty-five years ago. The Polynesians were 'The Lost Tribes of Israel' was one claim. Easter Island was peopled by St Brendan and his monks was another. No, they were from Outer Space! Thor Heyerdahl had sailed his *Kontiki* raft from the Peruvian coast into the great arc of those Tuamotu islands. Pacific peoples had come from the Americas, Heyerdahl had argued. We scoured everything botanical, linguistic, genetic, material, mythological, historical, anthropological, archaeological to prove him wrong. It was a wonderful intellectual odyssey. Knowledge knew no boundaries, no disciplinary boundaries, no limits to where encompassing Oceania might take us.

When there is no absolute time in such a space, no absolute dating (these were the days before carbon 14), no historical records—then one encompasses it with relative time embodied in typologies, distributions and the structural dynamics of change. The whole space becomes an exercise in surface archaeology. The whole intellectual endeavour becomes a maze of lateral pursuits. We needed a linguistic science to find the lineage of languages. We debated the great typologies of Pacific cultures— Melanesian/Polynesian/ Micronesian. How related are environments to social structures, we asked. What were the dangers of an anthropology that creates an ethnographic present that never was, somewhere between the before and after of the encounter? How do we read the memories underlying myth?

Forty-five years ago, we had a sense that Pacific waters were still uncharted. We were brash. We thought we had discovered something. What it was we would make by what we did rather than bow to some claim of territoriality that others might make. We felt that we had a lodestone in these uncharted waters. It was our history.

Anthropology scandalised us. We took British anthropology's rhetorical scorn for history personally, not knowing it for the politics of discipline that it was. We knew American cultural anthropology only in its most generalised form, and thought A. L. Kroeber as distant from an historical past as Oswald Spengler and Arnold Toynbee. We reserved our deepest scepticism for Pacific ethnography. It was essentialist in character, taking 'Polynesian' and 'Melanesian' out of time as if two hundred years of contact had made no difference. The ethnographers seemed to assume that there was nothing in between the 'now' of their observations and the 'then' of island cultures before contact. And when the ethnographers used Cook, Bougainville and the others as we did, we knew that *we* read our primary sources with much more of a sense of their conditioned, contexted nature than did the anthropologists. Anthropologists, we thought, stopped in the library and published sources. They did not seem to have the zeal to track down the unlikely letter or log or to chase home the past into all the nooks and crannies of personal, social and institutional life. We had the heady experience of knowing that there was not a cultural trait or ritual or legend or collected artefact that did not have an historiography. We *knew* that anthropologists had no patience for all the lateral pursuits that were essential to history. Every new source found raised a question about its relation to the rest, the interpretive framework into which it must be put, the contextual knowledge that would make sense of it.

We had R. G. Collingwood and his archaeology of Roman Britain to help us understand Easter Island, Marc Bloch and his study of feudalism to know what culture might really be. R. H. Tawney and Max Weber, with their delicious ironies on the unseen reality behind religion, informed our missionary studies. We stood on archaeological peaks with Sir Mortimer Wheeler and felt that we had been offered a kingdom. We even flew in a Tiger Moth with O. G. S. Crawford and saw *The Lost Villages of England* in the shadows on wheat and barley fields and marvelled on what new skills we would need to learn to write the history we wanted to write.

We learned how limiting it was to define one's history by the locale of its study—'Pacific History', 'American History', 'British History'—or by its period—'Eighteenth Century', 'Renaissance', 'Ancient'. These were years of innocence in which we read E. D. Merrill on botany, Bengt Anell on fishhooks, A. C. Haddon and James Hornell on canoes, Peter. H. Buck on material culture, Edwin G. Burrows on boundaries, E. S. C. Handy on religion, and Katherine Luomalo on myths, in the belief that we were doing history. We felt immodestly superior to the 'antiquarians' of the Pacific—Elsdon Best, Percy Smith, F. W. Christian. Their vast knowledge only served madcap theories about Polynesian origins and movements. In out-of-the-way places from Finland to New Zealand, from Leningrad to Valparaiso, men and women had collected the products of their experience of the Pacific. We felt that there was not an archive or a library or a museum, a learned society or a colonial bureaucracy in all of Europe and the Americas in which the ethnographic experience of the Pacific was not texted in some way. That immense variety of texts—logs, diaries, letters, journals, government reports, lectures, books, notes, written-down oral traditions, notes of memories—encapsulated the experience of those who made the texts, as well as something of the otherness of nature and cultures that was experienced. We felt that the peculiar joy of Pacific history was to catch the seers, the seen and the seeing, as well as the understandings of all those who looked on human condition and told us what it means. They were innocent times, magical times of intellectual purity, as if knowledge had no real consequences, as if living was a *Times Literary Supplement* crossword puzzle.

But there was a beach we needed to cross. It was the beach into Deep Time.

'Allow us to speak for ourselves', the Untouchable women of Lucknow said to the anthropologist R. S. Khare in 1979. 'Words mean so much to us.' 'Our words, crude and few, say well what we are. We do not need to borrow words from the learned.' That, I suppose, is a lesson that any anthropologist and historian must learn. Those whom we re-present don't need to borrow the words of the learned to say who they are. Their words are never-endingly subtle and manifold. The crudities and sparsities are ours, the translators, as we give their words typologies and grammar.

That culture is talk and living is story is the discovery of the 'learneds' of this twentieth century. Clifford Geertz, Jacques Derrida, Michel Foucault, Roland Barthes, Paul Ricoeur, Ludwig Wittgenstein have said it so.

Talk is never bare words, of course. It is all the ways words are symbolised. It is voice and gesture, rhythm and timing, colour and texture. Talk is tattoo. Talk is body paint and house columns. Talk is never just stream of consciousness either. It is shaped and dramatised—in a dance, a song, a story, a joke. Talk might seem to be blown away by the wind on the lips, but it never is. It is always archived in some way in the continuities of living. Talk joins past, present and future.

'My grandmother gifted me with a pure heart and a knack of "reading" a woman's belly with nimble fingers', one of the Untouchable midwives told Khare. Talk is reading and hearing too. As she went on, the midwife might have been Wittgenstein talking about reading the fictions of languaging.

> [My grandmother] used to tell me how her fingers 'saw' within the womb. Though illiterate, she 'read' like an Ayurvedic doctor, the full story of the mother and of the fragile life inside her. At ten, I remember I accompanied her a few times to her 'cases', just to move my trembling fingers over a mother's swollen belly, I felt so proud. My grandmother later taught me to recognize different signs and messages a pregnant woman's walk, cravings, limb movements, pains, and bodily odours emitted. [Brahman and Untouchable] are born the same way, covered by the same mucus, blood and fluids . . . With the first cry of the just-born, I thank God and look at my soiled hands with pride. Each time it happens I feel a joy.

Fingers that 'see' and 'read' are as chameleon-like as the words that describe them. Native tongues are just as semiotic. Living words weep and laugh, make *double entendre*, weave a double helix into gender, status and group.

It is a humbling thing to say, but a truth so obvious to a younger generation of 'learneds' in the development of an understanding of what it means to cross into Deep Time was hard learned by us, an older generation. But I can only speak for myself. And I can only speak of the past. I meet all my Natives, I meet all my Strangers, in libraries and archives. Historians never observe the past. They only observe the past transcribed, textualised, in some way. The past, for an historian, is always somebody else's history. That's true, of course, for the anthropological fieldworker as well. Life experienced is always in the moment-after, textualised in a story, an explanation, a recounted myth. But when the past is more distant, an historian has to be more intellectually puritanical. An historian has always to look for disturbances, re-textualising. In an historian's archaeology of knowledge, it is the tomb-robbers that are obvious, the disturbers. This breeds a certain scepticism about the continuities of culture. This scepticism, it seems to me looking back on forty-five years of representation in the Pacific, hasn't served us well.

When I began my experience of Pacific representations, we struggled with a name that came to us out of British anthropology and out of

Africa. It was 'zero point'. British anthropology did not trust history at the time. Or rather, it believed that there was only one sort of history worthy of the name. That was von Rankean, scientific history. This bred a sort of puritanical intellectualism.

The zero point was that dividing moment between a Before, when an indigenous culture was in its pure form, and an After of the encounter, when it was somehow adulterated. The zero point was a dividing line between authentic and inauthentic culture. In the Pacific, the zero point encouraged the 'as if' anthropology from the late 1920s through the early 1950s. Expeditions went to the Pacific islands and described cultures not in the Now, but 'as if' they were in the Before. Island cultures were frozen in an ethnographic present that had never been.

I suspect that each one of us experiences personally the disappearance of a zero point, that moment when the divisions between a Before and an After are blurred, that moment when a new 'I and an old I' merge, when apparent discontinuities are transformed in the continuities of living. The zero point disappears when my plagiarist, borrowing self merges with my creative inventive self.

That personal experience we have of the disappearing zero point is mirrored in a cultural way in the encounters between indigenous peoples and intruding strangers. To enter into Deep Time is to celebrate the creativity of that encounter

This is not as esoteric nor as apolitical a point as it might seem. In Australia and in many nations of the Pacific for most of this century and to this day there has been a strong belief in a zero point. There has been a strong belief among colonial powers that pure aboriginality belongs to the Time Before. Aboriginal cultures that have in some way transformed themselves are seen as bastard and illegitimate. The politics of the zero point is to be seen in our school textbooks over a hundred years. The authentic aborigines were the picanninnies and the nomads, not those down the street. Aboriginality in the zero point belongs to the museums of the mind.

I would like to say, 'no'. In cultural change there is no Before and After, only a Now. In cultural changes of the encounter, there is rarely a polarity between one way of doing things and another. In cultural changes of the encounter, beliefs, objects, words are not 'borrowed' from one culture by another. They are transformed, re-created. No belief, no object or word of one culture is nearer the reality it describes or encapsulates than the belief, object or word of another. Identity in cultural change is continuous. There is no loss of authenticity. Culture is as fluent as the languages that sustain it.

Encounters, by the prejudice of our established histories of them, are short, sudden and violent. In fact, encounters are slow, drawn-out. They belong to the *longue durée* of living. They never end. In a sense, too, they have no beginning. Encountering otherness, finding cultural identity in the mirror of otherness, seeing the metaphoric in something else—all these transforming processes are ever-present in culture. They are rarely episodic. They rarely turn around one event. This creative encountering is a repetitious, reflective thing. It happens not once, but a myriad of times. It is constantly renewed by story, dance, painting. It is re-presented. It is represented in all the social dramas of living. All encountering has continous theatre.

In the encounter, the zero point disappears in this theatre. Theatre does not need a building, but it needs a social space. It needs a space closed down by the willingness of an audience to watch and of performers to play. This theatre is a moment of in-between, a moment of seeing, a moment of theory. Every representation of this encounter, every painting, every carving, every craft, every song, every poem, every novel, every play, every dance is a moment of self-identification. A cultural self is recognised in the otherness of the encounter. This self is no Self with a capital S. This Other is no Other with a capital O. This self, like culture, is always clothed in particularity. That is the constant cultural miracle. Every difference has a sameness. Every smallness has a largeness. Every shape, every colour, every gesture has a theory.

The freezing rain on our backs chilled our bodies. Our spirits were numb, too. On the Friday of this holiday weekend, we had buried our oldest and closest friend. But we were a long way from his grave outside Melbourne. We were slipping and sliding in the wet clay and fuzzy underlay of the saltbushes at Lake Mungo in western New South Wales. We were on a pilgrimage to a much more ancient burial site, the graves of Mungo Man and Mungo Woman. Their bones had rested there for thirty thousand years, some say sixty thousand.

The seven of us were approaching the graves along the southern extension of the lunette of dunes that form the eastern edge of the ancient, dried-out lake. The vast arena of the lake bed had begun to glisten in the rain. It was easy to see that we were walking a shoreline. It was easy to sense the teeming aquatic life of many yesteryears.

The Walls of China were ten miles to the northeast. We had walked them the day before. We had wandered through this 100,000-year-old archive of climatic change. The eroded dunes are an earthen rainbow of greys, browns and whites as the blown debris of the lake in its different stages arched over one another. In the washes and on the flats it is difficult not to walk on shells and bones and an occasional stone flake. The dunes are alive with dead signs of living. The spirit of the place is patent to feel. The silence of its vast spaces is monumental. It leaves you alone with your communings.

We were more pilgrims than tourists. We had asked Dr Jim Bowler to be our guide and two custodians of the Muthi Muthi and Barkindji peoples to be our mentors. We had come to wonder and understand, to feel the timelessness of our land. Jim, a quaternary geologist, has been a student of Lake Mungo for thirty-one years. He it was who had discovered the fired and fused bones of Mungo Woman in November 1968 and had brought back Professor John Mulvaney and Dr Rhys Jones to rescue them with full archaeological proprieties. It was Jim Bowler, too, who five years later discovered the buried body of Mungo Man. It was a wondrous discovery, giving dates then of more than thirty thousand years, but which now he would probably extend to at least forty-three thousand years before the present. More importantly, the red ochre in the grave could only have come from 150 miles away. It was a sign of their carefulness to make that transition from life to death a cultural, ritual act. Forty-three thousand years ago, men and women made sacraments of their life passages.

The sun came out as we made our way to these sites. The vista was extraordinary. The whole top of the dune here had been blown away, leaving the oldest sands exposed. Small uneroded sand columns stood like miniaturised mesas in an Arizona desert. Freshwater mollusc shells, calcified pupa, bones of kangaroo and Tasmanian devil and otoliths, the almost indestructible parts of a fish's ear, litter the ground. Here and there is the shadow of 40,000-year-old wombat burrows, the bones of their owners still in the hub.

There is only an archaeologist's stake in the sand to mark the precise place of the ancient burials. The bones that were buried there are the cultural heritage of us all now. Their custodians are the Muthi Muthi, the Barkindji and the scientists.

This is as sacred a space as I have ever been in. Our Muthi Muthi and Barkindji mentors joined themselves easily to its timelessness. Here they were Muthi Muthi and Barkindji more than aboriginal. On this more than 100,000-year-old beach were the ancient relics of the Golden Perch and the Murray Cod they had caught and the grubs that they caught the fish with, the game they had hunted, the foods they had eaten only yesterday in their own lives, only lifetimes ago in their family memories.

It was hard for us to stay outside their experience. I can only speak for myself. I felt joined to the timelessness of the spaces around us. This was 'my' land I wanted to say, by right of inheritance, by the obligations of that inheritance. I have an identity determined maybe by First Fleets and national centenaries, but I also have an identity that is determined by the Land and all that is in it and on it.

The rains had set in at Lake Mungo and had made our direct road home impassable. We drove carefully in a wide circuit of this extraordinary landscape. 'Land', 'country', 'camp', 'home' are reduced to one term in first people's languages. Thus language fills the land with extraordinary intensity. Clan, family, person, people—fears, confidences, reason, emotions—fill the spaces with words and spirit. 'Old man', another old man told Bill Stanner, the anthropologist, 'You listen! Something is there; we do not know what. Something . . . like engine, like power, plenty of power; it does hard work; it pushes.'

2

Being There

Voices from the beach are hard to hear. They can be snatched from the lips by the wind or drowned in the white noise of the waves. There are also beaches on which voices are hard to hear because they are lost in a silence that clings like scented tropical air. It is the silence of vast spaces. It is also the cold silence of death.

'Being there' for an historian is that feeling for the past that can only be matched by the hours, the days, the weeks, the months, the years she or he sits at the desks in the archives. It is an assurance that one's extravagance with time there is rewarded with a sensitivity that comes in no other way. It is an overlaying of images one on the other. It is a realisation that knowledge of the past is cumulative and kaleidoscopic, extravagantly wasteful of energy.

'Being there' can also mean making a voyage to those places where the past is imprinted on the landscape. It is touching, feeling, smelling, hearing the past there, having the silence envelop one, crossing the beach and being conscious of one's intrusion. In 1974 I had the opportunity of 'being there' in Fenua'enata. Paul Gauguin and Herman Melville had 'been there' before me. I listen to the advice of the one and follow the practice of the other.

Enata (Marquesans)

Enata (Marquesans) settled their Land about a hundred generations ago. Archaeology tells us that the settlement was likely to have been between three hundred years Before the Common Era (300 BCE) and three hundred years into the Common Era (300 CE). There have been digs of what are believed to be first settlements at Ua Huka and northeastern Nukuhiva. We have told the story of first settlement in the prologue, 'A Most Remarkable Voyage'.

Linguistics and typologies of material artefacts and social institutions tell us a more surprising fact. This settlement on the eastern edge of Polynesia— let us call it Remote Oceania—anteceded the settlement of Tahiti, Hawai'i and Aotearoa (New Zealand). This settlement movement eastward turned back on itself and seeded the islands of the central, northern and southern Pacific and moved on further east to Pitcairn and Rapanui (Easter Island).

Archaeologists describe these earliest settlements, the progressive movement from the northeastern islands of Fenua'enata to the southwestern, and the evolution through nearly two thousand years of them all. But for more than two hundred years Enata culture at the end of that evolution has been described by strangers who have 'been there'. Thousands have 'been there' for the few days of their ship's stay. Hundreds have 'been there' for years—even lifetimes—as beachcombers, administrators, traders and missionaries. A few have 'been there' as professional observers—archaeologists, anthropologists, historians.

Early visitors easily identified Enata as 'Polynesian' in language, bodily physique and cultural characteristics. Enata women were the most beautiful in all the Pacific, they reported; their tattoos the most brilliant; their behaviour the most wild; their government the most chaotic. As accounts of the like of Robarts, Kabris and Crook and those they informed became public knowledge, the image of Enata as the prototypical cannibal islander and 'last savage' emerged.

The professional observers have always been teased by the nature of chiefly power in Fenua'enata and the dynamics in the environment that produced it—whether it was devolution from, or was on its evolutionary way to, the sort of chiefly power to be found in Hawai'i or Tahiti. Enata's custom of *pekio* (secondary husband) and whether it was truly polyandrous has been a matter of debate as well.

Missionaries had an interest in those essential parts of Enata cultural living that needed to be destroyed if Enata were to be civilised and Christianised. The list of core cultural things to be eliminated is long: tattooing, embalming the dead, singing and dancing, telling mythic stories, beating drums, anointing with *eka* (ginger), wearing pandanus-fruit leis and cloth covered in scent, *mau*, memorial feasts for the dead, war, *tapu* houses. In these things Enata lived, and then died.

Flying to The Land: Hiva Oa, Tahuata

December 1974

I am flying over an immense ocean. Not, like the yolla, shearing, arcing or knifing, to be sure. Actually I am sitting nervously behind two gesticulating French pilots. They point to every button on their instrument panel as if it is a subject of some great philosophical or mechanical crisis. It is December 1974. We have just taken off from Tahiti's Faa airport in a wet season storm. We are over this vast ocean on a northeast tack. That small part of it beneath our northeast flight over the 950 miles separating Tahiti from the Marquesas was the northern tip of the Tuamotu Archipelago, known in older sailing days as the Low or Dangerous Archipelago. Its seventy-eight atolls and innumerable hidden reefs fan a 1250-mile arc across the eastern approaches to the Central Pacific. Although it was my first time among them, my mind's eye had scanned them many, many times. I had mapped them in all sorts of ways—for the variety of their flora and fauna, for the variety of their cultural forms, for their populations and the relics of their populations, for the canoe voyaging among them.

My first images of the Pacific had come to me through the texts that innumerable intruders into this vast ocean had made of their experiences. I have never recovered from the historian's first excited discovery that most of history comes from unpublished sources—from letters, diaries, and logs imprinted as much with tears, sweat, blood and the dirt of time as by ink and pencil. I have always counted it the great privilege of an historian's life to finger these pages, sometimes for the first time after they were written. I have always felt as well that because so much of living is lost in the inscribing of it the historian's obligation is to saturate her- or himself in all there is. So history writing is as much a pilgrimage to all the places where these unique and disparate remnants of the past are to be found as it is a culling from books on library shelves. In the way of things, the history of strangers coming into the Pacific is to be found where they came from—London, Boston, Paris, Rome, Nantucket—rather than the places they came to. But here in a Twin Otter 20,000 feet above the sea, I am making a pilgrimage the other way round. I am flying to The Land.

In December 1974, I would not have called the islands I was flying to, The Land, Fenua. Nor would I have called the people who lived there, the Natives, Enata. I would have called them by the name Spanish outsiders had given them four hundred years earlier, The Marquesas, the Marquesans. But crossing their beach would be my learning experience. I would get the confidence and the courage to call them what they called themselves.

I am apprehensive. Fenua'enata, The Land and its Natives, had changed my life. But I had been to The Land and met its Natives only in libraries and archives. I know that I am stranger to them. I know the cost of every stranger's intrusion. The sadness of their story had affected me ever since I began to learn it. Inevitably I come with a sense of trespass. Their terrible story and my knowledge of it had been the capital of my life. The rewards of twenty years' study of them to this time had been great. Now I bring to them in my luggage the pride of my academic life to this time, my first book about them, *The Marquesan Journal of Edward Robarts* (1974). I know all my shortcuts in that book. I know all its tricks of camouflage for my ignorance.

Early in my studies of Fenua'enata, I had read Frantz Fanon's *The Wretched of the Earth* (1961). It had shaken me to my core. In a world of victims, he wrote, there are no innocents. No one can write two-sided history who in some way benefits from the power of the victors. No one can mediate between the disempowered living and the voiceless dead. All of us writing in a history so terrible as that of the Pacific—or of the Americas or of Africa for that matter—have had to resolve that dilemma for ourselves. No doubt we all do it differently. For me, giving the dead a voice has been reason enough for my history. I am with Karl Marx, too. The function of my history is not so much to understand the world as to change it. If my history by story and reflection disturbs the moral lethargy of the living to change in their present the consequences of their past, then it fulfils a need. I have not silenced any voice by adding mine.

I had failed rather badly in the photography classes I had taken in preparation for my visit to the Fenua'enata. I had been too timid to enter the private space of those 'interesting' faces of the poor and old and eccentric my teachers wanted me to invade. Now as the pilots begin to tap their compass and reach for their binoculars, I find my timidity is returning.

Still, I have my camera in my hand as we approached The Land, and my face pressed against the cabin porthole. Suddenly, through a gap in the clouds, I realise I am looking down on the one place in all The Land I had wanted to see, Vaitahu Bay on the island of Tahuata. At Vaitahu, the sad history of The Land had begun. Madre de Dios, the Spaniards had christened it with blood in 1595. Less bloodily, but bloodily just the same, James Cook had renamed it Resolution Bay in 1774. I have a slide of my

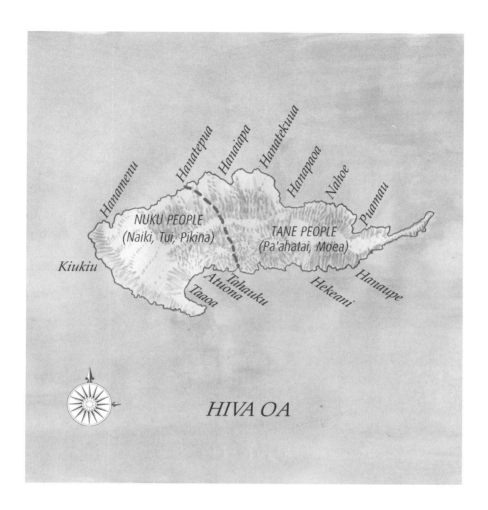

first sighting of a beach that has meant so much to me. It is a precious slide. Fading, though.

Seeing Vaitahu, however, does not mean that I am there. We land on Hiva Oa, the neighbouring island to Tahuata. The landing-strip looks as long and wide as an aircraft carrier. It is on the top of a ridge behind the village and beach of Atuona.

On the black sand beach at Atuona, Paul Gauguin had painted 'Riders on the Beach' in 1902. Two hooded riders—death on horseback—lead the other horsemen to an endless horizon. There is nothing 'real' in the painting, nothing of Atuona's black sand, dark tumbling rocks, closed bay. Differences are sponged out in his consuming effort to make this mythic and universal, a creation by the last savage of the last savages. Gauguin doesn't write his beach. He paints it out of what he calls his 'crazy imagination', filled with his own native myths, shaped by all the art history that has infused his life.

My first ambition is to walk the black sand beach at Atuona. Death had been frequent on that beach. The bay was called Traitors' Bay, for the fate of the several Euro-American boat crews that had been cut off there. But death had come more usually for Enata from canoes of their island enemies as they came 'fishing' for victims. In times of social crisis or in celebration of some sacred moment in their lives, Enata went fishing (*e ika*) for victims, *heana*. They would go raiding other islands, other valleys. They snatched their victims where they could, off the shore, from their houses. These *heana* were brought back, sometimes alive, sometimes dead, but always in the fashion in which fishermen brought back a catch of their most *tapu* fish. They were strung on poles, with large hooks in their mouths and baskets of bait attached to their limbs. When the victims had been killed, their corpses were mocked and derided. Parts of bodies were ceremonially eaten. Then they were strung up with other sacrifices in the *me'ae*, the sacred spaces of the gods.

Back from the beach—over Gauguin's shoulders as he painted—we walked the dusty roads and up the trails among the silent stone remains. Here and there a *tiki* head had been incorporated into a fence. The massive statues had long gone from this valley. You can see them in the museums of the world, staring wide-eyed and meaningless at the bored crowds. I liked the *tiki* in the fences and low shrubs better than all the *tiki* in the exhibition halls. The *tiki* in the fences had a modest dignity. Shadows and flowers gave them a life that spotlights and pedestals take away.

Everywhere in the valley of Atuona are empty stone remains. They were stone platforms on which houses once stood, or stone stages on which people had once danced and feasted, or stone altars in sacred places where sacrifices had been placed. They were scattered among the trees, overgrown and silent, all through the valley. They were relics of populations wiped out in the few short years of their encounter with Euro-American strangers. Diseases for which the people had no immunity killed most; but they died more horribly than that. In a cultural paroxysm in the 1860s, they killed themselves. When they had no explanation of why they were dying in such horrific numbers, they turned to killing one another for the machinations and sorcery they presumed were among them.

The missionaries early in the nineteenth century, hopeless in their efforts at conversion, had focused on destruction of the *tapu* system, which they believed was the key to native heathenism. They promised that the native dying would stop if the evil of the *tapu* was broken. They evolved a series of rituals by which the native gods were challenged to punish broken *tapu*. Men were asked to walk under women's most intimate clothing. Women were asked to walk over the most sacred objects. The effect was not so much change as emptiness and listless hopelessness. Enata were numb for a while, with liquor as much as cultural anomie.

Then in the 1860s, here in the valley of Atuona, there was a terrible revival of an old *tapu* custom, *e ika*, fishing for victims. In the cultural hopelessness of the 1860s, any rebirth of custom would be bastard. The revival of *e ika* was monstrous. Whatever balancing principles there had been to the death and violence of the old ways were now gone. This time, the killings had no ritual. They were not across islands and valleys. They were internecine, familial even, and orgiastic. In a population depleted in fifty years to three thousand from a hundred thousand, they now killed one another by the hundreds.

The death throes of this valley of Atuona were awful. It was and is today a place of extraordinary beauty, the sort of wild beauty that Gauguin ached to find. The peak of Temetiu dominates it. The wide sweeping southern arm of its bay bends out into the straits towards the neighbouring island of Tahuata. Its black sand beach collects the waves coming in on the southeast winds. Its river sparkles over a bed of stones. But its silence clings.

Among the silent stones, Gauguin's imagination does not seem so crazy, and nor his playing with the real so irresponsible. His cowled riders of death have a monkish feel, enough to remind us how much death those who preached eternal life had brought. The wash of his colours reminds us that any re-presentation of the past will have a dreamlike quality. The past has its own silences that never will be voiced.

Those last miles to Vaitahu were to prove harder to make than we had thought. It was a few days before Christmas. The islands had succumbed to a deeper level of quiet. There was a gasoline shortage, too. No one could guarantee a return from Tahuata to Atuona.

As we walked the dirt roads and trails, the women watched our passing with indifference. The children were more curious. Young men parked their motor scooters or tied their horses by the verandah of the general store. That store, a little larger and grander now, is still standing in its two storeys as when Gauguin shopped in it. We have his accounts for his purchases still. I note that on 26 December 1901, seventy-three years almost to the day that we bought our biscuits and our baguettes, he had an order for 34 litres of claret, 16 litres of rum, preserved butter, tins of asparagus, olive oil, a sack of rice, 2 litres of garlic, 5 kilos of onions and 12 kilos of sugar. I note too that his cuisine was not just French. It was provincial too: tins of tripe, tins of sardines, tins of sausages, litres of absinth, and cigarettes, many cigarettes. He was a very civilised last savage.

We paid Gauguin honour. We walked up the hill of Hueakihi to the cemetery. His grave is easily seen. Amid white cement tombs open to the sun, his is of reddish rocks and shaded by a frangipani tree. Seventy-five years after his death one of Gauguin's final wishes was granted. The cast of a favourite work, a ceramic sculpture he had called *Oviri*, was placed on his grave. *Oviri* was a favourite of Picasso, too, and inspired him. Gauguin had sculpted *Oviri* in Brittany on his return to France after his first trip to Tahiti, just before that terrible brawl that left him with a wounded leg for life. Gauguin thought it his finest work of art. He knew it was enigmatic, mysterious. '*Oviri*' in Tahitian means 'wild', 'savage'. The woman of the statue is indeed wild, a mixture of incompatible lore. She has the head of a mummified Marquesan skull. She crushes a wolf under her feet, just as those most unwild statues of the Virgin crush a serpent. Gauguin put his customary signature on the statue, 'PGO'. That reads as 'pego'. It is sailors' slang for 'prick'. *Oviri*'s wildness creates a disturbing restlessness over the grave. One cannot think that Gauguin's bones rest in peace.

We came down from Hueakihi, the hill of the cemetery, still on our quest to reach Tahuata. The mission compound is a square of two-storey concrete buildings, one a girls' boarding school, another the convent of the Sisters of St Joseph of Cluny. The church within the square is large and suburban. Robert Louis Stevenson, when he came to The Land, fell in love with the country churches the missionaries had built, often with their own hands. And it is true. Their white walls and peaked spires nestle comfortably against the green walls of the valleys they stand in. They landscape the ragged ridges around them. The church at Atuona is more nakedly intrusive, save for its carved wooden portals and its doors. There, the woodworkers, this time native and twentieth-century, wrestle with the syncretisms of their beliefs. In a religion as historical as Christianity the figures of the founders—Jesus, Mary and all the first holy heroes—have the shapes and particularities of their birth. But in carving them in wood, is it more important to catch the historicity of their bodies or the universalities of their spirits? The wood carvers need their freedom to link their own humanity to something that goes beyond it. They do it tentatively, with no extravagance or didacticism. I am not sure whether Gauguin would have been pleased or enraged.

This church and this mission are at the ends of the earth. The ripples created by the stone John XXIII threw into the pond of the Church's complacency are just reaching The Land. In 1974, Vatican Council II was not ten years complete. The Land had had its holocaust a hundred years before. Europe's holocaust was Europe's preparation for Vatican Council II. It gave the Church the courage—for a while at least—to listen to the silence of that horror and to respond to it. At the ends of the earth that silence was harder to hear. An expatriate mission church lived in the timewarp of its own expatriatism. When we went to midnight mass on Christmas Eve, Vatican Council II was eerily present in a distant way. The mass was demystified. The secret language of Latin was gone. The altar of sacrifice had become a table for communion. The priest's gestures and demeanour were open and inclusive, not divisive and self-important. But there was division nonetheless. The de-Latinised liturgy was doubly vernacular—French and Marquesan. Every French prayer and reading had a Marquesan echo. On the left of the church sat the sisters and the girls of the boarding school. On the right sat the Atuona community. The left was all French, hymns as well. The right was all Marquesan, hymns as well. The Lord, we assumed, was bilingual.

The rule of the boarding school prevailed for the girls. Not a word of Marquesan was even to be spoken by them while they were at school. The wood carvers, we felt, handled their double-visioned beliefs a little better.

Kindness does not have a pre- or post-Vatican Council II dimension, however. The sisters on our inquiry said that, yes, there were teachers at the school returning to Tahuata for the Christmas holidays and gave us their names, Melanie and Taro, and where we would find them. Melanie and Taro when we visited them agreed to take us to Tahuata but could not bring us back. In our desperation, we thought we would take the risk of finding another way back.

It took us several days to reach Vaitahu, however, and then only after dramatic rescues from a drifting, powerless boat we had boarded at Atuona. In the end we came to Vaitahu as the Spaniards had come four hundred years ago, and James Cook two hundred years ago. Like them we could not see the bay, hidden as it was behind the high bluff at its northeast point. But I knew it was there because I could see the effect of the blast of wind that tunnelled down from the mountains. Every ship that anchored there felt that wind and needed a double anchor on the sandy sloping floor of the bay to stay there. I don't know how many times I have written on card or paper a note from a log, a journal or a letter about the wind. Just seeing it on the waters outside Vaitahu was a thrill. I was nearly there where ten thousand times I had been in my mind.

We crossed the beach at Vaitahu in total disarray. Our experiences on the water had unsettled us. We needed an aggression for negotiating accommodation and transport that we did not have. Our softness bred distrust. But an old man, Teifitu Umu, took us in hand. He had rheumy eyes and feet swollen with elephantiasis. He is dead now, by a few months, as I write. With a shuffling walk he took us up the path beside the stream that flowed down the valley. From somewhere in my reading I remembered that this stream had become a flooded torrent in 1797 and had carried houses and their inhabitants into the bay.

Teifitu was a widower. Our appreciation of his kindness did not displace our dismay at the conditions of his house. But he had given us hospitality and we swallowed our qualms and used it. From the moment of our arrival a gaggle of children had also adopted us. They watched our social gaucheries with great amusement. The adults were more distant, but friendly.

After a sparse supper, Teifitu came to talk. In the growing dark, we sat at his table. I brought out my copy of *Edward Robarts*. I will never forget that evening as we bent over it and I tried to convey in my poor French and poorer Marquesan what its English said. He was clearly excited to talk with somebody with an interest in the island. He wrote his name in my diary, Teifitu Gregoire Umu, and then the line of his genealogy that took him back to Iotete, the *haka'iki* (chief) of Vaitahu, whose story I am about to tell. And to Iotete's father, Tainai, who had welcomed Robarts, Kabris and Crook. And to Tainai's father, Honu, who had welcomed James Cook. He

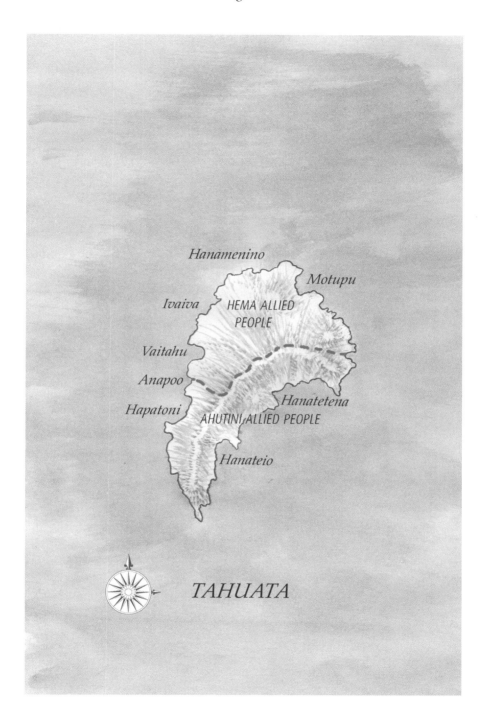

wrote down, too, the names of all the families still on the island. I have these pages still. I hold them precious, not so much for their information, but because they told me how much I didn't know and reminded me of my obligations in regard to silences that were not mine to break.

Things of the past—all those artefacts we call cultural—come into the present as 'cargo' across the beaches of island cultures. Their encapsulated meanings—status in a colour, cosmology in a shape, gender in a texture—are transformed in the new environment of the present into other meanings—of heritage, of evidence, of art, of loot, of souvenirs. The history of things will have to enfold the meanings of the present in which they were made and all the meanings of their successive presents.

It is the same with places. The history in places, especially in places of cross-cultural encounters, will take as much imagination as science to see. Blood and ashes are blown away with the dirt. Shouts and songs die on the wind. Pain and happiness are as evanescent as memory. To catch the lost passions in places, history will have to be a little more artful than being a 'non-fiction'. It will have to have, among other graces, a trust in and a sense of the continuities of living through different times, despite all the transformations and translations that masquerade as discontinuities.

Teifitu walked us round the sights and sites of the valley. Behind the beach of rolling stones in a cleared area, a breadfruit tree stands. Somewhere nearby the Spaniards said mass and killed those among Enata who jostled during it. Somewhere nearby they set up three stakes for three bodies. Who knows in what theatre or for what purpose, a soldier pierced the side of the body on the central stake with a spear. No word of whether water ran from the wound.

Deep in the valley at the end of a line of trees is a monument to three French soldiers killed in ambuscade by Enata in 1843. Teifitu showed us where and how the deaths occurred. When I asked him where the monument was for Enata dead, he shrugged his shoulders. No, there were no monuments, but there is memory and there will be history.

Make no doubt about that. There will be history. I won't be there to read it. Perhaps not you either nor your children's children. But these dead will be heroes for their resistance. If there is one thing we have learned in the Pacific, it is that if the Fatal Impact of the Euro-Americans killed hundreds of thousands of lives, it did not kill memories. These memories will undoubtedly serve their successive presents. These memories will be debated, revised. No doubt some day someone will start an archaeological dig around these monuments or the French fort. They will collect the musket balls and the sling stones, make their histories, build their museums. They will make two-sided history we have to hope.

The 'French presence' began on 1 May 1842, the name day of Louis-Philippe, France's uncomfortable monarch. In this improbable place, a backwater in the vast Pacific Ocean, Admiral Abel Dupetit-Thouars established an imperial presence for France with an occupation force of several hundred troops.

The Admiral took possession of Vaitahu with all the appropriate proprieties. He set up a flagpole. He beat the soil with his sword three times. He had the band play *Domine Salvum* for the king and the *Marseillaise* for his changed kingdom. After Solemn High Mass, he had the local 'chiefs' sign the cession of their land. The Ministre de Marine insisted that the documents be signed in triplicate. You can see the spidery scrawls and crosses still in the National Archives, Paris.

Taking possession of The Marquesas was easier than knowing what to do with them once they were possessed. The whole French caper was largely Dupetit-Thouars' idea. The French public knew nothing of it and were to be enraged when they discovered that they were saddled with the expense and tedium of their useless empire.

As Dupetit-Thouars saw it, there was nowhere else for the French to go in the Pacific. The British had narrowly beaten them to New Zealand. The Russians were developing Alaska and Kamchatka. The Americans were pioneering the Rocky Mountains and were the main influence in Hawai'i. On a map of Mercator projection, or in some model in a global strategist's head, The Marquesas were in the centre of the Pacific. They were on the crossroads between Panama and Sydney, Cape Horn and Shanghai. The British, Dupetit-Thouars said, would need a passport to traverse the Pacific.

But winds and currents and Great Circle navigation don't work like global strategists' models. The Marquesas remained as unstrategic as they ever were. There is an almost pathetic letter from Dupetit-Thouars to his Ministre de Marine as he arrived in Fenua'enata, explaining that now he had arrived there were some questions he would like to ask. There were ten islands in the *Îles des Marquises* and dozens of inhabited valleys, he reported. He would probably need about a thousand troops to control them. And, incidentally, what about laws? What systems of justice would there be? Who had power over life and death? Who owned the land? Should there be intermarriage? . . .

Those the French said they owned did not feel owned. In The Land, resistance was savage. At Vaitahu, the French made Iotete 'king'. They gave him a pasteboard crown decorated with glass beads and colossal feathers. They dressed him in a red shag coat with enormous gold epaulettes in the style of Louis XV. Someone among the officers said he looked like a Bourbon, if one forgot the tattoos. They had given him a flag, too, of red and white squares. It was the French naval signal flag for evening mess. They laughed and laughed at this joke on a cannibal king.

It did not take long for Iotete to realise that whatever greatness had been thrust upon him, he was greatly diminished. The French left two hundred troops in his valley. Only two hundred of his people had survived the 'ecological imperialism' that had come across their beaches in the form of diseases for which they had no immunity. The French soldiers made servants of them all and prostitutes of the women. The soldiers' hygiene was appalling. Iotete's people began quickly to die of dysentery. So Iotete took them out of the valley and retired to the mountains.

The sudden silence and loneliness of Vaitahu was disturbing to the French. This was not what empires were made of. They brought in enemies of Iotete and made one of them 'king' and decided to expel Iotete altogether from his island. Their military effort was singularly unsuccessful. Two of the soldiers, including a lieutenant, were killed. Then there was a siege of the soldiers' encampment. But the dysentery was killing Enata more quickly than the muskets. Iotete's people literally melted away with the flux.

So the French left Vaitahu. There are no Solemn High Masses for retreats as there are for possessions. There is no accounting for the costs of vicious absurdity, either. Perhaps it is the banality of their evil that should disturb us, not the scope of it. It is their bad faith in suggesting that it could not be otherwise. It is the immorality of doing to native peoples what their civilisation, their religion and their laws said they could not do to each other.

In this Silent Land, my memory is of sounds—of generators in the morning, of cocks crowing, of children playing, of coconuts falling, of the eternal rolling of pebbles in the waves on the shore. The silence, if I would be true to myself, was really in myself. The beach is always mirror to oneself. On a beach the reflections of self are as if in some Hall of Mirrors, distorted, caricatured.

Gauguin's Advice: 'Soyez mystérieuses'

January 1903

'This is not a book', Paul Gauguin protests in the first sentence of *Avant et Après*. In the last months of his life, he had turned to words rather than paint. But he struggles with words, doesn't want to be judged by them. 'This is not a book', he repeats mantra-like at each moment he expects his reader to be exacerbated by his discontinuities, whenever he presents himself brazenly as he is, without persuasion, without style, without art. Not a book, 'scattered notes, unconnected, like dreams, like life, made of bits and pieces'. But the bits and pieces of his life as he sees it now at the end of it are framed by the *Before and After* of his beach crossings on the margins of the civilised world.

Gauguin is writing this 'naked, fearless, shameless' self-portrait in a room on the top floor of his Maison du Plaisir, his 'House of Orgasm'. His 'House of Orgasm' is an island on an island. Cyclone and flood have divided it off from the little village of Atuona on Hiva Oa in The Marquesas. It is January, 1903. Gauguin had used this top-storey room as his studio for eighteen months. It is cluttered and disordered, a lumber room of special woods, a museum of finished and unfinished carvings and sculptures. There is a harmonium in the centre, an easel by the open window at the northern end. Padlocked chests and sets of drawers filled with prints and drawings. The walls are hung with eclectic reproductions of art—Hans Holbein, Albrecht Dürer, Pierre Puvis de Chavannes, Edgar Degas. Photographs of Parthenon friezes and Asian temples are hung there too. Gauguin always believed that the history of art and of cultures flowed through his fingers to his canvases.

His bedroom, accessed by a ladder he can now barely climb, is the threshold to his studio. There the walls are hung with photographs of his family, and a collection of lewd photographs he had purchased in Port Said. Gauguin would fondle and caress the women of the island as they ogled and laughed at the postures and contortions. It is a House of Orgasm after all.

In these last days he sets his painting of a Breton snow scene on an easel at the foot of his bed. It will be the last thing he sees before he dies. The snow scene is an icon of his *Before*, a reminder of how twenty years before he had challenged the virtuosity of Claude Monet and Gustave Courbet with his colours. He loved the edgelessness that colour gave to lines. Colour gave a dreamlike quality to shapes. When colours merged, sharpness had no space of its own. Defining lines were a trick of the eye. The trickster in the painter made it so. That is what Gauguin knew in the *Before* of his career. In the *After* of his beach, Gauguin now knows that edgelessness is not just a trick of the eye. On his beach, Gauguin has experienced a different order of things. The defining lines of the *Before* of his civilised world have dissipated in the wildness of his savage *After*. His older divisions between human and divine, living and dead, male and female, child and adult, landscape and person, are blurred now. There is a clutter of paintings in his studio, and packages of them in transport at sea to say it so.

Gauguin can no longer stand at his easel. The pain in his ulcerated legs is too great even with the morphine. He is breathless with angina. His syphilis is taking away his eyesight. His eyes look piggy behind the steel-rimmed circles of his spectacles. He knows he will not paint for much longer. He knows he is dying. His last painting has an awful realism his others don't possess. He paints himself as dead man looking. He throws away all the disguises of his other self-portraits and draws himself gaunt with pain, dried-up with discontents. Koke ('Wattle-Daub'), the islanders called him. Koke was his *patiki*, the shit name of a first tattoo. Gauguin's suppurating skin is peeling away like grey rendering on a wall. The sight and smell of it have driven the sex out of his life, have driven everyone away, everyone save one who was bound to him in a special way on his beach.

That one was Tioka ('Scooped-Out'). Wattle-Daub and Scooped-Out had a special relationship. They had exchanged names. Exchanging names like Wattle-Daub and Scooped-Out might not seem to have much aesthetic appeal. The exchange was a social grace nonetheless. The mutual gift of names embraced the whole person, all the person's rights and obligations, his property. It was never given lightly. It was given between equals but not necessarily between identicals. There was barter in it. Different advantages were exchanged. It was empowering, though. It was political, an alliance in the grassroots of life. It was an alliance steeped as well in all the cultural memories of how things used to be. Exchanging names was a very proper sacrament of beach crossings.

Tioka it was who found Koke dead in his bed, the body still warm, an empty morphine syringe beside it. It was 11 a.m., 8 May 1903. The Church with graceless haste performed all the proprieties for Koke's launch into eternity. There would have been no great confidence that holy water, oil and prayer would do their work. Koke would have been happier with Tioka's last rite. It had a savage, even cannibal, feel. Tioka bit Koke's skull in hope of some resurrection, in release of a troubled and troubling spirit.

'Mystery', 'mysterious' are words layered with thousands of years of meaning. At the heart of these meanings is an understanding that a mystery is the most complicated truth clothed in story or play or sacramental sign. Being mysterious means that there is work to be done—not just by the storyteller, not just by the author, not just by the priest, but by the audience, the reader, the believer as well. There are no closures to mysteries, only another story, another translation.

'Be mysterious' was Gauguin's advice. '*Soyez mystérieuses*' are words that Gauguin carved on the rosewood lintels of his House of Orgasm. 'I am not a painter who copies nature—today less than before', he was saying in another place. 'With me everything happens in my crazy imagination.' Colour was the instrument of his imagination. Colour itself was a language, a 'profound, mysterious language, a language of the dreams'. The ideas of a painting did not need words. Colour, with much the same vibrations as music, activated the more general meanings in what was being represented. It pulled out the interior force of things.

In these last months Gauguin was colouring-in the mysteriousness of his beach. The mysteries turned on the edgelessness of cultures in time and space. For all his talk of his never-ending voyage to the farthest savage land on earth, Gauguin never thought of savagery as a fossil thing, belonging to a time before. His models, the artefacts and persons he carved and painted from, never belonged to the past. They were always transformations and translations into the present. Savagery for him was the ongoing blurring of the edges of a civilised order of things. Savagery for him was always the incomprehensible. 'My Breton canvases have become rosewater because of Tahiti; [those of] Tahiti will become cologne water because of The Marquesas.'

Gauguin's bridgehead on his beach at Atuona was his name-exchange with Tioka. The equalities over which they bartered their friendship were basically two. Koke and Tioka were both *tuhuna* and *tukee*, craftsmen and tricksters. *Tuhuna* were skilled specialists. They had not only the skills in their hands to work the woods, the stones, the fibres, the colours of material culture. They held as well in their spirits the knowledge and lore that made every material object larger than itself, joined to the mythic understanding of what it meant, encapsulated with value and tradition.

Koke and Tioka were *tukee* too. They were both tricksters. Gauguin had been a trickster all his life. He was always in costume. Costume was his trickster's disguise, the theatre of his artistic world. He relished the ability to be saying something in the guise of saying something else. He marvelled at the trickster language of a disempowered Marquesan people. Their double play on words was a form of colonial resistance he understood. He joined them in it. He used his *tuhuna* skill to *tukee* effect by setting two statues, like two *tiki* in his garden, one of 'Père Paillard' (Father Lechery) another of Thérèse, his housekeeper-mistress. They mocked his enemy the bishop, cultivated gossip; made the bishop's people smirk.

Joined to one *tuhuna* by name, Gauguin quickly joined a whole network of specialist experts, each a trickster too because he had to practise what he knew under the gaze of the unseeing eyes of Church and State. Everything that joined the people of Atuona to a savage past was seen by the priests as subversive of their civilised future. Dancing, tattooing, singing ancient songs, stilt-walking, feasting to an old calendar of rites, all were forbidden. Even cats' cradles, the games to be played with string, were dangerous. Their figures held too many stories: there can be much politics and more tricksterism in children's games. So the specialist knowledge that made sense of these old ways had to be secured out of sight of authority and practised clandestinely. Gauguin made models of two of these carers of a sacred past. They were Haapuani and his wife, Tohotaua. Haapuani was *tuhuna o'ono*, a specialist on sacred songs and rituals. The suffix *tau'a* to Tohotaua's name marked her too as special. *Tau'a* of old were sorcerers, inspired prophets, diviners. Men and women *tau'a* were powerful forces. No life-moment was experienced without them. The women *tau'a* presided over that most dangerous and defining moment of life, birth.

Haapuani and Tohotaua were remarkable people. They each held their powers from their parents and from a long line of their parents' parents. Haapuani was of Atuona and the island of Hiva Oa. Tohotaua was of Vaitahu and the island of Tahuata. Tohataua had auburn hair. In 1595, Alváro de Mendaña's lady had fondled the auburn tresses of a young woman on the beach at Vaitahu. It is the way of things, and not unlikely, that red hair, a sacred sign, a *tapu* sign, marked a line of female *tau'a* through the centuries at Vaitahu.

Haapuani and Tohotaua were joined not just to the past but to the future as well. When Gauguin was long dead, and it was time for anthropological expeditions to catch what remnants of things past of Enata past was still left, Haapuani and Tohotaua would be their principal informants. The treasure of their knowledge now suffuses most understandings of Enata ways. Gauguin gave us a legacy of them as well in four brilliant paintings. If the Breton snow scene was an icon of his *Before,* these four paintings are icons of the *After* of his beach crossings. In them he colours his beach with his crazy imagination.

Gauguin's lustful predations on child-women came to an end in Atuona. He had a few months of play with a fourteen-year-old girl till her pregnancy and his decaying body drove her away. Vaeoho, the girl, was from outside the village of Atuona. Gauguin played the trickster to get her. He used the law against itself. The law said that parents who lived within four kilometres must send their children to school. He bought Vaeoho for two hundred francs' worth of cloth and a sewing machine. The accounts of it, together with all his other bills for his unsavage cuisine in this savage country, are still to be seen in the archives of the local store.

When Vaeoho was gone, Gauguin associated with a procession of older women. His views of them and theirs of him were unflattering. Tohotaua was different. Her beauty and her status were patent. With her he added a different sort of experience to his beach crossing. He became *pekio*. Edward Robarts had written many years before that the custom of *pekio* was 'a pill hard to digest'. *Pekio* were secondary husbands—a woman could have as many as ten or fifteen. Enata have been seen as one of the few polyandrous among many polygamous societies.

From the Strangers' and male-dominated side of the beach—inevitably all who came from outside Fenua'enata—the custom of *pekio* was seen as a trade-off by an Enata husband for the sexuality of his wife. For Enata of old, it was more of a woman's thing. The number of *pekio* was a measure of her power. Men bartered away much to benefit by that power. They crossed the beach between male and female and became something in-between.

Tohotaua stares dreamily into space out of the mustard- and green-tinted canvas of 'Woman with Fan'. Her breasts are bare. She is seated on a piece of salon furniture, ensconced by wild wooden arms. The white feather fan, which encapsulates her true native wealth and high birth, is decorated with a tricolour rosette. There is much crazy imagination in all that, and who will say with any sureness what it means? But that is Gauguin's ploy on his beach: to dream of how oppositions of beauty, power and tradition merge to create new beauties, new powers, new traditions.

'Marquesan Man in a Red Cape' and 'Bathers' are just as teasing. They are androgynous figures, double-gendered. Behind the bathers is a beach and in its surf, surfers. The beach at Atuona was the last space for native play where all else had been forbidden. The bather, too, is about to be naked, another thing forbidden by Church and State. The red *tapa* or bark-cloth cape is a *tapu* insignia. But nativeness in clothing requires a nativeness in wearing. Gauguin paints a man in fancy dress. The man wears something like a medieval singer's jerkin. Who will say what this crazy imagination means either? But if Gauguin had learned anything from his beach he had learned that divisions of time and space, of true and false knowledge, of gender and age and status, no longer set his world as they once did. Maybe these men-women, naked-clothed, archaic-modern figures are reflections of his redivided self.

'Be mysterious', was Gauguin's advice. I am inclined to take it. Beaches of the mind, like beaches of the body, being in-between, are more places of defining than definition. They are better experienced in story than in thesis.

Flying to The Land: Nukuhiva

January 1975

We had not finished with The Land. We flew to Ua Huka to join an old French naval landing craft for the five-hour voyage to Nukuhiva. The bare dry hills of Ua Huka are most untropical, more like Mexico, even to the corrals and all the other signs of a cowboy culture. We met up with a Swiss professor who was in high excitement at his time among the 'primitives', his word. '*Crains, crains* [skulls, skulls]', he kept saying—'in a canoe in a cave!'

Our berths on the landing craft, as it were, were a set of paladin-like seats high on the stern. We shared them with a French-Canadian missionary brother coming to inspect the mission schools. The landing craft dragged itself off the beach on its stern anchor and turned out of the cove and along the shore of Ua Huka. We stopped to pick some crew members from an islet alive with seabirds. New Year's Eve was on hand and

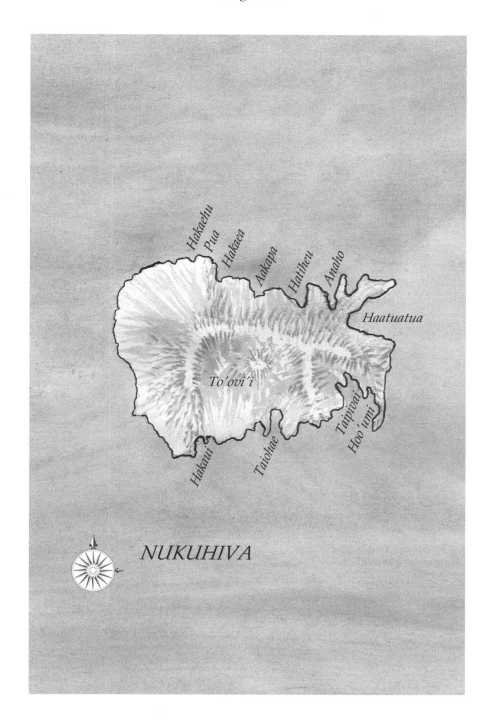

there would be a *koina*, a feast. The crew members had collected a boatload of eggs for it, as their forebears had done for centuries.

Then we turned to a hazy blue line of Nukuhiva to the west. It was three hours before we could discern anything of the island's landscape. We approached Nukuhiva from its southeast corner, and could see its north and south coast stretching away. All was abrupt cliff in the blue haze of the sea.

As we moved along the south coast, I began to recognise bays. Taipivai came first. Its valley and the high cliffs that hedge its waters stretch miles back into the hinterland of Nukuhiva. Taipivai was the valley which Herman Melville experienced as 'Typee'. He had run with Tobias Greene from the *Acushnet* in July 1842 and made his three weeks of beachcombing into a *Narrative of Four Months Residence Among the Natives of a Valley in the Marquesas Islands* (1846).

Typee was a brave book. It roused much anger for its immorality, but more because it challenged commonly held prejudices. Melville saw the beach as a tawdry place where nothing came across in beauty or fullness, where everything was a misanthropic, half-pointless, tattered remnant. He saw Enata in the rags of civilisation and saw the rags as a parable of the larger cultural dump The Land was becoming. To those who saw everything of civilisation as good and everything of savages as evil, Melville's perception that the good could be evil and the evil good was uncomfortable. The reading public denounced it as deceiving fiction.

As we passed Taipivai, I thought I could see the spit of beach and marshland which divided Taipivai from its neighbouring valley. I would want to see that spot. From that beach Herman Melville made his escape from his 'cannibal islands'. It was also on that beach that Lieutenant David Porter USN would land his marines in 1814 in what we in the twentieth century would call 'search and destroy' tactics against those who would not accept his intrusion on their land.

For me, it was a moment of tense expectancy as we first caught sight of the vertical lines of light-coloured rocks that were the navigators' signpost to the entry of Taiohae Bay. We then turned carefully through the narrow entrance and were overwhelmed, as every visitor must be, by the massiveness of the bay's encircling mountain ridge. It was as if we were in some giant's maw. There in front of us, jutting into the bay, was the small mound of Tuhiva. Fort Madison, David Porter had called it. Fort Collet was the later French name. For forces with cannon and artillery this small mound was of strategic importance. It commanded every part of the valley.

The *Kaoha Nui*, the other administration vessel, had just come to the pier a little before us. The crowd on the pier milled around shackled wild cattle that *Kaoha Nui* had brought. There were jeeps filled with butchered meat. The preparations for the New Year's Eve party were well under way.

We landed from the forward platform of our craft. Our companion, the mission brother, was ceremonially welcomed and almost disappeared among the green and purple leis piled high around his neck. We stood off awkwardly, hoping to ask somebody for somewhere to stay. The brother brought us to the bishop, Mgr Hervé-Marie Le Cléac'h. Recognition is not something I have come to expect, not then, not now. So let me record, not for the boast of it, but for the pleasure of it, that the bishop when he heard my name said: 'Not *the* Greg Dening'. *The Marquesan Journal of Edward Robarts* had come before me. It was one of the nicest moments of my scholarly and writing life. The bishop embraced me and excitedly went around the crowd telling them who I was and how marvellous *The Marquesan Journal of Edward Robarts*. For me, it was the beginning of a friendship I have treasured into the third millennium.

The bishop interceded for us with the administrator, a thick-set man in a perfectly creased khaki uniform, about finding us accommodation in the official visitors' residence. But the administrator rebuffed him. We gathered that had we been simple tourists we would have got it, but as I was a *monsieur*, a person of importance, our non-notification of our coming was taken as a slight. The bishop said that the administrator had been twenty years in Africa, and let us know with a gesture that this was the last outpost of French colonialism. There always has been an uneasy relationship between Church and State in The Land. The colony had been established when the animosities between black and red in Metropolitan France had been high. So the principal avenue at Taiohae is divided west and east by name. The west half is named Dordillon Avenue for the founding bishop of the mission and author of the Marquesan–French dictionary and grammar, Mgr René Ildefonse Dordillon. The east is named for Admiral Dupetit-Thouars, who brought the French here in the first place.

We ended that remarkable day on the porch of the accommodation provided for us. It was the most perfect place imaginable for me. We were given a house that looked out over the calm of the bay and through the narrow entrance to open seas stirred by the trades and the south wind. I was surprised that throughout Fenua'enata sight of the sea was always so blinkered. It meant that a ship or boat or canoe came suddenly into sight.

Whatever the purposes of strangers, whether they came 'from beyond the horizon' or more nearly from another island, first sight of them would always hold a moment's apprehension.

At the water's edge before us were the ruins of a stone house platform, a *paepae*. I knew immediately that it was that of Putahaii, a powerful woman of Robarts' and Crook's days. She was the mother of the *haka'iki*, the chief, of Taiohae, Kiatonui. With her range of *pekio*, or secondary husbands, with the network of the marriages of her children, with her many properties, she was a formidable force at Taiohae and through the whole island. Her house, Robarts had written, was exceptional in all of The Land. It was built into the water. I sat on the porch of our house that evening, the bay before me, framed by breadfruit trees and Putahaii's *paepae*.

I had come to Taiohae to put spatial images to my stories—terrible stories of invasion and massacre, stories that caught the metaphors of Enata living, stories of things I did not understand, of human sacrifice and body eating. I wanted to walk the four valleys that I had known from my readings were the residences of the four groupings of the Teii people of Taiohae. The spaces were not as I had imagined them.

In 1792, when a series of American, French and British voyagers each thought he had 'discovered' Nukuhiva, the landscape of Taiohae was lush, colourful and varied. It was alive with people, too, six to nine thousand of them. They died in catastrophic numbers through the next century. In the 1920s maybe there were twenty or thirty Enata at Taiohae. By the time of our visit the population of Taiohae was some hundreds, enhanced by the fact that the Catholic mission had established a boys' boarding school there for all the islands of Fenua'enata.

I found that the towering mountain ridges foreshorten all perspective. A grey-brown veil—no, a grey-brown shroud—of trees slips down the slopes of the ridges and over the distinctive features of the valleys. The French had imported mimosa—for the homely comfort of their troops of African and Mediterranean origin—and a thorny lantana—for a protective hedge against native incursions. The mimosa had spread like a spring tide in an estuary. It made a bland canopy over a landscape that had been coloured with the varied greens of the breadfruit, banyan, palm, banana, paper mulberry and ironwood trees among many, and the rainbow hues of hibiscus, gardenia and frangipani. Ironically the only part of Taiohae that was not shrouded in grey-brown was the park around the French administration buildings. It was aflame in December and January with poinciana. Beneath the mimosa canopy a forest of spindly boughs and trunks strangles what remnants there were of Enata past living.

I soon realised how leached of story, memory and history is a dead, veiled and strangled landscape. I felt very inadequate to my task. I felt depressed at my own silences. I did not know how I would give life to all the lifeless rubble around me or give voice to things so speechless. I know now, decades on from 1974, that I was at the nadir of my understandings. I had beaches to cross.

Our nearest neighbours were the dead. 'Royal tombs' nestled in the knoll beside us. We were settled on the lands of 'kings' and 'queens'. Empires need 'kings' and 'queens' to empower their possessiveness. When Admiral Dupetit-Thouars left Vaitahu, he came to Taiohae. He needed a 'king' who would cede the land and be responsible for the misbehaviour of his people. Temoana, the *haka'iki* of the Teii people in Taiohae, was an eager candidate for royalty.

Temoana's name meant 'The Immense Sea'. His life had been a pilgrimage across many oceans. He had crossed many beaches. He had been to Aotearoa (New Zealand) and Sydney. He had even visited Napoleon's tomb at St Helena. London had been his shame. In later years drink would make him remember with rage his humiliation in the exhibitions of his tattoos and the curiosity he became.

In 1839 a London missionary from Tahiti, Robert Thomson, brought Temoana back to Fenua'enata. Missionaries, like empires, need 'kings'. But Temoana had learned in his beach crossings that native politics were changed forever by the intruding strangers and he meant to use them to his purposes. The strangers' weapons made aggrandisement more deadly and their need for an ordered beach for trade and settlement favoured centralised authority. Temoana thought he could make a kingdom of Nukuhiva, like 'King' Kamehameha had done in Hawai'i, like 'King' Pomare in Tahiti.

I had a vague cultural map of Taiohae in my mind. The Bernice P. Bishop Museum, Honolulu, Hawai'i, had sent out the Bayard Dominick Expedition in 1920–21 on an archaeological and anthropological 'rescue' mission to The Marquesas. Scholars like E. S. Craighill Handy and his wife, Willowdean Chatterson Handy, made lasting contributions to our knowledge of Fenua'enata. In my younger days I was scornful and impatient with what they had done. Older now, I am more respectful and humbled by what they did.

A young Ralph Linton was their archaeologist. In later years he acted as psychologist to Enata polyandry and inspired some feminist polemics. Linton's archaeological survey of Taiohae and the description of beachcombers, missionaries and visitors gave me a start for my cultural map of Taiohae.

Each of the four groupings of Teii at Taiohae had their cultural markers around which their life cycles turned—their *tohua*, the dancing and feasting spaces; their *me'ae*, their sacred *tapu* spaces. There were remnants of more than a dozen of these structures around the valley, each imprinted in the cultural memory of centuries with a name, and with the name a story, and with the story a dance and a song.

Our house on the edge of the bay stood on the now dismantled *tohua* of the Hoata valley. Hopu-Au it was called. Down the road from us on Dordillon Avenue, in front of the old cathedral tilting into the ground and the new cathedral beside it, stood a plaza that had been Mauia, the *tohua* of Meau valley. A so-called 'sacrificial altar-stone' on the old *tohua* now sprouts a large crucifix.

There was one *tohua* that I especially wanted to see. It was high up on the trail to the pass over the ridge that led to the valleys east and west of Taiohae and across the deserted hinterland to the northern side of the island. The *tohua* belonged to the people of Haavao valley. Haavao was Temoana's valley and lay in the centre of Taiohae. The Haavao people got their eminence by residing astride this trail. They had built a fortified gateway through the narrowest passage at the height of the ridge.

Koueva was the name of the *tohua* I wanted to see. I had a story to tell of it. It was once large, though not nearly the largest on Nukuhiva. The dancing space was nearly 100 yards long and 30 yards wide. It was completely surrounded by platforms and terraces constructed out of large stones. The stone *tiki* that used to grace these platforms had long been ransacked, and, of course, all the wooden structures and their decorations had long rotted away.

Koueva had the appearance of a walled fortification, with narrow, easily defensible passages at its sides to give access to the open dancing ground. Indeed, David Porter had laid siege—unsuccessfully—to the largest *tohua* in Taipivai, Uahakekua, under the impression that it was a walled town. Koueva wasn't a fort, but it was the only place in Taiohae to which victims for sacrifice, 'fish', were brought. That is the story I wanted to tell, about a 'fishing' expedition in 1845.

Pakoko was *pahutiki*, 'wrapped in images'. His skin was his armour, like a crab shell, like a tortoise shell. There was no part of this skin that was not tattooed. Not his eyelids, not his lips. He was all *paka* ('crust'), *tifa* ('lid'), *po'o* ('skeleton'). Lightning struck out of the eye-spots in his armpits when he raised his spear to throw, his club to strike. Death's heads protected his back. Eyes flashed on his forearm. A filigree of half people that his mythical carers would make whole was an army on his body. The diagonal slash across his forehead proclaimed that there was nothing he would not revenge. It also said he was *pi'ee*, 'shit' of the gods.

Pakoko was *kikino*, 'rubbish'. The 'shitty snout' across his mouth said that. He was not chiefly, not *opou*, the one who answered first when the gods called. The first tattoo of the chiefly men was on the sole of their feet, so that they could walk on The Land without making it *tapu*. 'Rubbish' tattoos began with their face and spread over their body like diarrhoea, running shit.

In 1845 Pakoko was remarkable 'rubbish', though. He had been fully wrapped in images by the time he was eighteen years old. Other 'rubbish' took a lifetime, attaching themselves to the celebratory and mourning occasions, all the *rites de passages* of the better-born. Pakoko was in a hurry. He made his own occasions. They came quickly. He killed frequently, was always first in the alarums and excursions that birth and death and all the fears of a disturbed society brought.

Pakoko was in his fifties when the French came to Taiohae in 1842. He had lived all his days on a beach ever more intruded upon by strangers—the Russians in 1805, the invading Americans in 1814, British warships redeeming their losses from the Americans in 1815, Protestant missionaries from Hawai'i in 1832, Catholic missionaries from Paris in 1838. Every year brought more sandalwood traders and whalers seeking refreshment. There was hardly a year in which there were not thievings, killings, maimings, kidnappings and hostage takings. And always there were the ongoing deaths as the population slid away. The more divided Fenua'enata was, the less that the people understood what was happening to them. Sorcerers thrived. There was much 'fishing'.

Pakoko, wrapped in his images, also wrapped himself with intensity in the ways of Enata. He flourished his identity and difference in the faces of the strangers. He killed an American beachcomber who had stolen his pigs. He killed this thief in the proper Enata way, and 'ate' him. He laughed at the horror in the strangers' eyes that he should be a man-eater and told them the cannibal jokes they wanted to hear and tell themselves: how he didn't like white men—they were too salty. But he preferred British to French or American.

He laughed at the strangers' horror at him. But soon he learned that the strangers were enemies of them all, not just him. A year after he had killed the American beachcomber for stealing pigs, *tapu*, pigs being set aside for a feast—all 'rubbish' would have been killed for that—the USS *Vincennes* landed boatloads of sailors and burned fifty house in Taiohae. It was a lesson Pakoko learned well. Exemplary punishment has two sides to its beach.

When the young Temoana left Taiohae to pay his visits to London and Sydney, Pakoko stayed on. By attending to the cultural desires and political necessities of Taiohae, he gave himself a lift in social status. It was the Enata way. He was no longer 'rubbish'. He was chiefly. He wore the coconut diadem of rank. He carried a fan and a staff. He was now warrior-chief of the valleys of Pakiu and Hikoe. They were the easternmost valleys of the bay. They bordered the French encampment. Indeed the French would encroach one day on Pakoko's land because Temoana sells a part of it, Hakapehi, for 1800 francs. Hakapehi was at the foot of the escarpment that reached down from the ridges to Tuhiva, Fort Collet. It was bordered by a rivulet—the 'First River', the French called it, the edge point beyond which their soldiers might not safely go.

Among Enata, Pakoko has much cultural capital. Loyalties to him are broad across the whole valley of Taiohae. Pakoko is the personification of the old ways. The long grey-white beard he wears is an icon of that. And so is the *hami*, the white loincloth. It exposes how *pahutiki*, wrapped in images, he is.

Temoana, endowed by birth with a long reach back in time, hides his images under a colonel's red jacket and an artillery man's pantaloons. On the day Temoana gives Nukuhiva to the French on the gun emplacements of Fort Collet—Temoana in his regalia, Pakoko in his *hami* and tattoos—Pakoko snatches up a French flag and wraps it around himself. He mocks Temoana in the gesture. Temoana is wrapped in images of another sort, he is saying.

Temoana has sold out to the new. The whole valley knows it. They see it in his wealth, now cumulative to him alone, not distributive to them.

They see it in his drunken rages. They see it in the salary the French now pay him. They see it in the freedoms now denied them, so that the French can do their will more easily.

Let me tell the rest of Pakoko's story.

26 January 1845. Georges Winter, marine sergeant and interpreter, is on edge. There is trouble. He can sense it. For two years he has been the eyes and ears of the French. He had crossed the beach more than any of them, learning Enata language, making friends and exchanging names, talking with old men. He knows Enata's sullen anger. He knows when it is dangerous to be among them.

Now, beyond the parapeted palisade and ditch of the camp, the valley is seething. Behind the beach—now under Temoana's *tapu* and French edict not to be crossed—Pakoko's men are venting their rage. Their *haka* cries come through the trees. Their women had been forbidden to swim to the whalers in the bay, but had done so. Lieutenant Almaric, the French commander, had punished them by imprisoning them in Fort Collet. Two of Pakoko's daughters were among them. French officers might have their concubines, but ordinary soldiers don't. Pakoko's daughters are raped.

There had been trouble in the valley for more than a month, since Vahaketou, the chief fisherman, had died in a drowning accident. But no one dies by accident in these troubled times. Oko, the sorcerer, is back in the valley, they are saying. Oko is reported to have poisoned two hundred of his enemies. Who is to say he has not tricked Vahaketou into his death?

A year ago the French had bowed to hysteria and banished Oko. But now he is back. The French won't banish him again. They will take him up to the mountain tops where all can see and put a bullet into the back of his head.

Vahaketou had been a moderating force between Temoana's and Pakoko's factions. He was Taiohae's fisherman, a *tuhuna* or craftsman of peculiar independence. Many of the rituals of the old ways turned around him. He lived with seven or eight families on the far western tip of the bay. 'A small republic', Georges Winter described it as. It played a distinctive role in the politics of the valley. Vehaketou was in-between Temoana and Pakoko. Both needed his everyday skills as a fisherman. More importantly, they needed his *tapu* skills to catch devil rays and turtle, and to oversee the rituals of food and trade distribution.

With Vahaketou gone, the sullen anger of Pakoko's people becomes more threatening. There is no one to calm Temoana's extravagances. Cattle are stolen from the French encampment. There is fear in the air. Houses are

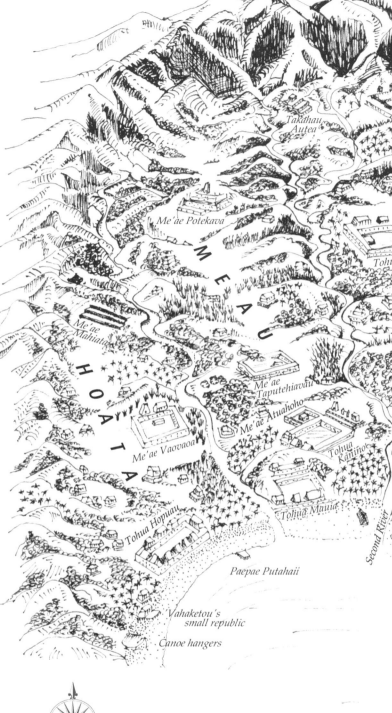

Takahau
Autea

Me'ae Potekava

M E A U

Tohua K

Me'ae
Mahiata

H O A T A

Me'ae
Taputehiavau

Me'ae Atuahoho

Me'ae Vaovaoa

Tohua
Kaninoe

Tohua Maiua

Tohua Hopuau

Second River

Paepae Putahaii

Vahaketou's
small republic

Canoe hangers

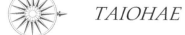 *TAIOHAE*

Me'ae
Paetekeika

H
A
A
V
A
O

P A A K I U

Koueva

Tohua Tahunui

Tohua
Tokahui

H I K O E I

Temoana's
House

First River

HAKAPEHI

TUHIVA

Fort Collet

Fort Madison

Saumerville

Madisonville

deserted in expectancy of retribution. Men and women collect at the dancing grounds. Their songs and shouts echo around the valley. Warriors are carrying clubs, rifles and makeshift weapons.

28 January. Georges Winter wants to wash clothes. He is free to go where he wants, but five marines fresh from Vaitahu and new to Taiohae join him. The 'First River' is a sludge of the sewage of the three hundred men in camp. Against orders they go on to the 'Second River' and on to Pakoko's land. Georges recognises that this is a mistake when he sees men running towards them, armed with whaling spades and scythes on the end of broom handles. He shouts a warning, but as he does there is a rifle shot and one of the troopers is dead, Private Alley, a musician. Georges' truncheon is no defence. Later he will have memories of Hutete ('The Huge One'), a *pahutiki*, wearing an immense panama hat and swinging a staff with a bayonet on each end at him. Georges escapes into a guava clump.

A straggle of bruised, broken and hacked survivors follow Winter back to camp. Three are missing. They find one body decapitated, another mutilated. They know where the other is, because they can hear the triumphant shouts as Pakoko's people take their 'catch' to Koueva. The French know it as a place of sacrifice. There the daughters of Pakoko are dancing naked around the body of Corporal Perrot, tied hands and feet to his 'fishing' pole. He would be 'eaten' on the morrow, the French believed.

Sorties from the French camp destroy all the houses in the now deserted valleys of Pakiu and Haavao. They waste the *ma* pits, the stock of fermented breadfruit kept for years, sometimes decades, against famine. Georges Winter himself retrieves the head of infantryman Raure. It is suspended in branches 30 feet high at Vahitapu ('Tapu Fish'). Vahitapu is an ironwood tree pushing against the back cliffs of Pakiu valley. The tree is full of skulls or warrior heroes and their trophies.

The French then launch a mortar attack from their blockhouse overlooking Haavao valley. They are pleased to report that their first volley lands directly in the middle of the feasting/sacrificing grounds of Koueva. Perrot's body is not hit, but they kill three men and a woman and wound many more.

For two weeks the valleys are deserted. The people have fled over the ridges and are without food or shelter in the To'ov'i desert area, or are beggars among their enemies. For a time they are defiant on the skyline of the mountains and shout 'Pakoko is with us. Come and get him.' The French disperse them with artillery fire.

Pakoko fails in his effort to get help from the people of the north and east, the Taipi and their allies. They still have a memory of the American David Porter's murderous foray through their valley in 1814. They do not know how far the French will go to capture Pakoko. In the end, to let his people return home, a sick and weak Pakoko surrenders to the French with six of his family.

Lieutenant Almaric, who will get a Legion of Honour for what he had done and what he is about to do—only to have it taken away from him because he did it all unlawfully—convenes a court martial in the block-house overlooking Haavao. This is war, he will argue, and he needs wartime powers and solutions. He doesn't want Pakoko as prisoner. He wants him dead. That is the way it swiftly happens. Pakoko and ten others are condemned to death.

It is Georges Winter who translates the sentence *'mourir soir'* for Pakoko. When Pakoko asks when it is to be, Georges says 'immediately', for fear of attack and rescue. Pakoko asks to embrace his wife and children, but is denied. *'Kao'ha*!—Farewell!', he says to those who condemn him. He is puzzled by French execution practices—the eye bandage and the tied hands. He won't have them. On the gun platform of the blockhouse, he faces his ten executioners with his fan and his staff. They shoot him at 3 p.m. It is Good Friday.

There are thousands on the ridge around. Great cries call out when it is done. The women dance naked. For another full day they mourn where they stand, until cannon disperse them.

For nearly fifty years, whenever alcohol freed them to rage, Enata would say to the French: 'You have killed Pakoko. You have cut off our head.' When it thundered, they would say: 'Pakoko is still with us'.

Pakoko's image-wrapped body, pierced now by ten bullets, is about to be taken away altogether. He doesn't need protection now. He needs freeing. His mourners, the women in his life, begin to free him immediately. They dance their *heva*, their most erotic dance, before him. He lies in his own house for many months before the women take him to his *fa'e tapu*, his sacred house, and, with their right tattooed hands, begin to *hoe*—to rub his body with oils and ointments. They are removing his tattooed skin. They put it into a special container, *hue po'o*, where its fluids are filtered. From time to time the women wipe this bowl clean with taro leaves and consume them. When Pakoko's body is cleaned of all its images and their power consumed, he is ready to be put into his canoe coffin to start his journey into freedom. Pakoko, *pahutiki*, is now *opou hou*, 'conceived for the first time' again. That is why when it thunders, Enata can say: 'Pakoko is with us'.

So we walk the valleys of Taiohae on hot, dusty tracks in January 1975, 130 years after these events. We move around to the western tip, to where Vehaketou's 'small republic' used to stand. Herman Melville will begin his adventures in The Land at this point: up to Koueva hidden in the mimosa tangle; over to the hillock where the blockhouse used to stand and Pakoko was executed. We climb back up to the cliffs of Pakiu where the ironwood tree of Vahitapu used to stand. Where the French set up their camp, other ruins overlay the old defences now—the remains of prison cells built for the revolutionaries of the Paris Commune, and the foundations for a cathedral that never rose above the ground. Down to Tuhiva, Fort Collet. There we stand, the past of this place all grey-shrouded around us. I feel unsure of how much I will ever see through this shroud, but I have long ways to go in crossing this beach in this new year of 1975.

In that January month, I had not far to go at all immediately, just down Dordillon Avenue to the house of the bishop, Mgr Le Cléac'h. A museum, an archive, a small library and conversation with a gentle, kindly man attracted me there.

'House Belong Memory', the Solomon Islanders call their National Archives. A mission archives is a special sort of House of Memory. Men driven by religious passions and a sense of calling put their daily experiences into diaries, letters, reports with a fullness others rarely have. They remain mysterious nonetheless, inaccessible in their certainties, sustained in cruel and uncomfortable circumstances by a spirit of self-sacrifice yet rarely loving those they sought to save. They are servants of a higher cause, but stern masters in all its human expressions.

There are papers of some forty missionaries of the Congregation of the Sacred Hearts of Jesus and Mary in the bishop's archives. Some of these religious were brothers who worked with their hands, building, farming, serving. Some were priests preaching, saying mass, giving sacraments. Some were intellectually curious, making dictionaries, writing ethnographies. Some were hard, narrow men, savagely sectarian; some were overwhelmed by what they saw as evil around them; some were priest-traders, priest-planters; some were poor, giving away all they possessed; some came from peasant stock in Belgium and France; some were more at home in the salons of Paris.

It is difficult to open a window on their souls. They are mostly very private public men. We never really get to know how difficult it was for them to stay celibate or sober. Or how they sustained their faith. They kept their secrets well. Their principal sin was that they maintained a mission and did not grow a church. Mgr Cléac'h, a theologian of a church made free by Pope John XXXIII and his Vatican Council II, had a belief that a church was seeded by the metaphors of understanding that reached deep into Enata souls. Art, song, poetry, language discovered the metaphors.

I have to confess that I retreated to the mission archives in some relief. Archives are my life. I love their cool quiet. Meeting the dead in archives is less traumatic than meeting the living on the beach. These archives looked out on a garden. *Tiki* peered in at me through the greenery. These were trophies, I suppose, of one religion's victory over another. They certainly don't create the fear that they once did in these priests whose lives I hold in my hands in their diaries and notebooks. When the light was right or when I grew stiff at the table, I practised my photography on the *tiki*. They still, over so many years, peer into my camera lens out of slides and photographs. I wonder what their eyes have seen over the centuries. Those that are very old are black and rough. They are not smooth, waxily shiny, precisely shaped like the *tiki*—of what?—just three or four hundred years ago. They are just as silent, though.

My notes grow thick. The priests whose diaries and letters I am reading came early in the mission—in 1838—before they could call on the French administration for help. Their real enemies were the English Protestant missionaries. They complain of their lies. They look for help from home in France to combat the slanders the Protestants purvey about the Church and the papacy—of 'Maria Monk' and 'Pope Joan'. They grasp at small successes—someone learns to make a sign of the cross. They are happy that their sacraments give them some statistics for their conversions. A dying infant baptised in secret is one soul saved. They don't dare say their masses in public. They are unsure what their vestments will incite or how much of the sorcerer Enata will see in their gestures.

There are priests who come later and stay a lifetime—Père Gérauld Chaulet, fifty-four years; Mgr Ildephone Dordillon, forty-two years; Père Jean Lecornu, twenty years. They were masters of Enata language. Their detailed knowledge and lists flood over me. Because of that I know the seasons and their harvests. I can look at the sea beyond the bay and know what signs it used to give the fishers. I can look at the moon and see something of what Enata saw. I know the rhythms of a day, the cycles in a life. I know the spirit life that mirrors every plant, every artefact, every sickness, every skill. I know especially those parts of living which these missionaries of change believe are obstacles to the grace of God that they are bringing. When they have the power to do it, they will go to what they see as the jugular of Enata living. My notes grow thick and my fingers tired.

There is a part of their writings that disturbs me and will do so for years to come. Père Chaulet, describing the obscene names given at tattooing—names referring to defects in a mother's pudendum, for example—and spelling out the rites of burial, suddenly breaks in with the names of those killed and 'eaten' in the valleys of Nukuhiva that year, 1862: at Aakapa six eaten and two others killed; at Pua, four eaten; at Hatiheu, four killed, two eaten; at Anaho, one killed; at Haatuatua, two; at Hoo'umi, three; at Vaii, four; at Hakaui, three. At most the population in these valleys at this time would have been four or five families. What misery would create this? Do I believe him? What does he mean—what do I mean—by 'eaten'?

There was some irony in the fact that our last meal in The Land was our largest and most delicious. The staff of the mission school and the bishop entertained us with gracious hospitality. It was ironic because we were about to lose every bit of it a few hours later as we returned to Ua Huka to catch the plane back to Tahiti. We climbed up the ropes on the side of *Kaoha Nui* like D-Day troopers. We did not take the advice of our hosts of a few hours before to scramble for seats in the lower-deck cabin. Instead, we stood romantically on the bare steel deck and watched the magical display of the stars. In the bay there was no movement of any sort. A group of Enata lying on the deck should have given us thought, however. They were seasick while the ship was still at anchor!

We knew why, the moment we reached open waters. We had to make for Ua Pou to pick up more passengers before trying for Ua Huka. The first part of our dog-leg voyage was across the seas and the weather. Instantly *Kaoha Nui* began to corkscrew in an alarming fashion. The stars were gone in a few minutes, hidden by the spray from the bow and rain on the wind. I am sure Captain Bligh would have described it all as 'only a gale'. It was enough for us. Dinner was gone in two minutes, and a hundred times over in the next three hours. Seasickness is the most selfish of all complaints. There was no room in my self-pity for anybody else. I clung to a stanchion and leant over the railing every few minutes—on the lee-side, of course. I read a lot about ship voyaging! I was hardly conscious, till I looked up and saw that Donna, my partner, who had been clinging to another stanchion was gone. So was everybody else. In terror that something had happened to her, I crawled over the unwalkable deck. I tumbled down the stairs and went around the passengers who looked like they were on some Stygian crossing. No one had seen her. I went to what passed as a toilet on the *Kaoha Nui*. At that moment Donna came out the door. I cannot really describe how she looked. She had just plucked up the courage to put her hand through all the filth in the washbowl to pull out the plug and had discovered why the plug was there. There was no pipe connected to the bowl. The filth had flowed all over her. We crawled around till we found space enough for our two bodies on the floor of the cabin. I have to confess that by the midnight hours when we reached Ua Pou, my ethnographic zeal had waned. We just lay on the floor while the 'mayors' of the islands—the *haka'iki* of old—met and talked.

After that, however, the *Kaoha Nui* turned into the weather toward Ua Huka. It will be hard ever to forget the euphoria we felt in the windless calm of dawn and the still of the bay at Ua Huka. Someone gave us a cup of coffee and a croissant. I found myself moderating my judgements about French empires.

Our flight back to Tahiti from Ua Huka diverted to the atoll of Takopoto, where we picked up a Protestant native missionary. He sat beside me in the plane and immediately pulled out Robert Levy's *Tahitians*. *Tahitians* is a psychological work about shame and guilt among native and converted Tahitians. I was reminded again that there are all sorts of silences to be translated between the Christian notion of guilt and the native sense of shame. I wanted to ask the missionary if Levy had it right, but I fear I kept my silence.

There had been one more moment of crisis at the 'airport' at Ua Huka when we discovered that our plane had been overbooked. For a time we feared that all our troubles to get to The Land would be repeated in trying to get away from it. Somehow we got on the plane. The only cost of that privilege was that they put our jiffy-bag luggage in the hold under a parcel of fresh fish. We thought we were deserving of some 'rest and recreation' after our expedition. So we had booked ourselves into a Tahitian resort hotel which we could barely afford. The look on the hotel porter's face when he took our smelly bags and looked at our clothing still unchanged from our night on *Kaoha Nui* told us we were crossing another sort of beach.

Melville's Praxis: Reading to Write

November 1851

14 November 1851 is a special day for Herman Melville. It is the official publication date of *Moby Dick*. On that day Melville drives his horse and dray from his home in Pittsfield, in the Berkshire Mountains, to nearby Lenox to have dinner with Nathaniel Hawthorne at the Curtis Hotel. Hawthorne has just finished *The House of the Seven Gables*. Melville had dedicated *Moby Dick* to him. 'In token of my admiration of his genius'. The two friends talk about writing. 'From my twenty-fifth year I date my life', Melville tells Hawthorne. 'Three weeks have scarcely passed at anytime between then and now that I have not unfolded within myself.'

Over the previous seven years, from his twenty-fifth year, Melville had written *Typee* and its near sequel *Omoo*. He had felt the genius within himself and wrote *Mardi* to prove it—not for the money that the public was prepared to pay, but for all his ambitions for American literature. *Mardi* was a commercial and literary disaster. In disgust he set himself to write something that the public would buy. He wrote *Redburn in* three weeks; *White Jacket* in twenty sittings.

Then having done his duty and now quite determined to be the self that had unfolded within him, he wrote *Moby Dick*, or 'The Whale', which was its original title. Now, at the Curtis Hotel, Hawthorne and Melville were talking of their deep-down ambitions, away from publishers and reviewers, away from that terrible culture of envy of the literary world. It is 'the happiest day of Melville's life', his biographer Hershel Parker, writes.

In his twenty-fifth year, in November 1844 to be precise, in a cold, most untropical winter, in his lawyer brother's Nassau Street office in Manhattan, on pieces of paper whose every space he scrimpingly fills, Herman Melville becomes a writer. He begins his first draft of ~~Tipii Tipee~~, *Typee*.

He begins to unfold the life that was in him. 'Unfold'. It is the right metaphor. The writer in him is unfolding the layers of experience within him: of ships—*St Lawrence* (a New York to Liverpool packet ship), *Acushnet* (a Fairhaven whaler), *Lucy Ann* (a Sydney whaler*), Charles and Henry* (a Nantucket whaler), *United States* (a US naval frigate); of captains—Oliver P. Brown (a Swede), Vincent Pease (Nantucketeer), Henry Ventome (English), John B. Coleman (Dartmouth, Nova Scotia, Nantucketeer), Thomas Catesby Jones (a fiery Virginian and violently contentious commodore); of beaches—Nukuhiva, Tahiti, Maui, Oahu.

Unfolding also are all the stories that had dramatised these experiences. Stories told to him in fo'c'sles, on decks, in the yards, in Seamen's Bethels, in gaols. Stories he told himself—in messes, parlours, at the family table. Stories whose fictions and dramatics got shaped with every telling. Stories whose audiences dictated their tone. Stories to entertain, stories to tease, stories to excuse. Stories honed in their telling, in their performance.

Folded, too, into his own life experiences were all sorts of vicarious lives from his readings. As he sat down to describe his arrival in his 'cannibal islands' in June 1842, he knew that he had been there in his mind's eye, sixteen years before, as a nine-year-old boy. That year he had a happy holiday with his eleven-year-old cousin, 'Langs'. Langs was named for Georg Heinrich von Langsdorff, a friend of Langs' father and Herman's uncle, Captain John D'Wolf. Von Langsdorff had visited The Marquesas with the Russian expedition of 1803–06. Langsdorff's book about that visit was *Voyages and Travels in Various Parts of the World*. Its English version had been published in 1813. *Voyages and Travels* was in Captain D'Wolf's library.

Langsdorff's story is all of tattoos and cannibals, taboos and language. Two beachcombers, Edward Robarts and Joseph Kabris, were his informants. The first thing the two boys would have seen in Langsdorff's book was an engraving of one of these beachcombers, Joseph Kabris. They had only to turn the pages and there were two engravings that caught the tattooed cannibals of The Marquesas forever, front and back, every space on their bodies inscribed with marks, as fully as were Melville's close-written pages later.

So at nine years old, Herman Melville met his tattooed cannibals, and his beachcombers as well. Langsdorff's book, forever on its shelf, is in the before and after of Melville's own beachcombing experience. Reading is a dance on the beaches of the mind. Recognition, transformation, future looks, backward glances, flits of memory and understanding are its steps.

No beach, certainly not Melville's, is pristine. A beach is always marked by footsteps in the sand of before, the wet soaking edginess of now, the vague future shapes beyond the dunes.

Most of the crew are on the *Acushnet*'s deck as she edges along the southern coast of Nukuhiva—filled with 'strangely jumbled expectations', the only writer among them says. Their gams ('gam' was the whalers' word for a pod of whales, in singing conversation always), their meetings with other whalers—there had been twenty-two of them—had filled their ears with yarns that gave an extravagance to everything about the beach they were about to visit—its dangers, its pleasures, its otherness.

The *Acushnet* had been at sea eighteen months from its home port Fairhaven, Massachusetts. She had 700 barrels of oil in her hold and had sent back 175 barrels by another whaler. At a guess, that is perhaps fifteen whales at 60 barrels a whale. At a guess again, that is forty-five frenetic days of chase, capture, cutting, boiling, cleaning up. The other five hundred days were search—in the South Atlantic, up the west coast of South America, around the Galapagos, along the equatorial line. Days of boredom in which men tested their sufferance of one another and teased the limits of power and authority over them. Days of ugly labour, engulfed in greasy black smoke, covered in the blood and slime of death.

They would have wanted to be alone for their beach experience, or as much alone as thirty men on a whaler can be. As the *Acushnet* turned into Taiohae Bay and lost her way in the protected waters, they found that they were by no means alone. In that vast volcanic cauldron, on their starboard side as they entered, were the ships of a French expeditionary force. Admiral Abel Dupetit-Thouars on his madcap venture of taking possession of The Marquesas for France and Louis-Philippe had arrived at Taiohae on 31 May 1842, just three weeks before the *Acushnet*.

His 1800 sailors, two infantry and artillery companies, and 400 troops had made their mark in that short time. They had forgotten to bring tents and hammocks. So the land in the eastern part of the bay was denuded of all vegetation to the end of the treeline on the slopes. Those ashore were tormented by the mosquitos and the curse of the island, the *noni*, a biting gnat. The smoke of constantly lit fires was their only repellent. Behind a deep trench, palm-leafed barracks and tiled warehouses for provisions and gunpowder were beginning to appear.

A small hillock jutted out into the waters of the bay. Its top was shaved flat and scarred with earthworks. Seven cannons dominated the scene. It was Fort Collet. Fort Collet divided the bay between a native (*enata*) west and a foreign (*aoe*) east. The natives called themselves Teii. '*Ma foi! Oui! Oui!*' ('My faith! Yes! Yes!'), they heard the French exclaim and called these foreigners *mafaui* for it.

Captain Pease of the *Acushnet*, no doubt realising that 2500 *ma-foi-oui-ouis* in the bay meant that supplies would be hard to obtain and expensive, anchored the *Acushnet* on the west, or native side. The whaler *Potomac* was already anchored there. The *Acushnet* and the *Potomac* were only the latest whalers of more than forty to have anchored at Taiohae in the previous twelve months. This was no pristine beach. The sands were a jumble of footsteps. This beach was a much negotiated space. It would be Melville's fiction to make it 'native'.

There would have been none of that Dionysian welcoming that had become one of the myths about arrival in The Marquesas. Melville was to have Dionysian memories, but these would be in a time-bubble in which somebody else's yesterday experiences had become his own of today. Probably some young girls and some older women swam out to the *Acushnet* and plied their trade. But that trade had become even more ugly and violent over the years. The rapes and kidnaps had become too ordinary, the diseases of the sailors too public, the brutal transience of the whalers' visits too obvious for the scene to have much charm. There were politics too. They could not see it from the decks of the *Acushnet*, but the beach before them seethed with politics. The beach was divided over what the intrusion of so many strangers meant and what it did to native life, and how it was to be managed, if not controlled.

The *Acushnet* had anchored at the extreme western end of the bay, opposite a collection of open sheds that housed a dozen or more canoes. There were war canoes, with their distinctive Marquesan washstrake and breakwaters. There were smaller outrigger fishing canoes as well. They belonged to a man called Vahaketou. This was Vahaketou's 'small republic'. Vahaketou was the *tuhuna avaiki*, the actual and ceremonial fisherman of the valley

Across the bow of the *Acushnet*—for more than two hundred years sailors have advised one another to anchor fore and aft looking north in

Taiohae—the crew could see an idyllic enough scene. A screen of trees—breadfruit, hibiscus, gardenia, coconut and myrtle stood behind a beach of smooth stones rolling in the waves.

There was a huge banyan tree, fifty yards across. It was alive with birds—the noisy yellow warblers (*komako*), green parrots (*kuku*), blue lorikeets (*pihiti*), flycatchers, kingfishers, pipers, and seabirds whirling and crying. Perhaps Melville didn't see the birds, though. The French officers, under all sorts of delusions about their length of stay and tropical plenty, were already moping over their rancid lard and vinegared wine. To cope, they had, in three weeks, blasted every bird out of the sky.

On the foreshore, midway between the canoe sheds and the banyan tree, stood the most obvious structure in the valley. It was a bastard of a house, an architectural icon of the littered spaces of a beach. It was an 'English' house, it was said. A door and two windows and divided rooms were the mark of its Englishness. Scavenged materiel from ships and past intrusions were its makings. There was a flagpole waiting for its flag, which the French were happy to give it.

It was Temoana's house. Temoana was *haka'iki* of Taiohae. We have met him. If Temoana had a beach of a house, Temoana also had a beach of a soul. He used to display it each evening for the 'Acushnets' and anyone else to see. He used to ride the foreshore on a white stallion that the French had lent him in a red colonel's uniform that the French had given him. The French had already given him much champagne and 1800 francs for the pieces of land on which they were building their barracks and fort. They were offering him a 2000-franc annual stipend if he would be their 'king' and sign their deeds of possession. He was playing hard to get. His wife had run away to another valley. He wanted the French to get her back first.

Captain Pease had decided that the *Acushnet* would leave Taiohae on 11 July. Melville was given shore leave with the rest of the starboard watch on 9 July. He knew the opprobrium of 'running away'. But he knew as well that someone's 'runaway' would easily become someone else's replacement crew. The turnover in places like The Marquesas was quick. There were eighteen 'runaways' at Taiohae alone in 1842. Melville would lose his 'lay', his share of whaling profits, but he probably owed the ship something too. Pease wouldn't just let him go. There was a beachcomber Jim Fitch—'Irish Jimmy'—policing the beach for the French and the whalers. He would return any 'runaways' to the ship. Melville if he wished to run away from the *Acushnet* would have to find some way of leaving Taiohae.

May to September were Nukuhiva's wet months. The *Acushnet's* starboard watch spent a wet shore leave under the canoe hangars. No orgies, no romance, not much joy. Melville and his mate, Toby Greene, slipped easily away, with some ship's bread, tobacco and a bolt of cloth for gifts in the folds of their frock shirts. They would have known that it would have been dangerous to come with anything else. It was safer for a 'runaway' to come near-naked to the beach.

Melville and Greene could not follow the four or five paths that led back from the beach to the interior of the valley and up the slopes to the mountain ridges around. They had to mount the ridge directly behind the canoe sheds.

Melville did not have to romance their dangerous, slippery trek in the dark on the edges of the high cliffs, uncertain as they were of where they were going, and what awaited them when they arrived. An ulcerated tropical sore on his leg added to the distress of it. His first steps across his beach heightened his fears of otherness. But hunger, pain, discomfort and disorientation condition his mind and body to some surrender of self. He will be grateful to these supposed savages who will save him.

Melville spent fourteen days among the Taipi, a week of them alone. The Taipi already had a savage reputation among Melville's future American readers. Lieutenant David Porter, commander of the USS *Essex*, had felt insulted by them in 1814 when he made a claim for the first overseas possession of an American empire on Nukuhiva, precisely where the French made a claim for theirs. Porter was defeated by the Taipi ambush and guerrilla tactics when he raided their valley to punish them. But he returned with an incursion force and burnt every house of the 2000-strong population of the Taipi and killed whom he could. Melville didn't have to elaborate the otherness of the Taipi. For American readers they already had the otherness of a native enemy.

Melville had fourteen days of native food, native habitation, native dress, native material goods. Fourteen days to enter the day-and-night cycle of native living. Fourteen days to catch something of the cycle of life and death, of dance and ceremony, of worship and government. These fourteen days were enough to pepper his story with reality effects. They were made the more real for him as a writer in his brother's Nassau Street office, because he could go back to Langsdorff and even David Porter. So his memory of his beach was like the line drawing of a colouring book. His reading to write gave him the brush to colour the details in.

Melville had had important experiences of otherness nonetheless. He learned that difference is a translation. The hospitality, care and comfort he received from these savages was civilisation in another dress. He won't find an entry into other people's metaphors—not by a long way—but it was a first step in a sense of the relativity of things.

Another realisation for Melville was that if there is civilisation on both sides of the beach, there is also savagery on both sides. He recognised the savagery in the French. He will see it later in missionaries. He sees it in himself. Here is how he describes his escape from the Taipi: Melville is fleeing in a longboat; Mow-Mow, his perceived captor, is swimming after him.

> Even at the moment I felt horror at the act I was about to commit, but it was no time for pity or compunction, and with a true aim, and exerting all my strength, I dashed the boat-hook at him. It struck him just below the throat, and forced him downwards. I had no time to repeat my blow, but I saw him rise to the surface in the wake of the boat, and never shall I forget the ferocious expression of his countenance.

It was the sort of violence, I have to say, that was a daily occurrence on these beaches. Melville's surprise was that he looked at the otherness of his beach and saw his own violence mirrored in the reflection.

CROSSINGS

An Archaeology of Believing

*All humanity is believing. Across times. Across cultures. All humanity has answers
to questions that never can be answered. All humanity has an ultimate metaphor for
what is. That metaphor might not be explicit—on the surface of things, easy to
see—but it is there. Being cross-cultural, it seems to me, means entering that
ultimate metaphor, translating others' metaphors into my own metaphor. Hearing
the silences in others' metaphors, so that I can hear the silences in mine. It is a very
humbling thing to discover that all our ultimate metaphors are equidistant from
reality. It is humbling to discover that the location of all our spiritualities lies in a
questioning that has no answer other than: 'Here I am. Here is my believing self.'*

*My believing self is not my beliefs. Beliefs are static, propositional, products of
closure. Believing is actual, processual.*

*Perhaps it might seem intrusive to present my believing self in the stories of
others' crossings, but there is a nakedness on beaches that I would share.*

A Brief Timeline

In 1948 I entered the novitiate of the Society of Jesus at Loyola College,
Watsonia, on the edge of the city of Melbourne. I entered with twenty
others, mostly straight from school, but also with some older men who had
returned from the war. Then followed two years of prayer, reflective reading,
testing of our vocation and decision. There was little formal study save in
Latin and Greek and in the constitution of the Society of Jesus. The novitiate
ended with the taking of the vows of poverty, chastity and obedience. Then
followed a year of humanities and language studies, French and German
added now to Latin and Greek. The year 1951 saw me begin three years of
scholastic philosophy. Our subjects included Epistemology, Ontology,
Cosmology, Rational Psychology, Natural Theology and Ethics, as well as
History of Philosophy, Science and Educational Methods. After completing
philosophy I was sent to teach in a Jesuit primary school for a year. Burke
Hall, it was called, a preparatory school to Xavier College.

To that date Canon Law forbade any student for the priesthood
attending a secular university where philosophy was taught. But in 1955 a
group of us were sent by the Jesuits to study full-time at the University of

Melbourne. Some did Classics, Literature, Psychology, Philosophy, Science, Mathematics. I did four years of History Honours, followed by a master's degree in Pacific Prehistory.

In 1960 I began theology at Canisius College, Pymble, NSW. I was ordained to the priesthood in December 1962 and then completed a final year in theology. The Department of Pacific History at the Australian National University, Canberra, offered me a research fellowship to work on the publication of Edward Robarts' journal. I held that until September 1964, when I took up a Saltonstall Fellowship in the Anthropology Department at the Peabody Museum, Harvard.

After completing all my doctoral studies and examinations, except my dissertation at Harvard, I started my return home to Australia by way of Hawai'i where I took up an appointment in the Anthropology and History departments in the fall semester 1967.

I returned to Australia to complete my final year of Jesuit studies in 1968. This Crossing is principally a story of that year. I took up a Senior Lectureship in Sociology and History at LaTrobe University in 1969, left the priesthood in 1970, was appointed Max Crawford Professor of History in 1971, retired from that position in 1991, and lived happily ever after.

I HAVE A SOUL, I think. My soul is my locating, searching self. It is not a soul that is 'saved'. Not an ethereal wispy, ghost-buster sort that eventually escapes this body and this vale of tears. A soul. A place of reflection where one knows oneself as is and would be. A place of commitment—and defection; of guilt—and innocence; of love—and hate; of truth—and lies; of believing—and knowing. My ambition always in writing ethnography is to locate other's souls, their searching selves, where they find themselves, as I do, always on the edge of understanding. Souls looking at one another out of the past or in the present is a kinder, less intrusive sort of ethnography it seems to me. The trick, of course, is to do it. My trick is to tell stories. Let me tell some.

It is 1955. I am in 'Hell'. Hell in this instance is the room in the seminary in which all the books we were forbidden to read were kept. We called it 'Hell'. I was a young Jesuit, four years into my training, then. Hell had a key. Hell was a locked room. I had to get the key to 'Hell' so that I could read Henri Bergson's *Two Sources of Morality and Religion* (1932), Alfred North Whitehead's *Process and Reality* (1929) and *Adventures of*

Ideas (1933) and Tielhard de Chardin's *The Human Phenomenon* (1955). Yes! Teilhard de Chardin, the pliocene age archaeologist who discovered 'Pekin Man'—perhaps the most famous Jesuit of us all—was forbidden reading.

Hell in the seminary was a highly elevated place. You had to climb rather than descend into it. It was in a tower overlooking miles of countryside to the mountains that ring Melbourne. 'Hell' was a peaceful, if dusty, place full of unread books. I remember the sounds of 'Hell'—the wail of the Hurstbridge train in the valley below, magpies warbling, crows chorusing.

I was researching a paper on process for my philosophy class. I still have the paper in my files. Process was to become the locating metaphor of my believing.

In 1948 I began a twenty-year pilgrimage in learning as a Jesuit. That learning pilgrimage did not end in 1968. It hasn't yet. But one cycle of it did end in 1968. That was my easy relationship with the Church in the priesthood. There wasn't a day in those twenty years in which I did not spend several hours engaged with my believing soul in prayer and ritual and giving some sort of public witness to what I saw in myself and the world. There wasn't a day in those twenty years, on the other hand, that I wasn't also engaged for many more hours with my knowing—as distinct from my believing—soul. Knowing—a consciousness enclosed in a myriad social and cultural systems; a consciousness that is always ongoing; a consciousness that is cumulative and kaleidoscopic. There was an extravagance in the Jesuit commitment to the double prongs of their lives—Believing and Knowing—for which I am eternally grateful. Eternally? I suppose that is the question.

Those twenty years began and ended with my engagement in the full thirty days of the *Spiritual Exercises* of Ignatius Loyola. At seventeen years of age I was engaged in the thirty days of solitary reflection to discover the spiritual courage to take the three vows of poverty, chastity and obedience that were the foundation of religious life. At thirty-seven years of age, the thirty days were to discover who I was as a believer after twenty years of engagement in a knowledge search that was inevitably relativising.

I have written in 'Ethnography on My Mind'—an essay in a collection of writings entitled *Performances*—how I think the *Spiritual Exercises* of Loyola shaped my thinking in an ethnographic way. The exercises were for us a daily performance. They filtered all our secular and religious learning. In 1948 the war was just over. The Holocaust and the war had raised unanswerable questions for all believers. Dietrich Boenhoffer was telling us that 'God was dead' and we knew what he meant. A religion that depended on an intrusive supernatural was no 'ground of being' in a world that had seen the evil we had seen. Our theology was teaching us to read our sacred texts—the Scriptures that infused our believing—in a new way. Literalism and fundamentalism, we understood, denied what we were learning about how human beings make metaphors of all last things. I have heroes among the scholars of sacred Scriptures whose names most readers will have no reason to know. Raymond Brown in his work on the Gospels, C. H. Dodd in his studies on the parables, taught us how to read our sacred texts without going into unbelieving free fall. One could be a scholar of the highest standards and be a believer too. In Scripture truth was in the metaphor. The wisdom and strength we drew on—the truth we saw in the literally untrue—was unending. We learned to make the metaphors of prophets, psalmists and ancient kings our own. Knowing Abraham and Isaac, David, Isaiah was to be as ethnographic an experience for me as field work in The Marquesas. We were postmodern believers before there was a word like 'postmodern' to describe us.

There was another strand of thinking that affected us. They were the European philosophers and theologians who were preparing the Catholic Church for Vatican Council II. Joseph Maréchal, Karl Rahner, Bernard Lonergan, Gabriel Marceau taught us to fly intellectually in a field of philosophy that most outsiders thought caged in by tradition and rule. If I could reduce all that was coming to us into a couple of sentences, it would be this. Humanity is part of a changing, moving, living active world. In that world we have to do not so much with inert substances, but with dynamic processes, not so much with things as events. Hence the 'ground of our being' is not an unmoved mover, a changeless essence, but a living, active, constantly creative, infinitely related, ceaselessly operating reality. The cosmos is alive.

Don't laugh at me. And don't ask for my scholastic syllogisms proving the thesis. But one of my most important insights turned around a Jesuit anti-Dominican thesis in scholastic philosophy: that there is no real distinction between essence and being, between defining qualities and existence. What is, is totally particular. There are no essences—things—distinct from their being. So when we translate our believing and knowing into words, our words are as alive as the cosmos. Any reading or hearing of words that freezes them is a sort of death, a sort of Terror as Jean François Lyotard has written.

There is Terror in all our institutions—church, university, state. The Terror is the template institutions put on living. The Terror, for that matter, is the template Theory puts on practice. Templates are dead words. Spiritualities will never be located in cemeteries of dead words, dead beliefs. Spiritualities live forever, are forever being transformed. It became my abiding ambition to describe the living spiritualities of both Native and Stranger as they are. Here is something I once wrote of that ambition.

. . . The thousands of eucharistic communions in my life, for all their scruples and arithmetic, have been sweet. Not mystic, I think, but sometimes moments of discernment, of cleared vision, occasionally even of a little breathless love. Why should I laugh at that? Why should I turn it upside down and say it is the effect of something else? Of deluded ambitions? Of subliminal class and sex? I have said to myself and to anybody who would ask, that I would like to describe religious experience as it is, not in terms of something else. It is an arrogance and sometimes a bore to begin with oneself. But I do not know where else to begin, where else to find the same, where else to find the different. Perhaps I should write a poem and by that be true to my particularities. But then again, I do not think my narratives of what it is to believe and hope, to be guilty and sad, to be sure and doubting—in different space and different time— is something less than a poem. Or should be. ['Soliloquy in San Giacomo', *Performances*, p. 272]

The year 1968 would be a fateful one for me, as it no doubt was for many others, but for different reasons. By 1968, when I returned to Australia from my studies in anthropology at Harvard, I had spent twenty years in preparation for what I expected to be my life's work—priest, scholar, educator. I had one more year of preparation to go. The Jesuits called it Tertianship, a third and final year of self-reflection and decision added to the two years of dedication in the Novitiate made at the beginning. Ordinarily, Tertianship would be done with others in seclusion and under the guidance of some master of spirituality. I had made some tentative arrangements to go to South America and work with those I had come to admire who came to be called 'liberation theologians'. But the Jesuits at home in Australia thought they had a need of me. There was a younger generation of Jesuits, still in their studies, who had been marked with the new freedoms in the Church and society of the 1960s. They came from a Catholic education system very different from that which had marked the generations before them. These young men had an engagement in scholarship and knowledge, but they came with a different sense of vocation than ours of previous years, no less idealistic, but less patient with institutionalisation, more eager to engage in their pastoral calling than to be holed up for years in studies.

Teilhard de Chardin had written: 'In the name of our faith, we have the right and duty to become passionate about the things of the earth'. The 'things of the earth' for Teilhard were primarily, of course, the deep-down fossils that bred his evolutionary, processual belief that the material world was not just signpost to but the expression of a dynamic divinity. For us, the 'earth' was not a fossil past, but our own humanity. Our belief in the divine began always there.

It is a peculiar sort of faith both to be a believer and to be passionate about the things of the earth. The 'earth' is full of mysteries, unsolvable for the most part. A voyage to the centre of the earth, to the resolution of even one of its mysteries, is a dangerous voyage for a traveller who believes faith solves all mysteries. 1968 was a year of my most dangerous voyaging.

The Jesuits asked me to come home and counsel two groups of their young men. They made me *Socius*, or Companion, to the Master of Novices, at the Novitiate, Loyola College, in Melbourne, and 'Spiritual Father' to a group of young scholars five hundred miles away at the Australian National University in Canberra.

The Master of Novices in the Jesuit scheme of things was responsible for the spiritual development of those beginning their lives in the Society of Jesus. His *Socius* traditionally focused on the novice's social and religious development—the nitty-gritty of discipline and rule, the externals of the spiritual life. The Jesuits, from the time of their founder, Ignatius Loyola, had always believed that physical space, time and the body shaped the spiritual. For my generation, twenty years before the young men now my responsibility, there was nothing ambiguous about the spaces and times of our lives. We were defined by the ways we walked, the modesty of our eyes, our formal dress, the bells that divided our days and our hours, the things we were allowed to talk about, the one page of a newspaper we were allowed to read once a week, the defined freedoms of our days off—the things we were allowed to do that we were not ordinarily allowed. We always referred to those defined in these ways as 'Ours'. 'Ours' were everywhere recognisable in their language, their posture, their attitudes, their assumptions. Loyalty and pride in being one of 'Ours' was a very real thing. Don't think that there were no freedoms behind these masks. There were great freedoms and joys. The choice to be bound so stringently was our own to make. All sacrifices are relative. The humiliations of having to ask for everything we used and to lead a fairly spartan existence was not poverty in any real sense. None of us starved. None of us were homeless. Our illnesses were cared for. Nonetheless, we had chosen to be poor for what any one of us would have said was an ideal—the love of God. Celibacy was no overriding issue— though the torture of adolescent bodies trying to be 'pure' was real enough. The true cost of celibacy was the deprivation of love and friendship. 'Charity', not love, ruled our lives: a carefulness for others, but also a carelessness for what really made someone else. Friendship was forbidden for what it would do to both community and celibacy.

By the time I had become *Socius* in 1968, nearly all the institutional savagery of these defining spaces was gone. The Master of Novices was a kindly, humane man, eager to promote the free spirits of the young men. I had no need in his eyes to humiliate the novices or to bend them to the letter of the law.

The other group of young men for whom I was Spiritual Father was a dozen 'scholastics', Jesuits in training, doing their undergraduate degrees at the Australian National University. Since the Jesuits had no house in Canberra, they lived in a wing of a Dominican monastery. It was not a happy union between the highly conservative Dominicans and young Jesuits who led a highly unmonastic life at the university. Their studies in science, mathematics, humanities and languages demanded a lack of routine that was foreign to the Dominican life. It was my duty to fly to Canberra every other weekend to counsel the scholastics on the double engagement of their lives—their secular studies and their religious duties of prayer, reflection and meditation.

All my life with the Jesuits I had admired the zeal with which they pursued secular learning. It was a serious gamble they took: that total engagement in secular learning would not shake religious belief. I suppose that it was their confidence in me that I had found a balance between faith and learning that led them to believe that I could counsel these young men well. It was not so clear to me. I was frightened at my responsibilities.

105

There was one important obligation on Jesuits in their Tertianship. It was to return to the *Spiritual Exercises* of Ignatius Loyola in order to renew the commitment made some twenty years before when one had done the full *Spiritual Exercises* for the first time. Now I did the thirty days of silence and prayer under the guidance of two men I admired greatly. Val Moran was an expert in Church history who was everything a humane historian must be. Bill Dalton was a professor of Scripture who had been my friend since he had taught me in primary school forty years before.

My thirty-day retreat was an important part of my voyage of 1968. All voyages properly have their logs. I would like to present some extracts of mine from those thirty days. I leave them as I find them, without correction, but demystifying an occasional allusion with a note in square brackets.

I began the Long Retreat last night, without much fear of the thirty days and without a very clear idea what I was doing it for or what I thought it would do to me. Some months ago I thought the Long Retreat would be a dramatic moment of decision. Indeed I had already debated whether it would be better for me to leave the Society and priesthood at its end, or whether I should remain a little longer, eking out the days of my usefulness. Now I do not feel dramatic at all.

The Pymble community [I had come from the Novitiate in Loyola to the theological college, Canisius, in Sydney] is relaxed and easy, a clear embodiment of all that Loyola isn't. They accept me. I think they admire me. They listen to me interestedly. I feel very much at home and feel that I have their sympathy. It is not a feeling that I have had at Loyola from *anybody*. So the atmosphere is congenial and has affected me with a peacefulness that thirty days cannot as yet disturb.

Last night I talked with VM [Val Moran] and WJD [Bill Dalton]. I told VM that I had long ceased to pray in the accepted mode, that I did not expect to pray that way in the Long Retreat. I was conscious of unorthodoxy, conscious that I had long since ceased to be able to feel sinful in any ordinary way. I told him that I hoped to see in what ways I stood in a personal relationship with God, in what ways I could be motivated. I wanted the role of Christ to be clear in my mind and I wanted to explore a spirituality of hopefulness and process. He listened—

he always does—suggested that the process from adolescence to now involved desiccation and rejection for us all. I felt that he sensed that there was more to my problem than that.

WJD was buoyant: expressed himself in almost as atheistic terms as I: we found our common experiences in relationship to law (purely a suggestive structure), faith (a working hypothesis), very much what I thought—except he thinks in a scriptural mode. He could not see the difficulty I have in the apparent hypocrisy of my life vis-à-vis the common life. Couldn't feel my protest against the structures.

I finished the evening with Daryl [my brother, now deceased, who was also a Jesuit, studying theology at Canisius] easily and sympathetically . . .

Day One. Today I began quietly—reading Stanley [David Michael Stanley, *A Modern Scriptural Approach to the Spiritual Exercises*, 1967], Rahner [Karl Rahner, *Spiritual Exercises*, 1965; *The Dynamic Element in the Church*, 1964] and Pettingren [Norman Pettingren, *God in Process*, 1967]. There were moments when some of their thoughts reached me, but they were few. Stanley's idea of the call to be Human and the risk involved in the call rang true. But they are still in an idiom and vocabulary that doesn't satisfy, and I guess at this moment I am frightened about the risk. I am, of course, holding back. I know it. Once in the day I thought that a full response would touch on greatness. I now know clearly the cost. It would destroy a thousand dreams and hopes. But I am frightened of these glimpses of 'greatness'. I have had them before, only to be deflated by the realities of non-retreat days and the emptiness of life.

Rahner's concept of only finding God in decision rang true, too, but again the decision is an act of courage that is beyond me at the moment. I cannot bear to *decide* and to leap and to find that across the other side I face only the old face of God which will melt away in the heat of the day. I cannot go back now to yesterday's religion. I am not sure what today's religion is or where it goes tomorrow. But yesterday's is barren and false, an idolatry that is less repugnant to me than the idolatry of self which might be my sin.

The day has been quiet. No peaks. No troughs. I was amused at dinner, as I listened to the record of selected ballet music to ponder the incongruities of *Cancan Moulin Rouge* with the solemn thoughts of the day.

Risk: the gamble in this life of faith and vocation is great, and yet it isn't. The risk is real. I have only really been happy in two ways in this life— no, three. Happy in love with Donna—intensely, sweetly, minute-by-minute happiness. Happy in my priesthood—in moments of giving, the moments of witness, the moments of community. Happy in personal achievement—the bittersweet and really the empty happiness of doing brilliantly, performing at the highest pitch—as student, teacher, professional.

Studded through all this is a great deal of blah. The gamble is really on the blah. The gamble is the emptiness and loneliness of this independent life. The gamble is a Pymble or a Loyola. You can be tossed into either. The gamble is in old age and a 'happy' funeral. The gamble is the continued fight for 'meaning', the endless fight for it today and tomorrow. The gamble is eternal youth or bleak years. The gamble is vision and plans. The gamble is effecting the dreams. The gamble for me is the nearness of the realisation of hopes and plans. What happens if religious life becomes livable, and I lose all the opportunity to negativise it, to anathematise it? What happens if I take the gamble and find that it was a myth? I lose what I have and I lose what I had.

The gamble is being yourself. WJD insisted yesterday evening that 'yourself' is situated in reality—hedged about with all the conditions as they are. There is no abstract vision of oneself that is not a delusion. He is right. He says what I say. What happens when you're a coward, and you're not sure whether you are being a 'realist' or a funk in not being yourself.

I feel right now that I should gamble by fighting all the structures. I feel absurd and getting the challenge and the denial that would make an exit the easier. Right now, all my life, the externals have got hold of me. I'm the 'perfect monk'—talk like hell about dreams, do nothing to make them come real . . .

Day Three. A little less restless and less sleepy today. A long talk with VM trying to describe my resistance, a nameless thing deep down within me, almost a physical feeling in the chest. I told him that the First Principles and Foundation [the leading meditation of the *Spiritual Exercises*] was meaningless to me. I had no way of translating them into meaningful terms except in a Tillichian type of philosophy. But that led me to the edge. I felt that I had got nothing out of the First Principles and Foundation. I'd not known what it was to 'praise, reverence and serve'. Val asked me if awareness of God didn't include praise and reverence. I replied that there was an awareness of God in me. I have some sort of unconceptualised knowledge of a presence—but that this was a *given*. It did not evoke reverence or fear or love. I did not respond to God directly;

nor felt that what I did morally mattered to him (tho' it mattered to me) nor did I find it fruitful to seek his will; nor did I seek to change it. I said that the afterlife was irrelevant to me. I could be what I am without any reference to sanction or carrot. Val thought that the only relevance of afterlife is the fact that my decisions here and now make me what I will be as I face death. But it is all a tangle in my mind . . .

Day Four. It's been Sin and Sun today—a beautiful, calm, sunny day—mesmerising me into sleep. Not a thing that I read, except a little of Paul in *Romans* and *Galatians*, and a little that I heard in community prayer got through. Maybe my conscience has been cauterised. Maybe I'm not a believer any more. But all Rahner's talk of the sinner just didn't ring true. I know I'm sinful in relation to the image I proffer and the reality I know. I know myself sinful in the ideals unrealised. I know myself sinful in the lethargy and cowardice of my life. But none of these things bear on God. The afterlife doesn't reach me, and the idea of a punishing God in this uncertain, unknowing world is an absurdity. If he is little enough to busy himself with Hell, then he is not big enough to be worshipped . . .

Yes, 'sinful' is a peculiar word. It is not merely guilt or freedom. I know that I have a measure of freedom and I know when I am guilty. At times I'd even be prepared to say that I was sinful in relation to the image I have of myself in Christ. He was the free man, the courageous one. He knew himself and could give himself. Having seen Christ, I know what it is to be sinful. But this does not move me out of the realm of man at all. I can say all that and still not believe that I have 'offended' God. I know all that Rahner has to say about 'offending' God—he translates it as the 'deification of finite reality'. Yes, I understand that man has a tendency to make idols, absolutes out of himself, out of things. That's his foolishness. He tries to make gods everywhere. Better that he do it nowhere. Hate God? I've never hated God. I've never hated anybody. The nearest thing to hate I've experienced is towards my self under the influences of 'Christian morality'.

Day Five. Last night I talked with the theologians about Prayer. Their worry was the role of Christ and the improbability of petitionary prayer. They worried for the Ignatian structure of prayer. I said that liturgically there is a need for structure. It makes human trust and human experience and the presence of Christ a possibility. There is structure in every aspect of life. In prayer? Not necessarily the same physical structure of preludes and imagination we learnt, but structure of attitude which makes reflexion possible. A structure of quiet and attention that lets a man know himself. Yet, I'm not sure whether I've said a single prayer (personal) since I began. I haven't addressed anybody. All I've attempted to do is to see reality (i.e. myself) clearly. That has been difficult enough. I am too disquieted to do it. What happens when I see it? I don't think I want to change it. Maybe if it is too ugly, I can summon courage to change myself. But I think more in terms of accepting. Knowledge is my main aim. Somehow I feel that knowledge gives me the key to God and myself. I suppose that is my old philosophy of the 'IS' and the 'GIVEN'. But new insight into self and the world, seeing new patterns of behaviour and response, knowing myself honestly, conceptualising all that I am and all that others are—I have no ambition beyond this. And I don't know if that is a prayer or if it is pure philosophy. It must be contemplation of some sort.

They asked if I thought prayer effective. I said that I thought it effective in myself (petitionary prayer) and in others when they were present or were conscious of my prayers. I do not believe that it *affects* the world by changing it directly. That alarmed some. It alarms me. I said I thought of it in terms of the absurdity that Christ's witness is. You do it knowing that its effect is minimal, not knowing how wide it will be. I pray in community. I feel myself extended to others in communal prayer, but I do not pray for others in the sense of asking God to do this or that. I do not ever pray for Donna in this sense. I only love her and worry for her and hope for her. I reach her in this way. I cannot reach her in a loop through heaven . . .

Days Eight and Nine. Two unmitigated disasters. Thoughtless and empty, lonely and desperate days. Tomorrow I will take a break.

Beyond this trouble I have felt weary with it all. The strain of being absolutely alone with myself has begun to tell. There are times when daydreams and reality mingle rather freely and times when a sort of consciousness that is on the edge of dream takes hold of me and I try to remember what thoughts I had seconds ago and they are gone, or weird stories and conversations take place in my mind, and an instant later, I am conscious, but not fully, to the point of recall of their strangeness.

Let me end my journal there. The further twenty days of the Long Retreat passed more peacefully. I had made the decision not to decide, but to let the events of my life unfold. Bill Dalton kept warning me that my impatience with the rhetoric of religion that did not describe the actual experiences of what it was to believe would inevitably lead to crisis. I knew that, but I did not realise how quickly the crisis would come.

My Long Retreat ended in July 1968. Almost immediately the Jesuits sent me to Brisbane, the capital of our northern state of Queensland. I was appointed as chaplain there to the University of Queensland, and to assist an old friend of mine, Brian Fleming SJ, at the Jesuit residential college at the University, St Leo's. Brian was a scholar of renown in French ecclesiastical history. He had been a hero of mine. I was about to bring him much pain.

At the University of Queensland I met up again with a group of Catholic scholars whom I had known as an undergraduate at the University of Melbourne in the 1950s. Under the leadership of a poet, Vincent Buckley, they had created an 'Intellectual Apostolate' way ahead of their times in the Australian Catholic Church. They were influenced by the 'Worker Priest' movement in France and the theologians and thinkers who gave the movement a *raison d'être*. For about five or six years at Melbourne, they gave a constructive intellectual outlook to young Catholics, bred in their schools on traditional dogma and apologetics. Now, older and more experienced in the reluctance of the Australian Church to embrace very much of Vatican Council II, they were nonetheless comfortable with the freedom that the Universal Church, as distinct from the Australian Church, seemed to enjoy. That comfortableness was shattered in September 1968 when Pope Paul II published his encyclical *Humanae Vitae*. *Humanae Vitae* turned back the clock in its edict of banning birth control. It turned the moral face of the Church away from the evils of global poverty, of violence within and between nations, of exploitation of the weak, back to the bedroom.

There was dismay among Catholics at the university at the encyclical. There were public meetings, debates. In Australia, there were no Catholic universities. In the USA, Catholic universities gave theologians platforms to question the theological basis of the encyclical. Nor were there any independent Catholic newspapers in Australia where the issue could be studied. Indeed, the Australian Catholic bishops added a protocol to the encyclical. All priests were ordered to preach the rationality of the Pope's stand against birth control.

It was this protocol that undid me. I was confident in my moral theology. I knew I could counsel in the confessional and outside it on the primacy of the individual conscience over universal prohibitions. What I could not do was preach that the encyclical was rational. Without making any public stand, I approached the Archbishop of Brisbane privately and told him my dilemma. Without a moment's discussion, the archbishop reached for the telephone and called my Provincial and told him that I must leave the archdiocese of Brisbane immediately.

One cannot abruptly leave a chaplaincy at the university in a time of turmoil without someone guessing that more is afoot. The newspapers pursued me—only one priest in Australia at that time had spoken out against the encyclical. I was chased to the airport, photographed leaving Brisbane, and had, not my fifteen minutes of fame but fifteen seconds, saying 'No comment'. Perhaps the fame was only fifteen seconds. The notoriety was much longer. A highly conservative politico-social-religious Catholic newspaper, *Newsweekly*, published a centrefold article on me under a picture of Judas.

I fled to Pymble. To the same room where I had done my Long Retreat. No sooner was I there, but the Cardinal's secretary rang my superior to say I must leave the archdiocese of Sydney. But it was not something he could force on the Jesuits, so long as I did not practise my priesthood publicly in Sydney—saying mass, giving sacraments, preaching, even addressing Catholic groups.

The young men at Pymble received me with love and admiration. There were a few older voices calling for my dismissal from the Society of Jesus, but I was left alone for the rest of 1968. I chose to do research in the great library of Pacific history, the Mitchell Library, Sydney. The turmoil of the year disappeared in the quiet of archives and library.

The sad truth was that there was nowhere in Australia where I could practise the priesthood publicly, save in Melbourne, to which I was about to go to start my academic teaching career at LaTrobe University. By a quirk of ecclesiastical red tape, I still had the 'faculties', the papers that allowed me to practise the priesthood, from the time I had been ordained in Melbourne in 1963.

I felt strangely free, though. I had not betrayed myself or the trust of others.

3

By Sea to the Beach

There needs to be some momentum in men's or women's lives to thrust them across a beach. Maybe fear or lust or the love of God pushes them into otherness. Maybe there is some immediate stress in the voyaging there. The threat of a mutiny, Robarts will say. The accident of a shipwreck, Kabris will lie. Maybe, as the young Crook believed, a man is predestined from before time began in a voyage towards salvation to this beach.

Whatever pushes men and women to strip themselves of all that culturally and socially defines them to immerse themselves in otherness, there are a myriad stories of how they got to their beach. Here are three of them.

Whalers and Missionaries

Following James Colnett's 1792–94 whaling expedition round the Horn to the Galapagos Islands, where he thought he had discovered the spawning grounds of the spermaceti whale, English whalers turned to the Southern Whale Fishery and the Pacific. In 1796 there were sixty vessels working these waters, twenty-three of them in the Pacific. The Atlantic, north and south, was a dangerous place in time of wars. The American whalers came later and in force. Between 1845 and 1860 there would have been seven hundred whalers in the Pacific at any one time. Three- and four-year tours were common. As the northern, central and Japan grounds were exploited, Hawai'i became a whaling emporium and chandlery. Visits to Fenua'enata were short and more for refreshment and women. A box of gunpowder would buy four nights with an older woman. A girl 'eleven and a half years and soft' was more expensive. The profits of the whaling industry were vast. The costs to sustain it with Pacific island supplies was relatively low.

Missionaries—Protestant, Catholic—English, Spanish, French, American—quickly followed the explorers, whalers and traders into the Pacific. The London Missionary Society (LMS) came in the *Duff* to Tahiti, Tonga and Fenua'enata in 1796. After Crook's failure, the LMS sent seventeen bewildered Tahitians to The Land between 1821 and 1834 to see if native missionaries could do better. In 1834, three Englishmen tried again at Vaitahu and failed, mainly, they felt, because Catholic missionaries of the Congregation of the Sacred Heart of Jesus and Mary had the unfair support of the French colonising power. In 1832 the American Board of Commissioners for Foreign Missions thought they would try their hand in Fenua'enata and sent three missionary families to Nukuhiva. They lasted only eighteen months. Much later, in 1853, the Hawaiian Mission Board, thinking that a Roman Catholic faith needed as much missionising as a heathen one, sent some native Hawaiian missionaries. This was perhaps the bravest and saddest of all the missionary efforts in The Land. All missions, Catholic and Protestant, were bedevilled—if this is the right word!—with the probem of how to bring universal truths clothed in culturally specific narratives across the beach. Almost all believed that civilisation came before conversion. Protestants thought that Catholic sacramentality had an advantage working on superstitious minds that the Word did not. All of them were assured that God worked mysteriously, but mostly through political systems.

'Call me Ishmael!'

Edward Robarts, Whaler

Call me Ishmael! No! There is too much ventriloquism in that. Call me 'Spirit of Ishmael'. I need Ishmael's eyes in the fo'c'sle. I need Ishmael's bare feet on the deck. I need Ishmael's voice to tell the story of this whaling ship. I need Ishmael's freedom in the telling of it—to move between a present discourse and a past narrative, to tell how large every trivial particularity really was. But I am two hundred years distant from the events I narrate. I know how the story ends. But even that is not true. The story isn't ended yet. I'll tread the decks of the *New Euphrates* like a ghost of its future.

Captain Henry Glasspoole was no Ahab either, though he had Ahab's propensity to retire to his cabin and brood over the bad luck of his voyage. But his first officer could have been Pequod. He was an officious, violent man. He thought himself a better whaler than his captain, and no doubt believed that on the next voyage a captaincy would be his. Certainly to this time—it is October 1798—the *New Euphrates* had had a miserable season. The few right whale they had chased in the Atlantic were virtually only practice. The practice hadn't done them much good. The first chase in the Pacific around the Island of Mochu ended with a smashed boat. The captain's boat at that. The first storm in the Pacific smashed the stern boat with all the whaling implements stored in it. Glasspoole was beginning to be seen as unlucky. It was a dangerous reputation for a captain to earn.

The whaler followed the cold artery of life up the South American coast. It had not been mapped yet, not given its name of Humboldt Current. But a whaling captain could see its way-signs. They led to the Tortoise Islands (Galapagos). 'Islands of Fire', 'Outer Islands' the Incas, rafting the same cold highway, had called them. 'The Bewitched' (Las Encantadas) was the name sailors often used. They seemed to drift in and out of sight as equatorial mirages as the strong currents of the Humboldt swirled at the current's journey's end and dragged ships with them every whichway.

The Galapagos seemed bewitched in other ways. 'Shores fit for pandemonium' Robert Fitzroy, the *Beagle*'s captain, would say. Charles Darwin, with hindsight, thought he had been 'brought somewhat near to the great mystery of mysteries, the first appearance of new beings on this earth'. Astonished as he was 'at the amount of creative force'—'if such an expression may be used', he rather coyly parenthesised—he nevertheless felt that the Galapagos were bewitched with a cyclopean air. The islands looked like some hell made of devils of satanic mills in the industrial valleys of Staffordshire, he thought. Herman Melville, too, found no charm in a landscape of bubbled lava, where 'the chief sound of life is a hiss'. For him, Las Encantadas was cursed by its changelessness, without season, without bloom, without green growth.

The *New Euphrates* hoped that their luck would change in the cold, calm sea around the Galapagos. There they surely would come across spermaceti. They didn't. They were out of season. In these first years of Pacific whaling, the pattern of the whales' travels were not yet known. When they were, it would take a short time to cut out 50,000 spermaceti from this coast of Chile and other Pacific grounds.

There were other hapless whalers in the Galapagos. Whalers with nothing to do are restless and dangerous. The empty barrels in the hold were a reminder that their 'lay', their very precise share of the profits of the oil that would be their only pay, would be small. Here off the Spanish-American coast there were other catches. The sea, even in the Age of Revolution and Enlightenment, was not yet a civilised space. It would take a few more wars, an understanding that empires were as much of sea as land, and more egregious losses of trade and capital to make the oceans a more civilised space. But in 1798 and for hundreds of years before and perhaps fifty years after, being out of sight of land, out of influence of law and order, the sea was a place of ambivalence. At sea disguise was ordinary. They could look the legitimate trader and demand all the courtesies and etiquette of diplomacy in port. Out at sea, seamen could change a flag, have no flag at all. Seamen could murder and rob, burn and loot. They could even have a passport to this mayhem. It was called letters of marque. Letters of marque might save a man from hanging as a pirate in a foreign port. They might give home governments a share of the loot, make robbery a sort of tax. Privateering, not piracy, they called it. There was even a flag for it, the 'budgee jack'. Fly the red budgee with the Union Jack and you were part of an 'as if' world that made any atrocity legitimate.

An 'as if' world of derring-do and adventure was the stage prop for the theatre of these waters, these islands, these coasts. These were the South Seas towards which Vasco Núñez de Balboa looked as he stood in a vast plain of stinking mud waiting for the tide to turn so that he could claim 'these austral seas and lands and coasts and islands with everything annexed to them' for the

Kings of Castile 'now and for all time so long as the world shall last until the final judgement of all mortals'. Not much would be allowed to stand in the way of enforcing that vision, not native people's rights, not human life, not danger and suffering beyond comprehension. And if hidalgo romance veiled the sordidness of it all, the challenges to it of monopolists, freebooters and buccaneers made a 'marchlands' of the sea, a regressive, bizarre, wild place where being 'civilised' was always compromised by the realpolitik of a harsh environment, where everybody went a little savage to survive. These were the seas of Francis Drake, John Hawkins, William Dampier, Alexander Selkirk, Daniel Defoe. Ah! Ishmael, as you would know, these are the seas in which the cultural thesbianism of derring-do makes ugliness look something different.

After one day of good luck for the *New Euphrates* when a pod of eight spermaceti came their way, there were no more. The crew earned their lays in the days of frenetic labour that followed—cutting the whales at the side, trying the blubber in clouds of black greasy smoke, stacking the barrels. But that gave them only a hundred barrels of oil, among 1100 empty ones. The crew of the *New Euphrates* in the idleness that followed began to itch to fly the budgee.

A whaling crew for a ship the size of the *New Euphrates* (286 tons) was larger by far than would be required to sail her efficiently. To the eighteen men that the three chase boats required, there needed to be added crew to man the ship while they were out, and to continue the trying of the blubber. Were she a trader and not a whaling ship, the *New Euphrates* would have needed less than half the crew, perhaps ten or twelve. That half number would have seen themselves differently, too. They would have seen themselves as true sailors. True sailors had nothing but scorn for whalers. True sailors had too much pride in their skills, too much identification with the lore of the sea to consider that whalers deserved their respect.

Space and its divisions, food and its quality, time and its filling are matters of prime importance for twenty men stashed in a fo'c'sle barely comfortable for ten. The privacy of a cabin or even of some niche deep in the bowels of the ship was seen as a privilege giving access to all sorts of other privileges. Between the aftercabin where the master and the few officers lived and the fo'c'sle where landsmen, ordinary and able seamen lived in layered bunks was steerage. The boat steerers, the cooper and blacksmith shared quarters in this in-between space, in token that the authority of their skills was something different from the responsibilities for order and government. There was another resident in steerage, more for protection perhaps than in recognition of his skills. It was the cook.

Edward Robarts was cook on the *New Euphrates*. Perhaps he had been a cook on all his voyaging before this Pacific one. We do not know. He had been on the slave trade to Africa out of Jamaica and Santo Domingo. He had visited St Petersburg and Rio de Janeiro. Perhaps these voyages gave him a sailor's as well as a cook's skills. Perhaps they didn't. Cooks on a whaler didn't learn sailhandling or boat-pulling or helmsmanship. They were not on watch where camaraderie and factions were born. The cook was a loner on a whaling ship, in-between the captain and his mess, whom he had to privilege in some way, and the fo'c'sle, whose appetites he was unlikely to assuage with rotten, rancid supplies. Unlike a cook on a naval vessel, who was likely to be missing something—an arm or a leg!—as a badge of his true seamanship, a whaling cook had nothing to show except the opprobrium of all the signs of his linkage with forces that managed men's lives uncomfortably. Robarts was small in stature too, a nuggetty, feisty man and know-it-all to boot. No one could have told him he was no sailor, not to his face at least. He knew instantly in every ship's crisis and before everybody else what was needed to be done with sail, helm and rope. While he admitted his language skills were only moderate, he claimed to get by in Russian, Portuguese (a little less comfortably) and French. He was a reader, of novels if you please. There weren't many novels available in his day, least of all to poor lads from Barmouth.

He was a Welshman. Maybe that was it. A brother of the Cheshire farmer's daughter he had wooed was a friend of his on the *New Euphrates*. He was the steward, as much an in-between role on a whaler as a cook. When the time came for Robarts to land on his beach, the steward wanted to come with him. Perhaps for the same reason.

These reasons began when the security given by the smooth running of the ship began to be uncertain. In the theatre of a ship, the fo'c'sle is the pits and the aftercabin the stage. Order in the *New Euphrates* began to unravel with dramas in the aftercabin between the captain and the first officer. A whaling captain's authority was different from, say, a naval captain's. It wasn't hedged around with formality. The aftercabin was a different sort of stage for the theatre of command than the quarterdeck. Also, a whaling captain couldn't afford to impose his will with institutional violence, such as flogging. He might be physically violent himself and impose his will by fear and the ways colleagues of the fo'c'sle fell back and away from a frightened man. But a flogging or a chained imprisonment required cooperation not just physical but psychological as well. A flogging required a ritual gaze for which there must be much theatre and many props. A whaling captain's authority was much more nearly negotiated—by being best at what they all did, by kindliness in harsh conditions, by conveying a sense of camaraderie in opposition to somebody else, the owners, other whalers, national enemies.

Such negotiations were not just between the captain and an undifferentiated crowd of a crew. The play was different down through the whole hierarchy of command as each level—first officer and the fo'c'sle, mates and their watches, boatsteerers and their boats, each domain of artisan skill, sailmakers, coopers, blacksmiths, carpenters—negotiated the order which they wished to impose. But the high drama of the ship was always in the aftercabin where two men, the captain and the first officer, each had responsibility in different ways for the whole ship.

The first officer's overall responsibility was the general industry and daily discipline of the crew. There was no problem for him in the frenetic moments of the catch and its aftermath. The problem was in the hours, days and, in the *New Euphrates'* case, the weeks in-between. On a sailing ship voyaging to some destination there is really no such thing as empty hours. All time is usefully filled with maintenance of the ship going forward to its appointed port. A whaling ship is different. There is no destination, just searching. With more than enough crew to maintain the ship, work has to be invented to occupy them. 'Puzzle work' was the phrase, useless, endless labour, with much undoing of what had been done. In the street slang of those much put upon them by the classes above them, 'puzzle' was a favourite word. 'Puzzle-cause' they called a confused lawyer; 'puzzle-text', an ignorant blundering parson. 'Puzzle work' came from one who didn't know how to order his domain. The first officer put all the crew, including those who had been on watch during the night, to puzzle work. When they grumbled and muttered, his abuse and threats became more exaggerated. Each task then became a test of his authority.

One day, just after breakfast, when the shouts, arguments and threats were at their worst, Henry Glasspoole came out of his cabin. The men complained to him directly about the duties the first officer required of them. Glasspoole cut across the first officer's responsibility by ordering that the ship be run from that time forward in its traditional way, 'watch and watch'. It was the right thing and the wrong thing to do. It satisfied a perceived injustice, but the negotiations of authority were turned around. Now the fo'c'sle negotiated the divisions in the aftercabin.

Glasspoole, being unlucky, did not need to be made a fool of as well. The first officer now had little authority with the crew. He was toadying to them one minute, raging at them the next. He committed the cardinal sin of power, giving orders that he knew would not or could not be obeyed. He was publicly and privately disloyal to his captain. When Glasspoole was prudent, the first officer was reckless. When Glasspoole wanted to gamble, the first officer didn't. There was a telling moment just after they had caught the eight spermaceti. It was the most dangerous moment on a whaling ship. The tryworks fires were ablaze. The decks were awash with the detritus of dead whales. A violent rainstorm erupted in a whirling wind. The hot oil began to splutter and the flames of the tryworks to spit. The ribbons of flammable substances led everywhere. Glasspoole called a halt, ordering the fires to be doused. The first officer, greedy for the oil so hardly got, countermanded Glasspoole to his face. Glasspoole shrunk away to his cabin. When nothing came of the storm, he looked more foolish still.

Fantasies about what this unsuccessful whaling voyage might become grew when a sister ship of the *New Euphrates*, the *Butterworth*, emerged from the mists around the Galapagos Islands. The *Butterworth* was a sister ship in the sense that she belonged to the same owners, Mathers and Anderson of London. She was in no way the same type of vessel as the *New Euphrates*. George Vancouver described her when he saw her in northwest waters as 'an English frigate of thirty guns'. Being a frigate she would have had a raised fo'c'sle and quarterdeck, three masts, and a true gundeck. Actually she was only British in the sense that she had been captured from the French early in the British–French War. She had speed and manoeuvrability. And she had guns. Captain Laurence Frazier commanded her. Captain Frazier wasn't Captain Glasspoole's retiring type.

The *Butterworth* and *New Euphrates*, now in consort, moved from the Galapagos to the Californian coast, still looking for whales. There they met up with another whaler, the *Liberty*, Captain Baxter. The *Liberty* was slightly larger than the *New Euphrates* and mounted fourteen guns, several more than the *New Euphrates*, but twelve-pounders rather than the *New Euphrates'* six-pounders. In their fantasies the three vessels became a 'squadron'. Out of earshot of Henry Glasspoole, everyone became an admiral of the line. If they came upon a Spanish vessel, the *Butterworth* would lay alongside to threaten with a broadside. The *New Euphrates* and the *Liberty* would take her by the bow quarter and stern, where the Spaniard's guns would be out of play, and would 'rake' her with fire.

Early one afternoon, the man at the masthead cried 'Sail ho!' It was their Spanish prey. Immediately everyone sprang into action, if we strip the word 'action' of the disciplined, honed character of a naval ship. The *New Euphrates* was a long way from being naval. Everyone ran every whichway, clearing the decks for 'engaging', setting the ship into faster motion. Robarts, being cook, had the run of the 'run', the narrow afterpart of the ship used for storing the accoutrements of battle—the boarding nets, the tubs of cartridges. He had just cooked the dinner that Henry Glasspoole was digesting on the cabin lockers at the stern windows. Presumably because the crew were doubtful about Glasspoole's reactions to this little bit of privateering, they had Robarts lock him in his cabin and sit on the hatch outside to prevent anyone letting him out.

Captain Frazier was an enthusiast for privateering; he brought the *Butterworth* close and hailed Henry Glasspoole. Henry was put out that he was locked in his cabin and pleaded through the door with Robarts to let him out, saying that he would not hinder them from engaging with the Spaniard. Robarts let him out. Glasspoole then had a conference with Frazier across the water. They decided to engage the Spaniard. The *New Euphrates* then gave three cheers for the *Butterworth* and the *Butterworth* gave three cheers for the *New Euphrates*. They then raised the budgee and the Union Jack.

They signalled the *Liberty*. When she came up, Captain Baxter told them not to be stupid. They were whalers, not privateers. He then hauled wind and was off. 'Coward!' they shouted after him. As they sulked and watched the Spaniard make sail, the first officer, no doubt thinking of his future captaincy with Mathers and Anderson, suddenly turned whaler rather than privateer and made Glasspoole look foolish again, persuading him to change his mind. This time when the crew grumbled at what he did, he had a cartridge belt around him and pistols in his hands. He shouted that he would shoot the first man who refused to brace up the yards and haul to the wind.

These aggravations did not have much time to fester. The three vessels moved south and west of the Galapagos for a few days. Then in the night they were hit by an intense, very local gale. The *New Euphrates* lost the jib boom and top mizzenmast in the wind, and then the tryworks and the cook's galley in the mountainous seas. Together with this gear on the upper deck, fourteen pigs and a collection of Galapagos tortoises were washed overboard. All the boats were stashed. In the middle of the chaos of the storm five feet of water was found in the hold and all hands were at the pumps. All hands except Robarts. As he climbed his way out of his steerage niche, a rolling bread butt took the ladder away. He lasted out the storm, sore in the cable tier dodging the rogue bread butt. No doubt he was thankful that he had not been in the galley when it went overboard.

In the morning the sea was eerily calm and oily. There was no sight of the *Liberty*, a little debris in the water, that's all. They had last seen her in the previous evening's dusk with all crew aloft fixing the night's sails. Part of the debris was empty sail casks. Two days' search found no more of her. They presumed she had gone down with all hands. The *Butterworth* was there, though. She didn't look a pretty sight with a broken mainmast trailing in the water beside her.

The two crews spent their time refitting the rigging and fishing and scarfing the masts. The *Butterworth*, being as nearly full of oil as she was likely to get, would soon be on her way home. Her trypots and works were transferred to the *New Euphrates*. It was the first officer's finest and most professional hour. He installed new goosepens—the water tanks beneath the brick base of the tryworks—and had the *New Euphrates* ready for whaling again. They were still pumping water by hand twenty-four hours a day. They spoke to another whaler of Mathers and Anderson, the *London*, Captain Gardiner. She had not felt the gale at all. She left them flying American colours—in case the Spaniards got too interested in her.

Captains Glasspoole and Frazier no doubt had instructions on where they should supply their ships on their years-long voyaging. It couldn't be the Spanish coast. There had been news in London at the time, brought back by the *Daedalus*, the supply ship to Vancouver's expedition to the northwest coast of America, of islands to the north of the Marquesas Islands which James Cook had visited in 1774. They decided to head for Santa Christiana, which the Spaniards had named in 1595, 'Ohittahoo'—as James Cook had heard Vaitahu—the anchorage on Tahuata.

The Pacific turned idyllic at this point. Dolphins, albacore and flying fish all around; seabirds in their thousands; smooth seas of the equatorial doldrums; prospects of a South Seas stay. But the crew of the *New*

Euphrates thought that they had unfinished business with the Spaniards and their first officer. Somewhere in these waters still was the unfound *Bounty*. Mutiny on a whaler was not nearly as hazardous as mutiny on a naval vessel. But there were violent men on the *New Euphrates* who could make it just as bloody. Robarts began to wonder at his fate if the fo'c'sle took the ship.

When the *Butterworth* and the *New Euphrates* dropped anchor at Vaitahu, about 20 December 1798, the first person to come aboard was a Hawaiian. 'Tama', 'Sam' or 'Tom' were his various names. He had already been to Boston. With his broken English, Tama acted as interpreter. Robarts saw a lot of him as he traded for refreshments, wood and water. It gave Robarts ideas.

'After the Quiberon Affair'
Joseph Kabris, Prisoner of War

Joseph Kabris went to sea out of the Channel Ports of France when he was fourteen years old. It was Year II of the Revolution. Louis XVI had died on the guillotine. His heir was dying in prison. The French émigrés across the Channel in England were plotting to come back. The English government, fearful of the possibility of their own revolution, plotted how they might use the émigrés to their own advantage.

The Channel was a borderland moat. The sails of the English blockading fleet were never really out of sight. The French revolutionary navy, culled of its experienced but royalist officers, was holed up in Brest. The harassing plays against the English were all made by small fast ships, corsairs, darting out of St Malo, Dunkirk and Le Havre. They scavenged the English coastal trade. It was a small-ship war, guerrillas at sea. The corsair captains were full of ruses. They knew the shoals and the seasons of these waters. But it was dangerous work. One hundred and forty of them were captured in these years. The corsair captains were all more experienced than their men, but the true sailors of the Channel ports, the fishermen, were too precious in a blockaded France to do anything but their trade. So the corsair captains snatched who they could, even a fourteen-year-old boy. Captain Renault of the corsair *Dumouriez* snatched Joseph Kabris.

The hinterland of the ports was, at this time, as savage a place as the Channel. There was a guerrilla war there, too. The Chouans, peasant insurgent bands, under eclectic chieftancies were ambushing convoys, cutting bridges, demanding protection money. The Chouans were the Whites, the anti-revolutionary terrorists, to the Blues, the *levée en masse*, the new army of the Revolution. This new army consumed the land like locusts and easily matched the terror of the Chouans. The general of this new army, in the hinterland behind the Channel, was the brilliant Lazare-Louis Hoche. He had taken on a task that Napoleon Bonaparte had refused, to search out and destroy the Chouans.

The émigrés in England, aching to return to France, thought their best chance was to make a Royal Army of these bands of Chouans. To do that they must land in France, establish a beachhead, arm and supply the Chouans, march them to Paris.

The 'Quiberon affair' was the bizarre and disastrous royalist D-Day of two hundred years ago. Messidor–Thermidor Year III, June–July 1795, was its date. Joseph Kabris dated the beginning of his voyage to his beach as 'after the Quiberon affair'.

Quiberon is a thin ten-mile-long peninsula bending south and east along the Channel coast, protecting a large bay with a sandy bottom, an excellent anchorage. The Mer Sauvage beats the swells of the Atlantic onto the sheer western cliffs of the peninsula. The peninsula lies on the southern coast of France's snout into the Atlantic, Finistère.

Quiberon Bay had an ancient air. On one side were the ruins of a monastery that Abelard had ruled. On the other were a thousand stones that were reputed to be the remnants of one of Julius Caesar's camps. All around were menhirs and barrows with their crouched dead, and runic columns. At the head of the peninsula was a low sandy isthmus, overlooked on the north by hills and commanded in the south by a fort. Fort Sans-Culottes it was called in these revolutionary times. Its old and about-to-be-restored name was Penthièvre. Its western ramparts topped the cliffs against which the Mer Sauvage beat. Its cannons and mortars on the eastern side controlled all of Quiberon Bay.

The invasion fleet was large, fifty transports holding 3300 fighting men, 500 assorted bishops, aristocrats and hangers-on, 300 horses, enough weapons, accoutrements and clothing for an army of 40,000 Chouans. They brought a portable guillotine, too. Three English ships of the line and six frigates escorted them. These were joined on the way by Admiral Bridport's Channel fleet. They brushed off a French naval assault out of

Brest. The French lost three vessels and retreated to Lorient, a little northwest of Quiberon.

They landed on the beach of the bay before Carnac, the site of Julius Caesar's camp. The landing was as brilliant as they had hoped. The republicans simply ran away. Ten thousand Chouans gathered within days and armed and clothed themselves, except for boots. The Chouans preferred to remain barefoot. The invasion would leave one hundred and fifty thousand pairs of boots on the beach.

There were too many generals among the royalists—Comte Joseph de Puisaye, Comte Louis d'Hervilly, Admiral Sir John Warren. They dithered in the delirium of their coming back. The only thing they did immediately was invest the *ci-devant* Fort Sans-Culottes. They took it easily. Looking down on a bay full of transports and warships and back to the Mer Sauvage with its roving gun-boats, the Blues saw no reason why they should stay and starve. The ease of this success seemed to freeze the invasion. The émigrés were dangerously confident that all Frenchmen were likely to think as they. Among the invasion force were 1600 French prisoners of war who had volunteered to join the invasion. For many of these the invasion was a ticket home and they melted away when the opportunity came. The same chances to change sides were given to the Blues who surrendered in the fort. It was they who would let the Blues back in. The royalists holed up in the fort and the small ports and villages to its south. Quiberon became for a time an émigré appendage on revolutionary France.

Lazare-Louis Hoche would be surgeon to this infected appendage. He cut it off with a revetment a thousand yards long on the hills of Sainte Barbe at the northern end of the peninsula. It was hard to build these fortifications in the running sands. His men cemented the sand with manure that they collected from the farms around. A great many royalists would die with their faces in the shit.

The royalist attempt to break out from Quiberon was the beginning of the end. Their columns lost their way in the dunes of the isthmus and then, clambering up the sand, were sucked in by Hoche retreating from his first lines till he had them all exposed and collected for an assault on the last line. His barrages of anti-infantry projectiles made a massacre. Hoche didn't immediately chase the Whites back across the isthmus. The guns of the ships in the bay controlled it too well by day. He waited till night to attack the fort. One of the deserting French prisoners of war, armed with the password, led a small force of grenadiers not through the eastern wall of the fort, but up the cliffs and rampart of the west. They took the defences by bayonet from behind, killed nearly all of the enemy, including the elite English marines. They then turned the mortars on the English ships in the bay. There had not even been enough time for the Whites even to complete the three-shot signal of their emergency.

Hoche's men simply rolled the émigrés along the peninsula, closing each small port as they reached it. The chaos of the panicked embarcation was complete. The fact that the commander, Comte de Puisaye, forced his way onto a boat in order to escape only served to damn him for the rest of his life. The Blues drove the whole invasion force into the sea. Those who surrendered they marched away in the dark, their women and children following in a near hysteria of mourning and fear. The lucky ones among the Blues, those not guarding the prisoners, enjoyed the mounds of supplies that the English blockade had denied them for years—hams from Cork and the best salt beef of Ireland. Beer. And coffee! The young among them had never even seen it because the English had all the coffee in the world. While they cooked and drank, they sang the hymns of the Republic 'in a thousand different keys'.

Those being marched away in the rain and dark began to realise that by the laws of the Directorate of Public Safety they were not the prisoners of war they thought themselves to be. They were dead men for coming back to France armed. Eight hundred 'traitors' were marched to Vannes. They were shot against the city walls, sixty a day.

The despair among the émigrés, their mockery by the Blues at so botched an adventure, the horror of its mopping up through all of Brittany—these were scarring social memories. Kabris had his own personal scars as well. So it was easy for him to begin his story in 1817 with the phrase 'after the Quiberon affair' and know the moods it dated. Sometime in the Quiberon affair he became a prisoner of the English. We do not know whether the corsair *Dumouriez* was one of the three French vessels lost in the attack on the émigré invasion fleet or whether he was captured in the first attack on Fort Sans-Culottes. The probabilities are for the former, as he was taken back to the naval prison hulks at Portsmouth. Forton, the prison especially erected two miles out of Portsmouth for the prisoners of war of the American Revolution, would have been the more likely place to which he would have been taken had he been captured in combat.

The sight of his prison would have given no comfort to a fifteen-year-old boy. The three dismasted hulks, the *Hero*, *Bristol* and *Prudente*, lay in line astern across the mudflats in Portsmouth harbour. Four more hulks would be added soon after his arrival. Prisoners of war were accumulating, and the conditions were worsening as the troubles with France dragged on. The protocols of imprisonment were changing also. The French, in the belief that their prisoners were being ill-treated by the English, refused to pay for them. Exchanges came to a halt. With six hundred prisoners to a hulk, many of them naked or near naked because they had gambled away or sold their clothes for food, and gaunt with the harsh prison diet, it was not a life that many survived for long. Money was essential, but on the hulks employment was virtually impossible to find unless one sold oneself to other prisoners or their guards. A little time after Kabris' imprisonment, the English government set up a Transport Office to reform the conditions of the prisoners of war. Corruption among the contractors, illegal payments demanded by the wardens, then became a matter of public outcry. Kabris would have experienced only the worst end of these conditions and not the reform.

With exchange impossible, the only way out for adult sailors was to take up an offer in English naval service. Not many of the French were willing to do that. Kabris endured six months of imprisonment. Perhaps because of his age, he was then offered the chance, not of naval service, but to join an English whaler on a Pacific voyage. It was the *London*, Captain Gardner. Her owners, Mathers and Anderson, sent her out in December 1795. It was to be a long voyage. She would not be back in London till November 1799.

We have met the *London* when it crossed paths with the *New Euphrates* and the *Butterworth* south of the Galapagos in October 1798. It had been surprised then to see the two whalers in such poor condition after the storms which the *London* had not experienced. It also heard then of the *Liberty*'s loss. We have to take note of that, because it clearly inspired Kabris to a little theatre in his story. He has nothing to say of his three-year voyage on the *London*, save that at its end when they were near the Marquesas Islands—he calls them the 'Mendoca Islands'—they caught six spermaceti. Before the crew cut them up and tryed them, the captain took advantage of the calm sea to feast his men. In the middle of that feast, with the ship's sails full spread, a violent gust of wind snapped the mast. Then Kabris, making a dramatic, even Shakespearean, beginning for his beachcombing, tells us that in the wild seas raised by the storm the ship was dragged onto a shoal and broke up. Kabris was able to grab hold of the wreckage of the ship's bridge—the *London* would not have had a bridge!— which he shared with the ship's cook, who could not swim. Together on this sort of raft, the pair floated to 'St Christine'—Tahuata. But Kabris confuses it with Nukuhiva.

The *London*'s story was less dramatic than that. In January 1799, she touched at Tahuata where Kabris deserted, perhaps because he saw how Edward Robarts was doing. Robarts was in his first weeks of this stay, and this cook, at least, had not come by shipwreck. The *London* then went off whaling in Marquesan waters. She was indeed dismasted and returned to Tahuata where Robarts, enjoying his first opportunity to act as a sort of agent to ships coming to his island, negotiated the acquisition of some seasoned wood to scarf the *London*'s mast. Kabris returned on board the *London*, voyaged with her to Nukuhiva, and there deserted again.

Kabris' voyage ended on the beach at Nukuhiva with some of the violence with which it had begun at Quiberon. The *London*'s crew, in a careless exchange of musket fire after a theft, killed a young woman. She was shot through the forehead. And a violent man by the name of Walker came off the *London* or was put off by her captain. He came to the beach armed with a musket. Coming to a beach with property of any sort was dangerous. Coming with a weapon was doubly so.

The 'Predestinated'

William Crook's Longer Voyage

'The Word struck hard—*Verbum percussit*', Augustine of Hippo had written in his *Confessions*, describing the impact of the Word of God on the world, the soul and the flesh. The Word, the abiding Christian metaphor for the Triune God in revelatory mode, is no gentle thing. The Word showed its force to young William Pascoe Crook in a chapel off Tottenham Court Road, London. William would have counted that moment to be the beginning of his voyage.

It was 1794. William was a boyish-looking nineteen years. He had walked to London from his mother's house in Falmouth in a fever of anxiety about his sinfulness and his salvation. In what ways he had 'stumbled' in his sinfulness he does not say. In the pursuit of holiness, sinfulness is fairly relative. It is a good guess that the prurient would not be greatly satisfied at knowing what his sinfulness was. It was just as likely to have been a despair that his inability to fulfil high ideals was a sign that he had not been 'justified' by a forgiving God.

The Word struck William through the mouth of the Reverend Moody and the scriptural text he preached, Matthew 4: 1–25. Matthew begins that chapter: 'Then was Jesus led up of the Spirit into the wilderness to be tempted by the devil'. And after forty days and forty nights Jesus came back to begin his preaching: 'Repent: for the kingdom of heaven is at hand', and choose his disciples: 'Follow me and I will make you fishers of men'.

Tottenham Court was a chapel of 'praying people'. John Wesley used to preach there. Affections—sorrow, joy—were no bad thing there. Its hymns could be heard half a mile away. The established Church gnashed its teeth at its 'low kind of language'. Cobblers, tinkers and old women 'feel the love of God in their hearts as they might do a cudgel on their head'. They heard the Word as if all the words of Scripture were literally true. The relativities and interpretations of a more comfortable church had no real play here. Enthusiasm was a dangerous thing when the poor and uneducated made their own meanings of the Word.

Young William's enthusiasm was without end. He suddenly knew that his repentance had been heard and that he was called to be a 'fisher of men'. Suddenly he knew that he could share the 'Elements', the bread and wine, in communion with the other 'saints' who knew that they too had been saved. He skipped home to the closet that was his room as a 'gentleman's servant', deliriously happy at his new certainties. He prayed that then and there he would die.

He didn't die that night as it happened, nor for another fifty-two years of nights. But the fire lit in his soul that day burned his whole life long. He would become a beachcomber for the Lord till the end. Not just in his first extraordinary adventure in The Land, but on the sandy coign of the first failed settlement at Sorrento in Port Phillip Bay (1803), in founding the first boarding school and Congregational Church in deadly, violent, convict Sydney (1809), in Moorea and Papeete, Tahiti (1815–30), back again to build a Congregational Church in the far reaches of Sydney Harbour at Watson's Bay (1841). Then to the raw shanty town of Melbourne where he built yet another first church. He died in Melbourne, 14 June 1846, memorialised in the cemetery with a 'eucalyptian' wooden monument that rotted away in far less time than his seventy-one years.

William took his calling to be a fisher of men seriously. His first impulse was to spread the Good News he had heard and to go on a mission somewhere, anywhere. Those whose business it was to missionise the world—in Africa, in the Americas—laughed at his youth and immaturity. But a certain Dr Thomas Haweis who had large plans for missions in the newest of the New Worlds, the South Seas, liked what he saw in William Crook. Above all, he admired his voraciousness for words of all sorts, in encyclopaedias, in dictionaries, in sermons, in books of theological reflections. Dr Haweis enrolled him in his School of Prophets, where William tried to learn a little Greek and Hebrew. He practised preaching there, learned 'navigation', debated the meaning of Atonement. When the time came he was chosen to be among the thirty who would be taken to the South Seas on the ship *Duff* to establish the first mission of the Mission Society, soon to be called the London Missionary Society.

'Predestinate' is a word that belongs to voyaging of an eternal sort. The end of the voyage, the destination, has been navigated with infallible accuracy from before all time. 'Predestinate', as any biblical concordance that William would have consulted notes, occurs only twice in the Word of God, in Romans 8: 29–30. 'For whom he did foreknow, he also did predestinate to be conformed to the image of his Son, that he might be the first-born among many brethren. Moreover who he did predestinate, them he also called and whom he called, them he also justified: and whom he justified, them also he glorified.' 'Predestinate' was a word that struck hard. To those who knew themselves as called, it was a voyager's passport to eternal glory.

Small wonder then that the thirty fishers of men who were on their way to the South Seas on the *Duff* looked at the lugubrious, emaciated face of Brother John Clark Jefferson with deep alarm as he suggested that the end of their voyage was not so accurately navigated after all. It was possible, he was saying, that even those who had been called could fail. Brother Jefferson had been an actor, a failed actor to be sure. The insincerity of acting had been his sinfulness. He would carry sincerity like a cross for the rest of his life. Right now he was being frighteningly sincere because other words of the Word had struck him just as hard as 'predestinate'. Hebrews

6: 1–8 for example. Those 'who have tainted the heavenly gift and have been partakers of the Holy Spirit, if they then commit apostasy, crucify the Son of God'. And Revelations 2: 2–5: 'I have this against you that you have abandoned the love you had at first . . . Repent and do the works that you first did. If not, I shall remove your lampstead from its place.'

These were not the Schools where philosophers argued whether angels as beings without space could occupy the head of a pin, or be numbered. Or whether the Creator had foreknowledge not just of what would happen but of *possibilia*, every possibility that could be as well, and whether such a sense of contingency didn't somehow wound the Creator's universal power. No these were the dark, cramped quarters of the lower deck of the *Duff*, their Meeting Place, where they prayed, communed, did their learning, debated the conditions of their life to come. With so much uncertainty in their lives, they did not need to learn that they were not really predestinated after all.

It was 23 January 1797. The *Duff* was in the high latitudes, 50 degrees South in the southern ocean, below the western shoreline of New Holland. The *Duff* was surfing the huge swells rolling eastward around the globe, coasting before the constant winds, logging more than a hundred miles a day. They were halfway along the huge 14,000-mile leg between Rio de Janeiro and Tahiti.

The missionaries were seasoned to their voyaging now, three months into it. The seasickness had gone. So had most of the squabbling that these complete strangers indulged in as they intruded on one another's living. They had composed themselves to the awesome power of the sea around them. They could even savour its beauty—the dancing tubes of the waterspouts, the vast shoals of fish that carpeted their way, the whales, the gambolling dolphins. The flying fish made flower gardens in the sea with their glittering colours. They had seen things outside all their previous experience. Some had appalled them—the naked slave markets and the open idolatry of Roman Catholicism in Rio de Janeiro. They had been terrified by the approach of privateer sails and had wondered whether the purity of their purposes should allow them to arm themselves—it did! They had established routines to make use of their daylight hours. Their prayers had an almost monastic regularity—6.30 a.m., 7 a.m., 5.30 p.m., 7 p.m. From 9 to 10 a.m., they learned Greek and Hebrew, 10 to 11 a.m. Tahitian, 11 a.m. to 12 noon 'navigation'—the mathematics of astronomy and surveying. From 2 to 3 p.m. they studied the islands they were approaching. That was the Order of their days. The reality that filled them was a little different. It was difficult to educate themselves in the abstract to a life that none of them had experienced. A sense of its impracticality fostered a lethargy and feeling of spiritual desolation when so much in their recent past had been all sublime consolations.

To tell the truth, most of them had lived the last nine months in an uncomprehending haze. Nine months ago, they had all been living very ordinary lives, as far north as Manchester, far south at Penzance, west in Dublin, but mostly in London, the Midlands and the southeast. All of them were artisans of one sort or another—carpenters, smiths, coopers, bricklayers, shoemakers, weavers, hatters, harness-makers, shopkeepers. The ministers of their parishes had seen them as 'pious', had broached the subject of a mission to them, selected them to go to London, 'charged' them as missionaries and farewelled them in the *Duff*. All in a matter of three months. None of them had any real idea of where they were going. Only four of them had wives, and one of these was a 64-year-old woman engaged and married in the last weeks before their departure. They all knew that there was no return from this mission. Their average age was twenty-six years. They could have no idea what a single life in an utterly foreign place would hold.

After Christmas, the *Duff* became a 'Church Afloat'. The brethren had to discover to one another their inner beliefs and to find a way by which they would be One Church. Words struck hard all through January. Even the mild celebration of the Lord's birth with 'a good cake' and a 'dish of chocolate' raised harsh, extravagant language. The modest Christmas cheer was described by some as 'rank idolatry'.

All through January of 1798, they threw words at one another like javelins—'Universal Redemption', 'Glory of Christ', 'Repentance', 'The Fall', 'Grace', 'Final Perseverance', 'Imputed and Imparted Righteousness'. They had been told that 'the best education for a missionary is none at all', other than learning to make wheelbarrows and plant turnips. They had only four ordained ministers among them. Their ordinations weren't recognised by the established Church because they had not been educated at Oxford or Cambridge. The opprobrium heaped on the thirty by the socially elite was as malignant as the support for them by the lower classes was sweet. 'Lower-class' the missionaries were deemed to be in language, dress and deportment. They were mocked for looking 'like petitioners at a gentleman's door'. There was an uncomfortable feeling abroad. In this Age of Revolution, God was becoming too accessible.

The missionaries had no referee for their theological divisions, no authority but themselves. When suspicion about the Arminianism of Brothers Jefferson and John Cock were raised, they turned to the captain of the *Duff*, James Wilson. Captain Wilson was a sturdy Christian. He had been a prisoner of French Catholics in India and had swum alligator-infested rivers to escape them. When he found God in London, there was no fluff in his piety. The Missionary Society put all decision-making on this mission voyage into his hands, including the management of a trip to China to get a load of tea that would pay for God's work.

Wilson was disturbed by the nascent divisions in the 'Church Afloat'. He wasn't for finesse in these sorts of things. He looked up 'Predestination' in the *Encyclopaedia Britannica*, whose second edition was in the ship's library. It was a very practical article for a very practical man, full of definitions and distinctions. 'Predestination', it read, 'was the decree of God whereby he hath for all eternity unchangeably appointed whatsoever comes to pass; and hath more especially foreordained certain individuals of the human race are to everlasting happiness, and hath passed by all the rest, and foreordained them to everlasting misery'. If you were Calvinist, this is what you believed. Arminians, Remonstrances, Dominicans and Jesuits believed otherwise. 'Are you Calvinist?', he asked the missionaries. 'The Missionary Society says you are. There you are then.'

Of Brother Jefferson, about to become Mr Jefferson because he was about to be excommunicated, Wilson asked: 'What's your definition of Imputed and Imparted Righteousness?'. Jefferson's answer didn't satisfy either Wilson or the brethren. Jefferson and Cock were told by letter that they were expelled and that henceforth no one would speak with them.

Silent isolation in such a crowded space seemed to have remarkable theological force. Jefferson and Cock recanted by letter, and happily, if such a word is appropriate for Jefferson's lugubrious character, proclaimed that they were saved forever.

The divisions among them were deeper than over matters of theological nicety, however. 'Separation' was one of those capitalised words that hit them hard. They must decide whether they would 'Separate' into different missions—Tahiti, Tonga or The Marquesas. A band of single missionaries had clearly decided to 'Separate', not so much *to* a different mission island, as *from* the married brethren among them. Their voyage had made it clear that the single men would have in some way to care for those that were married. Suspicions of such ungodly motivations for 'Separation' made them test themselves. They decided that the decision to 'Separate' should be made now, in these southern seas below continental New Holland, their destinations sight unseen.

On that condition, ten missionaries decided for Tonga, nineteen for Tahiti, and one, Brother John Harris, for The Marquesas. Why Brother Harris should be so idiosyncratically insistent on The Marquesas for his mission, we cannot say. It was a fervour, as we shall see, that wouldn't last one night on his beach. Young William Crook, sympathising with Harris in his lonely predicament, volunteered to accompany him.

That brave decision changed William Crook's life forever. It gave him a life of beaches. Its immediate consequence was to give him a sort of South Pacific cruise. He saw off the brethren at Tahiti, watched their first raw efforts at preaching the Word, realised the chaos of living on the edges of somebody else's culture. He sailed with the *Duff* westward to Tonga, entered the debate whether the Tongan missionaries should land armed, caught a glimpse of the surging native politics that would engulf them, must have sensed that these ten brethren were landing on their beach like loose flotsam and jetsam. Then there was a fifty-day circuit as far south as 40 degrees South to catch the westerlies, then north to the far edges of the Central Pacific, The Marquesas. Soon those still aboard the *Duff* played at being 'discoverers', putting the atolls of Timoe ('Crescent Island') and Pukarua ('Serle's Island') and the high island of Mangareva (the Gambiers) on their maps. The scenario of first sightings became familiar to them— armed figures on the beach defending their land, native incomprehension at their 'natural' gestures of giving and trade and peace, deserted houses and foreboding sacred places. They snatched at every sign that 'savages' had souls and reached out to something supranatural.

Came 5 June 1797—they had left London on 11 August 1796, Tahiti on 26 March 1797. The *Duff* found itself southwest of Tahuata. It wasn't where they wanted to be. They had to ply backwards and forwards against the prevailing winds to reach Vaitahu. (They preferred Captain Cook's name 'Resolution Bay' for Vaitahu. It would have been hard to establish their very Calvinist mission in a place with the Spaniards' very Catholic name of 'Madre de Dios'.) They took the pilotage of two natives who came out to the ship. They were grateful for it and admired their 'nautical skill' as they edged into the bay against the gusts that blew down the mountain ridges all around them. They anchored in 15 fathoms of water on a sandy bottom. Then they veered, or played out the cable to 185 fathoms, but dragged it back, no doubt with hard capstan work, to 35 fathoms. There they rested with a long taut line as darkness set in. As the sweet heavy air teased their salt-saturated senses, other teases came from the water around them. Young women had swum out to the ship and were calling—in a 'pitiful tone'—'*Vahine! Vahine!*—Women! Women!' But the *Duff* was not that sort of ship.

An Archaeology of Learning

I used to assure succeeding generations of my students that my best educational experiences had been my general examinations. None of them ever believed me. But it is true. I had four sets of general examinations over my twenty years of learning. After three years of scholastic philosophy at Loyola College, I had to defend a hundred theses orally in Latin for an hour before a board of three. After four years of history at the University of Melbourne, I sat for fifteen hours of written examinations which reviewed all subjects that I had studied in the first three years and then all four years. Theology ended at Canisius College with a two-hour Latin oral examination by a board of three that covered the seven years of theology and philosophy. Harvard's anthropology had two sets of general examinations, one called a Generals, the other called the Specials. There was no syllabus for these, only the knowledge that you would face an oral of two and a half hours in front of a board consisting, in the Generals, say, of an archaeologist, a linguist, a physical anthropologist, a cultural anthropologist, a social anthropologist, and in the Specials a board consisting of experts in your areas of choice—for me Oceania and South America. Candidates grew old waiting to declare themselves ready for examination. I was old enough already. I went for them after three years.

In none of these general examinations was the factual of prime importance. They were all exercises in synthesis, in an ability to declare a mastery over a field. Being rites de passage, *these general examinations would always have some moment of humiliation. At Harvard we tried to pre-empt these occasions by learning things such as all the principal publications of those prestigious gold-lettered names on the professors' doors down the stairway of Peabody Museum. My professor succeeded in surprising me by asking what were the principal anthropological works from Norway, then Sweden, then Finland, then Denmark. Mean! But I could boast about it for decades, couldn't I?*

Digging in the Mind

Johannes Forster, an 'experimental gentleman' on James Cook's second voyage of discovery, was perhaps the greatest mind to come into the Pacific in the eighteenth century. He never resolved one problem he had, however.

That was how to measure the temperature of the depths of the ocean without having his instruments corrupted by the surface temperatures as they passed through. Digging in the mind is somewhat similar to measuring the temperatures of the ocean. How does one reach one's mind of fifty years ago, when it is the mind of today that is doing the reaching? Am 'I' today what 'I'was fifty years ago?

Who am I to say that I am the same when my *faux pas* at last night's dinner table come to me at 3 a.m. and prompt me first to squirm and then to say that was not really me—now. Those of us who look back on lives that were closed down with rules, who remember how guilt defined our person, can get angry at the institutions that impressed themselves on us. But we mostly laugh at it all. None of us are likely to say that the 'I' who is the product of those years is crippled and disabled. Others, yes, destroyed, but not 'I'. Life can't be one long *faux pas*. Can it?

For myself, I think I made a crossing very early in life. It was my one big beach. All the systems that defined who I was—religious practices, beliefs of faith, ecclesiastical learning, rule of daily life—were closed. My crossing was to understand that nothing is in fact closed. All is open, but I am not less sure for that, less obliged, less self-demanding.

As I see it, openness is a demand that institutions—and there is no 'I' without institutions—accept the actualities of living, not their imposed 'realities'. Truth is in the metaphor, not the template.

If I ask myself where does an 'I' who finds sureness in unsureness, certainty in uncertainty, come from, I think that it is because for all my boyhood life I was in the care—educational, spiritual, pastoral—of priestly men. These were men who had loyalty to their calling and ideals, but who knew their own humanity to its core. As I dig in my mind, it surprises me that I recognise my 'I' in so many layers of its archaeology.

T HE WELCOME of the third millennium, New Year's Eve 2000, was special for me. I was on a high for days after it. I celebrated it in Sydney launching a book. Launching a book is not always a remarkable event and is not unusual for me at this stage in my career. It wasn't that. And the book was a dictionary of biography—like a telephone book, the old joke goes, great dramatis personae but not much plot. So it wasn't that either.

The Jesuits in Australia were celebrating their sesquicentenary. They were in Assembly, 180 of them. They had invited me to launch David

Strong's *The Australian Dictionary of Jesuit Biography, 1848–1998*, and to speak to them. The invitation was generous. I had been their colleague for twenty-one years. Not many institutions, in my experience, are prepared to risk hearing from their 'exes'.

There were 416 dead in the *Dictionary*. Of them, 139 had touched my life in some way. Facing 180 quick and 416 dead Jesuits was an extraordinary experience. The faces of the 180 quick and 139 dead were frozen in my mind as they were fifty years ago. The *bon mots* and *faux pas* of a lifetime flooded my mind. I kept asking myself what would it all have been, if it had been different? Would I want it to be different?

One hundred and eighty quick Jesuits are not actually young and numerous enough for them to expect with any certainty that there will be a bicentenary to celebrate in 2048. The Jesuits are in demographic slump. They are not reproducing themselves fast enough to continue their work in schools, universities, parishes, seminaries, social work and communications.

Their mood in Assembly was not actually sombre. 'As cheerful as a Jesuit at a funeral' is an old phrase used to describe victories of faith and hope over gloomy realities. Their mood wasn't sombre, but it was serious.

They had much to talk about. For at least fifty years they had been at the workface of a Catholic Church changed forever by the many holocausts of the twentieth century. Their history told them that they were born as champions of the Counter-Reformation in the sixteenth and seventeenth centuries. But for fifty years, at least, in the past century, they had been prophets of reformation, not apologists of counter-reformation. They had been out where the Church must—will—go. They had explored the reaches of ecumenism not just between Christian sects but across world religions. They had asked what it meant to divorce religious belief from class, gender and empire. They had confronted the contradictions of gospel values and realpolitik. They had made rituals that weren't ritualistic.

Jesuits don't, any more than the rest of us, live by such abstractions, of course. So these explorations and translations have had concrete and particular expressions: such as admonishing archbishops and popes for misuse of power; and advising believers on the ambivalence as well as the certainties of belief. They have given expression to what it will mean to have women's' ordination, a married priesthood, a gay apostolate, even Jesuit work without Jesuits. They have demanded that a church above all be a covenant of pilgrims.

It has always seemed to me that the Jesuits' world view essentially involved taking risks. They had gambled with me and lost. Now on New Year's Eve, they were gambling again. Not just in asking me to speak to them, but in inviting all those who had been with them and gone other ways over the last fifty years to share the Eucharist with them. We filled the chapel at St Ignatius College, Riverview, to overflowing.

We had shared an extraordinary, even mad, Kafkaesque experience. For me, it began in 1948 when, at seventeen years of age, I entered the novitiate with twenty others. Almost immediately we were given knotted rope disciplines with which to flog ourselves, and pointed wire chains to wrap around our arms and thighs. We were set to learn the pidgin Latin with which we communicated outside the hour or so of daily recreation. We were given score cards on which we would enumerate twice daily our personal faults and defects. We were given spiritual reading with innumerable stories of the extravagant behaviour of the supremely saintly. Every moment of the day from 5.25 a.m. to 9.30 p.m. was filled with prayer, reflection, instruction in the rules, physical labour. Twice a week we had 'quarters of charity' in which we would kneel before our peers and be told our faults.

You would think that we would be crippled for life by such extravagances. Maybe we were. But we lifted the chapel roof in song at Riverview, shared the bread and wine, embraced in the kiss of peace, we came out to greet one another with hugs, tears and laughter. Fifty years had greyed or thinned hair, lined faces and rounded figures. But a remembered gesture, a tone of voice, an angle of the head brought shouts of recognition. And stories.

'Remember the time . . . We were riding our bikes home in the dark down a mountain road and we hit a wombat. Our bikes flew into a farm dam on the side of the road. We took our trousers off to feel for the bikes in the water. The farmer came out with a torch and caught the three of us in clerical collars and trouserless in his pond.'

'Remember the time ... Bill Hackett took us to see a Christmas dawn over Port Phillip Bay from the You Yangs, he in a horse and trap, we on bicycles. Remember 'Spot' Sullivan teasing us to translate 'tit' and 'dugs' out of the *Aeneid*. Remember how he hated politicians, but wouldn't get absentee votes even though he couldn't get out of his room. We carried him down to the car, held him up in the voting booth. When we asked him how he voted, 'Oh!', he said, 'I just drew a golliwog.'

'Remember . . . Hugo Quigley, standing stark naked in the winter cold at the Port Melbourne Sea Baths, rubbing his bald pate to keep warm. Or Gerald Lawlor's retreat in a hot January at Loyola. He insisted we sit in the dark and contemplate our sins and flog ourselves vigorously for them. Or Harold Lalor's lectures on the Indonesian bombers warming up for a bombing raid on Darwin.'

Knowing that I was going to Sydney to launch the *Dictionary*, I had walked through the Kew Cemetery near my home in Melbourne past the Jesuit burial plots. I realised that my first experience of Jesuits being cheerful at a funeral was in November 1948. Father Johannes Peiffer was buried then. The *Dictionary* tells me that in 1900 he had come from Germany to work at Norwood, a Jesuit parish in Adelaide, South Australia. The 1848 revolutions in Europe had brought many Germans to South Australia. I met Father Peiffer at Caritas Christi, a hospice for the dying. A young man, Doug Boyd, and I were doing our novitiate hospital 'experiment' then. We novices were thrown into a number of extreme experiences as 'experiments' in the sorts of apostolic labours we might encounter as Jesuits. Well, they seemed extreme for closeted middle-class youth such as us—nursing in hospices for the dying, serving the homeless, teaching religion to young criminals. It was our first big adventure outside the novitiate, bathing in the admiration of the Sisters of Charity, enjoying the hospitality and the warming fire of the postmistress at the Watsonia Railway Station, doing spiritual obligations—spiritual reading, examen of conscience, rosary—in strange circumstances. The daily bath was Father Peiffer's great cross and humiliation. He used to say the sorrowful mysteries of the rosary while we bathed him. My companion, Doug Boyd, had a passion for entrepreneurial and scientific management not mentioned in the *Dictionary*. I experienced it as this early stage when he, as my senior, ordered me to collect all the false teeth in the wards and wash them in one basin. He did have the grace to give that sheepish smile of his as we measured a ward full of gaping mouths to see whose teeth were whose. One of the patients had an especially gaping mouth. His name was 'Rastus'. He had happened to put his head out of a manhole as someone else was putting a pickaxe in. We all knew 'Rastus' at Caritas Christi. In him we laughed at life in our stories. He was our clown.

Of the 416 Jesuits in the *Dictionary* 161 are Australian-born, less than half. I always thought that the greatest influence on my life were those Australian-born Jesuits, a generation of the 1920s, who were the first to complete their philosophy and theology in Australia. I always felt that there was a passion in them to imprint their Australianism on their religious life. They were practical, humane, sceptical of cant. They laughed at pomp and circumstance. I first met them as young men at St Louis School, Perth, where I began my education. St Louis was a remarkable school. The names of its classes—Elements, Rudiments, Grammar III, II, I, Poetry, Rhetoric—reflected the Jesuit ideal for a liberal education stressing linguistic, grammatical and textual teaching. The *Dictionary* describes Austin Kelly, the Jesuit rector and founder of St Louis, as 'lace-curtain Irish', and he certainly had a precious character. But the *Dictionary* also pays him the compliment of describing how he let men of talent go their own way. I think that these were passionate years in which these native-born and home-trained Jesuits explored the relevance of the *Ratio Studiorum*, their *Plan of Studies*. They were days, in a country without a Catholic university system, in which young Jesuits were trying to educate a laity beyond the level of apologetics. They did it through pious associations (always male) of the socially and culturally influential, through the institutes of social order, through intellectual and pious journals.

For a few hours outside St Ignatius Chapel, Riverview, we were high on the sweetness of our memories—of lifelong friendships born in extraordinary circumstances, of idealism lived out, of a spirit of self-sacrifice, of efforts to do something perfectly. That is the way it was. The tears and laughter said it so.

In an Archaeology of Learning of my own, that drive for knowledge fired by a sense of calling is my foundation stratum. 'AMDG—*Ad Maiorem Dei Gloriam*—For the Greater Glory of God' was our acronym for life. We headed every page of notes, every letter, every written activity with 'AMDG', or abbreviated to a simple cross (I still, after all these years feel my hand moving automatically to the top of the page to mark it in some way). We reminded ourselves in our daily meditation, our twice-daily examination of conscience, our frequent 'visits to the Blessed Sacrament', our quarterly three-day and annual eight-day retreats, and constant mutual exhortations that all we did had a higher purpose. Of course, we never measured up to our highest ideals—we went to sleep during meditation, we were careless in our pieties—but our failures were always there to prick our consciences. I do not believe that this was a fundamentalism, although there was always willing obedience to pietistic and ritualistic practices, always some comfort in the magical side of religion. It was not so much fundamentalism as highly motivated self-discipline.

In such a hot-house atmosphere it was easy to experience extreme pleasure in learning for its own sake. Among one's own companions, among senior older men, there were men of science and humanities who made contributions to secular learning—in astronomy, geology and Middle Eastern studies. There were men who became so expert in their hobbies—such as collecting ants and orchids—that the collections and their reflections on them are part of our Australian national heritage. There are men who were closed down by systems of piety in their early religious life, but who became liberated by changes in church and society. Professors of Scripture, of moral theology, of sacramental dogmatics, at the workface of their disciplines, imbued us with a sense that learning was a living, changing thing.

For ten years of my early religious learning—my novitiate, my philosophical and theological studies—we spoke, wrote, prayed, and to a greater or lesser extent thought in a dead language. Latin—'Dog Latin'—filled our days. Any conversation outside specified recreation time was in Latin. All lectures were in Latin, all note-taking, all scholarly debate, all constitutional and legal documents, all liturgy. It was a sort of pidgin, of course, as words of modern living were invented for a dead language. We giggled our way through our awkwardness. Then as our studies became more serious, we were proud that our life of learning could be so tough. We were proud, too, that we could speak to any nationality in our international society, though experience soon taught us that a Frenchman speaking Latin, or a German, or a Pole, were very different from an Irishman, an Englishman or an Australian. All Jesuits we knew as 'Ours', not without a touch of arrogance. We thought ourselves the best, although I have some pleasure in remembering that from an early time I had an urge to deconstruct institutional images and rhetoric. This urge matured in later years to a notion of institutional altruism, Institutional altruism is a notion that institutions should be anti-monumental. Institutions— churches and universities—should recognise that giving is better than taking, realism is better than hype. Recognition of error or wrongdoing, being humble, is no loss of face. Institutional altruism is the polar opposite to economic rationalism. About 1952 I began, at Loyola College, an annual journal called *Nostra—Our Doings. Nostra* was dedicated to the very ordinary happenings in our daily lives. It was a sort of ethnography of the everyday. It stressed the equality of all our experiences, from the 'brothers' doing their menial tasks to the 'philosophers' and their professors. I would say now that *Nostra* was holistic, compassionate writing—of mind, soul and body. Its ten or fifteen volumes are still in the Jesuit archives.

The post-war years of the 1940s and 1950s were years of slow revolution in the Church. Much of the revolution was about language. Language, vernacular language, freed us from the templates of law and rule and guilt that pressed down on our spiritual lives. It was hard to be multivalent and metaphoric in Latin. We savoured the new translations of Scripture. Ronald Knox was a hero to us as he tried to marry modernity with grace in his translations. The *Jerusalem Bible* (an English translation of a French translation of the Latin translation of the original Greek and Hebrew—well, not quite the original!) preferred not merely a new life to old words, but also the richness of a new understanding of what sacred texts might be. These were the years in which the participation of the laity in the liturgy was slowly being expanded. Congregations now recited first the Latin and then the English that once only the altar boys recited. The priest still stood with his back to the faithful, but there were more and more calls for the priest to engage in the sacramental mysteries with his full person in a less distant performance. It would be a long time before the Australian Church could shed itself of priestly exclusivity and let the laity play their rightful part. It is not done yet in Australia or the global Church. There needs to be another Reformation.

Words to us young apostles were important. We believed passionately that we had something to say about Jesus Christ, the Man of Freedom, the Man for Others, and the consequences that would follow in individuals and society on acceptance of him. I have my notes still of talks we gave to one another on the written and preached word in our 'Writer's Groups'. Words were our apostolate, we used to say. 'One drop of ink makes million think.' But what good was this passion if none listened to what we said or read what we wrote. We wrote papers to one another on opening sentences, adjectives, paragraphs. We preached to one another and critiqued our sermons. (Fifty years ago I heard our director of preaching—'tones', we called it—say what I heard an editor of the Bicentenary History of Australia instruct us in 1986. I didn't believe it fifty years ago. I don't believe it now. We should preach, we should write, they said, as if the congregation and the readers were twelve years old.)

If words preoccupied us, the Word mesmerised us. There wasn't a day when we did not choose some passage of Scriptures for our hour-long meditation in the morning. We were well trained in the first act of that meditation which we had learned from the Spiritual Exercises. 'Composition of Place', Ignatius Loyola called it—setting the creative imagination to work on the scenes in every event in the life of Christ. That imagination was fed with daily readings about the historical Jesus and the sites of his living. Then we emplotted that scene. We gave some narrative to our meditation, taking us to sorrow or gratitude or hope or love. Every word of the Word became busy with meaning upon meaning.

Let me stress again that this rock solid faith was not a fundamentalism. We were experiencing an exhilarating revolution in scriptural analysis. However unfreeing the papacy of Pope Pius XII was, he breathed life into every seminary in 1944—no, not every seminary, ours—with his encyclical *Divino Afflante Spiritu*. The encyclical insisted that the Word, if it certainly came from one divine origin, was a whole library of literary forms—poetry, epic, drama, parable, preaching, prophecy, historical reflection. Only a small part of the Word was 'historical'. Immediately, questions of facticity in the Bible became subsidiary to discovering what meaning was being purveyed to those who were hearing it for the first time thousands of years ago and to us now. Was Jonah swallowed by a whale? Did Peter walk on water? Did Jesus feed thousands from five loaves and fishes? The questions did not seem to matter. But the inspired meaning of the narrative did. The texts had a never-ending capacity to be enlarged. That was their strength. They buoyed us.

Meanwhile our performances in Latin undoubtedly tended to close down our philosophical learning and stultify our thinking. We had to put more energy into its expression than questioning into its understanding, certainly on basic presumptions. Our performances had theatre, nonetheless, and theatre has its own way of raising doubt. Our debates during three years of scholastic philosophy were by way of public defence and challenge of theses out of ontology, epistemology, cosmology, natural theology and ethics. Saturday mornings were devoted to 'repetitions', a centuries-old Jesuit pedagogic technique in which individuals were chosen at random to defend or challenge theses studied in the previous week. Once a month, and more importantly once a term and once a year, there would be public disputation before the whole philosophy school, and occasionally a 'Grand Act' was held before visiting professorial staff from other seminaries. There was much myth and history abut these 'Grand Acts'. Jesuit heroes, such as Robert Bellarmine and Peter Canisius, had done great things in these battles of belief in the Counter-Reformation. Monumental failures of those of us of a lesser breed became the stuff of whimsical tradition.

Public disputation—*Acta*, Acts—were a still-life of a way of learning of the Schools. Their formulaic nature supposedly allowed us to display their strict logic. Actually they only strengthened a sense that knowledge was a closed system but that we had the key to that system. A public disputation would begin with the 'Act' enunciating a thesis: 'Continuums (we would have said continua, I am sure!) are not (or are—I can't remember!) infinitely divisible'. (This is the old conundrum about the arrow never arriving because it has to go halfway first, after having gone halfway of halfway, etc., etc.) We disputed the proofs for the existence of God, the objectivity of knowledge, the nature of being. I have a thesis to be defended before me now, *'Ens vivens est essentaliter diversum a non-vivente, et est unum per se—*A living being is essentially different from a non-living being and is one in itself'. (Adversaries to this thesis are listed in my notes as Henri Bergson, George Cuvier and Herbert Spencer. We had long lists on our rogues' galleries. The church was—is—unforgiving on the slightest statement that could lead to the denial of some dogma. Whether these three denied that living beings were essentially different from non-living, I can't say. They would have been tainted in church eyes with their evolutionism.)

Having enunciated the thesis, the Act defined the terms, made a small statement about the significance of the question, described the propositions of the principal adversaries to the thesis, then proved it in syllogistic form. Share with me this example:

Major: Whatever has one principle of being is one in itself.
Minor: And: a living being has one principle of being.
Conclusion: Therefore: a living being is one in itself.

Then followed a series of syllogisms proving both the major and the minors of the original proofs.

Lined up against the defendant would be two or three adversaries in the flesh. These would be chosen from among one's peers. They would be very nervous young men, knowing that they could very easily make fools of themselves. These would come with a 'string' of syllogistic objections to the thesis. They would have made up the string themselves, or, more likely, have raided the collection of such strings handed down from one generation of philosophers to the next. The defendant would make distinctions in the adversaries' majors and minors. If the adversary was lucky, he would have foreseen these distinctions and could produce syllogisms against them till either the defendant or the adversary came to a point of self-contradiction or concession.

Unexpected or erroneous distinctions created turmoil. Everyone in the disputation then would be left dangling on the end of his own string of syllogisms. The greater percentage of these theses were unlikely to create any intellectual passion in us. We had little sense of the phlosophical world of our time. We rarely met our true adversaries—those we listed in our rogues' gallery, Kant, Hegel, Bergson, Bertrand Russell and innumerable others—in their own works. They came to us in headline bites in our text books. If I leave it there I will have left one stratum of my archaeology of learning undisturbed.

We were blessed to be taught by a professor of philosophy with great creative vision within this closed system of learning. Patrick McEvoy SJ was his name. He taught 'rational psychology' (theories of mind and intellect) and 'natural theology' (what reason could tell of the divine, as distinct from church dogma). McEvoy was an autodidact. He had never done postgraduate studies. But he was inspired by the work of Joseph Maréchal, a 'transcendental thomist' who tried to integrate Emmanuel Kant and Thomas Aquinas and who himself inspired the great theologian of Vatican Council II, Karl Rahner SJ. McEvoy was our line to Maréchal's aesthetically beautiful intellectuality. But it was not Maréchal's model of

146

understanding that inspired us, though we scoured the volumes of *Mélanges Maréchal* and wrote papers on Perfect Beatitude and the Metaphysics of Finality. What inspired us was the freedom it gave us to become engaged in a system of understanding that was not yet resolved but was in conflict with the essentially static nature of scholastic philosophy. We were in awe of McEvoy's brilliance. He would lecture to us in classical Latin for an hour without notes, demanding that we follow every step that he was taking. He had no patience with those he thought weak, but he would spend hours with those prepared to fly with him.

McEvoy was no ethereal spirit, though. Dishevelled would be the least extravagant word to use of the room he used to live in. Several cats and their breed lived in it as well as he. I have discussed the more exotic points of perfect beatitude while one of his cats gave birth to its litter beside us. He taught us a very physical biology as well as these things of the mind. I daren't describe the way in which he dispatched rabbits for our dissection or describe the smell of them as he taught himself their anatomy in his room. He was a constant smoker of self-rolled cigarettes and was never embarrassed for lack of an ash-tray. Inevitably he would make sure that the most squeamish of us had the task of pulling out a human brain from a garbage can full of formaldehyde in the classroom. A leading Catholic brain surgeon had given him a sampling of brains from his anatomy class.

My first introduction to McEvoy was in 1949. I was a novice, cleaning my shoes in the bootroom, silently with eyes down as required by our Rules of Modesty. The college dog, a Dalmatian, used to sleep there. It had all the weaknesses of the Dalmatian breed and needed to be put down. McEvoy came into the bootroom with a rifle and shot it down behind me and walked out without saying a word.

Thursday was a day off in the seminary. 'Villa Day' it was called, for the European Jesuits who would have had a villa house to which they walked on their day off from studies. We would usually take long walks in the bush and bike rides in the countryside around the college which was on the northern outskirts of the city. On Thursdays, McEvoy would take a select few on the back of a truck up to a property in the mountains which had been given him to clear. There, with the largest of mobile saws, he would fell fifty- and sixty-foot trees while we split logs and loaded the truck. McEvoy kept the college furnaces going for years. He also drove a heavy motorcycle around. We always had stories to tell of his adventures.

McEvoy was a shy man, socially inept, a terror in the weekly repetitions but gentle in examination. He was disorderly in his young days as a Jesuit. His superiors did not know whether he would make ordination. But he was simple in his religious duties—his daily mass, his reading of the office. He would attend all the community duties of prayer, meals and common recreation. And he was an obedient man. After twenty years of professing philosophy, he was sent by the Jesuits to a secondary boys' school where he taught small boys Latin for another twenty years.

In my Archaeology of Learning, I owe Pat McEvoy much. I owe him the inspiration of his teaching. I owe him the vision of my understanding of the nature of process. I owe him a sense of respect for simplicity in working through a life of faith and calling. Most of all I owe him the sense of rage I feel when in matters of the mind I hear someone judgementally ask 'Who said that?' before asking what it was that was said. Perhaps, after all, that is my first stratum of learning. Listen first. Criticise later.

4

Finding the Land

Fenua, The Land, is a 300-square-mile spot of earth, rock and vegetation in the middle of 643,000,000 square miles of ocean. It would have been a hard place to find, we have to think. It is nearly on the far reach of the most adventurous migration movement in human history. How Enata found Fenua and inspirited it is only one chapter in the story of how the Sea People of the West inspirited their Sea of Islands. It is a remarkable story. I would like to tell it.

Fenua (The Land)

Fenua was not, properly speaking, a name. Enata had no collective name for their islands. Fenua meant rather the earth, the land, something native. It also meant placenta, the nourishing envelope out of which one was born. The whole universe, Enata believed, was born out of the Earth seeded by the Sky.

Fenua was The Land as Enata perceived it, created it. *Tapu* was the central topographical concept that gave them a double dimension in time and space, but there were other ways in which Enata found themselves reflected in their environment. They found everywhere in their environment metaphors for male and female. A glittering leaf, a conch shell, a ripe breadfruit, an open bud, a red pandanus flower, to them was female. The male was the sun, a stick, a plucking-pole, the trade winds, a comet, pandanus roots. Their sexuality was explicit in word, gesture and movement. Enata lived closely to the dead, the enemy dead in their skulls, and the familial dead lying in their canoe-like biers. Stands of *aoa*, *temanu* and *maii* in closed valleys, cut off from the noise of wind and sea, made dark and silent glades.

Perhaps the environment was sombre to Enata, perhaps it was not. More certainly, they watched it very closely to see the portents it held. Their anxieties turned about war, death, sacrifice, exile, famine and pregnancy. These anxieties and fears gave noises, movements, colours and shapes enlarged meaning. To see the moon surrounded by yellow clouds, to dream of a body or of a fan or of losing teeth, to hear the cock's crow at night or rats scurrying in the roof, to find a leaf blown by the wind in one's path—these were presentiments of death. They would watch the colour and shape of clouds. Red clouds and hook-shaped clouds told them that somewhere men were looking for *heana*, victims for sacrifice. Late-ripening breadfruit, pounding in the ears, a dream of an old man's white beard would tell them that war was coming, and the clouds would tell them who would win. Dolphins stranded on the beach foretold of exile; red algae in the sea, of famine. Dream of germinating coconut or of pandanus, and one's child would be male; dream of ear pendants or of being beaten with needles and one boy child would die. The sun, the moon, the stars, the meteors, the buds and roots of plants, the behaviours of fish and animals held a thousand messages and Enata read them closely.

Enata saw the sea only narrowly. Sight of it was blinkered by the high arms of their valleys. The ridges of the mountains loomed high above every valley. Beyond the ridges was a no-man's-land where no one lived and no one went except to war and to waylay. Between the sea and the ridges Enata established their houses. They built them on stone platforms, *paepae*. They lived as if on islands within their own valleys.

Sea People of the West

I take the liberty of inventing a name, the 'Sea People of the West'. Such a name is not really mine to invent, either by right of scholarly knowledge or by right of a historical past that is mine. Scholars with far more knowledge than I have other names for my Sea People of the West—'Austronesians', 'Archaeo-Polynesians'. The islanders whose ancestors the Sea People of the West are as yet have no name for them, though I ride a wave of their energy as they seek a name in the past that will give them identity in the present. They seek a name for their ocean habitat that is theirs. 'Pacific', 'South Seas', 'Polynesia', even 'Oceania' are not theirs. 'Sea of Islands' they are suggesting is a name that taps a mythic consciousness of themselves. Both the 'Sea' and its 'Islands' raise poetry, song, dance, story, history and politics in them. My story, with all the clumsiness with which I enter somebody else's metaphor, is how a Sea People of the West became a Sea People in full and made a 'Sea of Islands' out of a sea of islands. My story is of how a Sea People encompassed their sea.

The 'Blue Planet' we call it now that we can see our earth from space. The Great Ocean—Moana—the Pacific—covers a quarter of the globe's face and gives the planet its blueness.

Two thousand years ago, the greater part of that ocean was uninhabited. Its islands were without the vegetation that would make them humanly habitable. The arc of the ocean's continental borders had been occupied through the millennia, but not the islands scattered across it. Forty-two thousand years ago—maybe thirty-eight, maybe fifty-two—a first people reached the southernmost point of the island-continent we call Australia, southwest Tasmania we would say. Or we could call it Toogee or Nuenonne country. As the first people stood on the southernmost part of the continent looking south forty-two thousand years ago, they would have seen the Antarctic reaching up to them in its ice-fields. The same global ice-age conditions that lowered the sea enough to make a land bridge to an island below the island continent, made the Antarctic mass and the glaciers that reached down to their shelters. The first peoples sheltered in caves in this southernmost region for five to ten thousand years at a time. They left their signatures on the walls of these caves by blowing red ochre and blood across their hands. They wave at us still across the millennia.

Fifteen thousand years ago a first people reached down through the Americas to the southernmost point in the east. Tierra del Fuego we call it.

The entry into the Pacific, as distinct from the occupation of its continental edges, has been by way of a tongue of islands—a 'voyaging corridor' it has been called. It curves southeast from the west into the Great Ocean. Beginning with Papua New Guinea, continuing through the Solomons and Vanuatu, this corridor of islands, each visible or nearly so to the one next to it, is closed on the last headlands of New Caledonia, Santa Cruz, and the Bismarck Archipelago by a vast expanse of water. For forty thousand years, the movement of the first peoples into the Great Ocean stopped at that point. Between 6000 and 3500 years ago that changed.

Let us savour the deep time in these forty thousand years. For forty thousand years—sixteen hundred generations—a people had looked eastward into the sea. They had occupied all the islands behind them for more than forty thousand years—for how much longer we do not know. Sixteen hundred generations had passed on to the next generation the knowledge, experience and wisdom with which they had imprinted their human spirit on their land- and seascape. This was the Homeland to which a first people would look back after their next step. They would call it Pulotu.

In Pulotu, the first people had domesticated the crops and animals that gave them life. Domesticated: there is so much in the word; breeding and selection, knowledge of the seasons, division of labour, ownership, control of uncontrollable forces, rules of behaviour, the multiple worlds of nature, humanity and spirits. In Pulotu, reefs, lagoons, forests and rivers became objects of strategies of exploitation. In Pulotu, these people were a Sea People in part. Through long experimentation they had evolved the watercraft and navigational skills to guide them between the small steps of sea in their corridor. In their next large step into the Great Ocean, they would begin to become a Sea People in full.

On this eastern edge of their venturing down the voyaging corridor, systems of weather and seasons reached out from the Asian regions behind them to the west. But also on this eastern edge, they caught the weather and seasons created by the vastness of the Great Ocean. Looking east the wind, and the sea with the wind, beat regularly into their faces from northerly and southerly directions. But from their backs the monsoonal seasons drove westerly against the regular easterlies. It was an annual cycle easily remembered. But there were other cycles every four or seven years, when the west winds won more easily and frequently over the east winds. We who live so far from the more particular signs of seasons and change have only recently come to recognise these other cycles. We call them El Niño. The fishermen on the far eastern edge of the Pacific on the coasts of Peru recognised the catastrophic consequences of El Niño, the warming of their waters, and the equally disastrous opposite, El Niña, their cooling.

Nearly as far as one could be on the Pacific away from Peruvian waters, other fishermen would have recognised these ordinary and extraordinary cycles in the weather. The cycles gave these seamen a westerly reach against an easterly regularity. The cycles gave these seamen a security that made their adventuring possible. They could sail to the east on a westerly with the assurance that an easterly would bring them home.

About six thousand years ago, after who knows how many exploratory attempts, settlement voyagers reached out across the 720-mile sea to the island clusters of Samoa, Tonga and Fiji. We have an invented name for these first people now. We call them Austronesians for their language characteristics. By any measure of achievement the Austronesians were the most adventurous people of all human time. By the end of our story they will have reached from Madagascar on the western edge of the Indian Ocean to Rapanui (Easter Island), the easternmost inhabited island of the Pacific. Between about 6000 BP and 3500 BP, the Austronesians were about to create a Homeland, Hava'iki. From it all islands to the north to Hawai'i, to the east to Rapanui, and to the south to Aotearoa (New Zealand) can be deemed to have originated—linguistically, genetically, culturally. This Homeland is a sea space enclosing many islands. The originating Austronesians were a sea people in ways no other human groups had ever been before.

The Hava'iki that the voyagers created was truly a sea people's Homeland. Their Sea of Islands around Samoa, Tonga and Fiji was an open sea. They needed the adventuring skills of blue-water sailors as well as the tidy, watchful skills of coasters.

Sixteen hundred generations had produced a cultural artefact of extraordinary genius. A canoe. A *va'a*, to give it its true name and not a name borrowed from the Carribbean and Christopher Columbus's first encounter with otherness. A **waga*, to give it a name that reaches back thousands of years into the Proto-Oceanian language spoken in Hava'iki.

The *va'a* had a variety of forms and functions. Single-hulled *va'a*, with and without outrigger, with sail or paddle, served fishing and travelling needs within the reefs. Outside the reefs, on deep-sea trolling, and indeed more adventurous exploratory trips of two or three weeks out and back, the single-hulled outrigger would be manned by specialist crews, carrying light supplies. Crews in single-hulled outrigger *va'a* probably reached out from the western edges of the Pacific to discover the islands of Hava'iki. But it would have been the double-platform *va'a tauna* that made the voyages for settlements and then undertook the trading ventures that joined the circuit of the Hava'iki islands.

The *va'a* of brilliant cultural genius was the *va'a tauna*, the double-hulled voyaging vessel. With no need of an outrigger, the two *va'a* were joined by a platform, about 12 feet wide and between 20 and 35 feet long. The platform could carry fifty to eighty people. Sometimes, if it were larger, a hundred. A shelter and a sand firepit might be put on the platform, together with cargo. More cargo could be stashed and sealed against water in the hulls of the two *va'a*, perhaps 75 feet long and 3 feet deep.

The most respected archaeologists and anthropologists of Oceania—Roger Green, Patrick Kirch and Geoffrey Irwin—differ in how they characterise the culture of Hava'iki. The differences do not greatly affect our story of the first voyage to Fenua'enata, except they mute somewhat our sense of certainty and affects the tone of our contexting voice.

The difference can be reduced to two questions. Firstly, is it proper to describe the Homeland in Near Oceania (Samoa, Tonga, Fiji) as a cultural and ethnic unit? Or should it be described as merely a trading circuit? Secondly, is this movement from the western edges of the Pacific first into Near Oceania and then into Remote Oceania (Fenua'enata, Tahiti, Mangareva) a smooth, gradual trajectory through three millennia? Or is it a movement with steps and pauses? The timetable for the steps and pauses would go something like this: 3500 years BP, the Sea People of the West reach out to Hava'iki. It is a reaching of two or three hundred years. Then there are about four hundred years of circuit trading through Hava'iki. Then come the first voyages to Remote Oceania. So the Sea People of the West are in their Homeland for about seven or eight hundred years before they make the most dramatic step of all, a settling voyage 4200 miles east to the far edge of the Sea of Islands.

I have no true expertise to bring to this debate. My images of the Sea People of the West come from the images of others, archaeologists and linguists. There is a famous phrase of one—Roger Green—that is borrowed by the others. The expansion of the Sea People of the West—it is I who call the Austronesians thus—'begins with Lapita and ends as

Polynesian'. Let me take the debate on the cultural and ethnic unity of Hava'iki no further than that.

Lapita was a reddish earthenware with characteristic geometric or 'dentate' (toothed) design stamped into the wet clay before firing. There are those who see in the geometric design the shape of an abstract face, the sort of face that will appear on later Polynesian carvings and tattoos. Pottery-making is not a cultural practice that we have come to associate with those we now know as 'Polynesian'. It died out, we now know, about two thousand years ago. Wood, stone, gourds replaced it in the portfolio of domestic utensils. We don't really know why a skill like pottery-making disappeared—it will disappear in Fenua'enata, too, But we know that in the early stage of the Sea People's expansion the most highly decorated Lapita pottery was an item of extensive trade over the whole Homeland. After several centuries of activity, the trade seems to fade away, and the production of the local and less ornate style of Lapita pottery continues, again for several centuries, until all pottery-making disappears. Let me say that the trade in prestigious cultural items that could only be obtained by adventure voyaging is an important characteristic of the Homeland.

It is not correct to think of a disappearing cultural trait, even as valuable trait as pottery-making, as a sort of cultural decadence. Other skills are developed, other resources are exploited, as social structures evolve through the centuries and new and more fashionable ways are developed to express in material ways the immaterial forces of power, status, gender and expert knowledge. The dynamics for the evolution of the root culture for 'Polynesia' are under way in Hava'iki. It is this root culture that the first voyagers will take with them out of Hava'iki to the far edges of their Sea of Islands.

We peer back into the millennia of that root culture in two ways. Archaeologically, first. There are more than twenty-five archaeological sites in Hava'iki that give us dates and stratified deposits. Linguistically also. An older linguistic method which we called in my younger scholarly days Glottochronology has become much more sophisticated. Linguists these days call it the Comparative Method. Glottochronology gave us a sequence and provenance of island languages. The relationship in the temporal order of Hawaiian to Tahitian, and of Hawaiian to Fenua'enata, for example, told us with some certainty that there was contact between these three groups of greatly separated islands. Comparative Method is focused on the rooted meanings of words in the languages. We get descriptive vocabularies of a language 2000 to 3000 years old. It would be remiss of me not to say that I am dependent in all this on the brilliant work of linguists such as Andrew Pawley and Malcolm Ross.

Archaeology tells us the Sea People in their Homeland lived in permanent hamlets and practised both a maritime and an agricultural economy. They held rituals and buried their dead in their houses, **fare*—a root word. The **fare* will become the assembly places of Samoa and Tonga, places where the ancestors live on in the posts, as they did in their houses. Those who leave Hava'iki will develop the monumental places of sacrifice we know as 'Polynesian' in Hawai'i, Tahiti and Fenua'enata. The underground oven will be a distinctive mark of the Sea People in Hava'iki and all over the Sea of Islands. As will tattooing, known from the finding of needles in archaeological sites. And, of course, there is trade across open sea in Hava'iki.

Linguistics, as well as archaeology, gives us access to the vegetable, animal, fish and shellfish life that sustained the Sea People. More importantly, linguistics tells us that birth order and the ranking of siblings was the dominant rule of inheritance. In this cultural feature, there were not only seeds of tensions as firstborn and later-born competed for land and power, but seeds also of adventure voyaging as later-born went looking for their own land. There was what has been called the Founder Effect, as the Sea People saw that the *mana*—the personal power—of the originating ancestors was made present in those who could claim to be in their line. Linguistics tells us, too, that a series of critical roles in society began to emerge in Hava'iki—the *ariki*, the firstborn in a genealogical line with the founder; the *tuhuna*, the craft expert in various domains of living; the *tuhuna pu'e*, the sea expert with control over navigation and the building of *va'a*; the *toa*, warrior.

It is the marvel of a first voyage and the transformations that follow a first landing that excite my imagination more than anything else about islands. I have told the story of the first voyage to Fenua'enata in the prologue of this book. The marvel of that first voyage is that the men and women who came on it had millennia of past culture in their heads and in the small cargo of their canoe. It is not reasonable to think that there was a flood of such voyages from Hava'iki to Fenua'enata. So the one or two 'first' voyages were the seed of the two thousand years of culture to follow, not only in Fenua'enata, but also to the north in Hawai'i, to the east in Rapanui (Easter Island), to the southwest in Tahiti and the far southwest in Aotearoa (New Zealand). These 'first' voyages to Fenua'enata were the seed, too, of all the metaphoric variations of what we call 'Polynesia'—in language, religious belief, government, mythology, everyday practice. All these empty land spaces in the vast ocean were made into new/old islands by the seed of those 'first' voyages.

Moana was a sea of thousands of islands. But it wasn't the Sea of Islands. The Sea People of the West would literally have to make the Sea of Islands. That is their great cultural triumph. The first creative step in that triumph was the first voyage from Pulotu to Hava'iki. The second step was the first voyage from Hava'iki to Fenua'enata.

Homeland

The Homeland—Hava'iki, as Enata called it—is shrouded in a mist of memories two thousand years old. A few recognisable names and more unidentifiable archaic titles come out of that mist. These are the places of origin or places of visit of Enata *atua*—the ancestors possessed of supernatural powers expressed in the triumphs of their heroic voyaging.

It is not myth that takes us back two thousand years, though. It is archaeological science. We have archaeological images of Hava'iki, the Homeland, at about the year zero of the Common Era (0 CE). Our dating is not precise. There are many more archaeological digs to be made on many more islands for our dating to be more precise. It could be three hundred years Before the Common Era (300 BCE). It could be three hundred years into the Common Era (300 CE). What is certain is that within that span of six hundred years that most remarkable canoe voyage whose story I have told occurred between the Homeland in the west—the islands we know as Samoa, Tonga and Fiji—and Fenua'enata in the far east of Moana, the Great Ocean. It was a voyage of some 2173 nautical miles across open sea.

What is remarkable about this voyage is that it was intentional. It was a voyage of settlement. Aboard this first canoe from the Homeland to Fenua'enata were men and women, animals, male and female, and vegetation in sufficient number and quantity to endow an ongoing human habitation with foods that had given subsistence to the Homeland peoples for millennia—pigs, dogs, chicken; taro, yam, breadfruit, banana.

About five hundred years after this settlement voyage—or perhaps, because of the margins of error in our understanding, a thousand years—

about 800 CE, occurred another equally remarkable settlement voyage, between Fenua'enata and Hawai'i in the north of 1885 nautical miles. I will tell the story of this second voyage anon.

These stories need to be told. When Fenua'enata was 'discovered' eighteen centuries after Enata themselves had discovered their islands, the concerted opinion of Euro-American strangers was that Enata voyaging skills were poor. Their canoes were considered to be the least seaworthy of all Polynesia. Enata did not show that relationship to the sea and sailing of the Tongans, Fijians and Tahitians that had been the object of admiration of such eminent navigators as James Cook. You will have seen that I tell a different story.

Vava'au, the first settlement *va'a*, lands its crew and cargo in a bay on the southern side of Ua Huka. In time Enata will call the bay Hane. Let us imagine that we are standing on the top of an archaeological mound in Fenua'enata. Hane is at the bottom. There will never be, of course, an archaeological mound like this one. Everything of Enata cultural history is beneath our feet. In reality there are thousands of archaeological mounds in different places in Fenua'enata. We have shuffled them into one. The top surface of this mound has a precise date. It is the year 1800 CE. It is really Edward Robarts, Jean Kabris and William Pascoe Crook who are standing on the mound. You and I are looking around through their eyes.

What we see is what most outside scholars today would call the end of the Classic Period of Enata culture. In fact Robarts, Kabris and Crook are symbols of the beginning of a new 'Colonial' Period when Enata are no longer alone to develop their identity. Beneath our feet are the deposits and all around us are the remains of the four hundred years of the Classic Period. We see the triumph of Enata architecture—the massive *tohua* (dancing grounds) of Vaihaipekua (Taipivai) and Taaoa (Hiva Oa). We see fortifications on the ridges where there is access to the valleys. We see *me'ae* with their huge stone *tiki*—now mostly in the great museums of the world. We will notice some extraordinary structures. In Hane, the valley where *Vav'au* landed, there are some thirty-three pits, mostly upland of the valley, and another thirteen pits in house platforms. They enclose 243 cubic yards of space to store, if needs be, the *ma*, the fermented breadfruit, for decades. The *ma* pits are a sign of both an environmental condition and a fundamental cultural characteristic of Fenua'enata. These islands on the edge of the equator and within the reach of El Niño are subject to periods of severe drought. Enata must always look to the future and preserve enough food to survive. Besides, the population has soared. There is competition for resources. Competition brings conflict and war. War, ironically, focuses on destroying the enemy's most valued resource, breadfruit.

There is a unkempt feel to these triumphant remains we are looking at. In 1800 CE the energy it had taken to make these great structures seems to have gone.

We can drop a number of timelines from top to bottom of this archaeological mound. Only one, radio-carbon dating, gives us firm dates. The others—proto-linguistics and cultural typologies—give us relativities. We get insights into the cultural processes at work once Fenua'enata became relatively isolated from the rest of Oceania. Let us plumb our mound.

Radio-carbon dating gives us the reasonable certainty that *Vav'au*'s settlement voyage occurred between 300 BCE and 300 CE. It is a vague sort of certainty to be sure, but all that we have. A series of other radio-carbon dates from Ua Pou, Nukuhiva, Ua Huka and Hiva Oa allow us to do what archaeologists love to do, periodise the two thousand years that followed the settlement. With the cautionary proviso that the edges of the periods are blurred, let's list them: a Settlement and Development Period (300 BCE – 300 CE to 1100 CE); an Expansion Period (1100 to 1400); a Classic Period (1400 to 1800); a Colonial Period (1800 to the present).

A thousand years for the Settlement and Development Period is forty generations. We cannot think that the story of these thousand years is ever told in the bare description of material artefacts that come from ancient grounds: shell peelers, coral scrapers, stone adzes, bone tattooing needles, sea-urchin abrasers, pearlshell trolling lures, augers, bone-reel ornaments, pig, dog, fowl, fish, turtle and human bones (cannibalised human bones). We can follow population movements back from the edges of the sea up the valleys. Domestic utensils will tell us of a move from a maritime, sea-edge economy to an arboriculture of breadfruit and coconut, the beginning of irrigation agriculture and pondage. We begin to see distinctive Enata stylishness in the way they begin to tang their adzes and move from a quadrangular to a trapezoidal shape. These thousand years are not static.

We have access to the immateriality of that cultural history through a recently developed science called proto-linguistics. Proto-linguistics is the science of discovering the baseline vocabularies of languages at the point of dispersal. So we have the possibility of catching something of the language of the *Vav'au*'s crew as they left on their settlement voyage. It is not just the words that should interest us, though. It is also the creative imagination that those words clothe. So we have all the Proto-Oceanian terms for *va'a* parts and seafaring; all the terms associated with the breadfruit and coconut culture and other horticulture; we have terms for that material culture that will not survive archaeological deposit—barkcloth, mats, baskets; we even have the words of a pottery industry that itself will not survive.

The *Vav'au* crew bring with them terms describing social relations, too. Let me indicate the proto-words with an asterisk. **Ariki* (chief), **tufunga* (expert), **toa* (warrior), **tautai* (seaman-navigator), and key sibling kin terms—**tuakana* (male's elder brother, female's elder sister), **tahina* or **tehina* (male's younger brother, female's younger sister), **tuanga'ane* (female's brother), **tufatine* (male's sister), **kainanga* (land-holding descent group), **kainga* (minimal descent group with land). We have no assurance that the meaning given to these words two thousand years later is the precise meaning possessed by them in Proto-Oceanian. In fact, we know that the meanings will be subtly different all around Oceania. A dozen island societies will play out their distinctive metaphors on the primary proto- meanings. Each *va'a* in the dispersal from Hava'iki to Fenua'enata will hold on to its traditions in a slightly different way. Each will let the forces of their island environment and their historical evolution play their variations. What stays the same is the thrust of their resolution of universal problems of humankind.

Let us turn to the terms of religious beliefs and practices. *Vav'au* brings with it some basic understandings—of **atua* (deity), **'anga'anga* (spirit, soul, corpse), **fai* (performing rituals), **mori* (offering, act of worship, removing taboo). We find terms for the rites of the kava bowl. We find **renga*—the saffron-coloured stain from turmeric, the root of the ginger plant, *Curcuma domestica*.

A twofold world came with *Vav'au* to Fenua'enata. It was a world particularly experienced and ordered, expertly known, commonly known. And it was also a world, just as particular and multiple, but outside the immediately experienced world. This other world was experienced indirectly—through the immediate world. I am reluctant to call this the world of 'gods' because of all the presumptions the word 'gods' holds. Let us use the Enata word, *atua*, or a word favoured by a scholar, Douglas Oliver, with far more experience in this than I, 'godliness'. 'Godliness' describes the blurred edges of the two worlds where the *atua* who have a powerful presence might be the never-human beings that created the world, or be beings that infused particular aspects of the natural world—winds, ocean, rocks—and the human-made world—*tiki*, burial places, reflecting bowls of water. Or indeed, they might be humans—chiefs, firstborn women of high descent—possessed of such a supranatural presence that they were *atua*. Enata lived in a natural world full of godliness.

Vav'au came with a pantheon of *atua*. It is impossible to move back through the evolution of that pantheon to the set of *atua* that came in the minds of the crew of *Vav'au*. What is remarkable is that wherever one looks in both Near and Remote Oceania, this proto-pantheonic set evolves in different ways—in Hawai'i, Aotearoa, Tahiti, Fenua'enata. What is remarkable is not so much the evolution as the fact that the fullness of the proto-pantheonic set would have come to Fenua'enata in one *va'a tauna* and spread out to the rest.

There were two proto-Oceanic words that came with *Vav'au* that we might reflect on—**mana*, **tapu*. They were instruments of understanding and control in Enata's double world of infused godliness.

Efficacy in living—in leadership, in fighting, in food production, in avoiding disaster—was never a matter of contingency. Nor was it ever fully or only humanly achievable in Enata understanding. The powers that efficacy signified were always a sign of godliness. *Mana* was that godliness. It came by birth in a line that was godly in its founder. It came by ritual insertion in which the *atua* were made temporarily or permanently present. It came by invocation. It came by being possessed. Enata would not be Enata without the idea of *mana*, the recognition of *mana*, the managing of *mana*.

Mana, as a cultural reality in Oceanian society, was not a very useful nor easily understood concept for the Strangers that came to Oceania. *Tapu*, *kapu*, 'taboo' was. 'Taboo' was very early recognised and used in the encounter as a thing, a place, a behaviour that was forbidden. Ships captains, missionaries, colonial administrators immediately realised that having the signs that made something 'taboo' brought discipline into the encounter. But the inviolability of things 'taboo' was only part of the cultural reality of *tapu*. In fact it is William Pascoe Crook and Temotete who give us understanding of *tapu* in Fenua'enata.

'Taboo', as some thing or some action forbidden, was perhaps the most noteworthy Oceanian contribution to Western vocabularies. It is William Pascoe Crook who tells us that *tapu* was not so much a prohibition supported by supernatural and social sanctions as a positive quality possessed by things and persons in their relationship to the source of their sacredness.

Seen from the negative perspective, 'taboos' were listed by many visitors as irrational rules that were burdensome, superstitious and capricious, symptoms of moral depravity and of social oppression. The only rationality visitors could imagine for them was that 'taboos' were the means by which men dominated women. For those familiar with the images of Judeo-Christianity, it was easy to interpret the restrictions among Enata as if women were unclean. Women could not go on a *me'ae*, sacred place, or walk over places where food was cooked. Women could not touch the *hami* or loin-wrap of men: men could not touch the *ka'eu* or waist-cloths of women. Men could not take up nor put their hands under the mats on which women slept. Women could not eat food prepared by men or food cooked at men's fires; men ate in separate eating houses. Male and female were forbidden all social and sexual intercourse at moments of social importance, such as preparation for war. Women could not enter fishing canoes. Women in menstruation were threatening, and curses that referred to female genitals were the most powerful.

Yet the notion of *tapu* was far wider than a device to regulate relationships between male and female. Ultimately it was the individual person who was sacred or *tapu*, free from illicit encroachment. There were two mysterious seats of a person's power—the head and the genitals. The social protection of the individual's personality turned around all that belonged to these two areas of the human body.

Every individual's head was *tapu*, so that there were elaborate rules to protect the personal space that surrounded it. Anything that covered the head or was in the hair or passed over the shoulders belonged in a direct and immediate way to that person, so that to lose it was dangerous, to capture it or take it was a rape of personality, to step over it was a personal desecration. Elaborate precautions were taken in the disposal of anything that touched the head. Shaven hair would be buried in sacred places; lice would be eaten; women would be careful to push aside leaves that had fallen on paths, lest they step on something that had been over another's head. Women would be confused on shipboard by the possibility that they might be standing on the deck above the heads of men below.

Tapu was imposed in the Fenua'enata by giving one's name or the name of members of one's descent line to the object under *tapu*. A name was, in a sense, the person. When objects were named in *tapu*, there was a clear extension of personal space to them. These *ad hoc* proceedings by which special trees or places or products were made *tapu* were supported by more permanent procedures in which certain types of foods and places, species of plants and animals were attached to the personality of individuals in their sacred roles. Whole categories of goods and foods were reserved for *haka'iki*, chief, or for *tau'a*, sorcerer, or for other special groups of males, or for men as distinct from women. Turtle, bonito, albicore were species that were attached to social definitions of individual persons. Some foods, such as breadfruit, most fish, taro and yam could be eaten indiscriminately by anyone, if the right social forms were observed. Some foods, such as chicken and squid, were the exclusive prerogative of the male. Others, such as pork, were mostly exclusive to males, but on occasions were allowed to women. Some foods were the exclusive property of certain ranks of males. The reddish hue in some chickens, fish, bananas and pigs marked them as belonging to the *haka'iki*. Some foods, while not exclusive to any rank among the males, could only by eaten by men of equal rank together.

With *tapu*, then, Enata were provided with a topographical and social map in which places, plants, trees, fruit, fish and cultural objects were recognisable extensions of social identity, and in which rank and hierarchy were as discernible as they were in the social unit. Since social identities had a temporal as well as a structural dimension, birth, death, marriage, tattooing, naming, piercing of ears, circumcision, puberty of individuals were hedged about with *tapu*. These *tapu* were narrow or wide, according to the rank and position the individual possessed. And since this temporal process belonged to social units as well as to individuals, the occasions on which the unit performed its social functions were also surrounded by *tapu*. House-building, the learning of songs, the exercise of skills in the making of objects such as canoes and ornaments, war and sacrifice, the collection of critical crops, the first use of productive instruments such as fishnets, were all invested with a sacredness that flowed out of individuals in their relationship to the principal source of *tapu*. In time and space, in the individual in his personal and social dimension, in the established roles of the group, a sacredness was invested whose strength could be measured by its extension and by its exclusiveness.

It is not to our purpose to unravel the evolution and historical development of everything that the voyage of *Vav'au* seeded in Fenua'enata. We will see what evolved when we stand with Robarts, Kabris and Crook on top of our archaeological mound in the year 1800 CE. Our narratives of beach crossings principally concern an encounter of Strangers with an Enata culture nearly two thousand years *in situ*.

It is to historical events that I would turn. They occur around the years 400 and 800 CE. It is likely that these events happen within four or five hundred years of the settlement of Fenua'enata by *Vav'au*. They are historical events in the sense that they actually happened, not historical events in the sense that we can give an actual history of them. We have to account for them, though. Accounting for them will require imagination. Not fantasy. Imagination.

For about four or five hundred years, twenty or thirty generations, Enata are in The Land. They have come to know The Land in all its seasons. They know that when Mataiki (Pleiades) have set and the sun has reached its zenith over their islands before moving north—on 9 March in our calendar in our time—the winds will move. *Tuatoka*, the east-southeast wind, begins its seasons (from March to September). 'A'ina kanau'u', they will say. 'Almost to the south.' With this almost-to-the-south wind comes rain, and the seas turn with the wind. Then, when the sun reaches its zenith over their islands on its way south—22 September in our calendar in our time—the constant *tuatoka* wind turns to east-northeast. 'A'ina tiu', they say. 'Almost to the north.'

On the wind change to the east-southeast in March come more frequent west winds. Then long flights of migratory birds—first the Pacific golden plover (*Pluvialis fulva*—*kolea* in Hawaiian), then the long lines of the bristle-thighed curlew (*Numenius tahitiensin*—*kioea*) and the ruddy turnstone (*Arenaria interpres*—'*Akekeke*) move from south to northwest. They will return from northwest to south six months later. The golden plover moves between the northern and southern summers. It collects in Hawai'i before flocking to Alaska for a northern summer nesting.

The birds in their millions come and go from pit to pit in the night sky—from Big Dipper to Southern Cross. They give clear signs of land to north and south. About four or five hundred years into their settlement of Fenua'enata, Enata begin to follow the birds northward, probably on the turn of the wind to the east-southeast and in the season of the west winds, in March, in *Poke*, as they come to call the month. They can tack along the east-southeast and west winds, north and south, out and home. The first followings of the birds would have been exploratory. A few days' sailing north would have taken them over the equator and into the night sky of the northern hemisphere. It is a sky that they had never seen before. In the pit of the north sky was a star that never rose or set. It so narrowly circled a northern darkness that it appeared to be stationary. In the south Crux circled a pit in the sky. They have a guide for north–south voyaging.

Some centuries after the settlement at Hane, Enata are restless again. With the certainty of a landfall, a direction given by the plover, and a trust in their way-finding abilities, Enata set out on a settlement voyage with a cargo as full as their first settlement voyage to Fenua'enata. The story of this settlement voyage from Fenua'enata to Hawai'i is another monument to the genius of the Sea People of the West. There will be another settlement voyage perhaps a hundred years after the settlement voyage to Hawai'i. It will be across 2200 miles of open sea to the loneliest island on the globe, Rapanui (Easter Island). It will mark the end of three millennia of a most extraordinary human migration.

Well, not quite the end. The east-northeast winds from September to March of each year spill over Fenua'enata and on southwest over the Tuamotu and Tahitian islands. In August–September of each year, the shearwaters, the yolla, also move southwest in their millions just north of Fenua'enata. They fly on to Aotearoa (New Zealand), to the Australian coast and to the islands near my house beside the beach. About 800 CE, a settlement voyaging *va'a*, directly or indirectly from Fenua'enata, arrived in Aotearoa. Then perhaps the Sea of Islands was settled in all its parts. Except for one mysterious issue, the sweet potato (*Ipomea batatas*). The sweet potato comes with its name, *kumara*, from South America. We know it had reached as far west in the Sea of Islands as Mangaia by 800 CE. How it came, we really do not know—probably by an accidental raft voyage to Fenua'enata. Patrick Kirch proposes that, whatever the way of its initial introduction, it is probable that it was followed by a return visit to the Peruvian coast from Fenua'enata. The world gets smaller all the time. Forty years ago I made a survey of the accounts of all first visitors to islands of Polynesia. I wanted to discover where the sweet potato reached before the arrival of the Europeans. Here is my list: Mangareva, Fenua'enata, Rapanui, Pitcairn, Hawai'i, Tubuai, Mangaia, Tahiti, Mehetia, Aotearoa, Atafu, Fakaafu, Rotuma, Tonga, Samoa. The world indeed gets smaller. The Sea of Islands now belonged to the Sea People in full.

I promised that I would tell the story of the settlement voyage from Fenua'enata to Hawai'i with imagination. I cannot tell it without changing voice and narrating a crossing of my own.

CROSSINGS

Way-Finding

I meet all my Natives—I meet all my Strangers—in the library. I do all my sailing there, too. For me, one of my most exciting voyages has been an armchair one. But libraries are truly magical places. In libraries you can 'armchair' your way onto a thousand voyages. Like this.

Way-finding

'Way-finding' is the the word that modern islanders use to describe their craft and the craft of their ancestors in piloting their voyaging canoes around the Great Ocean, the Pacific. They prefer to call themselves way-finders rather than navigators. Navigation is a more universal science of instruments and the application of systems of time and space as broad as the cosmos itself. Way-finding is a more interpretive craft, closer to the signs the systems of the cosmos imprint on the environment. No navigator—certainly none of the pre-eminence of a James Cook, let us say—would distance himself from the myriad of signs in sea and sky, in wind and water, that tell him where he is. But a navigator has the security that the system he applies in his voyaging has a life outside himself—in a book, an instrument, a map. For a way-finder no knowledge, no image is stilled either in time or in space. The temperature of the water, the movement of the waves, the seasons of the stars, the patterns of the winds, the habits of the birds, are all in his head. And it is a knowledge that comes to him not through his own experience alone. It comes to him down through the ages of his line of masters and apprentices. A way-finder finds his way with style, as a surfboarder rides his wave with style. No voyage is ever the same. His way is always different, but always ruled by his confidence that he will find it.

I prefer, I must confess, to be a way-finder than a navigator in all my voyaging through learning and knowledge. Metaphors are the trade winds of my mind. Models are the doldrums.

IT MIGHT TAKE some imagination to see the great domed Reading Room of the Victorian State Library as a beach. But it was a beach for me one day in 1958. I remember it well. I made a crossing that day.

It was a wet day. Rain dripped from a great height into buckets strategically placed on the floor. I was seated at my favourite reading table—if Karl Marx needed to sit always in the same place in the British Library, we lesser beings have a right to use the same sort of security blanket. The green leather of the reading table was inscribed with various initials—presumably of persons even less secure in their identity than Marx or I. 'Foo' had been there, too, proboscis and all. A number of damp and odorous homeless men sat around me. They had come in out of the rain, spied my clerical collar, and felt it would somehow protect them from the ire of the librarians, who sat high overlooking us in the axle of the library's radiating spokes of reading tables. No doubt Jeremy Bentham inspired more than prison wardens when he planned a geometry of total surveillance.

The State Library was born of the wealth of the gold rush and the ambition of Melbourne to become the southern hemisphere's most civilised city. It was a magical place for me. I loved the heavy silence of its great space. It was a silence you could feel on you shoulders, something like standing on the edge of the Grand Canyon or in the Australian bush. The few sounds there have a distant feel, like children's voices in a schoolyard far away.

The hours I spent reading in this library rolled into days, into weeks, into months, maybe even into years. You could squirrel away stacks of books on your table, against the time it took to search for some volumes, against the volumes that were lost forever somewhere in the stacks.

This rainy day in 1958, I was in the beginning of research that would occupy my energies for years. A curmudgeon of a scholar, Andrew Sharp, had written a book entitled *Ancient Voyagers of the Pacific*. There were no 'Vikings of the Sunrise', he declared. No navigators sailing deliberately to its remote islands. The islands of the Great Ocean were peopled by accident, certainly in its margins—Hawai'i, Rapanui (Easter Island), Aotearoa (New Zealand)—and probably those in the centre of great clusters of islands, such as Tahiti, Tonga, and the Fijis. Traditions to the contrary were just myths.

We younger scholars did not sense at the time how devastating and political a conclusion that was. It struck heavily at the island peoples' idea of a cultural identity for themselves.

My first academic publication was to be a review essay of *Ancient Voyagers in the Pacific*. Essentially, the essay was a denial of Sharp's central thesis. I still have Sharp's stinging rebuke in my files. The faded blue aerogramme is a sort of scout's badge of adversarial academia. I keep it proudly because I knew I was right.

In fact I knew I was right on this wet day in the Reading Room of the Victorian State Library. On this particular day, I read Harold Gatty's survival pamphlet for crashed airmen during World War II, *The Raft Book* (1943). It was full of the lore Gatty had learned from islanders about all the signposts to be found at sea—ocean swells and the shadows islands made in them, clouds and the colour of the lagoons reflected in them, birds, migrating or returning to land to roost, orienting stars. It was an enlightening moment for me in cross-cultural history. It was a moment of solidarity with experiences I had never had, a moment of trust and imagination. Anyone engaged in cross-cultural research will know that it is not the mountains of texts of the encounter between indigenous peoples and intruding strangers that are the problem. It is the depth of the silences. I thought my best chance as an historian of hearing what those silences hid was to learn a bit of anthropology.

It was not as if history lacked anything. History as a discipline excited us greatly at the time—the compassionate history of R. H. Tawney, the thinking-person's history of R. G. Collingwood, the brilliant narratives of Thucydides, the humanistic archaeology of Mortimer Wheeler and Glynn Daniel. We could read Max Weber on the intertwining of religious belief and economic realities and think we could write better mission history for it. We could dig up a neolithic lake villages in our minds and know how to read human agency in the shape of a Tahitian house complex. Above all, we knew that there wasn't a narrative that we could write that wasn't in some way shaped by a living discourse about Machiavellian Florentines or English civil wars or Athenian democracy that was ours to join.

No part of living is really compartmentalised, however, certainly not one's religious beliefs from one's secular learning. And there was also a paradigmatic shift suffusing religious thinking all through these years. Europe's inability to deal religiously with the Holocaust was driving the paradigm. It was hard to believe in an interventionist God amid such evil. Of course, the death of God didn't begin there. Dr John Hawkesworth, the editor of James Cook's journal of his voyage of discovery in the *Endeavour*, got himself into a lot of trouble for even suggesting that the naturally high tide that saved the *Endeavour* on the Great Barrier Reef could hardly be described as supernaturally providential. The death of God didn't begin there in post-Holocaust Christianity, but the birth of the present does. A sense of an ever evolving, present-participled present— an ethnographic present, I would now like to say—was growing in me. It is a processual present, never static, never really in polarity, always being changed by itself. I went to read anthropology at Harvard with a philosophy and theology of process in my mind and spirituality. It is what anthropology would always be for me: a narrative of the present moment, in the past or now. On my way to Harvard I made a pilgrimage to Teilhard de Chardin's grave. He was a hero to me, a man of faith at the limits of science and learning. His writings were still on the Vatican's Index of Forbidden Books at the time. The Jesuits had misspelt his name on his gravestone.

In 1958 my scholarly goal in life was to learn all I could about island people from what the early explorers, missionaries, traders and beach-combers saw and wrote of them. I began an exhaustive reading of what these sources could tell me of 'the geographical knowledge of the Polynesians'—the islands they knew outside their own, their deliberate and accidental voyaging, their motives for voyaging and their navigating methods. It resulted in a map recording some 215 deliberate and accidental historical voyages in the Central Pacific. My conclusions were that the 'Polynesians' were rarely daunted by voyages of about 300 miles in open sea. They were never really daunted by being blown off course. They had confidence in what more recent voyagers among them would call not navigation, but way-finding, their ability to make a landfall if they came within 100 miles of an island.

The early explorers—the British, the French, the Spanish—all made diligent inquiries as to where other islands were to be discovered. James Cook was lucky. He met up with up with a most remarkable man. His name was Tupaia. He is a hero of mine. I met him in 1958 and have loved learning more of him ever since. Andrew Sharp's approach to Tupaia was one of distrust. Mine was one of trust. I would like to tell Tupaia's story and the new beaches to which it took me.

Tupaia was a priest from the sacred island of Ra'iatea in the Tahitian cluster of islands. He was a priest in the formal sense of that word. He was a man of establishment, a guardian of tradition, a master of ceremony and ritual, a man of sacrifice. Saying Tupaia was a priest, we are saying that he was not a prophet. The gods did not possess him, make him shiver and quake and speak in tongues, manipulate good and evil fortunes. No, Tupaia was a priest, a political manager of supernatural worlds.

Tupaia was a priest of 'Oro. 'Oro had come to the sacred island of Raiatea on a rainbow. 'Oro, as a feathered basket *tiki*, travelled around the islands in his canoe called *Rainbow*. Rainbows, feathers, canoes—all of 'Oro's symbols were of crossings, between heavens and earth, air and ground, sea and land. 'Oro's temples were places of crossings. They stood on points of land looking to an opening in the reef. Taputapuatea was their name, Sacrifices from Abroad. Taputapuatea had narratives in their architecture about crossing beaches, about encounters in place, about assuaging violent power. 'Oro's canoe, bearing sacrifices on its prow, would beach itself on the seaward side of Taputapuatea. Standing on a stone between the seaward side and the landward side, his feet too sacred to stand on the ground around, the *ari'i nui*, the high chief, would eat the eyes of the sacrifices. The violence in him would be softened by that. He would then be wrapped in the feathered symbols of 'Oro, be given his titles, and established in his authority by that. Then in a world turned upside down, he would have shit and semen poured over him, and be taught his proper place in the order of things: be made the shit of gods.

On the landward side of Taputapuatea was a place of communion. Sacrifice and communion always go together. It was a place of feasting. It was also a treasure house of sacred paraphernalia and memory. It was a place where traditions were sung and souvenirs of encounters were kept. A portrait of James Cook by John Webber was kept in the Taputapuatea at Matavai through all these years. And the red hair of the *Bounty* barber. And the skulls of two mutineers killed on the island. Taputapuatea were Pacific representations of the sort of crossings that in an island world had to be made between sea and land. They were a liturgical map of the beach.

Tupaia was the manager of the theatre of these sacred spaces. In fact, in 1760 he had brought from Raiatea one of those stones on which the *ari'i* stood to receive the sacrifices. That stone was the foundation stone transported from Taputapuatea on Rai'iatea to Taputapuatea on Tahiti. If I had space, I would tell you how significant an action I thought that to be. I would tell you Peter Brown's story. Peter Brown is an historian of the ancient church. He has a story of how altar stones with their martyrs' relics were the building blocks of a universal church, the materialisation of extended centralised powers (*The Cult of Martyrs*, University of Chicago Press, 1981). I would tell you David Starkey's story. David Starkey is an historian of the kings of England. He has a story of how the Privy Council, the carers of the king's excreta, became the political extensions of the king's body ('Representing through Intimacy', in I. M. Lewis, ed., *Symbols and Sentiments*, London: Tavistock, 1977). I would tell you Jean-Christophe Agnew's story. Jean-Christophe Agnew is an historian of the modern capitalist economy, of bank cheques, currencies, stock exchanges and the like. His story is of how it is in theatre that we experience the virtual realities of the civilising processes (*Worlds Apart: The Market and the Theater in Anglo-American Thought, 1550–1750*, Cambridge University Press, 1986).

That will be my point about Tupaia. He knew the civilising processes in his own native islands well. Tupaia knew the virtual realities of abstractions, the subjunctive world, the 'as if' world of the reifications of state, kingship, law, economy. Tupaia knew the fictions of his languaging. Tupaia will easily translate flags, uniforms, military order and the theatre of power into something he understood. That will be his triumph.

Tupaia first met this other world in July 1767. It was at Matavai on the northwest coast of Tahiti. Captain Samuel Wallis' *Dolphin* had been anchored there for a couple of weeks. They had been a terrible few weeks. The 'Dolphins' had killed they did not know how many islanders—as many as a flock of birds, a shoal of fish, the Maohi, the Tahitian islanders, said. Tupaia came to Matavai when the relations between the English and the Maohi were more settled. He came with Purea, whom the English took to be Queen. They presumed they had killed her King in the first massacre. Queen Purea, they would say, gave them Tahiti. Tupaia came with Purea from the Taputapuatea he had established for her. They came with Purea's son, who held from his father and his mother the highest title on the island. They had already begun their translation of their encounter with the English. They would incorporate the flag of possession that Wallis had erected in Matavai into the sacred feather girdle of 'Oro that would be wrapped around the *ari'i nui* on his Taputapuatea stone. James Cook would later see it among the sacred treasures of 'Oro's temple, and William Bligh was to draw it.

When Tupaia boarded the *Dolphin*, the 'Dolphins' sensed he was of superior rank, even a priest. They gave him the name Jonathan. Tupaia was curious about everything on board the ship. He learned things by touching and handling them, sometimes the hard way—that teapots held boiling water, for example. A cameo portrait of Wallis' wife sent him into raptures. It was a fascination with representation that never left him, as we shall see.

The officers of the *Dolphin* fussed over him. They sat him down to dinner, a large dinner—chicken broth, roast fowl, roast pork, roast yams, plantains, bananas, soft bread, biscuit, apple pudding, apple pie, and a cup of tea. Tupaia mimicked the etiquette around the table, and was embarrassed when he got things wrong, like putting his fingers in the butter, or as they invited him to do for the laugh of it, wipe his mouth on the tablecloth, since he did not have a pocket handkerchief such as they used. There is much of the civilising process in the private spaces of good table manners. Norbert Elias has taught us that. There is also much hegemony in the laughter at bungled native mimicry of civilised ways.

The 'Dolphins' decked out 'Jonathan' in a complete suit of clothing before they left. In this garb and to their patronising smiles, he returned to the beach and there delighted a large crowd of islanders with the theatre of his encounter.

Tupaia's next encounter was with James Cook and Joseph Banks. His political status had changed between the visit of the *Dolphin* and that of the *Endeavour*, but his usefulness to Cook and Banks was greatly enlarged. He was their guide, interpreter and informant. In the end Banks decided to take Tupaia back to England. He would not cost as much as the lions and tigers his neighbours collected, Banks had mused.

Every encounter of the *Endeavour* with indigenous peoples from that moment on was mediated by Tupaia—through the Central Pacific, all around New Zealand's north and south islands, all along the eastern coast of Australia. By the time they leave Australia, Tupaia's body is scoured and bruised with scurvy. It has no immunity left against the fevers of Batavia. Tupaia is one of the first of Cook's thirty-six men to die there.

But not before leaving us with a brilliant heritage. That will also be Tupaia's triumph. In the great cabin of the *Endeavour*, Tupaia saw James Cook bending over his chart table. He saw Sydney Parkinson, the painter, at his easel working his oils and watercolours. So Tupaia makes a map of his ocean world. And he starts painting. In his map and paintings Tupaia equips himself with new skills to represent something old within him. They are Pacific representations of extraordinary brilliance. They are translations of culture. Tupaia translates his metaphors into somebody else's.

We don't have Tupaia's original drawing of his map. We have only English interpretations of it. Or rather we only have English misinterpretations of it. Tupaia's ocean of islands arcs across 4200 miles of the Central Pacific, from The Marquesas in the east to the Fijis in the west. There are islands to which he himself has sailed—most remarkably, those taking ten days' sailing to the west from which it takes thirty days' sailing, against the prevailing winds, to return. There are islands 350 miles across open sea to the south to which he pilots the *Endeavour* with pinpoint accuracy. There is knowledge of the ages in the map, and history of a century or two. A great number of the seventy islands on it (he originally named one hundred and forty) we can't identify. This is probably because the names are as archaic as the knowledge they represent. I would like to argue that they are something else as well. Tupaia's map is a Sea of Titles, or of sacred places where titles reside.

As Tupaia acts as the master of ceremonies for all of Cook's encounters with indigenous peoples, he insists on the protocols that needed to be observed. Respect and reverence in body gesture and pose, exchange of true gifts not trade, and obeisance to the true titles of the place in that sacred space where they resided. In all of Tupaia's encounters, he would engage himself in discussion of the titles and origins of the places he visited. It made him famous throughout New Zealand. Among the Maori he was remembered for generations longer than Cook. The Maori named a cave for him where he slept, a well that he dug. They give their children his name.

For many years we have had a series of paintings from the *Endeavour* identified only as the work of 'The Artist of the Chief Mourner'. But just a few years ago, a note was discovered in Joseph Banks' papers saying that 'The Artist of the Chief Mourner' was Tupaia. By that they become an extraordinary archive of the 1769 encounter. Like his map of the Sea of Titles, Tupaia's paintings focus on the larger narratives of Tahitian life.

We have his map-painting of Taputapuatea. He draws the seaward sacrificial space separate from the landward feasting and memorialising space, with 'Oro's canoe, *Rainbow*, in-between. We have his depiction of long-distance navigational canoes and, in the background, the vegetable foods they brought, plantain, coconuts and breadfruit. We see the meeting place where their stories were told. And the war canoes. We have the theatre of Tahitian memories—the musicians and the dancers. When Tupaia is in New Zealand, we have the theatre of gift exchange, with the prominent depiction of the eye, the source of power. On the Australian coast, he is intrigued by the primitiveness of the canoes and the utter nakedness of the people. And he sees people's eyes. He always sees the eyes.

All the way from Tahiti to Batavia, in whatever direction the *Endeavour* sailed or whatever foreign lands they reached, Tupaia always knew the direction of home, and its distance. When they reached Batavia, Tupaia noticed immediately that the many different peoples—different in their colour and their appearance—wore their own distinctive native costumes. Tupaia looked at himself and saw himself in the slops of ship's clothing. He threw them away and dressed himself in his native *tapa* cloth. That was his last gesture of identity. He died wrapped in the red *tapa* of his *arioi* and priestly status.

When I began my studies of the encompassment of Oceania by the islanders themselves more than forty years ago, two other young scholars were making their first contributions at the same time. Marshall Sahlins and Ben Finney. I was jealous of them both. Marshall had just written 'Esoteric Efflorescences on Easter Island' in the *American Anthropologist*. It was part of his library-oriented doctoral dissertation on *The Social Stratification of Polynesia*. I was jealous of him because he was reading everything that I was reading and was reading it differently and more creatively—wrongly, but more creatively. I decided that anthropology helped him do it. So I went off to Harvard to acquire anthropological reading skills. I didn't know what those skills were, but I hoped that they would teach me to read the silences in other cultures.

Ben Finney had just written an article on ancient surfboard riding in Hawai'i. I thought surfboard research was a pretty good lurk. But it was the beginning of a career in which he has wedded theoretical knowledge with practical skill. These days he calls it 'experimental archaeology'.

Finney was about to construct a Hawaiian double canoe. It was a replica of King Kamehameha III's royal canoe. He tested it in Californian waters. His purpose was modest: to test whether shallow-rounded hulls would give resistance to leeway, and whether the inverted triangular 'crab-claw' sail would drive the canoe into the wind.

When Finney brought his canoe to Hawai'i from California, Mary Pukena Pukui, one of Hawai'i's traditional scholars, called the canoe *Nahelia*, 'The Skilled Ones', for the way in which the hulls gracefully rode the swells and drove into the wind. Already the project was getting larger than itself. The admiration caught in the name was a sign of deeper cultural and political forces beginning to be focused on the question of how the Hawaiians, Tahitians, Maori and Samoans encompassed Oceania.

By 1975 Finney, now supported in and eventually relieved of his leading role by native-born Hawaiians, turned to the construction of an ocean-going canoe, *Hokule'a*. *Hokule'a* means Star of Joy, Arcturus, the zenith star of Hawai'i's celestial latitude. The overriding ambition of all *Hokule'a*'s great voyages was that they be performed as much as possible in the way in which they were performed a thousand years ago. *Hokule'a* has now voyaged to nearly all parts of the central Polynesian Pacific: Hawai'i–Tahiti–Hawai'i; Tahiti–Rarotonga–Aotearoa; Samoa–Aitutaki–Tahiti.

These voyages have been an extraordinary achievement. There is no point in being romantic about them. The thirty years of this odyssey have had their pain and conflict, their tragedies and failures, their political machinations, their greed, their absurdities. But they also have been courageous overall triumphs, tapping well-springs of cultural pride in a sense of continuity with a voyaging tradition. This has been not just in Hawai'i, but in Tahiti, Samoa, Aotearoa as well. Everywhere it has gone, it has been the same. The landfall has been a theatre of the identities of island peoples now and in the past.

Deep in the mythic consciousness of the peoples of the Sea of Islands is a series of crossing metaphors that have served their understanding of themselves. Each metaphor, embodied in story or artefact or ritual, described some bridging process—between sky and earth, human and suprahuman, sea and land. The voyaging canoe embodied something more. It embodied the people of the place. Owned in its parts by individuals and families, the canoe was a map of the whole temple congregation or political unit. In its name was a heroic ancestry. Its voyaging was always epic—from or to Tahiti ('A Distant Place'), to or from Hava'iki ('A Sacred Homeland'). Its launchings and arrivals were always larger than ordinary, always celebrations in places of power and significance, always occasions of memory and rite.

Hokule'a was launched with ceremony in March 1975 at Kualoa on the north side of Oahu, a beach full of *kapu* for the People of Old of Hawai'i. Signifying actions can sometimes seem awkward: out of season as it were, divorced from present times and contexts, antiquarian mimes. The meanings of the signs aren't seen immediately and directly. They strive too hard to be didactic. They cease to be sacramental—effective of what they are signifying in the signifying—and become merely symbolic. Ritual and theatre lose their cathartic effect if the ritual becomes ritualistic, succumbs to formalistic repetition, if the theatre becomes too theatrical, overplaying the words, gestures and signs. At *Hokule'a*'s launching, the *kahuna*, the master of old knowledge, sang the chants and blessings that had been rescued from oblivion a hundred and fifty years ago when the Hawaiian People of Old embraced the literacy that was the single greatest import of the strangers. All the proper garlands and proprietary parcels of sacrifices were used. *Kapu* were conscientiously obeyed. The moment was as inventive of solemnity and full of distractions as is every cultural act. The thousands of spectators on the beach gave *Hokule'a* their own blessing with cheers.

The catharsis of the launch was more long-coming in its effects than in those minutes on the beach at Kualoa, however. The politics of dispossession were strong in Oceania in those years. Bikini and Muroroa and their mushroom clouds still overshadowed the islands. The *kamaiana, maohi, enata*—the native islanders of the Pacific—were asking what a 'world encompassed' really meant for them. Hawaiians, Tahitians and Maori were asking what joined them together in the Sea of Islands. When *Hokule'a* arrived in Tahiti at the end of its first successful 34-day voyage, the peoples of the Sea of Islands were joined by their ancient mastery of the ocean and their cultural memory of it. The launching ceremonies of *Hokule'a* lasted from March 1975 at Kualoa, where thousands saw it take to the water, to June 1976 at Papeete, where thousands welcomed it after a voyage which they believed re-enacted the voyages of their ancestors.

It was James Cook who began the debate on the 'Polynesian Problem'. How was it, he asked himself, that every island he 'discovered' in the vast Pacific was already peopled by natives whose physical appearance was similar and who seemed to speak the same language in dialect? He carefully watched their sailing techniques, asked what other islands they knew, admired their ocean-going canoes when they scooted past the *Resolution* in a good breeze. He even let Tupaia guide him over 300 miles of unknown seas to a new 'discovery' of Rurutu. He was impressed that in the east, the Tahitians, and in the west, the Tongans, could name hundreds of islands in a great arc around them. He wanted to believe otherwise, but in the end, probably persuaded by the 'experimental gentlemen' around him, he concluded that the dispersal of the Pacific peoples must have been largely by the accident of seafarers lost in storms.

James Cook began the debate. He certainly did not end it. Andrew Sharp tried to in 1956 with his *Ancient Voyagers in the Pacific*. Sharp's scepticism prompted the armchair research—including my own—into the distances the Polynesians could deliberately sail and their motivations to such dangerous enterprises. But two brilliant books, Thomas Gladwin's *East is a Big Bird* (1970) and David Lewis's *We the Navigators* (1972), sent the debate in a different direction. They described the extraordinary achievements of island navigators reading the swells in the sea and the stars in the sky. Gladwin especially showed the ways in which such complex knowledge might be transmitted through generations and be systematised on principles different to the global navigation principles of the Europeans.

Computer simulations of Pacific voyaging came early into the debate. But hundreds of thousands of deliberate and accidental voyages simulated in the computer did not resolve the matter. Or rather, they left scholars with the remarkable conclusion that not one of the accidental simulations reached the three outer points of the Polynesian triangle—Hawai'i, Rapanui, Aotearoa. By the computer, voyages to the edges of the Sea of Islands were all intentional.

Let me tell my story of the historic voyage from Fenua'enata to Hawai'i. It is a story born of the confidence created by a most rewarding intellectual engagement in the issue for so many years. I have suggested how the voyaging to Hawai'i would have begun by Enata observing the bird migrations into the northern hemisphere. I can only imagine how it ended. *Hokule'a*'s homecoming voyage from Tahiti to Hawai'i in June 1980 helps me do it. It begins in Matavai Bay, Tahiti, and ends thirty-two days later on the Big Island of Hawai'i. I would like to join it in the last days of its voyage to Hawai'i. About that time, the courses of *Hokule'a* and the voyaging canoe from Fenua'enata seventeen hundred years before would have coincided.

Nainoa, a young man of Hawaiian birth, twenty-five years old, was the navigator of *Hokule'a*. Nainoa had apprenticed himself to Mau Piailug, the Micronesian navigator who had taken *Hokule'a* to Tahiti in 1976. Mau had also given David Lewis much of his navigator's lore. Nainoa has no Hawaiian tradition of navigation to call upon. That's gone, or rather, it is too deeply embedded in mythology and the language of the environment to be of much use. Nainoa has virtually to invent his own system. He does not do it by learning Western celestial navigation. He avoids that. But he uses the Bishop Museum Planetarium in Honolulu to set in his mind the night skies. He can simulate the rising and setting of the stars for all seasons in Hawai'i and in different latitudes. He creates for himself a star compass and sets it in his mind, as is done in all systems of oral memory, with a metaphor. His metaphor for *Hokule'a* is *manu*, a bird with outstretched wings. He has not just a star compass in his mind—different from the ones we know of in Micronesia—but a directional compass, as well. It has thirty-two settings, or 'houses' as he calls them, more regular than the traditional settings. He sets himself to remember the rising and setting of stars, sun and moon in these houses. He also sets himself to calibrate his hand to the two great determinants of the Hawaiian latitudes, the North Star and the Southern Cross. When he is not in the planetarium he is in the seas around Hawai'i, experiencing the swells made by the dominant weather patterns and their seasons. He also experiences the seas created by the changing winds and movements made by the backlash of the sea against island shores and in the island shadows. Navigational lines in his system, latitudinally, north and south, are relatively easy. But his movements east and west along a longitudinal line are far more complex, involving dead reckoning of distance sailed and the relativising of theorising and settings in his star compass. That will be the greatest anxiety of his navigation. He has to make landfall upwind of his destination, northeast of Tahiti, southeast of Hawai'i. Downwind, if he ends up there, will require tacking.

Nainoa has 2000 miles of an arcing northwest sail to Hawai'i from Tahiti and the seas northwest of Fenua'enata. In this vast open sea huge forces are at work, especially in the clockwise systems of winds and currents of the northern hemisphere and the anti-clockwise systems in the southern, and the doldrums between them. Nainoa's knowledge can't just be local. It must be global and encompass the great regulators of time and directions—sun, moon, stars.

Each dawn is a precious time. The sun in its rising sets up a relationship with the swells of the ocean and its low shadows help the sight of this relationship.

1 June 1980. They are within six days of a Hawaiian landfall. Nainoa says:

> Dawn. The first rays of dawn hurt my eyes to maintain the sailing course. I have an uneasy feeling this morning for I know that the thin sheetlike layer of cirrus cloud that moved in last night means a change of weather—a change from the regular trade that can make navigating difficult.

Nainoa had difficulties in the night identifying the stars in the breaks of the cloud.

They are now in the last three days of the voyage from Tahiti to Hawai'i. These are the miles in which the voyaging canoe from Fenua'enata would have been looking for signs for a landfall. Nainoa is tired and anxious. He hardly sleeps at all at night and not more than an hour at a time in the day. For ten days high clouds have obscured the stars. He has steered mainly with the sun and the moon. The moon in its crescent carries the sun's shadow vertically near the equator, then more angled as they move north. The full moon on the horizon gives them a steering target. Dawn is the most important time, not just for the compass point of the sun's rising, but because the angle of the sun makes reading swells and seas and the weather of the day come easier. Mau, the Micronesian navigator, has thousands of dawns at sea in his mind. The Southern Cross as it moves lower and to the west convinces Nainoa that third-last day that they are 530 miles southeast of Hawai'i. But they see a land dove during the day. How could it have flown that distance between dawn and dusk?

They have passed through the equatorial doldrums. They have passed through that part of the ocean where the northwest swell of the northern hemisphere moves over the southeast swell of the southern and has given the distinctive pitch and roll movement of the canoe. Nainoa has learned to feel these different motions of the canoe from Mau Piaulug—by lying prone on the decking. Now they are at the most anxious time of their voyage, wondering whether they should trust their calculations and turn westward in the Hawaiian latitudes. In way-finding each day and night is a new calculation, a new assessment. Nainoa will find, when the voyage ends, what errors he made each night and morning in his placing of *Hokule'a*. He will find that his actual course weaves a line east and west over his presumed course. He will find too that his errors were random.

What seemed undeniable in Sharp's argument was that errors were cumulative and, once committed, drove canoes into oblivion. But the discovery over all of *Hokule'a*'s voyaging is that errors are random and tend to counter one another. But that does not relieve the tension at moments of critical commitment.

Tropic birds are plenty, but these are no sure sign of the direction of land. But there are *manu ku*, land doves too. The *Hokule'a* crew know land is near. They catch the angle of the North Star against the horizon and get a clear sighting of the Southern Cross. These convince them that their latitude calculations are right. On the second-last day Nainoa says they are 200 miles from the Big Island, but he nervously changes his calculations to 290 miles.

He tells of a moment in which he was close to losing confidence. The night was black, the winds strong, the waves twelve feet high.

> You keep the record of what you have done in your mind all the time. It is your history. If you forget it, you are lost. Keeping thirty days in the mind is difficult. We had two choices—to sail or to drop the sail and go nowhere . . . I gave up . . . I just gave up forcing myself to find answers. When I gave up forcing myself to find answers, somehow I knew. Then there was a break in the clouds and the moon showed— exactly as I thought it was supposed to be. Even when I saw it I was surprised. That's my most valued moment, that one.

All day on the last day, the clouds on the horizon seem stationary. Clouds at sea move. Clouds over land stay still. There is something different about the setting sun. They cannot say what, its colouring perhaps, as it catches the air around and above Hawai'i. They alter their course a little in its direction. It is in the right house of Nainoa's compass for land.

Then a stationary white cloud opens up and reveals the long gentle slope of Mauna Kea on Hawai'i. Nainoa says to himself:

> The way-finding at this moment seems to be out of my hands and beyond my control. I'm the one given the opportunity of feeling the emotions of way-finding, not yet ready to have a complete understanding of what is happening. It is a moment of self-perspective, of one person in a vast ocean given an opportunity of looking through a window into my heritage.

I think he is correct. All over the Sea of Islands, island peoples saw themselves in their canoes—in the canoe's making, in its parts, in its launching, in its voyaging. The canoe was an icon of all sorts of continuities of identity, an icon of a conjoining past and present. I don't have difficulty in believing that island peoples can recognise themselves in *Hokule'a* and embroider that recognition with all sorts of rebirths of traditional arts and crafts, with dance, poetry and song. Whatever the transformations of modernity that masquerade as discontinuities—religion, science, politics—the theatre of *Hokule'a*'s re-enactment is directed to that recognition, a new and an old encompassment in one.

Early in 1995, the theatre of re-enactment of voyaging canoes came to a climax. Seven voyaging canoes of the Sea of Islands collected at the sacred island of Ra'iatea in the Tahitian group, in preparation for an epic sail from Tahiti to Fenua'enata and then to Hawai'i. Three of the canoes were from Hawai'i—*Hokule'a, Hawai'iloa* and *Makali'i*; one from Tahiti—*Tahiti Nui*; one from Aotearoa—*Te Aurere*; two from Rarotonga—*Takitumu* and *Te Au o Tonga*.

By 1995 the voyages of the canoes from north to south, south to north, east to west, west to east, had long outlived their function as simply an argument against Andrew Sharp's denial of their possibility. They had become signs of the living vitality of a long cultural past. They had become empowering metaphors of identity. And that identity was a conjoined one—not just a sense of the legitimacy of their continuities within their individual island cultures. An identity of a shared nativeness to the Sea of Islands.

Taputapuatea on Ra'iatea was an ideal space to play out that conjoined identity. It was always a space larger than itself, always reaching out as well as receiving. It was the ritual ground of 'The Friendly Alliance' of islands. The mythic chants that were sung there were anthems of union and treaty. The themes of these chants were recognisable as far away as Aotearoa, Tonga and Hawai'i. It was Havai'iki (Sacred Home) to many Tahiti (Distant Places). Taputapuatea bred other Taputapuatea by establishment in shared foundation stone. 'Oro, its god, was a power over distance.

Catharsis, it seems to me, is not a piecemeal thing. It is whole and one. It is the reduction of complexity to simplicity in an instant. Rituals, on the other hand, can be piecemeal, blaring, empty, contradictory, driven by many forces. So the ritual at Taputapuatea to welcome and send the voyaging canoes from all over the Sea of Islands was uncomfortable, hot and boring to many there. The French officials, especially in Polynesia, are inclined to speak of such rituals as 'folkloric'. They bend to the politics in them with some cynicism, born of the belief that they are at least a boost to tourism. At Taputapuatea, anti-nuclear protest songs competed electronically with ancient chants and fundamentalist Christian hymns. The experiences of the thousands there were kaleidoscopic. But the catharsis was not. As the thousands took their leave, the social memory of it was one. They had looked into the past and seen the future. They were confident that a living culture was a metaphoric thing, and that they had seen the metaphor at work in their Sea of Islands.

The memories of Enata's first voyage to Hawai'i, three hundred years after the settlement of their Land, have long gone. We have to think that there was no return voyage from Hawai'i. The contrary forces of wind, weather and ocean were against the possibility of such a voyage, There are mythic memories in Hawai'i of voyages to Tahiti and back. Linguistics and anthropology tell us, too, that there was at least one voyage from Tahiti to Hawai'i. The Sea of Islands then seemed to have been encompassed. The far edges of that Sea became isolated for a thousand years. Then the Strangers came.

Honu

Timotete

5

Encompassing the Land

Encompass: to enfold a space with knowledge and the human spirit. The Land, now found and settled, is inspirited by Enata for perhaps 1800 years till that time in our story when Robarts, Kabris and Crook cross its beaches. That timespan is roughly that between Julius Caesar's invasion of Britain and the reign of King George III. That should warn us that any still-life image of Enata cultural ways over a few years is unlikely to be true to its 1800-year history. The ethnographic present of my description of the Land encompassed belongs to the years 1796–1814. I hope to offset the limitations of such a framing of a frozen moment in cultural time. I offer a 'map', a 'Brueghelesque painting', and a story of one year in the life of one man as a ethnography of how Enata encompassed their Land. What a 'map' and a 'Brueghelesque painting' might be I trust will become clear.

The Beach

The beach must have some priority in any story of beach crossings. Its deep time gives everything that happens on it a context. But in encounter history, the beach tends to lose its priority. The skewed nature of the sources tend to turn the storyteller to where the dramatics are explicit in the journals and papers of those who are literate. I will turn that around if I can. I know that there is a time coming when the descendants of the Sea People in their Sea of Islands will call on the deep time within them and write their histories with the proper priorities. That writing of a Native's rather than a Stranger's history has already begun.

But that does not relieve me of the responsibility of doing my best to tell my stories with their true context. I am loath to write descriptions of Enata ways frozen in a moment that never was, and divorced from my stories. So I experiment in describing Enata culture in such a way that the description will become memorable as the context of the stories I will tell in more focused mode.

I draw a 'map' of Fenua'enata. I do a 'Brueghelesque painting'. A 'map' is an outsider's view of a cultural territory. It is an attempt to describe the grammar of a culture, the system that gives all its particularities meaning. A 'map' gives the roles, rules and structural relationships that make a particular way of living distinctive. A 'map' is not necessarily true to an insider's understanding of how things actually are. Who among us does not feel that every effort of somebody else's to describe who we really are is not a caricature? Living is full of contingencies that demand interpretations of roles and rules rather than literal obedience to the 'map'.

A 'Brueghelesque painting' is brimful of living, kaleidoscopic, full of contingencies. But it is also framed. It is artful. I trust that the artfulness of my 'Brueghelesque painting' will prompt a viewer to realise how much else there is to be shown.

I hope to offset the otherness of my storytelling in these ways.

A 'Map' of Fenua'enata

We are standing on the top of our archaeological mound. It is crowded. Not only William Pascoe Crook, Joseph Kabris and Edward Robarts are there, but hundreds of others. All of them have put their experience of the otherness around them onto paper or canvas. They have written letters, journals, logs, notes, reports and scientific papers telling what they have seen. Sometimes these have been published. Mostly they have not. It has been a privilege in my life to hold most of these thousands of pieces of paper in my hands and to have read them. They rest now in the great national and university libraries and archives around the world—London, Paris, Washington, Los Angeles, Boston, Cambridge, Oxford, San Francisco, Sydney, Wellington. Or they are looked after in missionary archives—Rome, Honolulu, Taiohae. Or in small historical societies, whaling and maritime museums, learned academies—Cornwall, Connecticut; Nantucket, Falmouth, Greenwich, Washington Naval Dockyards; Nanterre, Rouen.

There is another group elbowing their way on to the top of our mound—the professional observers. They come to Fenua'enata with a sense of rescuing a dying culture in the 1920s and 1930s—the German Scholar Karl von den Steinen, the Americans E. S. Craighill Handy and his wife Willowdean, Ralph Linton, the French scholar Louis Rollin. Then there are the archaeologists—Robert Suggs, Yosihiko H. Sinoto, and the adventurer-scholar Thor Heyerdahl, and his colleague Bengt Danielsson, who spent the rest of his life in Oceania and gave us so much. Then those of us of a later, but not necessarily of a last, generation who see everything through the words and images of all of those who have gone before—Nicholas Thomas, Alfred Gell, John Kirkpatrick . . . and myself.

Too many eyes for any one vision of Fenua'enata? Yes, but they are the means of our 'being there'.

'Being there', being in touch with the real in a past that is beyond our experience and memory is reached, I like to think, by story. I would like to reach the real in Fenua'enata in an ethnographic present that could be defined as being between the years 1796 to 1814 by telling stories. I will tell them shortly. Before I do, I want to present a cultural 'map' of Fenua'enata, to make the reading of my stories easier.

William Pascoe Crook's 'Account of the Marquesas Islands' is our principal means of 'mapping' Fenua'enata. Remember though that the 'Crook' of the 'Account' is the beach-experiencing, twenty-year-old whitesmith

187

missionary, and the library-experiencing and text-composing intellectual doyen of the London Missionary Society, Samuel Greatheed, and the fifteen-year-old Enata boy-informant, Timotete.

That the Enata were 'savage', not just heathen, was Wlllliam Pascoe Crook's discovery and revelation in his 'Account'. That is one way in which he 'maps' Fenua'enata. His was as curiously a paradoxical discovery, as he was a curiously paradoxical man. He was confronted with scenes of extravagant violence and carelessness for life and person. Yet he was totally dependent on Enata's respect for him, whatever the disturbance of his presence. He reads their public cultural mask as violent, lewd, a contradiction to every Christian and natural virtue. But he also has a story to tell of their persons and their kindness and gentleness to him. He gives us the image of a most unmissionary missionary, as he joins forays and feasts wrapped in a woman's *ka'eu*, with a dog at his side. He loses himself among Enata, with few of the boundaries that missionaries usually make, more like a beachcomber than a man of God. That makes his 'map' special. He is a participant in what he observes. And he learns, as so many have learnt because of that participation, a little cultural relativism. He learns that others have different metaphors for the same values as his.

Crook arrived, as it turned out, at the beginning of Enata's dying. Calculating from his guesses, we could say Enata numbered some 50,000 to 75,000 in 1796. Within a hundred years they were less than 2000. Crook arrived in a period of terrible droughts and famines. And, with the intrusion of foreign diseases, the population did not recover from its downward trend from that date. His ethnography was not written as a monument to what was lost and gone. But neither does it seem to have been written as a weapon to destroy a heathen culture. It is remarkably lacking in diatribe and judgement. It is more willing to accept differences as an intellectual puzzle than to report them as fuel to fire anti-heathen enthusiasms. The 'map', the ethnography, is a monument nonetheless. Enata of 1796–97 only have existence in the records of those who came to change them. Enata and Aoe have a bound-together history.

There is a touch of brilliance in the 'Account' of the Fenua'enata which marks it as one of the most original, the most informed and the most insightful of all eighteenth-century ethnographic descriptions of the peoples of the Sea of Islands. Joseph Banks, Johann Reinhold Forster and William Anderson of the Cook expeditions, William Bligh and James Morrison of the *Bounty* and William Mariner, a beachcomber in Tonga, are among the most noted ethnographers of the time. All of them, with the exception of Morrison and Mariner, were shipboard commentators. While Banks' and Forster's contributions to botanical sciences were more lastingly significant than Crook's, none of their descriptions of Sea of Islands societies and environment have the fullness and sureness of the 'Account'. These observations are remarkable for a 19- to 22-year-old artisan of Plymouth with little education and exposed to culture shock that not many others might have endured.

There are two other significant qualities in the ethnography. One is that it offers an interpretive unity to the observed data. *Tapu* is 'mapped' as a structurally differentiating concept by which Enata themselves and the outside observer might make sense of Fenua'enata culture. The other significant quality of the 'Account' is that it offers not only a 'map' of the social structure of the Enata, it also gives a history of their actual social relations. Their society is drawn not merely in terms of its roles and rules. It also describes that society in terms of the idiosyncratic ways in which actions were performed by individuals. Being participants, making acute observations, seeing the general and describing the particular, are all ethnographic graces of high degree. And William Pascoe Crook had them all, no doubt assisted by the mature judgements of Samuel Greatheed and the linguistic knowledge of Timotete.

So let me draw a 'map'—a 'map'? No! A section—of Fenua'enata by courtesy of Crook, Robarts and all the rest.

Small universes

A universe—the kit of culturally identifying characteristics—is full but it is small in number of persons or in space. Such small universes boil with energy.

A cultural universe for Enata consisted in having these roles: *haka'iki* (chief), *tau'a* (sorcerer), *tuhuna o'ono* (ceremonial priest), *toa* (warrior), *tuhuna* (craftsmen), *pekio* (secondary husbands), *kai'oi* (dancers). This world is gendered, male, female and in-between. It is also divided by those who are *tapu* permanently or temporarily, and those who are common.

Crook tells us that there are some one hundred and fifty distinctive Enata groups distributed through the six inhabited islands of Fenua'enata. Population figures are notoriously unreliable for the eighteenth-century Pacific. Crook works on 'fighting men' as the basis for his estimates. So he tells us that Tahuata had 1200 and Nukuhiva 6000 fighting men. Hiva Oa, which he knows less well, has 10,000. Fatuiva, Ua Pou, Ua Huka, of which he has only hearsay knowledge, he thought had 5000, 1200 and 800 respectively. A multiple of three for every fighting man would make the total population of Fenua'enata in 1796–97 75,000. A population of 18,000 for Nukuhiva would seem about right from the estimates of Robarts, Langsdorff of the Russian expedition of 1803, and David Porter in 1813. By 1832, forty-five years, this 18,000 had dropped to 5331; by 1855, to 2700; by 1872, to 1568.

In 1796–97, the 18,000 population of Nukuhiva was divided into more than twenty communities, each with a full kit of Enata cultural roles. They were separated from each other by the physical barriers of mountain ridges and the social barriers of endemic hostilities. Crook listed thirteen groupings among the 4000 population of Tahuata.

The more largely populated valleys of Nukuhiva—Taiohae and Taipivai—would have had about a thousand people each. They in their turn were divided into five groupings. Again each had a full cultural kit. Maybe there would have been about fifty families in these small groups. More likely there would have been only about twenty-five households of twelve people.

William Alexander, a missionary from Hawai'i in 1833 on Nukuhiva, despairing at finding any authoritative figure who could govern the community or lead a conversion, characterised Enata as having 'a wild spirit of independence, accompanied by an unusual degree of self-consequence'. Many other visitors commented on the frenetic energy of Enata's cultural, political, and social systems. Let me illustrate that energy with another pointer in my 'map': the *koina* (feast).

Koina (Feast)

The *koina* was an ever present reality for Enata in its preparation, in its happening, in the debts of social obligation it left behind. Virtually all important moments of an individual's life and death, and all occasions of note in the social group, were celebrated by *koina*, large and small. Peace, war, death, birth, marriage, puberty, tattooing, naming, circumcision, friendship, departures, exchange of property, were all occasions of *koina*. The universal manner in which contracts were made, alliances established, occasions celebrated was to collect together in carefully defined groups, participate in the bounty of the individual or group responsible for the *koina*, and make the occasion memorable with chants and dances. The scale of these *koina* varied greatly. Some were celebrated only by a family; some were celebrated by groups of the *tapu* class. Often the people of one *haka'iki* would feast together. Sometimes a whole island would come together. The essence of *koina* lay in the accumulation of social energy and material wealth so that it could be expended to the social prestige of individual and group. Months would be spent in collecting and laying aside food, in learning new dances and songs, in ornamenting houses, in constructing and repairing *tohua*. The *koina* itself would last for days and sometimes for weeks.

We do not have a precise calendar of *koina* in this early period, only an assurance by both Crook and Robarts that feasting was constant. David Darling, a London Missionary Society missionary, recorded events from May to August 1835 in the valley of Vaitahu on Tahuata. Iotete was then successor to Tainai, who in Crook's and Robarts' time had been *haka'iki* of the valley, and whom we are about to meet. Iotete was a transitional figure and suffered the tension of playing *haka'iki* in the changing conditions of cultural decline. He had declared to the missionaries that his people were dying because they had stopped feasting. On 13 May, Iotete's wife began building a *tapu* house to hold a *mau*, or a memorial *koina* for her father. At the same time a *koina hue* was being prepared and celebrated in nearby Hanamiai. A *koina hue* was a competitive *koina* in which two parties tried to outdo one another in feasting, dancing and chanting. On the 16th a *hoki*, a dancing troupe, of thirty men arrived from Hiva Oa and spent the day beating drums, chanting, dancing. As they danced they would call on the names of persons from whom they expected to get pigs or cloth or ornaments. A few days later a canoe came from the east coast valley of Hanateio with food and kava for a *mau* and for some unnamed occasion for Iotete's son. After a week's feasting and intoxication, Iotete had his head shaved in preparation for going to Ivaiva to plant sweet potatoes. Because of a sudden need to complete a canoe for a raid on Hiva Oa, on 5 June all the kava was burnt. The canoe makers needed to be released of the *tapu* necessary to drink kava in order to be established in the *tapu* necessary to build a canoe.

On 30 June a messenger from Hanatetena, a valley on the east coast of Tahuata, arrived begging for dishes for a *mau* in memory of their *haka'iki's* father. It was to be a very great *koina* to which most of the island would go. Some of the women had begun to learn new songs and for this they had made themselves *tapu*. Begging (*moko*) was a ritualised part of the *koina*.

The *haka'iki*, or a representative wearing his ornamentation, would formally visit different parts of the island and ask for food or utensils or *tapa* cloth. He would ask for quantities proportioned to his rank. On 3 July another messenger arrived at Vaitahu, this time with an invitation to attend a *koina* at Hanatefau.

The women, who were learning new songs, were adding to their repertoire the songs of a Nukuhivan woman who had visited them on a whaler. The women constantly rehearsed their songs for the people of the valley, because Iotete's approval was needed before they could present the songs at the *koina*. On 9 July, there were two *mau* on the island, one at Hanatetena and another at Hanaiopu. Both were for *haka'iki* many years dead. For both, pigs were sent from Vaitahu as tokens of respect. At this time Iotete himself was building a *fa'e taina* (a ceremonial *tapu* house) for another *haka'iki*'s sister's child. On 14 July a new fishing net was put into the sea for the first time and a large number of fish were caught and distributed to highly ranked *tapu* men. In the meantime preparations for the *mau veahue* for Iotete's wife were becoming more intensive. A number of men had become *tapu* in order to go fishing in a new canoe for this *koina*. There were two more *koina* in preparation on the west side of the island and two on the east. The two on the west were merely feasts for friendship; the two on the east were memorials. Again on 17 July a number of young men at Vaitahu became *tapu* in order to be tattooed. They began the first day with a *koina* and songs. The next day, Iotete's wife finally had her *koina*. It was 'for the purpose of showing the rank of those for whom it was designed', wrote Darling. Only two or three women were present. Still another *koina haaepa* was held on 20 July to allow Iotete to go to a great feast. He had been in *tapu* from dances and needed a *koina* to relieve him of that *tapu*. The day after this, a messenger arrived from Hapatoni with an invitation to Iotete and his family to go to a *koina* to consecrate a *tapu* house called *fa'e fanai* that was being built for the next child that Iotete's wife would have. The *haka'iki* of Hapatoni, a valley hostile to Vaitahu, was nonetheless going to adopt the child. News also came of another *mau* at Hanaiopu. In the next week there was more tattooing and a *koina* at Hanamiai. Two messengers from Hanatetena came on 6 August. They were dressed in their best finery and cried out their invitation in a loud voice. Their *mau* was to commemorate a great *haka'iki* who had been lost at sea some time before. At this time, said Darling, nearly all the people had become *kai'oi*. They feasted, he said, 'for showing off and for exalting themselves in the eyes of the other parts of the island: it arises from a spirit in Iotete to show as it were his greatness'.

Contingency

Contingency I see as a creative cultural skill that Enata used well. A 'map' of Enata culture would say that title and authority descended through a *haka'iki*'s firstborn child. Contingency means that being 'firstborn' was as much a matter social recognition as actually being born first. Adoption, multiple marriages and infant marriage were used to manipulate rules to the opportunities of a political moment. Fatherhood itself was a social attribution when the twelve-month-old infant was said to father the child of an adult woman.

Contingency was the ability to see the *haka'iki*'s real authority and bend to it when others were more wealthy or more physically powerful. Contingency was the ability to see when and where godliness was in human or in nature, when the spaces of *tapu* worked and when they did not. Contingency was the ability to let cultural things lie fallow for a time and find them renewed with intensity.

Common people

Crook saw the fundamental social division among Enata as being between the 'common people' and the *tapu* group. He meant by that distinction something more than an economic and social division between wealthy and poor, powerful and weak. Not all commoners were poor or without power and social prestige; the most *tapu* men were not necessarily the wealthiest. For Crook, 'common people' were those who could lay no claim to an extension of their personal *tapu*. Among them were the socially depressed and women, but also among them were men who had given away their *tapu* to become *pekio* or *kai'oi*. These men were not necessarily socially depressed.

Crook gave no word for 'common people'. That group of them who were socially depressed were known as *mataenata* (the sly people), *vaitahu noa* (common water), *kikino* (poor, mean), *tupe noa* (insignificant), *maunoa* (dark people). They were servants. They fetched wood and water, collected breadfruit and coconuts, and lived on the properties of landowners and guarded them against theft. They dressed food, nursed and minded children, watched the fruit. They had no separate households nor could they be said to have married. They were subject to sudden retribution from landowners for thieving and carelessness, and were sometimes arbitrarily killed by the powerful. Different social behaviour, exposure to sun and weather, different diet, different codes of beauty established a discernible physical difference between the 'common people' and the *tapu*. Langsdorff in 1803 saw them as small-bodied, with a belly disproportionately large, of slow and trailing walk and of a dark colour. They contrasted with the light-skinned, well-formed women and the tall, strongly built men of the higher classes. From among them *heana*, the victims for sacrifice, were likely to be taken. Their death as *heana* gave them status. In the land of their afterlife, Hava'iki, they lived with the chiefs.

Women

Women were the other commoners in Crook's sense. We have seen that women's sexuality was a threat, but only one of many, to *tapu*. Crook's own account makes it clear that there were some women who at times were *tapu* and others who, while not *tapu*, were socially and politically much stronger than many males. He wrote of girls of principal families being removed to *tapu* places at puberty and their menstruation being used as a means of reckoning time for some period afterwards. Young girls were under *tapu* to learn song. Women of rank built their own *tapu* houses in which they held their own memorial feasts, *mau*. Yet it was true that there was no *tapu* which male and female would share. Those social customs which were seen as specifically female, such as the bleaching of skin with *papa* juice, were taken as signs, when used by males, that they had given up their *tapu* status.

Kai'oi

Kai'oi were a group of young men and women who were excluded from the *tapu* class by virtue of their assumption of certain female ornamentations and cosmetics. They danced and sang at the *tohua* during *koina*. They lived together in houses they built especially for themselves which, according to David Darling, they called '*tute auri*', a word, he said, that 'conveys the idea of regardlessness'. There they would prepare their dances and learn their songs.

Pekio

Pekio have always been a mysterious institution in Fenua'enata ethnography. They shocked the sensibilities of early European visitors and were the object of their prurient curiosity. Polygamy visitors could understand, but polyandry was, as Edward Robarts said, a 'pill hard to digest'. They saw *pekio* as secondary husbands. The Russians said gallantly that a *pekio* was the 'guardian of the Queen's virtue who was rewarded by the enjoyment of that which they protected'. Later anthropologists seemed happier to rationalise the custom as a social mechanism by which a greater number of males was given access to a scarce resource in a demographically unbalanced society. Other anthropologists have accepted the fact that the *pekio*'s sexual function was probably subordinate to their economic and social function. Edward Robarts, who lived with the same families as Crook, stressed the role of *pekio* as substitute in those skewed marriages between infant males and mature women. *Pekio* acted as genitors of children who would nevertheless gain rank and status from their infant fathers. Crook had a more structural perception of *pekio*. Introducing the concept of *tapu*, he wrote that all men employed in the service of women lost their *tapu* status. *Pekio* were *tahu ahi*, firemakers. They were common among the wealthier families and Crook was scandalised to note that some women had many *pekio* in succession. The wife of Kiatonui's youngest son was reported to have had forty. *Pekio* did not necessarily lose personal prestige with their *tapu*. Crook reported them as confidential friends of the husbands, and Kiatonui's *pekio* was a wealthy man with much property. He also seems to have acted as warrior in Kiatonui's place. Kiatonui had more interest in priestly ritual than in fighting.

Names

For Enata, names were important but not permanent. They exchanged names for one thing, and with the names, titles, rights to hospitality and sanctuary, whole networks of consanguineal and affinal kin. They liked a descriptive name, pertinent to the character of the person who carried it or to the occasion on which it was acquired. A man might be called Tuhuka ('Wise'), or Tutaikivi ('Birdshit') for his tattoos, or Opevahine ('Woman's Arse') for his looks. A child would not carry its father's name or even say it. To do so, they said, was *kaikai*, eating his flesh. Enata took a new name at every remarkable occasion of their lives. It was as if these moments were new beginnings and individuals were constantly being remade by the circumstances of their lives.

Life's passages

There were many occasions in an individual Enata's life that were marked in a special way. Birth, puberty, tattooing, marriage, death were the most notable occasions. Most males of the *tapu* class would have a superincision (a single longitudinal slit in the foreskin on the dorsal aspect of the glans). Most males would also be tattooed because there was some social opprobrium directed at those that did not. However, not every individual was 'born', 'married', or 'died.' 'Birth', 'marriage', and 'death' were social acts. They were performed only for individuals whose status was established and reflected in the ceremony.

No doubt every individual, *kikino* and *tapu* alike, was born with such ceremony as protected the mother from dangerous spirits and gave the child its first care in washing, anointing, massaging and purging. For those who were to be born into the high *tapu* status or into some close relationship with those who held *tapu*, the moment was more careful. A special house was made. Everything that concerned the child, its food, its clothing, the disposal of the birth remains and its own excrement were surrounded with the strictest *tapu*. Gérauld Chaulet, a Sacred Heart missionary, described the ceremonies surrounding the birth of a *tamahaka'iki*, a firstborn son of a *haka'iki*. The ceremony was called *kohihika* and was the making of a chief. For a whole year the infant was separated from the community in an isolated house deep in the valley. The house was called *fa'e hakaiko*. Five days after birth, or after an initial and brief suckling, the child was taken to this special house by *tuhuna makuvaipu*, a priest who would live with the child for a whole year. *Koina haikai pito mavae*, a sumptuous feast in which the *makuvaipu* was fed on turtle, the most *tapu* of catches, marked the moving of the child through the roof of its birth-house (not the door) to its residence. The mother and all the people of the area were present. They were dressed in white *tapa*, their foreheads decorated with kava leaves. Nothing profaning could take place in the valley, no fires, no rubbing with oil, no noise. Through all that first year there were special *koina*. At first there was *koina pitopiki* to celebrate the first bathing, then a more splendid *koina vaihana* when the child was bathed more publicly. About the eleventh month the child was displayed in an obelisk-shaped hut (*fa'e pukoo*), dressed in the turtleshell diadems and white beards that were the *haka'iki* insignia. Finally, the year ended with *koina ohohava*, a profanation ceremony that ended the long *tapu*. In these ways the child was set apart, displayed in its sacredness, made the focal point of those who in coming together acknowledged their common interest, was invested with the symbols of *tapu* but not the actuality of power, and finally was made in the image of Enata's expectancies for their *haka'iki*. He was 'born'.

Adoption, a characteristic custom through all the Sea of Islands, was developed to a high degree among Enata. Children would be solicited before birth and even, at times, before conception. At adoption, there would be a formal exchange of gifts in *koina* between the contracting parties. Their size and value was determined by the relative rank of the parents. As distinct from name exchange, social relations in adoption were not so much added as transferred, so that the adopted child was fitted precisely into its new family. Later missionaries were scandalised at the melodramatic possibilities such strict transfers entailed. Brother in this new relationship might marry natural sister. Mostly observers were amazed at how skewed relationships became by the practice. Young children became grandparents; brothers became cousins. Observers were a little disturbed to see how easily a child might be separated from its natural mother. They were consoled by the fact that the adopted child was treated with full affection and care, as if the fiction of their new status was 'real'.

Enata were also discriminating about whom they ceremonially 'married'. *Kikino* were not married at all. The liaisons they established among themselves were loose and involved no exchanges. Of their family structures nothing can be learnt at all. Among the *tapu*, relationships were more structured but not necessarily more permanent. Both Robarts and Crook described the exchange of gifts that occurred between families whose sons and daughters were seen to be married. Of the examples of marriage we have within the *tapu* group, we have cases of alliances that lasted through the lifetime of two persons, and cases of successive alliances. There were marriages between two infants who returned to their parents after a stay with one another for a short time. There were marriages between infants and adults. If marriage alliances had political and social functions, the union, however, seemed less important than its product. The first child of the union, whether conceived in it or not, was the valuable element. Their child accrued what was sacred in both its parents, enlarged the *tapu* of each of them, became a focal point for all who were related to them. The child was also attached to the land. The land that was the child's was marked out at birth. Trees whose produce was exclusively the child's were planted. Even secular exchange of land was not ratified until continuity was established by the new owner having a child. Between grandparent and grandchild there was a special relationship. The soul of a grandfather was believed to be transmitted to the body of a grandchild, and an unfruitful wife was sometimes made to lie beneath the corpse of her husband's father in order to become pregnant. It is clear from naming practices that between firstborn and their grandparents there was an exchange of names and an exchange of dignity.

Sacrifice

Small sacrifices, with every man his own priest, were a constant and daily practice among Enata. Every first morsel of a dish would be flung into a corner or into the thatches for the *atua*. More ceremonially, portions of a crop, especially of breadfruit, and of a catch, especially of fish, or portions of the first fruit of some instrument such as a net or a canoe would be placed in sacred places. Nothing in the commentaries of Strangers suggests that these divine tariffs played any more than an incidental part in Enata's daily and religious life.

There were other sacrifices, however, that demanded a far higher emotional involvement. There were *heana*, human victims that were sought in times of crisis, such as the failure of the breadfruit crop, or the death of a *haka'iki* or *tau'a*. It is difficult to come to a full understanding of *heana* because the practice was associated with the eating of human flesh, and Enata reacted very sensitively to strangers' disapproval of the custom and revealed little. In fact sacrifice of *heana* was merely an extension of that ceremonial setting aside of portions of important foods and products already mentioned. When *heana* were taken, most would be eaten and some would be taken to the *me'ae* of the *tau'a* where they would be hung with other offerings. Although Stranger observers used such words as 'altars', there is no evidence that Enata developed any conceptions or rituals of mediation in sacrifice.

The dominant idiom in the pursuit and capture and dispatch of *heana* was a fishing one. The chants in the canoes as they set out in pursuit of *heana* were fishing chants, and the *tapu* activities surrounding their departure and return were the same as those used in fishing for turtle (*honu*), which was the most *tapu* of all catches. The *heana* itself was referred to as *metau heana*, hooked victim, and its capture was symbolised in the fishhooks and lines that were placed in its lips, eyes, ears and nose after death. The fruit of the *noni* was put in the *heana*'s mouth as bait for other *ika*, and two small baskets (*kete hakaoho*), containing hooks and bait, were attached to the *heana*'s arms. The bodies of *heana* were given the reddish tinge of the *fanatoto* fish by being covered with red ochre (*kaaea*). The red flower of the *koute* (hibiscus) was put in the ears of *heana*. In the end *heana* were strung on trees in the *me'ae*, just as sacrificial fish were strung in the fishermen's sacred place.

The number of *heana* is impossible to know. One hundred to two hundred a year throughout all the Fenua'enata would probably not be too large an estimate. *Heana* were most likely to be women of the poorer class, as these were most exposed to capture when they collected shellfish along the shore or roots and berries further inland.

Haka'iki, tau'a, tuhuna

Missionaries and administrators looked for political centralisation. Traders looked for that sort of authority that would make trade on the beach orderly. Perhaps that was why the role of the *haka'iki* was seen as paradoxical. Strangers looked for conspicuous display of wealth that might signify high political status, but they could not see it in the tattoos, the reddish *hiapo tapa* cloth or the *pavahina* (old men's white beards) that were the symbols of *haka'iki* status. They looked for an authority that could transmit instructions along a permanent structure of command and that could support that structure with force. So they could not recognise non-administrative authority as expressed and legitimated in the cycles of exchange that marked moments in the life of individuals and of the group.

The truth was that the *haka'iki* were at the centre of Enata society in time and space. They anchored the present very firmly in the past. Not only were the *haka'iki* the latest in a long line of significant figures going back to the *atua*, all of which played their part in ensuring good crops and full catches, but *haka'iki* also continuously drew the attention of their groups to this fact by the constant memorial feasts to their dead ancestors. *Haka'iki* were at the centre of all movements of material goods. They did not accumulate wealth so much as act as the instrument of its distribution in the feasts which were a highly developed feature of Enata society.

Crook's description of the *haka'iki* role and their concrete actions makes two points. Firstly, their authority was not disturbed by a wide dispersal of ownership of property or by a wide distribution of important roles and skills, or even by competition from junior descent lines. In any grouping of Enata there could be individuals who exercised physical force and resolved conflict without reference to the *haka'iki*. There could be individuals who exercised critical roles, such as priest, warrior, fisherman, who were not *haka'iki* or even in the *haka'iki* family. Yet all individuals exercised their roles and their skills and enjoyed the resources of their environment only under the *tapu* of their *haka'iki*. The second point of interest to come from Crook's description was that personality had an important part to play in the interpretation of the *haka'iki*'s role. Kiatonui on Nukuhiva preferred ceremony to fighting. Tainai on Tahuata was a restless pocket-Napoleon. Yet both expressed their position in the structure of Enata society with the same cultural metaphors of *tapu*, feast and sacrifice.

Tau'a was another pivotal role in Enata society. Edward Robarts called *tau'a* 'prophets'. He had no intention to make the theoretical distinction between prophet and priest. He was only describing the *tau'a*'s role as diviner and medium. The distinction, however, between prophets (*tau'a*), men of disturbance who had direct contact with the divine, and priests (*tuhuna o'ono*), men of establishment who were guardians of what was traditional and ceremonial, was quite apt for Enata society.

Crook said that *tau'a* were completely distinct from *tuhuna o'ono*. No person was both. Among the *tau'a* he saw a distinction between *tau'a atua*, who were living gods, and the more numerous male and female *tau'a*, who were sorcerers. Later descriptions distinguish a wide range of the latter according to their different sorcery practices. The only tasks *tuhuna o'ono* and *tau'a* had in common, according to Crook, were in curing diseases. However, there is some suggestion that, while *tau'a* used mainly magical means, *tuhuna* used medical lore and surgery. The *tuhuna*'s other functions were to remember, teach and sing sacred songs and to give every social act under *tapu* its meaning with their chants.

Tuhuna were an integral part of ordinary social life. Junior as well as senior members of the *haka'iki*'s descent line were widely represented among them. Crook insisted that *tuhuna*, as distinct from *tau'a*, did not inherit their roles. *Tuhuna* achieved their role and eminence in it as a social goal. *Tau'a*, in one sense, were outside ordinary social life. They were a frightening, demanding and erratic force in Enata society. Permanently or temporarily possessed by gods, they announced the desires of the gods (*atua*), divined the future, controlled maleficent forces. They were, however, also part of daily anxieties and their alleviation. Offerings of all sorts were made to them. They killed, maimed and made sick those who did not placate them. Above all, in times of crisis they called for human sacrifice. Their own death was always a signal that men would come fishing for sacrificial victims.

Neither *tuhuna o'ono* nor *tau'a* represented a challenge to the central position of the *haka'iki* in the social reality of Enata. The *tuhuna o'ono*, as well as the secular *tuhuna* (craftsmen), were participants in the *tapu* of the *haka'iki* and had no basis outside him to challenge him. It was his line they celebrated in genealogy and song: it was the occasions in his and his children's lives that they ritualised. The traditions they guarded belonged to him. The rhythm of social life they marked found meaning in his *tapu*. *Tau'a*, on the other hand, had an idiosyncrasy that denied them a structural challenge. They became wealthy with their sorcery and were perhaps in that way a potential political threat. But they were also factionalised into competing guilds of sorcerers and were neutralised as centres of political tension. If their hold over Enata minds was strong, their calls for sacrifice and war were in the end a means for the *haka'iki* to demonstrate and reinforce their own *tapu*.

Haka'iki, tau'a, tuhuna—and indeed, *toa, pekio* and *kai'oi*—were closely bound together. The bond was *tapu*. They were not bound in some pyramid of social power which others shared in some graded and lesser degree. The factors that distributed social capital, such as personal skill, force, inheritance and marriage, affected *haka'iki* and all alike. There were, indeed, individuals who might outstrip *haka'iki* in all areas of social capital—save one, *tapu*. Because *tapu* was the currency that gave all else value, the economic, political and social powers of *tau'a, tuhuna* and *toa* were meaningful through the *haka'iki*.

In the *haihai heana*, the sacrificial ceremony, the *tuhuna o'ono* chanted a litany. '*Metau a Tavaki. Etué tike. Metau a Taiko. Etué tike*—This hook belongs to Tavaki. What a fish! This hook belongs to Taiko. . .'. Down through the long line of *atua* and forebears, each had helped catch this *ika* (fish). The hooks belonged to the *haka'iki*'s line, and their qualities were enumerated. The genealogies themselves were a line and the *haka'iki* its hook. '*Etué. Amo mai te aku*', they chanted as they brought the *ika* to the *me'ae*. 'What a fish!', they sang and made an onomatopoeic litany on puns on their words for fish, the sounds of pleasurable eating and the poles that held the *heana*. The *haka'iki* was the support of his people.

Vaitahu and Taiohae

1790–1806

Enata in 1797 had been settled in the valley of Taiohae on Nukuhiva for probably 2000 years. The valley of Vaitahu on Tahuata was probably settled for 1500 years. The people at Taiohae, when we come to know them, were the Teii—in age-old hostility with the Taipi. The people of Vaitahu were the Hema. They too were in constant war with their neighbours on the island, the Ahutini. Hema and Ahutini had broader alliances across the two islands of Hiva Oa and Tahuata. Hema were Nuku. Ahutini were Tane. Nuku and Tane were the legendary brothers who were founders of their peoples, as Taipi and Teii were of theirs in the north.

The Nuku in the south comprised the Naiki, Tui and Pikina people in the northwest and southwest valleys of Hiva Oa (Hanamenu, Atuona and Taaoa) and the Hema and Mioi on the western coast of Tahuata (Vaitahu). The Tane comprised the Pa'ahatai, Etuoho, Vaiui, Moea and Ha'amau on the northeast and southeast valleys of Hiva Oa (Puamau, Haneuapa, Hanamate) and the Ahutini who occupied the southwest, southeast and northeast valleys of Tahuata (Hapatoni, Hanateio).

So the groupings in the northwest–southwest of Hiva Oa, and the southwest of Tahuata were in loose (we will see how loose) alliance as Nuku. The groupings in the northeast–southeast of Hiva Oa and in the southwest–southeast–northeast of Tahuata are in similar loose alliance. William Pascoe Crook, as we shall see, crossed his beach principally among the Nuku (and the Teii at Taiohae). Edward Robarts crossed his beach principally among the Tane (and the Teii at Taiohae). Jean Kabris crossed his beach principally among the Tane on Tahuata and the Taipi on Nukuhiva.

1790. Anchor at Vaitahu. Look at the head of the bay, eastward. To the left, and north, is a high rocky headland reaching out beyond the beach. To the right, and south, another less prominent headland reaches out beyond the beach. Beyond that southern headland is another inlet. It looks deserted, and it is.

Fortified Pass

Path to Hapatoni

Path to Hanate

Me'ae Iomavaepu

Tohua Tenuu Apita

Tohua Vahanekua

French Ambuscade

Tahus Waters

Paepae Tainai

Paepae Hitihiti

Tohua Tutukokina

French Fort

Tohua Vahiuhi

Rolled stone beach

Josiah Roberts'
Shipyard

Hanamiai

VAITAHU

Beyond the beach, the broad face of the valley angles back. The ridges on either side narrow till they run into the wall made by the mountain ridge that is the spine of the island, north and south. At this point the ridge is 3300 feet high, and 15 to 35 feet wide. The top is often lost in cloud. When it is not, there are two or three palisaded structures to be seen clinging to the side of the ridge. They are fortifications, large enough to be places of refuge. They guard the tracks that go east into a valley called Hanateio and south to a valley called Hapatoni. East and south are enemy territory. The Ahutini are always threatening.

At Vaitahu, the vegetation reaches down to the foreshore. There are no habitations to be seen. It is too dangerous to live close to the water. There are a few fishing *va'a* on the beach. There are another twenty or so *va'a* in the valley hidden away or disassembled. They are too valuable to be left where raiding parties can destroy them.

A stream runs down the valley. It runs deep into the rocks, a sign that it rages at times. This stream is Vaitahu, 'Tahu's Waters'. Tahu is an *atua*. He babbles. That is the godliness in this stream. It babbles. Tahu is the *atua* of the *kai'oi*, the libertine young men and women of the valley. He needs to be present for successful abortions. It is not right that the sexual freedom of the young should lead to birth.

There is a house visible on its stone platform. It is close to the water in the lee of the northern headland. It has a decayed, unkempt, look. Actually it is more monument than habitation. This is Paepae Hitihiti. Hitihiti was a seventeen- or eighteen-year-old Pora Poran with a penchant for travel and a sense of theatre. James Cook took Hitihiti with him on his circuit of southern waters in 1774. Hitihiti would one day dramatise his travels in the theatre of the *ari'oi*—Tahiti's equivalent to Fenua'enata *kai'oi*. He had arrived with Cook at Vaitahu on 8 April 1774.

Hitihiti had much to tell Enata of these strangers who were the first to come from beyond the sky for centuries. He would have told them—because it was a horror that had entered his soul—how one of Cook's men, Richard Pickersgill, had bought from the Maori the head of a young boy killed in battle at Totara-nui, a bay on the northeastern tip of the south island of Aotearoa (New Zealand), and had the head with him on the *Resolution*. Hitihiti would have told how another of Cook's men, Charles Clerke, had carved a slice of flesh from the cheek of that head, then grilled it over a fire. When Clerke offered the barbecued flesh to a Maori, the Maori took it and ate it with rapturous expressions of pleasure, licking his fingers. A bit of theatre in itself. No doubt the Englishmen didn't see the mockery in it. Then Clerke offered the cooked meat to other sailors—some of them vomited in response—then to Hitihiti. Hitihiti stood transfixed, 'as if metamorphosed into a Statue of Horror'. He then burst into tears and told them all 'they were Vile men and he was no longer their friend'.

So Enata heard from someone who could speak and understand their language their first truths about the strangers. They were cannibals! There was more. Hitihiti brought with him red feathers from Tonga—from Hava'iki no less. Legendary heroes had gone to Tonga from Fenua'enata in search of red feathers. Hitihiti had done what heroes had done. They kept Paepae Hitihiti *tapu* for decades after.

In 1790, Honu, the *haka'iki* who had welcomed Cook and Hitihiti to Vaitahu, was recently dead. The turmoil of the 'fishing' expeditions that followed his death was over and the cycle of memorial feasts was begun. His body lay in its *va'a* in the *tapu* house among the compound of houses that were his son's. His son, not his firstborn child, but his firstborn male child, was now *haka'iki* of the Hema at Vaitahu. His name was Tainai.

We have portraits of Honu and Tainai. Honu's portraits are a drawing attributed to William Hodges, the artist of the *Resolution*, and an engraving after another portrait by Hodges. Honu looks grand, even arabesque, with flowing cloth over his shoulders and chest. He is wearing his *uikawa*, a pearlshell and tortoiseshell head ornament, an object of much comment by Cook's people, the like of which is now to be found in many museums around the world. The coconut-fibre band around his forehead is topped with tail feathers of the frigate bird. His tattoos as represented by Hodges look more like a phrenologist's map of the skull than any indigenous design. Honu wears a crescent-shaped wooden gorget studded with the red and black seeds of the *Abrus precatorius*. One has the feeling that this is a studio portrait with the ornaments, no doubt on the table before Hodges, superimposed on his memory of Honu, 'The Chief at Sta Christina'.

Tainai's portrait is more realistic. It was drawn by a somewhat distraught and ill-fated young man, William Gooch, in March 1792. No 'noble savage' here. Just a scruffy, bearded, totally tattooed wild man. He is leaning on what looks like a spear with a pig's head hanging from its tip. Had he looked a little closer, young William would probably have seen that it was not a pig's head but a human skull with pig's tusks attached as incisors, pearlshell in the eye sockets and a wooden snout in the nasal fossa. The 'spear' was a 20-foot *toa* wood staff. It was a *kouvai*, a sort of bishop's crook or royal sceptre, a staff of power and authority. Tainai was to give his staff to Captain Wilson of the mission ship *Duff*, in exchange—we might wonder—for William Pascoe Crook.

Tainai had few other external signs of his chiefliness. He wasn't a man for bodily ornament. No exotic hairdo for him, either. No topknots. No shaven skull and horns of hair. No elongated earlobes. Visitors to his island used to remark that he could readily disappear into the ruck and turmoil of an Enata crowd.

Tainai was more a man of action than ornament, although he was *pahutiki*, 'wrapped in images'. Ornament enough! He made the lines of power in Vaitahu run through him, nonetheless. He was not born to power, as perhaps our 'map' of Fenua'enata suggests a *haka'iki* should have been. He was not firstborn. Three sisters were born to Honu before him. His eldest sister was called Vahinetapu, 'Sacred Woman'. Tainai, like his father, Honu, would also have a firstborn daughter. She would be called Vahinetapu as well. There is another axis of power at work at Vaitahu.

Listen to William Wales describe a visit by Honu to the *Resolution*. Honu is almost certainly accompanied by his daughter Vahinetapu. I wish I could describe the gestures and bodily movements, the personal spaces, the looks and glances, and hear the talk that drew Wales to his judgements about Vahinetapu, but I can't. Our gaze is too fogged and filtered when the experience of otherness is put on paper.

> Hitherto we had not been indulged with the sight of one Woman since we came to these Islands: but this forenoon a party of several Hundreds of the Natives came down with one of their Chiefs at their Head in great pomp and form, and amongst them one Woman. She certainly was, or appeared to be considerably on the wrong side of thirty; but notwithstanding that was in the opinion of Most who saw her one of the most beautiful women that has been seen at any of the Islands in these sea. She was clad from head to foot pretty much in the same Manner, and with the same sort of Cloth as the Women of Otaheitee are. She was remarkably fair; but had some freckles on her Nose and Cheeks, and her Feature[s] were extreamly regular, soft, and agreeable, and her whole deportment meek affable, and apparently, modest in the Utmost Degree so that if this was a just sample their women must be exceedingly desirable. There was along with her a Man who carried in his Arms an exceeding beautiful Girl about

Tainai, haka'iki of Vaitahu

6 Years old which they gave to understand was hers, from this circumstance & the attention which seemed paid to her by those which were About her I concluded that she was of some Rank amongst them & that Curiosity had brought her down, rather on this day than any other, as thinking probably it might be done with more safety: but some of our Gentlemen, who it must be owned are much quicker sighted, in matters of this sort than Me, were *positive* she was brought down for a *certain purpose*, and I was near getting my self into danger by doubting it. All that can be said to the Matter is, *that if it was so* either the Women of this Island are ill qualified for, or the Men who brought her down were bitter bad judges in the Choice of a Whore seeing that there did not appear to be the least spark of Concupiscence in any one feature or Action; on the contrary her whole Person and demeanour bespoke her one of that sort of Women which a Man of any tolerable degree of Modesty could never think of Attempting with success.

Tainai's principal heritage from his father Honu was an island cleared of one of Hema's main enemies, the Tupohe. Honu literally cleared Tahuata of Tupohe. Some 2000 of them were killed. Only a niece of Honu and her *pekio* survived by fleeing to Hiva Oa. In the way of Enata politics such a final solution to everlasting hostilities was only possible with a sudden imbalance in power relations. The Tupohe were allies of the Ahutini in their enmity to the Hema. The Ahutini turned on the Tupohe and now, with the Hema as allies, did most of the killings of the Tupohe.

The destruction of the Tupohe left Tahuata's sixteen inhabited valleys divided between the Hema and the Ahutini. They were neighbours in their principal valleys of residence, the Hema at Vaitahu, the Ahutini at Hapatoni. Their valleys were divided by a high ridge with its fortifications. Their two bays on the southwest side of Tahuata provided the only feasible anchorage for the Strangers' ships that after 1790 came ever more frequently. If they came from the southwest, they would happen on Hapatoni and anchor there. If they came from the east around the northern tip of Tahuata, as they more usually did, they anchored at Vaitahu.

Tainai's story through the twenty-five years of his life, 1790–1806, turns around his management of the old realities in The Land and the new realities of the Strangers' intrusions. These intrusions are sometimes measured in days for the ships that suddenly appear in the bay, and in years for the beachcombers, missionary and secular, that stay on the island. The glimpses that the Strangers get of Tainai's story were partial and focused fundamentally on his relationships with themselves—how they managed the chaos of their visits, how they were supplied, how they prevented and punished thefts. A story of Tainai that is less tangential to the old realities of The Land has to be a little 'Brueghelesque' in ambition. It has to catch something of that sixteenth-century Dutch artist's particular and total vision. Our canvas of old realities in The Land will be a still-life composition of the places, people, occasions and objects, small as they may be, that represent some sort of totality of living in The Land. Let's paint it.

A 'Brueghel' for Vaitahu

On the edge, all round the canvas, are the vegetation, the land- and sea-creatures that sustain Enata living in all its aspects—in their seasons, in their catastrophes, in the craftspeople that exploit them. In the body of the canvas are a small group of persons acting out all the sacramental occasions of living that inspirit an individual's and a community's life from birth to death and beyond. Here, too, are places, sacred and secret, open and public, where the social dramas of living are played out. In the centre we can make out Tainai, playing out the ways the networks of power at Vaitahu run through him. Scattered about in the bottom corner of the painting are a series of frames depicting the theatre of the Strangers' intrusions.

Something Brueghelesque will always be kaleidoscopic. Perhaps living is kaleidoscopic. There needs to be some theatre in a painting, though, some way of reducing what we see into one understanding. Perhaps even a sentence. A sentence for my 'Brueghel for Vaitahu' might be: There is an extravagance in living and dying that dooms Enata to disaster.

Everyday living

A 'Brueghel' of Enata living at Vaitahu that frames Tainai's stories would be a very full frame of stills. There would be hidden sacred spaces deep in the valley where the *tau'a* lived in isolation. His share of sacrifices—human, animal, vegetable—are around him, in the shadow of gigantic trees. The *me'ae* would be more public, marked by their wooden pyramids decked with white cloth pennants, skulls, rotting sacrifices. The priests' assistants, *moa*, live there. The priests themselves—*tuhuna o'ono*, keepers of the sacred traditions and masters of ceremonies—merge with the population but are recognisable always by their coconut-leaf caps. Scattered around the valley are residences in small compounds behind stone fences. In each compound are a number of houses raised on their *paepae*: a sleeping and resting house, a *tapu* house where men eat and the owner keeps his valuables. Nearby is a house for the dead. There would be space for an earth oven, a pound for the pigs. A small plantation of breadfruit trees, one planted for each birth in the family, is close by. All around the valley would be temporary and permanent *tapu* houses, inviolable to all who are not in *tapu*. Tattooists and their apprentices would be there, working on coteries of eight to ten clients benefiting from some celebratory occasion in the *haka'iki*'s life and sharing his patronage. The tattooing expert himself would perform his art on the socially elite—he could do a quarter-inch band across the face (the *kutu epo*, 'shitty snout') in two to three minutes. His apprentices would be more painfully slow on those less socially eminent.

All the other craftsmen (*tuhuna*)—the canoe builders, drum makers, fan makers, hair workers, ornament makers, surgeons and healers—would appear on the painting in their special houses, stonewalled around, *tapu* signals in place. The fishermen, a distinct and separate group as perhaps fishermen always are, occupy spaces for making and equipping the *va'a*— the ropes, nets, hooks. They might be seen bartering their catch on the beach. But the sea and many of its creatures were owned as particularly as the land. So if there were turtle or rays or red-coloured fish, or a wide range of others to be caught or places in the sea to be fished, there were sacred songs to be sung before the fishing and division-of-catch rites in their fishermen *tapu* houses. A 'Brueghel' would catch the night-fishing with candlenut torches and the driving of porpoises into nets with a beating of stones underwater. How shall we catch the conch shell sounds, the screaming and whirling of gulls, the wild movements of the canoes when the yellow-fin tuna spawned in the summer months?

There are other *tapu* houses scattered around the valley, for young girls in their first menstruation, houses for birthing, houses for preparing the dead. The *kai'oi*—the young dancers—and the *hoki*—the theatre groups— also had their special places where they learned old songs and dances and composed and choreographed new ones.

There would be groups in our painting of Enata amusing themselves— flying kites, spinning tops, swimming and surfing, fighting sham battles, juggling, wrestling, stilt walking, skipping, cat's-cradling. There would be clusters of people harvesting the breadfruit. Clear skies and brilliant stars were good predictors for the main harvest, Te Mei Nui, in January and February. Te Mei Nui was the first of four croppings. Enata counted the years by the Te Mei Nui and counted the breadfruit—maybe four hundred to a tree, maybe three to five thousand in a family *ma* pit. Nothing was done without ceremony—not the picking of the breadfruit with net-poles, not the opening of the initial pit (*tahou*), not the transfer to the principal pit (*ua-ma*), not the opening of the pits for use. Nothing was eaten, no social or personal action done, without addressing the *atua* in some way. Cursing the breadfruit was the worst crime. Anyone would be strangled on the mere suspicion of it.

There would be grimmer scenes in our 'Brueghel'—of Enata hanging themselves from trees, throwing themselves from coconut palms or off cliffs, poisoning themselves with *eva* (*Cerberus manghas*). Those occasions we have record of turn around infidelity in marriage and shame and loss of face. Tainai's third wife committed suicide when he discovered her infidelity with a *tuhuna* from Fatuiva. There is some doubt about that. Perhaps Tainai simply killed her.

The universe of Enata might seem tightly framed by their valley walls, but they had nonetheless a sense of their whole Land, from the uninhabited island of Eiao in the north to Fatuiva in the south. We must put into our 'Brueghel' an inset of travellers. The season of westerly winds, November to February, signalled the beginning of trading voyages—to Eiao for stone for adzes, to Fatuiva for their brilliantly carved festive bowls, to Nukuhiva for *eka*, the perfumed saffron-coloured cosmetic with which they anointed their bodies. The prestige for bringing some news or displaying some new object was worth the risk of open sea voyages. Putini, Kiatonui's brother-in-law from Nukuhiva, took a tour of the islands to show off the goat he had acquired in 1798. *Hoki*, the dancing troupes, would tour and make theatre of something remarkable, such as the arrival of a ship and the strange things that happened during its stay.

Then there were the émigrés, those that leave the islands forever. Robarts tells us of hundreds from Nukuhiva in a year. For them the gamble of a voyage into the spill of islands to the south and west was worth the risk when confronted by the catastrophe of a famine or a war. We hear little of them, except sometimes a later traveller would catch up with their descendants or survivors, or would find a connection in a shared genealogy.

My 'Brueghel' of Vaitahu is a close-worked canvas of Enata living off the land and sea. Detail will overwhelm us if we try to picture The Land as Enata actually saw it. For myself—a product of an industrial, urban culture, distant from nature around me—the marvel of this island world is how it was so completely known and exploited. I marvel that the most common foods— breadfruit (*mei*), banana and plantain (*meika*, *huetu*), coconut (*ehi*) and taro (*tao*)—were distinguished as thirty-four, seventy-five, fifty and thirty varieties respectively. Touch and smell helped make even finer distinctions by the size and shape of fruits and foliage, the texture of skin and bark, the height of the tree, the time and length of maturation and fruiting. The secondary foods— roots, tubers and corms, fruits, nuts and condiments—were less specifically distinguished, at least in the records. There were foods—some fifteen of them—too fibrous to be attractive in time of plenty. They were the starchy buds and roots of ferns, the nuts of palm and pandanus, small shoots, bitter fruits, small cucumbers and others that were difficult to collect and took time to prepare. These were turned-to between seasons, or in time of catastrophe. They tended to grow deep in the valleys or in the mountains.

There were certain trees and plants whose uses were so multiple that they could be said to be totally exploited. The coconut (*ehi*) was one of these. Its nuts and buds were food; its oil was cosmetic, medicine, waterproofing, embalming; its nutshells were cups, containers, graters; its husk was fibres, cordage and lines; its leaves were thatching and were woven in baskets, fans, mats, torches; on the spines of its leaves Enata hung their candlenut lamps and the seeds and flowers of their *hei* (garlands and crowns). There were many ceremonial uses of the coconut palm also, as *tapu* signs, as dress for *tau'a*, as covering for the dead, as signs of peace and treaty. The breadfruit (*mei*), pandanus (*haa*) and hibiscus (*hau*) had almost as many uses. From them also came gum, bark for cloth, and a large variety of instruments and household wares. Each different wood was adapted to its special purpose in size, strength, grain, hardness, spring and flexibility.

As there were individual trees that were totally exploited, there were industries that exploited a whole range of resources of the environment. Fishing was one of these. Enata used a number of narcotics in their fishing: *hutu* (*Myrtaceae, Barringtonia speciosa*), *kiki* (*Leguminosae, Thyncosia punctata*), *kohuhu* (*Leguminosae, Tephrosia piscatoria*), *kokuu* (*Sapindaceae, Sapindus saponaria*). For their nets and lines they drew not only on the coconut (*ehi*) and hibiscus (*hau, hau kua*) but also on a number of other grasses, vines and trailers: *kakao* (*Gramineae, Miscanthus jacopus*), *kiki, koke, pakoko* (*Leguminosae, Phaseolus amoenus*), *papa* (*Leguminosae, Phaseolus adenanthus*), *pute* (*Urticaceae, Boehmeria platyphylla*), *to* (*Gramineae, Saccharum elistichophyllum*). For canoe hulls, outriggers, floats, paddles, bailers, prows, sterns and sewn sections they used hibiscus and breadfruit and also *hutu, maii (Combretaceae, Terminalia catappa), manee (Rhamn aceae, Alphitonia marquesensis), mio (Malvaceae, Thespesia populnea), netae (Leguminosae, Erythrina indica), pukapuka (Hernandiaceae, Hernandia nukuhivensis), temanu (Guttiferae, Calophyllum inophyllum)*. They caulked the hull with coconut fibres and mosses (*inu, Hymenophyllaceae, Trichomanes latiabiatum*), and sealed it with coconut oil. For gums to bind their sennit, fix their hooks, append their *tiki*, they chose from among the resins and saps of trees already mentioned—*hiapo, ihi, kokuu, manee, mei, vi inara*—as well as *moua* and *tevai (Euphorbiaaceae, Santalum freycineti)*.

To many observers of the late eighteenth and early nineteenth century the most noticeable physical feature of Enata was their tattoos inscribed in the black dye taken from the *ama* nut. Tattooing, however, was only one part of Enata's preoccupation with the decoration and beautification of their bodies. They worked feathers, shell, bone, hair and teeth into an extraordinary range of headdresses, bands, ear-plugs, necklaces, armlets and anklets. Still more extraordinary was the number of sweet-smelling, pleasant-looking ferns, shrubs and trailers they worked into *hei*, crowns and wreaths. Feasts and ceremonials were special occasions for decoration.

Skin bleaching was a noted cosmetic practice among Enata women. Male dancers would also bleach their skin with the juice of the *papa* vine (*Phaseolus adenanthus*) or *paku, tuhia (Cruciferae, Cassia occidentalis)*. There were also stains, mostly yellow, with which their bodies were painted: *eka, mio, pini (Bixaceae, Bixa orellana)*, depilatories, *puka (Hernandiaceae, Hernandia nukuhivensis)*, cleansers, *tutu (Melaiceae, Colubrina asiatica)* and a large number of scents that they mixed with coconut oil, or sometimes with *upere (Meliaceae, Ricinus communis), aunona (Rutaceae, Pelea fatchivensis), kikapakuee, kokopuhi (Zinziberaceae, Zinziber zerumbet), kokuu, meie, meie parari, mio, niou, temanu, terepota*. Enata were attracted by the ways in which oils and stains heightened the effect of tattoos. Only when Strangers came did they discover that coconut oil had a disagreeable smell. The need to celebrate and decorate died as quickly as they did. They learned a new use for the coconut tree from Strangers. They made *namu*, coconut toddy, from the fermented sap from a tree's tip. The drink annihilated the joy of display and of giving in the feast (*koina*) and loosened their hatreds.

The implements of everyday life were too many to list. The need to find substances to bind, support, contain, cut, dig, lift, strain, stir, insulate, shelter and cover drove Enata to discover in their islands the fibres, leaves, woods, seeds, saps, fibres that would solve their problems.

For their fibres and cordage they looked to *ehi, hau, kiekie, mouka (Cyperaceae, Cyperus pennatus), pakoko (Leguminosae, Phasseolus amoenus), papa, pute (Urticaceae, Boehmaria playtyphyilla), tao kape taa taa.* For bedding under mats on the stones of the *paepae* they used a variety of grasses, sedges and ferns: *aumakamaka (Polypodiaceae, Teitoria jardinii), haiki (Gramineae, Cyperus compressus), huetu, kirika (Asdepiadiaceae, Asclepias curassivica), moukutai (Gramineae, Pennisetum identicum), pakihi (Geraniaceae, Oxalis corniculatus), paheutute (Gramineae, Eragrostis xerophila).*

Leaves had very specialist uses. Cooking in banana (*meika*) and taro (*tao*) leaves gave different flavours. *Hau* leaves were used for platters, *kape* for packages, *ti* leaves for cooking and the lining of the *ma* pits, *vahake* for parasols and shelter. For baskets, mats, fans and heavy textiles there were *ehi, haa, hau, kohe, pia, puehu, vahake.* For the heavier woods from which they constructed their houses, weapons, wooden bowls and platters, drums, *tapa* beaters and firelighters, they turned to coconut, breadfruit, rosewood (*mio*), pandanus (*haa*), ironwood (*toa, Casuarinaceae, Casuarina equisetifolia*), soapwoods *kokuu* and *tiatia (Dodonaea viscosa)*, borage (*tou, Boraginaceae, Cordia sebestene*). In building their *fa'e* or houses, for example, they would use breadfruit tree for the endposts, fan palm (*vahake*) for the ridge pole, hibiscus for the rafters and bamboo (*koh*e) for supports. The making of bark cloth was perhaps not as highly developed as elsewhere in Polynesia. *Hiapo* (young banyan), *mei* and *ute* were the three trees used to make different grades and colours of cloth.

Botanical chemistry, however, was an area of special knowledge of Enata. They showed it in three particular areas: in the dyes they used, their medicinal plants, and the poisons they were reputed to know. Enata extracted black, brown, red, yellow magenta and blue dyes from a large number of lichens, creepers, gingers. They had no fixatives and only one bleach (*kokui, Sapindaceae, Sapindus microcarpa*).

With the residence of Europeans in the islands, a different medical lore came very quickly across the beach. But missionaries, soldiers and sailors also looked to Enata to cure their own ills. Enata looked for new cures for the new diseases the Strangers brought. Stringents, diuretics, purgatives, liniments and poultices are to be found among indigenous medicinal plants. And so are relieving medicines for toothache, headaches, ulcers; soothing for burns, inflammations and wounds; curatives for rheumatism, fevers, tumours. Most observers of medical practice in Fenua'enata were distracted by the magical element in most cures. Sickness, death and accident in Enata's eyes were a consequence of sorcery. Observers failed to record how the sick helped themselves, and the sorcerers helped their magic, with medicines.

Enata knew their environment more than as merely source for exploitation. Much of it had for them a deeper meaning. They connected it directly with their broader perception of how their world came to be and was sustained. Each part of it had its own legendary story of its origins. Out of the environment they drew their metaphors, above all those metaphors that described and distinguished male and female. Parts of their environment they associated with their social divisions. Each would know what belonged to certain *tapu* groups, who might eat what and with whom, who might prepare what to be eaten by whom. Each part had its use beyond its use as food or medicine or material. There was a long list of nightshades, storkweeds and other plants whose bad smell would keep away the gods: *akautuhia* (*Leguminosae, Cassia occidentalis), kenae, kotuna, hei otona, kohuhu, vau, kava, pukavapui, tattare, pahuauta, mani, noni*. There were the poisons which, if not used as poisons, were known and used by the *tahuata'a* in their *nani kaha* (sorcery): *hoaau, hutu, kaha, keoho, kokui (Sapindaceae, Sapindus microcarpa), pakoko, puhatu, puka (Hernandiaceae, Hernandia peltata), tama, teve, tue*. Finally, there were the ceremonial and ritual uses. Sometimes the ceremony would focus on the plant itself, as in the drinking of kava (*Piperaceae, Piper latifolium, P. methysticum*). More often the ceremonial occasion demanded a special leaf, oil or dye, and the plant was known for its special use. *Ehi* (coconut), as we have seen, was perhaps the most widely used tree in ritual. Others included *aoa* (*Moraceae, Ficus marquesensis*) for burial of the dead; *tapa kaupe* (*Apocynaceae, Carissa grandis*) at childbirth; *kekevaemoa* (*Lycopodiaceae, Lycopodium cernuum*) for embalming the dead.

Roland Barthes used to berate historians and novelists for the use of what he called 'reality effects', superfluous factual detail that gave the illusion of reality to a story. I hope my 'map' and my 'Brueghelesque painting' are not 'reality effects'. I see them more as stage-props in the theatre of my storytelling. I have a story of Tainai to tell first, then of the Strangers who came to Fenua'enata, then of Crook, Robarts and Kabris as they cross the beach. I hope my 'map' and my 'Brueghel' give the beach the priority it is owed.

A Year in the Life of Tainai, Haka'iki of Vaitahu

September 1797

A *tau'a* of the Hema is dead. He is *atua*, man-godly. The breadfruit crops have failed. A shiver goes through the valleys of Tahuata. The priests decree the number of sacrifices. The news is quickly over the ridges to enemy territory. At Vaitahu, the *kikino*—the poor and expendable—know they must hide.

There is need for speed if *heana* are to be caught before the news reaches Hiva Oa. Tainai gathers two or three of the most feared warriors in the valley, has the priests decorate the *va'a* with skulls, *tiki* and *pavahina* (old men's grey beards). The priests sing their songs over the expedition, the same songs they sing for catching the most sacred of catches, the turtle.

The 15-mile passage in the dark to Hiva Oa is never easy. The winds race down the funnel of the straits between the two mountainous islands. The Pikina will be the pool from which they will snatch their victims. The Pikina are an old enemy. They have devastated Vaitahu at least twice in the last ten years. They come across in force from Taaoa, the neighbouring valley to Atuona on Hiva Oa. They are an inland people, but there will always be some who live dangerously close to the sea.

Tainai's raid is swift and brutal. The *heana* are night-fishers with their torches, or they are on the shore, or they are asleep in their houses. Four— three men and a woman—are taken, killed in a welter of blood, their bodies thrown into the bottom of the *va'a*. The voyage home is filled with triumphant chants. Each hook that is put into mouth, ears, and anus has its own derisive song.

There is a crowd on the shore at Vaitahu when they return in the dawn. The crowd has seen the white streamers flying from the stern. They are the signal for a catch taken.

The four bodies are thrown on to the shore and their hands and feet bound to their poles. There is a frenzy in the screams and shouts. There is fear, hope, abuse and derision in the tumult. Small boys mutilate the corpses, play with their genitals.

Life is on edge at this time at Vaitahu. Three breadfruit crops have dried up. The fish have disappeared. There are dead unburied in their houses. The dying are a skeletal presence. The wealthy and powerful have insurance in their *ma* pits, but those who have no carers—whether by familial obligation or through coalitions of self-interest—have a lonely and painful time. They are mocked for their helplessness, pushed to the ground in bone-rattling falls. There is not much mercy in Vaitahu when life is on edge.

The four *heana* are taken to the *me'ae* in procession. They are slung on their poles like a catch of fish. The *moa* have prepared the ovens and then prepare the bodies. The noise is ferocious—drumming, shouts, priests chanting in an unintelligible language, old women dancing naked. Public nakedness is derisive. They deride death. They deride the *atua*. When all is on edge, it is the attention of the *atua* that they want, not their blessing. The priests take their share of the victims and eat it, first the brains out of blackened skulls. They are all engulfed in the noise and smells and sights of life and death.

October 1797

The Ahutini erupt out of Hapatoni and occupy Anapoo. They destroy the coconut palms. It is more harassment than invasion. They are testing Tainai. These years, the Hema at Vaitahu are getting most of the spoils. The Ahutini want a share of them. They know Tainai will ransom Anapoo. He does. He will give Ahutini the large axe that Captain Wilson of the *Duff* gave him. Not yet. He has something to do with it first. Kill a thief.

The fruit of Te Mei Nui, the great breadfruit crop, are forming and holding. There will be a crop. The sacrifices of six weeks ago have worked on the *atua*. But now the crop has to be defended. Landowners through the valley will abide no thievery. Tainai kills a thief with his axe and feasts on his body. Uniua, Tainai's cousin, also kills a thief, a woman this time. She is eaten too. Then Uniua kills the woman's mother. She had allowed a child of Uniua in her care to be burned. Then Tainai kills her son for no apparent reason other than that he can do it without fear of retribution. The family is wiped out. It had no important connections.

Tainai seems to have no rivals in the valley. Perhaps his violence ensures that. Within the valley he knows when and where to control his violence in everyday conflicts. He isn't the wealthiest man in Vaitahu, nor the largest landowner. The population of Vaitahu is probably too small to sustain a rivalry between Tainai and his siblings' lines. The five members of an older generation and the twelve members of Tainai's own generation occupy the principal social roles—*atua*, sorcerers, priests, craft experts.

Tainai to this time is his own *toa*, warrior. The inter-island, inter-valley, inter-grouping marriages of his family create networks across entrenched hostilities. It is an insurance when living is so full of violent death.

Mid-November 1797

Two guests at Vaitahu, a priest and a principal man, cross over to Hiva Oa to visit relatives at Taaoa. They are seized in the night by raiding Naiki from the valley of Atuona. They are taken back to Atuona alive. A priest and an expert craftsman from Vaitahu sail dangerously in a small canoe to Hiva Oa to beg for their lives. To no avail. They are already killed and eaten.

Late November 1797

Vaitahu is on edge again. The murders of the priest and *tuhuna* on Hiva Oa won't be avenged, but the strongmen of the valley are thirsting for blood. A score of victims is the boast of their warrior lives. Victims, too, are capital. They can be traded for food in time of want, for booty in time of plenty.

Tainai leads a night expedition that includes his brother and several others who are his stalwarts. They raid the Tipai. That the Tipai are the group from which the two sisters who became Tainai's second and third wives come, doesn't seem to matter. The Tipai are conveniently adjacent on the southwest coast of Hiva Oa. They belong to a more or less permanent pool of enemies to be fished. Fourteen *heana* are caught asleep in their houses. Natuafiti—Tainai's brother—captures a young man who is the son of his daughter. His daughter, a *vahinetapu*, resides with her son among the Tipai. Natuafiti lets the young man go free. Ordinarily, if he had not killed him he would have at least scalped him of his horn of hair—a trophy for any warrior—but not this time. There is too much godliness in the relationship.

The fourteen *heana* are brought back alive to Vaitahu, subdued and hopeless in the bottom of the canoes. On the beach several of the captives are traded for a quantity of *ma* in its pits to Mauatiti, a wealthy strongman, and his collection of his friends. It is still a time of famine. Food is a good barter for fame. Mauatiti and his friends will strangle their barter and eat them.

As the sorry catch of *heana* are driven up the path beside the stream at Vaitahu to their place of execution, one of them, a woman named Titfau, calls out to a woman who had once been her mistress at Vaitahu. 'Fitiatupu', she calls. Calling a name is one of the protocols of protection. Fitiatupu is a woman of eminence, the wife of Tainai's brother Puaka. She runs out of her house and pleads for the victim's life. Tahaiti, her captor, refuses. On the way to the slaughter place and ovens, a severe storm intervenes. Titifau is tied naked to a tree while her captors seek shelter. Her former mistress sends her *pekio* to free and hide her. She will be sheltered for some months until she can be secretly taken back to Hiva Oa. All that time the family of the captors and the rescuers eye one another, neither party daring to take the matter further. Meanwhile the thirteen other captives have met their fate. Some of their bodies are still hanging in the place of sacrifice, their skulls have been added to the warriors' collection.

January 1798

The great breadfruit harvest is abundant. The sacrifices to the *atua* have done their work. The Ahutini raid again, as far as Hanamiai this time. Tainai repels them without casualty and dances his boasts at their retreating figures. They will never take Vaitahu.

February 1798

There is a newcomer in the valley. Auhe'e is his name, or 'Sam' as his sailor colleagues call him, or Tama as Enata do. We have met Tama. He is the much travelled Hawaiian whom Captain Asa Dodge had taken to Boston. Dodge now listens to his request to let him off the *Alexander* here at Vaitahu. Tama comes to Vaitahu in the splendid array of scarlet regimentals. He brings, too, the first musket with powder and balls to Tahuata. And a chest full of clothing. More than that, Tama brings stories of foreign places that Enata can hear because he speaks a language they can understand. He tells them that the Strangers have no gods. He has been to their lands and seen for himself. He tells them of what happened when the Strangers came regularly to Hawai'i, and they remember what Hitihiti told them about what happened when the Strangers came regularly to Tahiti. They hear of 'King' Kamehameha in Hawai'i, as they had heard of 'King' Pomare in Tahiti. With the wealth, the weapons and the beachcomber-warriors that the Strangers bring them, these *ali'i* or *arii* (*haka'iki* in Enata terms) become 'kings'. They overturn the political status quo. They end the endless hostilities with final victories. They make kingdoms not just of neighbouring valleys, but of neighbouring islands as well.

Tainai hears the stories and begins to dream of kingdoms. Tama tells of battles and wars, and the tactics that win them. Tama can throw a spear further than any Enata. He has a musket. Tainai, who combines the role of *haka'iki* and *toa* in his own person, now makes Tama *toa* of Vaitahu. He and Tama also exchange names.

Early March 1798

Tainai is seeking an alliance with the Pikina. Negotiations are delicate and the gift-giving extended. He is to bind the alliance with the marriage of his eight-year-old son to an infant daughter of the *haka'iki* of the Pikina. She is still at her mother's breast. The time has come for the ceremonies. A large double *va'a* is loaded with the customary gifts—rolls of white *tapa* cloth, domestic utensils and carvings of the most expert *tuhuna*, trading items from the Strangers' ships. Tainai, his *pekio*, his brother and his son board the *va'a*. The seas are too rough to cross to Hiva Oa directly. They coast slowly up the shore of Tahuata, spend a night in a northern bay, Hanamenino. Next day they cross to Hiva Oa and down the coast on the southeast wind. The sea is still wild. Puaka, Tainai's brother, spends the voyage on the outrigger to keep them from overturning.

At Taaoa, the marriage is sealed simply enough, with the presentation of the gifts and the delineation of the properties that each of the couple will own in the other's valley. Pahevi, Tainai's son, is made to sit with his infant bride who is in her mother's lap. They all sit together on a most dangerous piece of cloth, the white *tapa* cloth that the bride's mother wraps turban-like around her head. The priests have their song to sing. There is roast pig and plenty to be feasted on. Tainai's party stays the night and returns to Vaitahu the next day.

Late March 1798

Tama persuades Tainai that his wars with the Ahutini are small-time. The Hema and Ahutini should have more strategic targets. In alliance, they could be a formidable force. They should do what they did in Hawai'i, fight together and descend on a common enemy, the Naiki at Atuona.

The Hema and Ahutini then collect a fleet of thirty large *va'a*, and a force of nine hundred warriors, decked out in their finery. But there is no real proportion between the show and all its noise and the success of the expedition. The nine hundred kill only one Naiki. When they bring the corpse back to Vaitahu, the Ahutini claim it and rush it off over the ridge to Hanateio. Tama is chagrined and plans to do better next time.

April 1798

Tainai is not inclined to see the son he has just married off as his heir. For heir, he looks to the *tapu* line of the women in his family, the *vahinetapu*. His eyes turn to a twin boy—the more godly for being a twin—among the Ahutini. Peiteitei is his name. Tainai adopts Peiteitei, brings him home to his household at Vaitahu. Then he does something so extraordinary that we don't really know what he is doing.

In early April, Tainai with his brother Patou and a cousin make their way over the ridge behind Vaitahu to the valley of Hanateio. His other brothers come with him, but they will be spectators of, not participants in, what is to come. Tainai's sister's daughter lives at Hanateio with her husband. Her husband is the father of Tainai's adopted son, the twin Peiteitei. Tainai's niece is about to give birth. She is in the *tapu* birthing house, *fa'e taina*. The *tapu* signals are all around. The sign of a new birth— the turtleshell and pearlshell diadems—is above the entry way. A special matting is on the floor and over that is a covering of white *tapa* cloth. Old women have cleaned the hut of spirits and act against encroaching uncleanliness.

Tainai and his two companions are taken to a special house. There they are rubbed with *eka* and coconut oil. It is a rubbing that feminises the male dancers and the removes the *tapu* from *pekio*. All the threatening qualities of Tainai's *tapu* are thus removed. He is common for a time. The three men squirm beneath the mat and the *tapa* cloth. Tainai's sister's daughter, with the help of her husband at her back, then gives birth over the heads of the three men. It is a boy!

May 1798

Tama, in full regimentals this time and with his musket, assembles another fleet and a force larger than the previous one of nine hundred warriors. But this time Tainai's nephew by his *vahinetapu* sister is killed in the first skirmish. The allies are able to retrieve his body. Tama, pausing to load his musket with powder and ball, is seriously wounded in the leg and laid low with a slingshot. His warriors, pursued by the taunts of their enemies, are forced to carry him ignominiously from the field.

With their general incapacitated, the Hema men are forced to stay on Hiva Oa until he has recuperated enough to travel. So the women of Tahuata cannot mourn over Vahinetapu's son. They walk from Vaitahu to the northern valley of Hamenino on Tahuata. There they catch a fisherman's canoe to Hiva Oa. And there they perform their naked mourning dances over the corpse.

Hiva Oa is in turmoil. The warriors of the alliance of the Teia, Pikina, with the Hema and Ahutini are still raiding the Naiki. But four Ahutini, deep in Pikina territory, quarrel with their allies and are killed. The Ahutini and Hema then fall on the Pikina in revenge. 'Multitudes' are slaughtered. Vahaniuau, one of the principal men at Vaitahu, delights in killing the *haka'iki* of the Pikina and carries off his body with all its ornaments to Vaitahu. It is into the Pikina *haka'iki*'s family that Tainai married his son.

Tama's fleet, now laden with corpses, returns to Vaitahu. There they meet up with four Pikina men who were at Vaitahu begging for ornaments so they could go properly into battle with their allies. Tainai's younger brother kills all four.

June 1798

There is land under dispute at Vaitahu. Takaha, a priest who lives with Tainai's mother (Honu's widow) is killed in a quarrel with its owner. Pahaumuma, the owner, clubs Takaha to death. But Takaha had previously given some offence to a female *tau'a*, the sister of the *atua* Tuaapuameini, who had power over all the breadfruit trees of Tahuata. It was a dangerous family to offend. She had caught Takaha's soul in her cupped hand and had smothered it. His clubbing death was just the playing out of her sorcery. The whole valley knows it.

Tainai cannot ignore the killing of his mother's partner. But Pahaumuma is a powerful man. He constructs canoes. His daughter is married to Tainai's nephew and namesake, Tainai-Moheop. The valley is bitterly divided over the affair. Powerful coalitions are opposed.

One side—Pauhaumuma's—is almost a league of junior descent lines. Tainai's younger brother is among them, and the leading men of families of the younger brothers of Honu are with them. So too are families that would boast of their *atua*—godliness. The other side—Tainai's—is composed of his other brothers, cousins from the other families of Honu's siblings, and husbands of Tainai's daughters.

The two sides confront one another in open violence, but the fight, as so often in these conflicts, is reduced to a combat between two champions— Pahaumuma and Tainai's brother-in-law Tahoputona. Pahaumuma is knocked down by a slingshot. Tahoputona rushes in to finish him off with his spear, but Pahaumuma is rescued by one of his warriors.

The two groups pull back from the abyss. Tainai, with the slight advantage of Pahaumuma's wounding, claims the disputed land. But Pahaumuma makes him an offer he can't refuse—three long clubs, two hogs, three *peue* (headdresses with frigate-bird plumes) and, most valuable of all, a sperm whale tooth. The whale tooth is almost too much for Tainai. He has a prized possession too, a cat. He gives the cat to Pahaumuma. Actually, Tainai believes he has a monopoly on cats. But nobody has a monopoly on cats for long. Rats thrive on the filth of living and detritus of sacrifices at Vaitahu. Cats thrive on rats.

Tainai has another dozen years of his life to add to this one. They won't be largely different. The cycle of wars and raids will intensify before it abates. There is a madness in that intensity as Enata learn to trade their supplies to Strangers' ships for muskets and other savage killing instruments, such as whaling spades.

No story I can tell can hope to discover what it means to live with death looming so persistently and so violently. I wish I could say that the coming of the 'civilised' moderated this 'savage' violence. It does not. The Strangers' intrusion is callous and ugly.

CROSSINGS

'Ethnogging'

*'All tricksters are "on the road". They are lords of in-between', Lewis Hyde writes.
He gives us a book of stories about the kind of imagination that stirs to life at the
beginning of a journey. He calls it* Trickster Makes the World *(1999). He is
thinking of the tricksters Coyote, Hermes, Mercury and more. 'The road that
trickster travels is a spirit road as well as the road in fact. He is the adept who can
move between heaven and earth, and between the living and the dead.'*

*Educators, it seems to me, need to be tricksters. They need to educe—to draw
out—the creative spirit in those they educate. Some of my own students—I use the
term 'my', knowing that they never really are 'mine'—have remembered the heady
days when we educated one another. They have said of me:*

> *Dening remained inscrutable, offering no definitive solutions, and never
> allowing us the sense of having finally arrived at the right answer. There was
> a peculiar motion of the swivel chair, a particular way of staring out into the
> twilight (we used to meet at 5.15 p.m., and the pigeons would be beginning to
> roost outside the window) which managed, by neither affirming nor denying,
> to convey the sense that of course there was much thinking left to be done,
> many other aspects to be considered. Hence the famous sense of something
> elusive, just out of reach, something perhaps ultimately inexpressible. But out
> of that elusiveness was conveyed to us a sense that there were things that
> mattered, that intellectual work was important, that the pursuit of
> understanding went beyond the process of debunking, or of revealing the
> duplicity or self-interestedness of actors in the past. [M. Cathcart, T. Griffiths,
> G. Houghton, V. Anceschi, L. Watts and D. Goodman,* Mission to the South
> Seas: The Voyage of the Duff, 1796, *1990.]*

*Let me bask a little in the creative skills of these students, 'ethnogging'
something of our mutual educational experiences. The trickster in me had a phrase
for these exercises on the beaches of the mind: 'cognitive dissonance'. Let me tell
some stories of its practice.*

Observing the Other: Observing the Familiar

We budding anthropologists at Harvard in the 1960s, anticipating the coming fieldwork in Bougainville hamlets or Yucatan villages or Brazilian forests or Kalahari deserts, laughed a little nervously at stories about our forebears that told how unprepared they went into the field and yet produced such masterpieces. Was it really true that Franz Boas, when asked by Margaret Mead what she needed to take into the field, replied after long consideration, 'Plenty of sharp pencils'?

We drew comfort from the prefaces of great books such as E. E. Evans-Pritchard's *Nuer*. He suffered 'Nueritis' in his tent, he tells us, frustrated at his own inability to enter the otherness of the people he was observing. We learnt that one way to bring our readers with us was to bare our souls, although not many of us would be likely to reveal, even posthumously, the inner ugliness that Bronislaw Malinowski revealed in *A Diary in the Strict Sense of the Term* (1967). Perhaps no scholar liberated us more in this respect than Clifford Geertz. 'Early in April of 1958, my wife and I arrived, malarial and diffident, in a Balinese village . . . We were intruders, professional ones . . . we were non-persons, spectres, invisible men.' That is how he begins 'Deep Play: Notes on the Balinese Cockfight' (*Daedalus*, 1972). Then followed the story of how he and his wife panicked and ran away when the police came armed to break up the cockfight. Their fear and panic delighted the Balinese. 'They gleefully mimicked over and over again our graceless style of running . . . In Bali, to be teased is to be accepted.' Clearly, that is one way of crossing beaches.

The familiar is more difficult to observe. The theatre in everyday life is too close for comfort. Sincerity is best an unthinking, unconscious virtue. When we unravel our scheming nature in every social act, there is the sudden possibility that we are responsible for what we do. Discovering our own bad faith is very unsettling. Politics begins there. We begin to change the world in changing ourselves.

IT IS 1967. The Vietnam War grinds hopelessly on. I have just finished my anthropology degree at Harvard. I am flying home via Hawai'i where the Anthropology and History Departments at the University of Hawai'i have offered me a short-term appointment. The airports are filled with young men and women in military uniform. Hawai'i is a giant military camp, a giant military hospital.

I come to the University of Hawai'i with large ambitions to teach a new sort of history. 'Ethnohistory' I call it, until the politics in the name disturbs me—there is no reason why the history of first peoples in Oceania or the Americas or Africa should be 'ethno' and the history of empires and conquerors just 'history'. 'Culture contact' won't do either. Cultures don't come into contact. 'Contact' is too wimpish a notion for the story of the violent encounter between the islanders and intruding strangers that I have to tell.

Thirty-five years on, I still won't have a name for it. Maybe 'anthrohistory' would do. 'Anthrohistory' suggests that both sides of my story—of natives and of strangers—are equally subject to my anthropological and historical gaze. But give something a name, and someone will create an association, a journal, and department, and will begin to put boundaries about it. I'm not into boundaries around knowledge.

'Double-visioned history'? I would settle for that, if only to challenge the presumptions of so much single-visioned history that seems to dominate. It would have to be 'multi-visioned history', though, wouldn't it? Our gaze on the past is gendered, coloured, aged, classed, modern and postmodern—multi-visioned. 'Cross-cultural history'? Yes, if it is accepted that all history across time and space is cross-cultural. Just 'cultural history'? Why not? So long as we don't waste time debating what 'culture' is. At my last count there were 366 discursive definitions of 'culture'. Let me make it 367 and leave it. Culture is talk. Living is story.

The History Department at the University of Hawai'i did not know what to do with me. The 'Pacific' history they taught was about empires, navies and wars. Not much 'ethno' at all. The Anthropology Department set me to teach first-year ethnology, Ethnology 101. My class was made up of Samoans, Tongans, Filipinos, Chinese, Japanese, Portuguese Macaoans, Hawaiians and a few sun-dazed and waterlogged Anglo-Americans. The textbooks set—not by me—were formulaic descriptions of island societies. There was not much incentive in them to enter into cultural differences. None at all to translate the differences into some representation of otherness.

So I started a practice in Hawai'i that I followed for the rest of my teaching academic life. I taught 'culture' by asking my students to describe

226

it. I taught the past by asking them to tell something of the present in story. 'Ethnogging', my later students used to call it with affectionate disrespect.

To 'ethnog' meant being observer of, not spectator to, life's experiences Our cultural antennae are at their peak as observers. Every trivial detail is larger than itself in an observation. We see the interconnectedness of things. We read gestures with the same astuteness that we need to survive culturally in everyday life. We see the multiple meanings in every word. We are catching meaning in the context of the occasion. Above all, as observers, we are reflective. We see ourselves mirrored in our own observations. We know our honesty. We know our uncertainties. We know our tricks.

I was persuaded to the practice of 'ethnogging' by a cathartic pedagogic experience. It involved a Hawaiian-born student. I had asked my students to describe something culturally different or out of the ordinary in their lives. The cultural difference did not need to be great— something across gender, religious belief, language, ritual, ethnic custom. Some did marriage ceremonies. Some did *luau*, Hawaiian feasts. Some did their 'pot' parties. A couple of Buddhists did the Sunday mass I used to celebrate at the Honolulu cathedral. The Hawaiian-born student wasn't much into study of any sort. He 'didn't know what to do'. I asked him what he did on Sundays. He said that he used to play touch football on the beach at Kaneohe. 'Do that', I said.

The Sunday morning beach game was played between Hawaiian-born young men and the US marines based at Kaneohe. There was not much love lost between them. The Hawaiians were resentful that their island had become an army camp. The marines were resentful at the ingratitude for the sacrifices they were making and at being made to feel strangers in their America. The 'touch' in the touch-football was a pretty relative concept. The games were violent, full of subliminal hatred.

I remember very well my student's discovery that a touch football match was so much larger than itself. It was a parable about something else—about identity, about political domination, about macho gendering. He came to realise this. Then he confronted with some relish how he would make a narrative that matched the excitement of his discovery. He had to perform his experiences, make theatre of it.

He had to be a storyteller first of all, a short-story teller. He had to make 'an experience'—in John Dewey's phrase—out of a continuum of experiences of consciousness. In some way he had to frame what he saw, give drama to it by giving it a beginning and an end. If he were good enough, he would be able to make his short story a parable of all that he wanted to say. He would have to find the rhythms and silences in his words to tease and intrigue his readers. And he would soon learn that he himself was an empty vessel until he joined his experiences to the experiences of others—of Clifford Geertz, for example or Oscar Lewis or E. E. Evans-Pritchard. Observing wouldn't be enough. He would have to become a reader.

I was to leave Hawai'i for the traumatic year of 1968 in Australia. 1968 was a prelude to my full-time academic teaching life. Jean Martin, founding professor of sociology, and Alan Martin, founding professor of history, at LaTrobe University had offered me while I was still at Harvard a joint appointment in sociology and history at their new university. The three years they gave me at LaTrobe were seminal years in my academic life. There is something very sweet about the beginning of educational institutions. There is nobody there to say 'this is how we do it'. Every year is different as the achievements and failures of the last year are measured against the highest ideals. And the students are all there because they want to be, not because some social imperative tells them that they should be there. They are risk-takers. It is wonderful to teach risk-takers.

My immediate task at LaTrobe was to establish a cross-cultural 'Pacific' history course in the History Department and a cross-disciplinary course on Papua New Guinea in the Social Science School. But my most important, and most interesting, task was to direct the senior students in sociology in 'Social Theory' and the senior students in history in 'Reflective History'. Reflective History was a name I invented in place of 'Theory and Method of History'. Theory and Method was a subject that Max Crawford had created for senior undergraduate history students at the University of Melbourne in the 1930s. I suspect that it was a world-first creation on his part. It certainly bred a world-wide interest in 'theory and method' as his students spread themselves to many British and US universities. I never really believed that historians *did* 'theory' or that method study was rewarding. Reflective history was what they actually did. They wrote their histories and discovered both their own presence in them and the discourse that made sense of their histories.

What surprised me in educating these two streams of sociology and history students separately was how quickly their disciplines socialised

228

them. I suppose my first efforts in 'cognitive dissonance' were directed at destabilising them in the unreflective certainty that such socialisation gave them. Nothing destabilised them more than a demand that they read outside their discipline and, even more, that they cease and desist in *doing* papers and essays and instead *write* sociology and history. One *does* essays and papers for readers who are paid to read and examine them. One *writes* to intrigue. One *writes* not by continually saying 'I'm coming! I'm coming!', but by being there directly. One *writes* by being an honest reader oneself, knowing when I skim and skip, knowing that I rarely read a book in one sitting, knowing that I need signposts and memory stations, knowing that I need epigrammatic thoughts to round off a reading.

I had never expected to return to Melbourne University. My professor, remember, had told me that being engaged in cross-cultural history and doing anthropology would be the end of my academic career. So I was stunned when Melbourne offered me the chair of history in 1971. I then felt ashamed of myself that I accepted the offer so readily. I owed so much to Jean and Alan Martin and felt that I had let them down. They both had long-term visions for universities and their disciplines. I came to Melbourne with the sense of freedom and excitement that they bred in us all. There was more reflection on and experimentation in the educational process at LaTrobe than would happen in the older universities for many years. And I had started life-long friendships with scholars and writers like Rhys Isaac and Inga Clendinnen. We attended one another's classes. We read one another's writings. We fed one another with readings. We didn't believe that disciplines, departments and universities should hedge us around. We 'blurred genres' with excitement. We debated ideas. Above all we enjoyed our students.

I had been one of the first cross-discipline appointments in the humanities and social sciences in Australian universities. I had also been one of the early flow-backs at the professorial level from the new universities to the old. I came to Melbourne with strong anti-territorial values and the belief that the only way for change was through institutional and departmental altruism. Altruism is seen to be a wimpish sort of philosophy in the hierarchies of privilege and the competitiveness of economic rationalism. I soon discovered that the worst job in the world is being head or chair of department. I made many mistakes that I deeply regret. But I also discovered that there was considerable freedom in being a professor. I didn't need to drag a department along with me to enjoy that freedom.

It had always interested me that the anthropologists I greatly admired—Mary Douglas with her fluid notions of structure, E. E. Evans-Pritchard with his entry into other cultures through their metaphors, Victor Turner with his notions of theatre and social drama—all had a Catholic religious element in their understanding, either by birth and education or by conviction and conversion. I had always seen in them a sacramental theme in their perceptions, a sense of how the ultimate truths in life are played out in sign. Sacramental theology is centred on the effectiveness of material signs on the spiritual. Catholicism is built on sacramental realism. A sacrament is defined as a sign that effects what it signifies in the signifying. So the signifiers in baptism, confirmation, marriage, eucharist, reconciliation, ordination and extreme unction left, as it were, an indelible mark on the soul. Inevitably, 'ethnogging' tended to focus on the sign-scenes of living—the rituals that defined or maintained relationships—lifting one's hat to a 'lady', walking always beside her on the kerbside (not that any of my students would have experienced such gestures, but their quaintness helped me make a pedagogic point!)—or rituals of transience from one state to another—getting married, being buried, being convicted, being hospitalised. So an 'ethnogger' had to describe these in-between spaces where language, dress, gesture and commitment to the theatre of it all made something 'as if' very real indeed.

I suppose I was never innocent in all this. I was never far from my need continually to display the creative freedom in the human endeavour. Say it was my never-ending search for ways to define human responsibility against the awful social forces that seem to take it away. The Holocaust was never far away from my mind, nor the terrible things that happened wherever empires met indigenous peoples the world over. Jean-Paul Sartre's notion of 'bad faith' and Hannah Arendt's 'banality of evil' had struck deeply into me. It wasn't accidental that *Islands and Beaches* began with that terrible scene on Vaitahu Beach when, after singing High Mass, the Spaniards put three bodies of those they had killed on three stakes and pierced the heart of the middle one with a spear. It wasn't accidental that I began *Mr Bligh's Bad Language* with the execution of the three *Bounty* mutineers. In my eyes these were studies in institutional 'bad faith' and the complex interplay of signs (that worked immediately) and symbols (with more conscious attention to their meaning), and the need in 'ethnogging' ritual to describe the perceptions of all the participants.

Of all the pleasures in teaching that remain in my memory, two stand out. One is the 'contract' with my students that the year's course would not end in essays or examination but in a book that they must edit together. Whether it would be published was another thing altogether. They must write it to be read. My side of the contract was that I would take them to Sydney for a week or two of research in the Mitchell Library. We would stay across Sydney Harbour at Manly, have our seminars in the ferry coming and going, work all day in the library, taking lunch in the Botanical Gardens and talking our book there. I wanted them to have for a time the pleasure of total engagement in research, to confront the advantages and difficulties of teamwork. I am proud to say that a couple of books were published out of these classes.

For ten or fifteen years classes of mine would 'ethnog' Anzac Day. On 25 April every year, Australians celebrate the landing of the Anzacs (the Australian and New Zealand Army Corps) at Gallipoli in 1915. That landing, fifteen years after the Australian federation, is seen as the bloody birth of a nation. The military failure of that mission only helped to confirm the 'Anzac spirit' of sacrifice, as well as mateship, scepticism towards authority and the rhetoric of elite power, and individual 'Aussie' initiative. Returned soldiers from all wars prepare for weeks for Anzac Day. Each country town, where the losses of World War I were hugely disproportionate to population sizes, has its monuments to which the parades are directed. In Melbourne there is a Shrine of Remembrance. Harsh and heavy, all contradiction in architectural design, a ziggurat on top of a columned temple, the Shrine stands on a rise that dominates a wide boulevard leading into the heart of the city. There are two ceremonies at the Shrine on Anzac Day, the dawn service and the march.

Twelve of us stand awkwardly in the pre-dawn cold, a crowd of some thousands around us. We are in the forecourt of the Shrine of Remembrance. Its ziggurat tower is a dark shadow against the lightening eastern sky. We can't see the Shrine's carvings and statues—Justice, Peace, War, Sacrifice. These symbols had seemed distant and rhetorical when we had sat among them in the light in the week before Anzac Day. They were not sacramental at all. Now in the darkness they become a more sacred space. The crowd around us is nearly silent. Cigarettes glow in cupped hands. The Eternal Flame flickers in the darkness. Those standing around it are caught in a Goya-like painting of the awful things that happen in the dawn's half-light. We who have never stood in a trench looking out to an attacking enemy, have never prepared to make a life-and-death leap over the parapet, are overwhelmed with a sense that if we have no personal memory of these things, a memory nonetheless hangs in the air around us.

The trumpeter's Last Post and Reveille from the darkness of the parapet penetrates our spirits. The sparsity of the ritual makes it the more unritualistic. Maybe effective signs are made with simplicity. Symbols are more long-winded.

The thousands, a red poppy in hand, file through the Shrine at the simple ceremony's end. We feel a little intrusive as observers, as if we are using others. We are a little shocked, though, as two women in uniform ask the women students among us to go to the very end of the line. Males first! We would debate later how sacramental this gesture was!

When we have dropped our red poppies into the well of the Shrine, where a ray of light strikes a message of sacrifice on the eleventh hour of the eleventh day of the eleventh month, we are surprised to find ourselves nearly alone. Then we realise that the crowd has assembled again, this time in playful mood at the barracks a little way from the Shrine. There behind trestle tables, 'ladies', grey-haired and of the generation of the older men around them, are serving strong, stewed, sweet tea into large old railway cups. It is a scene from hundreds of wartime railway stations and wharves as troops on the move were served some comfort. All around there is much playing of old roles—saluting, standing at attention talking to officers, using nicknames, relating stories that must have been told a thousand times raising guffaws of laughter. There are perennial and expected practical jokes. A hired Rolls Royce turns up and takes away those least likely to have a Rolls Royce. These old faces told the young faces in our group that they were there to celebrate the gallantry of the defeat at Gallipoli. There is a sense of innocence and purity in their motives for going to war. The evil of war is none of their making, the brilliance of it is. They share memories with comrades that they could never share with others.

We have several hours before the march. We huddle over breakfast and talk long about signs and symbols, myths and legends. There is never any doubt that we have entered for a few moments a sacred time, a sacred space. Whether we have a theory that would explain it all, that is another thing. Whether we could best describe what we had experienced with a poem or a play or an ethnography, what narrative strategies we would employ to catch the truths we had seen, that also is another thing.

Many weeks ago we had joined a group of returned servicemen— maybe a naval vessel or a battalion or a squadron. We had joined the committee meetings preparing for the reunions after the Anzac Day march, hearing their stories. We now join them again at the head of the march. We know in an instant that the assembly for the march is its most important moment. As old mates cluster in assigned places, the empty calendar of their lives is filled with stories of the past year. It is a networking moment of communication—about recent dead, of fortunes won or lost, of disabilities. Widows, sons and daughters take somebody's place. Medals are not buried with the dead. They are handed on. Grandchildren, awkward in their self-importance, would be there all bedecked with ribbons and medals. The years of their war experience had put all their lives in step, made a march of it.

We walk along with our group through the crowd, sampling this man's or that woman's response to the day. On the fringe of the crowd there are always other, caricatured 'diggers', out of their units, usually showing their medals, but always showing signs in their dress, or in their gestures, or in the things they said to nobody in particular, of not being part of the rest. Sometimes their otherness cannot be avoided if they catch an eye. Sometimes they are so distant within themselves that they do not have an eye to be caught and to catch. They are the walking wounded of war.

The Anzac Day march does not end in a large assembly. Nor is there a show of martial might. The current military on this day are servants with respect of an older generation. The marchers pass the saluting post and wheel left past the Shrine, off to their reunion places. If ritual can make sign and symbol in negative, then perhaps the turning away from pomp and closure at its end makes it a sacrament more of peace than of war.

We who are 'ethnogging' it all stay back to see its end. A phalanx of the socially elite, politically powerful, the representatives of State, Church and Society, form a square. It is a sort of map of proper power. They salute the Queen and the nation and have someone spell out didactically the meaning of the day. Their speeches are heard with only moderate sufferance by the crowd, who are now drifting off to football games or horse races or to pubs and picnics. This last act of the ritual looks like a rather private affair for public figures. We do not dare ask them if they believe in it or not. They look patient but a little bored. We think that for them it would have been a bigger sin not to have been there than not to have believed.

The memory of the fifteen years when I took successive years of students through these experiences are precious to me. I knew that I had allowed some to enter a mystery. The important things in life are sacramental.

History—the transformation of a past, no matter how recent a past, into words or paint or dance or play—is always a performance. It is an everyday performance as we present our selective narratives about what has happened around the kitchen table, in the courts, to the taxman, at the graveside. A quite staged performance when we present it to our examiners, to the collegiality of our disciplines, whenever we play our role as 'historians'.

All my teaching life I have asked my students to perform their history, to 'make' their history, not to 'learn' it. There is always a gamble in performance. A performance is always to somebody. A performer always has performance consciousness. 'Ethnogging', in my view, is not a presentist infection. It is not done out of fear of not being able to know the past. It discovers to us how hard we have to work to give back to the past its present. My students always discovered how difficult it is to describe the present. They approached the task of describing the past with a bit more humility. When they had done the one, I always made them do the other.

6

The Strangers Come

There is no memory among Enata of the first Strangers, the Spaniards, who came from beyond the southeast sky twenty generations ago. At least there is no memory that later Strangers' questions could prompt. There is a name—Fitipiti ('Belonging-to-the-East')—floating in the mists of time. Who they are, when they came, no Enata can say.

There is a memory of 'Tuti' (Cook). Strangers always ask about Tuti. This man can show the scars that Tuti's 'thunder' left him. 'Tuti' killed, they remember, that one's brother, this one's father. They can even show the 'nail'—the stanchion of the Resolution's *gangway—that a man was killed for taking.*

Now, in 1791, Honu, the haka'iki *who welcomed Tuti, is recently dead. Tainai, his son, still has Vaitahu under* tapu *in preparation for Honu's* mau, *his memorial feasts.*

Then, on 15 April 1791, another Stranger's vessel from the east appears in the waters between Hiva Oa and Tahuata. It is the Hope *(Joseph Ingraham), an American trader. Then a French trader, the* Solide *(Etienne Marchand), 13 to 20 June 1791. Then an English naval supply ship, the* Daedalus *(Richard Hergest), 22 to 30 March 1792. Another American trader, the* Jefferson *(Josiah Roberts) will stay three months from 11 November 1792 to 24 February 1793 to construct and launch a small schooner. Enata will quickly learn that American, English and French Strangers have different tribal characteristics. Let us look at them managing this new phase in their lives.*

The Godliness of Strangers

No doubt it served many a Stranger's self-delusions to be called a 'god'. James Cook certainly seemed to enjoy being identified as the god Lono by the Hawaiians. Perhaps the rigours of ten years' Pacific exploration and hero-worship at home will do that. Actually, I believe, Cook was remembering what Tupaia the Priest had taught him about the protocols of crossing a beach at Ra'iatea in the Tahitian islands in 1769. The first thing to be done, Tupaia showed him, was to pay respect to the divine titles to the land in their sacred places. The second was to give true gifts, not to trade. Cook was being polite at Kealakekua Bay in Hawai'i. He probably was also trying to avoid all the disasters that had dogged his voyages when his men had crossed beaches violently and without protocol.

Look onto a beach from a ship. You look through a glass darkly. Every part of what you see is coloured by all that makes you who you are—your language, your institutions, your myths, your memory, your daily experiences. Everything different is shaded into familiarity. You cannot be a 'god' in any other way than the way you know 'gods' to be. The other cannot be made different in any other way than by making it somewhat the same.

Look out from a beach to a ship. It is the same. Otherness only makes sense if it is a version of the same. Those that 'come from beyond the sky' are *atua*. Those ancestors who 'came from beyond the sky' in the original settlement, they were *atua*. As were any who went to or came from the Homeland, Hava'iki. That sorcerer demanding sacrifices is *atua*. That *tiki* is *atua*. All the spirits who inhabit the natural world are *atua*. The *haka'iki*'s dead father is *atua*. Sometimes that very human *haka'iki* is *atua* too. These ignorant Strangers who cannot even speak are *atua*. Translate the word '*atua*' as 'gods', if you like, but see what Enata see when they see *atua*. The godliness of *atua* is shared and experienced in many different ways. Enata aren't deluded in its variety. That is *atua*'s metaphoric strength.

The Hope, Joseph Ingraham

15 to 20 April 1791

The *Hope* was a 70-ton brigantine—a hermaphrodite brig as the Americans called it. Two-masted—square-rigged on her foremast, schooner-rigged on her mainmast—hermaphrodite. The *Hope* was well armed: twelve carriage guns and six swivels. The islands were dangerous places. By 1791 two traders had been cut off in Hawai'i. But 'sixteen young men all in high spirits' was how her supercargo Ebenezer Dorr described the *Hope*'s crew. Joseph Ingraham was the twenty-year-old master, a man with an eye for detail and a sense of history. He would leave a four-volume journal of this voyage.

Thomas Hanskynd Perkins, in the early days of amassing his fortune as a Boston trader, built the *Hope* for the China fur trade. He was one of the first to respond to John Ledyard's report on the possibilities of trading otter furs from the Northwest Coast with the Chinese. Ledyard had been on Cook's last voyage and had seen how Cook's crew had traded otter skins with the Chinese for as much as $800 each. The Chinese to that point were uninterested in any other trade than gold bullion. American traders quickly sent out vessels to trade with the Indians on the Northwest Coast for skins to trade with the Chinese and to bring home tea, ivory, wallpaper, pictures and porcelain. Perkins had sailed with Captain James Magee on the *Astrea*. He knew the profits. He knew the risks. This was venture capitalism.

If an ethic of Enlightenment science and empire suffuses the first exploratory entries of the Strangers into the Sea of Islands, it is the ethic of the trading venture that colours the subsequent encounters. The trader's encounter on the beach is always transient. His relationship with the islanders has no future unless he is hoping to return to the same place safely. What he does to endanger others who follow him is the others' risk. His trade is a thing of the moment. He won't be there to fix any imbalance. *Caveat emptor* is his cry to natives totally ignorant of what it is they must beware of. The relativity of prices is his profit. The worthlessness of what he trades is never a measure of the worth to him of wood, water and food to the bottom line of his profit. Out here on the beach, there is no one to police his conscience. His immorality has no cost, to him at least.

That is not to say there were no decent men among the traders. Joseph Ingraham would be one of them. More bemused at the strangeness of what he saw than curious of its humanity, he would keep his distance from the beach at Vaitahu. Thomas Perkins, the *Hope*'s owner, was wary of native cunning. He had not expected Ingraham to call at The Marquesas. 'I absolutely forbid letting y'r anchor at any' of the Hawaiian Islands', he instructed.

This first venture of Perkins would not be a happy one. Even though Ingraham would collect fourteen hundred otter skins and sables off the Northwest Coast, the venture would lose $43,000. But this was because they had failed to consider the international jealousies of the Chinese and the Russians. Ingraham was perceived by the Chinese to be a Russian smuggler. But our interests are not on the full trading venture.

Only one crew member of the *Hope* went ashore at Vaitahu. 'Opye' is how he is registered on the *Hope*'s muster roll. Opai was Hawaiian. Kalehua, 'Jack Ingram', were his other names. Kamehameha, Hawai'i's 'King', wanted a navy. He had sent various of his subjects off to learn seamen's skills. One of them was Opai. Robert Gray brought Opai back to Boston on the *Columbia*. With 'Jack Atu', Opai was the first of many Hawaiians to come to New England. Their first appearance, parading in feathered helmets and cloaks, caused a stir. They seemed like 'Apollos', a staid New England newspaper mused. Opai sailed out of Boston to the Carribbean and to St Jagos in the Cape Verde Islands. There he collected a pet monkey and seeds of orange, lemon and lime that he hoped to take back to his native Kauai.

Ingraham wanted Opai as an interpreter, but his language skills were never great. On the *Hope*, he spoke a nearly unintelligible mix of Kauaian dialect and sailors' slang and never really did communicate well with Enata. There were too many things to be seen, he told Ingraham, but Ingraham thought he had too close an eye for the 'ladies'. Ingraham also thought that Opai would be a better interpreter if he wore his native dress, a *maro*. Opai was of the opinion that his best suit of American clothes better declared his status. Let us say that, whatever Opai's linguistic skills, Tainai would have been very interested in what he had to say of 'King' Kamehameha.

Ingraham took the *Hope* down the Atlantic to the Falkland Islands, where he sealed without great success, then around the Horn and across the vast space of the Pacific to Fenua'enata. He was four months into his voyage when he sighted Fatuiva and sailed down the straits between Hiva Oa and Tahuata. The 'sixteen young men all in spirits' would have had high expectations of the South Sea islands they were about to see for the first time.

The old man stands unsteadily in his *va'a*, rocking in the waters offshore from the island of Hiva Oa. The hull of the *Hope* towers over him. The old man is Naiki from Atuona. He doesn't know that the Strangers are American from Boston. He knows what to call their vessel, though. It is *ihepe'a*, a sailing 'ship' ('*hepai*' is the word the French will collect). He had the word from the *tuhuna* of the last Stranger's voyaging *va'a* to come to these waters seventeen years ago; 'Tuti', James Cook, had given it to them.

The old man is mystified by the gestures of the *tuhuna* of the *Hope*, Joseph Ingraham. But they seem friendly gestures. Ingraham throws a white cloth, a handkerchief, into the water. The old man has only one thing on his person to give in return, but, in a sense, it is his most valuable asset. It is his grey beard. The beard is an ornament full of time and tradition. It is part of every solemn moment in Enata living. Any voyager, the old man must assume, would value it. So he 'twitches' off part of his grey beard and throws it into the sea. It is an invented ritual, but it brings this out-of-experience of the encounter into the experience of everyday. The old man hasn't known what is expected of him. He does what he can. Then he makes it a moment of offering. He makes his companions throw coconuts and red *tapu* fish on to the deck of the *Hope*. Ingraham reads the old man's gesture not as an offering, but as a trade, and gives them nails for the food at his feet. Enata immediately weave the nails into their hair and beards. The nails join the teeth and shells already there. For a time the men from Atuona stretch out of their *va'a* and peer through the stern and port windows of the *Hope*'s great cabin. Then the *Hope* moves on to anchor in Vaitahu.

At Vaitahu the *Hope* is welcomed by about twenty single and double *va'a*. Again a white-haired, grey-bearded old man welcomes them, this time venturing onto the deck of the *Hope*. We have to think this old man is the man-godly *tau'a*, Toouiviatua, Tainai's uncle, the *atua* of Vaitahu valley. As he stands there on the deck, the old man trembles violently. He is *atua* in the presence of *atua*, those who come from 'beyond the sky', like his hero ancestors. He trembles. He does not know what powers he has over them, what powers they have over him.

The people of Vaitahu look out at the *Hope* from their beach behind the rolling stones and strong surf. Only the adults have seen a *ihepe'a* before, but all of them know what happened when Cook's *Resolution* was in the bay. They have danced and sung his visit many times. They've made stages in their *tohua* like a ship. They have laughed at the mimicry by the *hoki* (the theatre groups) of the Strangers' strutting ways. They have mocked their inability to speak a language that all can understand. They know the power of muskets and cannon, the Strangers' 'thunder'. Thunder, they have known over the millennia, is a godly power.

They can see how the *Hope* is different from the *Resolution*. There are no uniforms. They know the function of flags. The *Hope*'s, at its stern, is not the same as the *Resolution*'s. They recognise the postures and gestures of authority and know that it is Joseph Ingraham in charge. They know what the Strangers will want—water, wood, food, especially hogs. They know that the Strangers will respond to the cry '*taio*—friend', and '*tapu*—taboo'. They don't yet have a sense of transient trading. All their exchanges are based on long-term relationships, an expectancy that an imbalance in the value of what is exchanged will be adjusted in time. The Strangers will ride roughshod over their values, will fish where they have no right to fish, will eat what they have no right to eat, will go where they have no right to go. So there is a sense that this disregard of property is mutual. They will learn painfully that it is not.

As the *Hope* anchors, Enata counsel among themselves about how the Strangers should be met. Ten men—Tainai must be among them—dress as they must for any confrontation, but are not armed. They have skulls at their waists, old men's grey beards on their arms, frigate-bird feathers on their heads. And of course they are 'wrapped in images'. The eyes on their tattoos flash their warnings, shout their courage. The ten men come forward in a canoe, plaintain branches in their hands. The branches are substitutes for the human sacrifices that *atua* would expect. There are also foods that the *atua* demand—hogs, breadfruit, fish. There is no worship in these offerings, only respect for powers that are not yet known. The Strangers are men, as the *tau'a* are men, but they have a power that must be managed.

When Cook was in the bay, Enata hid the women away, except for Vahinetapu whom William Wales described. Perhaps it was a *tapu* time unconnected with Cook's visit. Perhaps with *atua* in the bay it was dangerous to expose the women. With the *Hope* it was different. *Atua* could be managed with more than offerings. *Atua* had all the passions of humankind—anger, irritation, lust. When the ten have made their offerings, suddenly the water is filled with young women. They are the *kai'oi*, the young dancers. Their ages are from eight years to twelve, barely into their puberty. All the older women, beyond those years of freedom, hold back. They see immediately from the reactions of the Strangers that the girls are likely to assuage their power.

Hear what one of the Strangers, Ebenezer Dorr, says of the *kai'oi*:

> The girls were permitted on board without any hesitation. They were in general small and young, quite naked and without exception the most beautiful people I ever saw. Their shapes and features were exquisite beyond description. They being naked there was no deception of dress. Their complexion varied, some of a copper and others as fair in complexion as any of ourselves. Their hair was various colours, long and fine, wearing it flowing in its natural curls. Of the ornaments we could not see any and suppose but few are worn by them, unless printing or staining [tattooing] is admitted as such. On the whole their beauty and gentleness with the rest of their charm was such that few could but admire them and none resist the impulse of the moment. They do not appear to have any idea of shame or criminality.

Of course, a sense of shame and criminality is a two-sided virtue. The next Strangers to arrive—the French—would be even more orgiastic in their response to the *kai'oi*. They would go away realising that their predecessors in the *Hope* had brought more from the seaboard towns of the United States than beads, mirrors and nails. They brought 'the itch' as well.

The rest of that first day was spent to Ingraham's satisfaction. Enata swam hogsheads of water through the surf to the longboat, and flotillas of *va'a* brought wood and supplies. When the chaos around the *Hope* became unmanageable and Enata appropriation of whatever was moveable too steady, Ingraham would brandish a musket and everybody would jump overboard. Ingraham was reluctant to fire his muskets in order to avoid the example of Cook, 'who', Dorr writes in his journal, 'in general leaves some mark of violence behind him wherever he goes'.

There is little sleep on the *Hope* that night. All night long, far up the valley, there is the beating of drums, shouts and singing. They could see the flames of fires through the trees. Ingraham orders the cannon to be loaded and fused and the matches to be kept lit. He has the four-pounder fired regularly to scare away anybody in the water.

Enata were living through what must have been a remarkable day in their lives by doing what they knew best—feasting, dancing, singing, displaying what had been won from the Strangers. They had stories to tell of extraordinary sights, none so remarkable, perhaps, as a pet monkey. It belonged to 'Opye'. He was lucky not to have it stolen.

All four of these first Strangers' vessels to visit Vaitahu were using Fenua'enata as a supply spot on their way north to Hawai'i and the Northwest Coast. None of them, for reasons of trade or diplomacy, wanted to call in at Spanish ports on the South and North American coast. Turning north after Vaitahu, they inevitably came across the northern Marquesas Islands. They each believed that they had 'discovered' them. But Ingraham was the first. His newly established United States inspires the names he gave his discoveries—Washington, Federal Islands—'in honour of our new, equal and liberal constitution, which I hope will be as permanent as the island itself', comments Dorr. They 'take possession' of the islands, as 'discoverers' are wont to do. That they did take possession would be an issue of national pride for some years—in Massachusetts at least. Enata 'gave them a song' in return, Ingraham writes, and discovered that the nails that were given them did not float.

The Solide, Etienne Marchand
13 to 20 June 1791

While Thomas Perkins was building the *Hope*, a 37-year-old Frenchman was dreaming of a much grander trading venture. Etienne Marchand was born on the outer edges of metropolitan France, in Grenada West Indies. He would die on its edges too, in Mauritius, soon after his venture, in 1793. Looking in from the edge seemed to bind him more closely to the centre. He was proud in these early days of the Revolution and he dreamed of making these early years of the new nation even more glorious.

By chance Marchand had met up with Nathaniel Portlock at St Helena in 1788 when he himself was on his way home to Marseilles from Bengal. Portlock had been on Cook's last voyage and had seen the possibilities of the China fur trade. He had immediately gone out on trading ventures and was at St Helena homeward-bound after his second venture. Marchand listened carefully to what he had to say and hurried home to Marseilles with a plan for the French trading company Maison Baux for whom he worked in Bengal. The plan was ambitious, an expedition of two vessels to the Northwest Coast. The Pacific was on the minds of the French in these days. La Pérouse's two-vessel expedition had got lost some time in 1788. Joseph-Antoine Bruny D'Entrecasteaux, in search of La Pérouse, would enter the Pacific from the west a little after Marchand would enter it from the east.

Marchand's ambitions were curtailed somewhat by the turmoil of the times. Instead of two vessels, there would be only one. Still it would be a trading venture on the grand scale. The *Solide*, 300 tons, especially built, would be copper-sheathed. It would have two captains, three lieutenants, two surgeons, three volunteer scientists, and thirty-nine crew. The *Solide* was seen as the acme of modern French ship-building, with special attention to ventilation and other aspects of the crew's health. It would be Marchand's boast that there was no sickness in twenty months of the *Solide*'s cruise. They left well supplied—500 chickens, seven pigs, thirty sheep—about ten chickens for each man, one-seventh of a pig, half a sheep.

Marchand's expedition was venture capitalism touched with the altruism of science. There would never be a trader as meticulous as he in giving the world the benefit of his experience—in navigational detail, meteorological and astronomical observation, in the carefulness of his description of native custom and island environment. Marchand was also quite intent on letting the islanders speak for themselves as much as he could understand them. The names they gave to their islands and bays had priority over those he invented. He had other sensitivities. He would not 'take possession' of islands already possessed by those who had discovered them. But he had his ceremonies of discovery. He was proud to raise the tricolour in the islands he thought he was the first European to see. But he would not fire a volley of muskets in celebration. He did not want to be the first to do so in these islands he thought so peaceful and friendly. With some ingenuity he left three sealed bottles containing documents describing his 'discoveries' and gave them to an old man, a woman and a young girl.

Marchand's expedition, conceived in a time of peace, was delayed till the conflict between Britain and Spain over Nootka Sound, a trading station on the west coast of what is now known as Vancouver Island, British Columbia, Canada, was resolved by a piece of artful ritualism. Vancouver raised a British flag once and pulled it down to demonstrate their right to be there. Then the British and the Spanish simultaneously withdrew from Nootka.

On 14 December 1790, Marchand took the *Solide* through the Straits of Gibraltar, then down to Cape Verde Islands and on to the Pacific around the Horn. By the time the *Solide* reached Fenua'enata, 13 June 1791, their principal need was water. The Spaniards in 1595 and the English in 1774 had described the stream of Vaitahu and a spring out of the southern hillside of the bay. The French were confident of being supplied.

The *Solide* is French. Enata don't know that. But they see a difference between these Strangers and the English and American Strangers who have come before them. There is the different flag, the tricolour.

There are more subtle differences that Enata see. These Strangers are close observers of body language and the relations among men as expressed in space and gesture and dress. When there is no language shared—though this is a difference, too; these Strangers are eager to share language and have a good ear for Enata tongue—the readings of all cultural talk are much closer. There is more carefulness than suspicion in these Strangers' body language. Their watchfulness is less aggressive. There is no part of Enata's living that is not of interest to them. Their gaze is as admiring as it is curious.

One incident illustrates this. A sentinel guarding the water casks drops his blunderbuss. It accidentally discharges into a crowd of Enata resting beneath a tree. A young boy is hit. There is no panic. It is seen as an accident. The next day the *Solide*'s surgeon, Claude Roblet, goes ashore to see what he can do. He finds the boy's arm broken with the ball. The wound is already excellently bound and the break splinted. A great crowd surrounds Roblet and the boy and watch in utter silence as the surgeon re-cleanses the wound and binds it. Roblet is *tuhuna*, expert, and the crowd knows it and is appreciative of his concern. He is shown lance wounds and skull depressions from slingshot wounds, and some trepanning surgery, and what seems to him an inordinate number of eyes missing from their sockets. He sees only one deformity, a man with slender legs. The common height is 5 feet 8 inches and few men are less than 5 feet 4 inches. (The French foot was slightly larger than the English, 0.3248 metres to 0.3048 metres. The common height was 1.830 metres, Roblet was saying, and few men were less than 1.732 metres.) He sees the variety of hair colour among the women—flaxen, auburn, black. He notices the class difference in skin colour among women. The wealthier express their wealth in dress and ornament and are almost as pale as the French. They protect their skin from the sun with a sort of parasol of leaves.

And another incident. Marchand is taken to see the *tau'a atua*, Touiviatua, in his residence behind a four- to five-foot stone wall. They meet in the deep shade of a *temanu* tree. The old man looks wretched. The grey-bearded man who stood on the deck of the *Hope* is still trembling! He is clearly uncertain whether the godliness in himself matches the power of the godliness in the Strangers. He addresses Marchand as 'Otōouh'— '*Atua*'. It is a nice moment for those of us who think there is no degradation to indigenous culture in their perception that the Strangers had the sort of godliness that came with knowledge, power and marvellous things.

The *Solide* was welcomed into the bay with lines of chanters and dancers decked out in all their finery. Conch shells blew loud, and the beat of the welcome was slapped out with right hand against the crooked left elbow. There was no mistaking the meaning of the invitations being given in the gestures of the girls and young women. Nor was there any mistaking the welcome the young men from the French provinces offered these creatures whose beauty they had never seen before and whose sexual freedoms were beyond their dreams. The Frenchman didn't need to dive deep into their belongings to give the women trifles that pleased them. The scenes on the *Solide* were orgiastic, even extending to the tarry-top, a platform on the lower masthead. It became a temple of Gnidus was one comment. (A reference, I must confess, that I have never been able to follow.) Perhaps that was one of the things that made the Frenchman seem different to other Strangers. They entered the sexual abandonment of the *kai'oi* with spirit. The French themselves, however, were not above being shocked at seeing men and women among Enata 'gratifying themselves publicly amid the loud plaudits of both sexes'. They tell of seeing four old women hold down a girl who was barely into puberty, while a young man performed 'unnatural' acts on her.

Marchand turned *Solide* north, because he too was trading in furs and did not want to meet up with the Spaniards. So Marchand 'discovers' Nukuhiva and Ua Pou. He will happen to meet up with Ingraham in Canton and be disillusioned of his exploratory achievements.

The Daedalus, Richard Hergest
22 to 30 March 1792

I feel a sadness as I go to my notes to tell William Gooch's story of his beach crossing at Vaitahu. Not that this particular beach crossing is sad. It is frivolous and trivial, if anything. The real tragedy of William's story is his death at Waimea on the Hawaiian island of Oahu. That is still two months away. *Pahupu*, Hawaiian warriors 'cut-in-two' by their tattoos, would kill him there, together with Richard Hergest, the naval commander of HM Supply Ship *Daedalus*. Manuel, a Portuguese sailor, one of those who had replaced those who had run away from Hergest's unfortunate captaincy at Rio de Janeiro, would be killed as well. No, my sadness here comes from my memory of a growing attachment to young William as I felt I got some lien on his life from the relics he left of it. Out here on the beaches of life it is not often one gets a glimpse through the window of the soul of one making its crossing.

William is twenty-one years old. He is the son of William and Sarah Gooch, the only child now that one sister had died at birth and another of smallpox. William is the light of his parents' lives. His parents are poor. His father is barber to the socially elite around the village of Brockdish in Norfolk. Old William is also churchwarden. His grave and his wife's and daughters' nestle against the grey stone wall of the Church of St Peter and St Paul he served. I've made my pilgrimages to them. I've also walked the ruins of the *heiau*, the sacrificial temple on the heights over Waimea, where I suspect the bones of young William have long become dust. For that matter, I have walked the spaces of Gonville and Caius College, Cambridge, and the university where William had his academic triumphs. He ended his university career as Second Wrangler, the second most honoured student of his year. (William Wordsworth was Hoi Polloi, among the also-rans in the same year.) You cannot tell true stories—make history—without a sense of place. You cannot make history, either, without being joined in some way to those you write about. I used to be good at the things William Gooch used to be good at—the 'Acts', the formal disputation in Latin of a thesis against the syllogistic objections of an opponent. I know the triumphs and frauds of that academic theatre.

If the entry of a poor scholar and barber's son into the exotics of a Cambridge University college was a cross-cultural experience, William Gooch's academic triumphs immediately offered him another beach to cross. George Vancouver, already on his way to the Northwest Coast, is in need of an astronomer and surveyor. William's professors at Cambridge have the ear of the Astronomer Royal, Dr Nevil Maskelyne. Maskelyne is chair of the Board of Longitude which makes the appointment. Sir Joseph Banks is on the board, as well as several professors of mathematics and astronomy from Oxford and Cambridge, the First Lord of the Admiralty and the Secretaries of the Navy. Gooch's first experience of the gestures and postures of the new world he is entering are Sir Joseph Banks's 'sly looks' which intimated that he knew by what sort of machinations young Gooch would get the appointment. William sat waiting for the board's decision with Jesse Ramsden, the maker of the 'universal theodolite' that Gooch would take with him to the Pacific. (It would cost one Enata man a musket ball in the shoulder for attempting to steal it.) William's cabin on the *Daedalus* would be packed with the artefacts of the most brilliant astronomical artisans of his day—Jesse Ramsden's azimuth, John Dollund's achromatic lens, John Arnold's and Thomas Earnshaw's precision clocks, Edward Nairne's 'philosophical apparatus', that is, dipping needles, pocket compass, magnetic bars. Packed with them would be telescopes and sextants, bottles of quicksilver, surveying chains, coloured wedges to darken the sun, and a whole library of the latest astronomic almanacs and texts. Gooch's beach was packed with instruments of practical knowledge. Dr Maskelyne was clearly nervous in entrusting such treasures to a novice astronomer and would spend years making sure he got every one of them back after Gooch's death at Waimea. You will find most of them still in the world's museums and historical society collections. Gooch himself hardly lived long enough to appreciate their artistry. For most of the last nine months of his life they were more instruments of 'fagging' than things of beauty. The records of his 'fagging'—in his ten-digit calculations from these instruments of observation—are still to found in his two volumes of workbooks in the Board of Longitude archives.

That was how I first met William Gooch—in these workbooks—in his endless pages of untidy calculations, in his doodles, in his practising of his signature—William Gooch, W. Gooch, W. G.—in notes to himself of what to tell his parents, notes about the new love of his life, Sally Smithson, 'Miss Goody Two-Shoes', whom he had met just before leaving for the Pacific. There are also drafts, written in Greek letters, of recriminatory messages to Richard Hergest, the commander of the *Daedalus*, whom he had thought to be his friend.

Poor Richard Hergest! George Vancouver would say after Hergest's death that he was his most 'intimate friend'. Vancouver and Hergest had been together as midshipmen on Cook's last two voyages of discovery. Everybody in the Royal Navy probably knew of Richard Hergest. After the death of Cook at Kealakekua Bay on the island of Hawai'i, Hergest had chased the man, 'Britannee', who they thought was Cook's killer, had levelled his pistol at Britannee's head to execute him, and had the pistol misfire. The Admiralty had qualms about sending him out to the Pacific again. Hergest proclaimed to anyone who would listen to him that the only way to deal with savages was with violence. Vancouver had asked for Hergest to come with him on his expedition but had missed out because of the alarms of a new war with Spain. But when he needed to have a supply ship follow him, Hergest was put in charge of the *Daedalus*.

Poor Richard Hergest, I say. He was not allowed to open his sealed orders in the *Daedalus* until he left Portsmouth. Then he discovered that he wasn't actually going to join Vancouver. He was to remain commander of this 312-ton, pug-nosed, Whitby-built, copper-sheathed trader on lease to the navy. He was to meet up with Vancouver in Hawai'i or on the Northwest Coast, deliver his 160 tons of material in the *Daedalus*—material badly and dangerously packed, as they were about to discover. Then he was to ply between the Northwest Coast of America and the new convict settlement of Botany Bay, bringing cattle and sheep to the latter and returning with whatever Vancouver needed. No glory of discovery for Hergest. Not even the comfort of navy life. He was doomed to an ugly trading sort of life at the ends of the earth. He wept copious tears at the thought, and took his anger and disappointment out on all around him.

Hergest was no man for beaches. The *Daedalus* was not a 'hermaphrodite brig'. It was a mixed-up vessel nonetheless. It was on lease to the navy from Alexander Davison, who was steadily amassing a vast fortune as Lord Nelson's prize agent, transporting convicts to Botany Bay and, as England prepared for the Napoleonic wars, becoming very practised in shady dealings for which he would eventually be indicted and shamed. Even the innocent William Gooch could see that Davison was a 'dirty rascal'. Hergest agreed. 'Mr G., that Davison is a merchant and merchants are such damned strange sets of animals as perhaps you've never dealt with.' Merchants and navy didn't mix. Hergest was a navy man on a most un-navy ship. He didn't cope well with the freedoms his non-navy crew thought they had. William Gooch would be Hergest's only real companion on this long voyage, but it was a companionship that blew hot and cold. Hergest had told Gooch the moment he met him that he would be a brother to him. It was an intruding and then retreating brotherliness, though, not at all conducive to a smooth relationship. They would die together at Waimea in one of its lows. Hergest could not get any of the crew to come ashore with him. He was forced to ask William to accompany him. As they walked to their death at Waimea, they were probably trying to retrieve a relationship that seemed irretrievably broken when Hergest told Gooch that he would give a bad report of him to Vancouver, thus ruining a career not yet begun.

The six-month voyage of the *Daedalus* to Tenerife, Rio de Janeiro, the Falklands, around the Horn and across the southern Pacific to Fenua'enata had been miserable and uncomfortable for Gooch. He comforted himself with the spaniel puppy given him by Captain Thomas New, Alexander's representative on the *Daedalus*. 'Tio' they had called him for the Tahitian word for 'friend', *taio*. He found comfort too in his letters, more to Miss Goody Two-Shoes than his parents. He used his astronomer's skills and his traveller's tricks to join their lives in real time. His are trusting letters, written with the knowledge that Sally would not believe all his self-deprecation. Trustful too in showing his anxieties and his loneliness. He has a softness that beach crossers shouldn't have.

On 22 March, just a day before they see Fatuiva, William tries his hand at a first bit of serious astronomy, measuring an eclipse of the sun. The same eclipse, seen by Enata, must have been awesome prelude to a Stranger's visit, we have to think. Gooch's 'fagging' for this astronomical event is frenetic, pages long. Mixed up among his calculations are all sorts of observations. Lists of Enata words—about the body, clothing, numerals one to ten. Drawings—of tattoo designs, of the *Daedalus*, of Falkland Islands sealing. There is our drawing of Tainai—Gooch calls him 'Taoo'. He writes a couple of Latin phrases: '*puella osculis dilectissima*—delicious girls with kisses'. There are many notes in phrases: 'amorous female offended at inattention'; 'afraid of dogs'; 'bones in ears'; 'clap hands for music'. The otherness of it all is kaleidoscopic.

It is dark, near midnight, before they drop the anchor and get it to hold on the sandy bottom. They had passed Vaitahu by, thinking it too small for

Cook's description of Resolution Bay. Then they had to battle back and tack painfully against the wind buffeting down the valley. Canoes had followed them down the straits between Hiva Oa and Tahuata. They now cluster around, the natives singing and clapping. The *Daedalus* crew had hardly settled at 4 a.m. when the anchor cable snapped. Hergest takes the *Daedalus* out to the open sea and turns her around in the dawn light. Then he asks the crew if they smell smoke. Yes, they say. They have smelt it since they anchored. They think it comes from native fires on the shore. Hergest goes to Gooch's cabin.

Gooch smells smoke too. The pair follow their noses to the great cabin. There they discover to their alarm that smoke is coming from the deck below. They open the scuttle and smoke pours out. Their alarm now is very high. The gunpowder is stored in the hold from which the smoke is coming. With the gunpowder casks are packed stores of all sorts—against all naval regulations. They cannot get the gunpowder out quickly. They form a line to the main deck and hand all along it. When the gunpowder is out they discover the leaden floor of the hold nearly too hot to stand on. The fire is a further deck below. They guess that all the water they shipped in coming around the Horn has gotten into the bedding they are bringing to Vancouver. The wet filling of the bedding becomes a compost and spontaneously combusts. The one thing they cannot afford to do is to let air onto the combustion. They bore holes through the leaden floor and pipe water on to the fire until they are sure that it is out.

Meanwhile, the crew not assisting at the fire—there were thirty of them—were doing two things, getting the longboat ready in case of the need to abandon ship and bringing the *Daedalus* back to its mooring. They grasp at the fact that Captain William Bligh was either at Tahiti or about to arrive there. The Admiralty had sent Bligh out to Tahiti in the *Providence* and the *Adventure* to collect the breadfruit that he had failed to deliver in the *Bounty* to the slave plantations in the West Indies. There was a chance that the *Daedalus* longboat could take them to safety in Tahiti. But it isn't needed. There is one last frustration after their nervous night. Enata have stolen the buoy holding the anchor cable. Enata don't want the *Daedalus* to go away, though. They replace the buoy holding the line to the anchor cable with a piece of wood.

The decks of the *Daedalus* are a chaos of gunpowder barrels and rescued cargo. The crew are throwing the wet, burnt bedding overboard, cursing the navy dockworkers for storing it so badly. Enata splash around frenziedly in the water thinking that the waste might be valuable. They try to clamber aboard from all sides to take the pickings on the deck. Hergest's dog Bot frightens off some. Hergest shoots a man in the shoulder to retrieve a theodolite and another in the calf through the side of a canoe to rescue a blanket. Disorder is matched by the bizarre—men tie ship's biscuits into their necklaces, nails into their hair.

That afternoon, no doubt weary after their sleepless night fighting the fire and still alarmed at how close to disaster they had come, Hergest and Gooch go ashore. Hergest, whose imprudence will be the death of him in Hawai'i, makes no preparation for what is nearly inevitable. Enata mill about the pair in near hysterical excitement. In the heat, and with the smells of rancid coconut on tattooed bodies, the unintelligible shouts, the pulling and pinching, the unmistakable invitations of the young girls, William's aplomb dissipates. Maybe he is too polite in such a foreign place to face them with stern authority. Maybe all the tensions of this unhappy voyage come to a head. Maybe the otherness of it all just enfolds him. He dissolves into tears.

Such lack of control outrages Hergest. It is not gentlemanly to lose face in this manner, he shouts. It is like losing one's self-control in face of a London street rabble. As he berates Gooch, someone in the crowd takes advantage of his distraction and snatches a fowling piece from his hands. In a rage he orders the sailor following them to fire his musket into the crowd. Luckily—Hergest then realises—the musket misfires. Luckily, because they all would be defenceless if the crowd turned on them.

They hurry back to the boat, fire volleys of musketoons and muskets over the crowd's heads and return to the *Daedalus*. There Hergest orders four cannons to be fired deep into the valley. It is where most Enata habitations are. It is an irrational and disproportionate action, a collective punishment that is theatre to nothing but power. He sheepishly reports it in his journal, knowing how it will be seen in the light of his violent approach to natives. He thinks nobody is injured in his salvo. At least nobody is reported as such.

A crowd of Enata come down to the beach carrying their proxy sacrifices, plantain branches. Hergest takes it as a sign of peace. When two of whom he thinks are 'lesser chiefs' come aboard *Daedalus*, he takes them hostage until his fowling piece is returned.

Gooch recovers his senses back on board the *Daedalus*, even if his relationship with Hergest is further damaged. He pursues his curiosity about Enata from the *Daedalus*. Enata are curious at his curiosity. They see him writing his notes with his pen. 'Epartoo', '*patu*', they say. 'Tattoo'. They lie down on the deck and invite him to do his tattooing on them. There are certain things Gooch doesn't want his mother to see. These he writes in Greek letters. So in Greek letters, he describes how Enata men tie back their prepuce over their glans, and he remarks how ordinary it is to see a man carrying on a conversation with a friend while tying up his penis.

On 24 March, Hergest turns the *Daedalus* north to Hawai'i, and like Ingraham and Marchand before him 'discovers' Nukuhiva, Ua Pou and Ua Huka. But this time there is an apprentice map-maker aboard. William Gooch leaves us our first map of these northern Marquesas—Hergest Islands, Vancouver will call them in honour of his most intimate friend. Indeed the fag book has six sketches—our first for these details—and small descriptions of the bays along the southern coast of Nukuhiva: Hakaui (Trevennen), Taiohae (Port Anna Maria), Hapa'a, Taipivai and Hoo'umi (Comptroller's Bay). Gooch goes into both Taiohae and Taipivai in the longboat surveying. He remarks how in both bays, especially in Taiohae, Enata are along the shore in their thousands, dressed for the most part in white cloth and in long lines dancing and clapping. Dr Maskelyne won't be happy in the end with his map-making, but William, exhausted by it all, feels he has come of age as an astronomer.

The voyage to Hawai'i begins badly. Tio, Gooch's spaniel pup, is lost overboard. Hergest won't listen to him and is taking the *Daedalus* too far to the west. They will have to tack back against the prevailing winds to reach Hawai'i. It is a delay in meeting up with Vancouver that will prove fatal.

Hergest is threatening to report that Gooch is unsuitable to be the astronomer for the Vancouver expedition. The great cabin of the *Daedalus* is a tense and unhappy place. Hergest and Gooch aren't talking. They correspond in a code of English written in Greek letters. Nothing augurs well for whatever is to come.

The Jefferson, Josiah Roberts

11 November 1792 to 24 February 1793

Josiah Roberts has an idea. He wants to trade for sea-otter skins on the Northwest Coast. Better to have two ships for that, a mother ship to store the skins and a smaller vessel to navigate the bays and rivers. Roberts has one ship, the 150-ton *Jefferson*. His idea: take a prefabricated schooner in the *Jefferson* and put it together on a Pacific island. Which island? Hawai'i is dangerous. No news of Ingraham in Boston yet, but The Marquesas are islands being talked about in trading circles. Roberts will do some sealing in the South Atlantic, provision if necessary at Valparaiso, and scout the possibilities of Resolution Bay on Woahoo (Ohitahoo, Tahuata).

The voyage does not begin well. The *Jefferson* runs foul of a rope while moving from Rhowe's Wharf to Long Wharf in Boston Harbor. A man is killed. The ship is well crewed—thirty-six men, twenty-four for the *Jefferson* and twelve for the schooner they will build. Theirs would be a long voyage, three years and eight months. Twenty of the thirty-six won't live to return to Boston.

They spend a cold two and a half months at St Ambrose Island, collecting 13,000 seal skins. At $60 a hundred in Canton for the skins, they have made a good start.

Nearly a year after leaving Boston, the *Jefferson* is working its way past Fatuiva and Hiva Oa. All crew are quartered to its eight guns, which are loaded with grape. They are delighted with Resolution Bay. 'As good a bay for anchoring as any I ever saw', Bernard Magee, the first officer, writes in his journal. Not an assessment with which many coming before or after him would agree, but they are also looking for a site where they can erect their shipyard. They think they see a spot tucked against the northern promontory. The water is deep to the shore there. They can build a wall of stone to hold their slipway.

The welcome of Enata to the *Jefferson* is as excited as ever. The water around the ship is filled with men and women holding calabashes of water, fish and fruit. There are many canoes too. When Enata clamber aboard the *Jefferson*, pilfering is rife. A compass and glass lamp go quickly. A musket is taken through a cabin window but dropped to the floor of the bay. There is a strange air of inconsequentiality in the disorder. It is a strangeness that will bedevil the men of the *Jefferson* the whole three and a half months of their stay at Vaitahu. It will help excuse their own savagery. Nothing they do has a long-term effect. No one among the natives seems to have responsibility for anybody else. Everything in the natives' relationship is as slippery as quicksilver.

On this first day on the deck of the *Jefferson*, an Enata man steals the cooper's cask axe. Bernard Magee fires the full charge of his musket into the man's face and neck. Whether he kills him, Magee doesn't say, or what happens next. Within minutes, however, Enata are negotiating the exchange of a twenty- to thirty-pound hog at the price of an axe. The hog is expensive, the 'Jeffersons' learn, because of the recent visit of the *Hope*, the *Solide* and the *Daedalus*, but Enata do not give them the ships' names. Tainai is on the deck telling them so. Tainai is chief, they know. But he has no authority. More a 'father of a family', they think. They are not sure what this will mean for their future relationships in the bay.

It is Tainai, though, who helps them select the site for their shipyard in the northern corner of the bay. It is beside Hitihiti's *paepae*. There is great excitement about the strangers building a ship at Vaitahu. Enata help bring the frame and masts ashore. It will be a 20-ton schooner. They discover that they do not have enough timber in the prefabrication by about one-third. They will clear the valley of the best timber to complete the job. They will need about 700 bushels of charcoal to forge the 'towees', the iron adzes with which they will trade on the Northwest Coast, and the schooner's ironwork. (A Winchester bushel in use in the United States at the time was 2150.4 cubic inches. They were needing about 300 cubic metres of charcoal.) They will clear the side of the hill above their shipyard for that. The extravagant call of the Strangers' ships on the natural resources of the islands will change the landscape very quickly.

There is much else that the 'Jeffersons' will garner for the *Resolution*— that is what they will name their vessel. They will require sealing for the hulls and decks and provisions for the coming voyage. Thirty-six men, with a taste for meat and vegetables that Enata count as special, puts a strain on everyday subsistence in the valley. Those on the edge—the *kikino*, persons of low status—who suffer most when abundance is low, begin to become resentful. The Strangers' intrusions become trespass when they take trees not theirs to take, when they go where they have no right to go, when they eye women not to be eyed, when they interrupt the seasons of remembrance and festival. There is a growing resentment in the valley. There are several skirmishes around the shipyard as Enata try to steal what is lying around. Several Enata are killed. No numbers are given. The 'Jeffersons' are not long at Vaitahu when their black chef tries to run. Roberts—'Kopati', 'Old Dried Up', Enata call him—immediately goes to Tainai with an armed group and threatens dire revenge if the cook is not returned. He is back within two hours, bound and trembling at his experiences. It is enough to scare off any other attempt at running away.

The Strangers obey their own taboos. There is no labour on the Sabbath. Half the crew are given shore leave for an afternoon. The rest no doubt do what sailors always do on Sundays, wash and mend their clothes, yarn, carve scrimshaw. The rest days are dangerous days. On the first, two men go into a *tapu* place, a *me'ae*. They are attacked. The musket of one is taken and his arm broken with the musket used as a club. The other has his two pistols stolen. When an armed party from the *Jefferson* comes to rescue them, they are ambushed by stone-slinging Enata. The 'Jeffersons' are surprised at how long it takes, even with their musketry, to make Enata back away.

Two weeks into their stay, a large crowd, many from different valleys on Tahuata, collects around the shipyard. They shout what are clearly insults and threats. Roberts sends the longboat to shore with swivel guns and musketoons. Enata attack the shipyard all of one long afternoon. Nine are killed and many more are wounded. The cannons from the *Jefferson* finally drive them off. Tainai is wounded in this skirmish. The Strangers also believe that they have killed his father and his brother. Tainai's father, Honu, wasn't killed but his brother Tupahui was. When Crook and Robarts come to the valley six and seven years later, the memory of all this is still clear.

The next day Enata collect on the hill over the shipyard and pound those below with their slings. Then they roll down large boulders, but they are driven away with concentrated fire. It is all slightly bizarre. Tainai comes aboard the *Jefferson* to have his wound dressed by the surgeon. Everything calms down as if nothing had happened. Soon after, large seas in the bay break down the stone wall holding the slipway. Enata enthusiastically repair the damage.

The building of the *Resolution* is much slower than they had planned. On 2 January 1793, they are alarmed by the sound of conch shells. Enata gather in all their war regalia and sing war songs along the shore. The 'Jeffersons' are not in danger of attack, however. Canoes from Hiva Oa—Pikina and Tui probably—have landed somewhere on Tahuata. If one could guess at what was motivating the attack, it was probably bravado. The Pikina and Tui would show the Hema and Ahutini how to deal with Strangers. Tainai is half hopeful that the *Jefferson* will join the fleet collecting in the bay. But his twenty-five canoes and perhaps two hundred warriors must do their attacking for themselves. They sail out to the north to do battle with the Hiva Oans.

With the men out of the valley, the women swarm over the *Jefferson*. There is some suggestion that the visit of the *Jefferson*, unlike the visits of previous ships, is raising tensions between the men and women of Vaitahu.

With the *Resolution* near completion in the first weeks of February, Roberts is thinking of his voyage to come. On board the *Jefferson* are five young Enata men. They do such services as fishing and collecting provisions. They had been promised a trip to America. Because Roberts was eager to acquire hogs, he listened to the five's plan to go ashore at midnight and steal the hogs they needed. Roberts was too smart by far. Two of the five, who slept on the floor of the great cabin, took two muskets and some cartridge boxes, and all five disappeared into the night. They were probably the first firearms with ammunition to come into the possession of Enata. It is probably not a moment to celebrate. Enata would become obsessed with this weapon of death. It would make their darkest hours even darker.

Roberts had met up with a man from Nukuhiva who had lived at Vaitahu for ten years. Tuhimatatini was his name. Tuhi took Roberts to the top of the hill behind the shipyard on a clear day. There he showed him the mountains of the island of Ua Pou peeking above the northwest horizon. Tuhi agreed to pilot Roberts to Ua Pou and Nukuhiva. Roberts would be another to think he had made a 'discovery'.

The first attempt to launch the *Resolution* failed. It settled into the soft bilgeway and couldn't be moved. It was 7 February. The carpenters lined the bilgeway with oak planking. The next day it poured with rain. Finally, with the enthusiastic help of Enata, well used to large-scale cooperative works, the *Resolution* slipped into the bay. The great crowd of Enata, left alone on the shore, looted the yard with glee. All that the 'Jeffersons' could do was commandeer canoes and nets and threaten to destroy them unless the more valuable of the equipment was returned.

It took two weeks to 'boot-top' the *Resolution*, that is, to cover it with a mixture of tallow, sulphur or lime and resin and paint it. Then they rig and load it with wood and provisions. The *Jefferson* and the *Resolution* left Vaitahu for Ua Pou on 24 February. For a brief time two of the islands they would see carried the names of the two ships.

Roberts sails first for Ua Pou. Tuhi gives them the Enata names of all these 'discoveries'. Roberts, not knowing that Ingraham has given these Washington Islands the names of the heroes of the American Revolution, gives them all another round of revolutionary names. Tuhi gives them small indications of population numbers and provisioning possibilities, pointing out the uninhabited islands which were visited seasonally for turtles and birds. For some reason the two ships move on to the southwest corner of Nukuhiva. Roberts sends Magee out in the pinnace to search out an anchorage. Tuhi goes with Magee. Magee takes the pinnace northward along the western coast of Nukuhiva. This is the most unpopulated coast of Nukuhiva, except for a number of small fishing colonies. They are in any case driven back by an northeast wind and land in a small bay—'rockbound', without beach. There they meet people who offer them baked fish rolled in leaves. These people are deeply admiring of everything about the pinnace, especially the ironwork. They seem attracted to the muskets. Perhaps the gestures of the boatpeople indicate that they are weapons. Tuhi asks that the muskets be fired. They all jump immediately into the water and come up holding their heads in their hands. Tuhi is greatly amused. When these fisher people learn from the 'Jeffersons' that they have come from Tahuata, they show a Nukuhivan uppitiness. Tahuata, they indicate, is a small-time island.

Tuhi takes his leave of the 'Jeffersons' at this point. They leave him with gifts of a blanket, a hat, a hatchet, a knife and a looking-glass. Tuhi is one of the first Enata mediators. We know him by name, but that is all.

Roberts takes the *Jefferson* and the *Resolution* to the Northwest Coast. He will have a financially successful voyage. The sea-otter skins they trade cost him $6. He sells them in Canton for $20. In human terms he is not so successful, but we do not know how he calculates such costs in his bottom line. The *Resolution* is lost in a wild sea with all hands on the Northwest Coast. Another eight of his crew perish with disease and by accident. Still Roberts' voyage is well celebrated in Massachusetts. The adventure in venture capitalism glosses over the human pain in the profit made with a sort of mythological and historical glow. Another sort of 'boot-topping'. The twenty lives of the crew lost and the fifteen or more Enata killed certainly are not accounted for in the final cost of a trading voyage.

CROSSINGS

'Remember me?'

'Remember me?' It is an unnerving question coming at the end of a public lecture or over a supermarket trolley or at a funeral or on the street. Forty years of teaching puts thousands of faces into the mind's bank. Not all their names are retrievable.

Those who ask 'Remember me?' don't often let one dangle long in embarrassment. Even a flicker of puzzled recognition will evoke a follow-up declaration. 'I was in your Social and Reflective History class.' 'You took us to Sydney to work in the Mitchell Library. We were going to write a book, not an essay.' 'We did an ethnography on Anzac Day. We stood in the rain at the Dawn Service. We were both in tears.' 'You said something I'll never forget.'

Teaching is a hard life. Those you teach come and go in short cycles. All the long-term goals you have for your students can never be seen to happen in those short moments. Hearing 'Remember me?' is a teacher's gift, a sense that something that had been seeded and cultivated has been harvested.

Footprints in the Sand

A footprint in the sand can be disturbing. Man Friday's footprint certainly disturbed Robinson Crusoe's sense of ownership of his island, as Paul Carter has reflected on in *The Lie of the Land* (2000), his splendid study of the different footprints on the Australian landscape. There is nothing so pristine as an untrod beach. To see footprints on it brings the disappointment that one is not after all there first.

To discover that the past belonged more to those on whom it impinged than to those who had the academic skill to tell its story was something like seeing footprints in the sand to those of us who try to write encounter history. It demanded a more generous understanding of what history might be, as island people tapped their cultural memories in song, dance, poetry, art and craft. It demanded as well that one could not tell the story of another's past without sharing in some way their language. Another people's language is truly their footprint in the sand. It holds the other's metaphors. It frames an historical past and all the events in it as surely as my language frames my history of them.

For nearly forty years now I have been responsible for educating young men and women to their highest degree of skills in their chosen field of endeavour, the writing of history. I have urged them always not to see the footprints in the sand as some sort of trespass on their beach. Because all education now is global by way of our journal writing, our book publishing, our conferencing, our associations, our exchange lecturing and our examining, I can claim that—perhaps not for forty but certainly for twenty or thirty years—I have said to all young island scholars as well that they must not see footprints in the sand as trespass. Sometimes they have been offended when I tell them what I have told my own students: 'If you look too long at your navel, you will only see a belly-button'. They are offended, they tell me, because 'navel' has been one of their great cultural metaphors. Each of their islands in their Sea of Islands is 'The Navel of the World'.

Maybe. But we all have to cross beaches sometime. It gives me the greatest pleasure in recent times to see the young scholars of the Sea of Islands reading the footprints in the sand that world literature, world neomodernity, world representational art have left on their beaches not as trespass but as signposts. They can read these signposts through the deep metaphors of both Sea and Land that give them their identity from the past. They are comfortable with ways of understanding whose borders are in flux. They see their Sea of Islands out of both their roots and their routes.

'REMEMBER ME?', a young real estate agent asked me when he had sold me a house. Indeed I did. Remembering him took me back to 1954. I had been sent to teach small boys, aged between eight and twelve years, in a Jesuit preparatory boarding school. Burke Hall, it was called, for the real estate agent who had contributed generously to its establishment. The headmaster at the time was the Reverend 'Chips' Carpenter SJ, an eccentric English Jesuit from Bath, full of delusions of social grandeur. He put me in charge of about sixty junior boarders, none older than nine years. I had one dormitory of seven- and eight-year-olds in a high state of trauma at feeling somehow disposed of by their parents. This meant waking them at 6.30 a.m., seeing to their ablutions, watching their piety through morning mass, snatching breakfast before overseeing the polishing of their shoes. Then, after the day's classes and sport and study, seeing them to bed after showers. Smells, they say, linger longest in memory. The smell of wet small boys in large number has lasted a lifetime with me. Father Carpenter had made me sports master and yard master. He assigned me six classes to teach each day. The matron had had a car accident the week before the school year began. So he made me matron as well.

Among his many eccentricities Father Carpenter used to get what he called 'headaches' on weekends and public holidays. 'Gregory,' he would say to me, 'get rid of all these boys'. I and about two hundred boarders used to roam restlessly around the suburbs like the Lost Tribes of Israel, sometimes paper-chasing, sometimes creating chaos down at the Saturday matinee at the local cinema. If you haven't taken two hundred small boys to a Saturday afternoon matinee, you cannot really say that you have experienced life. These were the days of serials—'Speed Gordon', 'The Lone Ranger'—and Fitzpatrick travelogues. These were the days when ice creams and lollies were bartered down the aisles at intervals. These were the days when those who sat in the stalls lived in mortal fear of what would come down on them from the balcony. These were the days when a brave organist would rise out of the orchestra pits and defy the hordes.

In the first weeks of first term, Father Carpenter called me into his office and confided to me that one of his friends among the socially elite had told him that there was a poliomyelitis epidemic raging through Melbourne. I must cancel all inter-school sport. Of course, I stopped all matches, although I had many mystified return calls from other schools saying that they could not confirm my rumours. I put all my energies into organising a highly complex internal school competition in all aspects of cricket—bowling, catching, batting, running; ten-over matches, one-day championships. In March a large headline in the local newspaper read: 'Lowest Polio Episodes in Three Decades'. It did not persuade Father Carpenter to return to inter-school competition. 'By order of holy obedience', he said, invoking my vows, 'I command you to cancel all matches this term'.

I had been made sports master, but not grounds master. In the middle of my frenetic efforts to have the whole school entertain itself, the grounds master decided that the bottom oval needed reseeding. He hired a horse from Murphy's Grain and Fuel on nearby High St and began ploughing the bottom oval. That meant that I had only one small oval for sport. One day I had fifteen cricket matches on it.

One evening as I was lining up the boys for rosary at 5.15 p.m., a small dayboy came shouting: 'Sir! Sir! The horse is out.' Out the horse was, on Studley Park Road, a principal thoroughfare passing by the school along the ridge of a hill, then down a steep gradient into a large junction, then off again towards Murphy's Grain and Fuel. It was the peak traffic hour. I joined the procession behind the horse, in my clerical dress and gown, the small boy at my side. A car pulled out and offered to drive us around the horse. So on the top of the hill over Kew Junction I stood in front of this huge horse-led procession, stopped him, and walked him back to school, to something like the 'Trumpet Voluntary' from honking cars.

Then some years ago I bought a house in Kew. The young real estate agent who sold the house to me, when he learned my name, said: 'Remember me? I helped you catch the horse on Studley Park Road.' Sometimes men will come to me and say: 'Remember me? You taught me "The Marseillaise".' 'Remember me? You used to tell us serial stories down in the yard on wet afternoons.' But 'Remember me? I helped you with the horse' is the nicest of all my 'Remember me's?.

The world of educationists seems to be divided as to whether it was Ignatius Loyola, the founder of the Jesuits, or Adolf Hitler who said: 'Give me a boy of seven and I will make him what I will'. I hope it wasn't Loyola. His Jesuits, no matter how competent they were with young adults, were inept with small boys. Burke Hall was a rude, ugly place without a touch of femininity. I had been a boarder there myself when I was twelve years old, and loathed it. The only good that came to me out of my schooling and teaching there was that I knew what 'total institutions' were long before I read about them in Erving Goffman's *The Presentation of Self in Everyday Life* (1959). I learned much about total institutions— the theatre of them, the counter-plays of those in their tight hold, the boundaries of private space created even under the most public gaze. I learned to read gestures and looks, to know the distinction between power and authority. I learned, too, that pain inflicted did not itself create memories or seed revolt and mutiny. What hurt, what made memories and mutiny, was opening a wound into the soul, adding guilt or shame to the pain. I would be able to write of the theatre of command and violent punishment on the *Bounty* in *Mr Bligh's Bad Language* (1992), of the rituals of Cambridge University college life in *The Death of William Gooch* (1995) and indeed an ethnography of Jesuit education in *Xavier: A Centenary Portrait* (1978) and *Xavier Portraits* (1993) because of my experience in the total institutions of schools and seminaries.

Boarders used to be at their most miserable coming back to school after a home weekend. There was one small boy always totally distraught at coming back to Burke Hall on a Sunday evening. His parents would bribe him back with bags of candy—'lollies' in the Australian dialect. Dormitories were places of the highest discipline. Places of absolute silence. Eating was especially forbidden. Food was absolutely prohibited in the dormitory. This small boy would secrete his lollies all around his bed, and eat them in the dark. After many warnings and threats of punishment, I was confronted with the necessity—or so the advice on disciplinary theory that I was given told me—of my first strapping. Each of the Jesuits at Burke Hall, not the lay teachers, was armed with a leather 'strap', two inches thick, four inches wide, two feet long. It was a symbol of our power to punish boys. Some never used it. Some carried it ostentatiously. Some joked constantly about it and revelled in their reputation as a frequent user of it. I remember my first use of it on the small boy as if it were yesterday, his wriggling figure, my hand on his wrists, his clenched fist trying to avoid the strap, and his tears. I don't think it was too violent, and it wasn't done in anger. I think I succeeded in perhaps one and a half of four strikes. But I had nightmares about it for many years after. Some years ago, when I was welcoming postgraduates to the History Department at the University of Melbourne, a mature-age student came up to me and said 'Remember me?' It was the same little boy grown to middle age. I told him of my nightmares. He couldn't remember a thing. I suppose that is a comforting 'Remember me?' for a teacher too.

My 'Remember me's?' these days are likely to come from the other end of the educational scale, those senior undergraduates and postgraduates who have elected to go one step further in their learning. That extra step will inevitably mean an engagement in a partnership between supervisor and student in research for two, three, six years and more. This partnership can be a delicate one. If life intrudes on any study, it certainly intrudes on postgraduate studies. I am not being falsely modest if I say that I never believed myself to be a very good supervisor. My scholarship was too maverick, my picture too big, my demands of reading beyond their topic too large for many of my students. But I read with pride the 'Remember me's?' that come in the form of acknowledgements at the beginning of masters' and doctoral theses and the pages of now some dozens of books on my library shelves.

These students can learn all that they need to learn in their reading. I always felt what they really needed from me was inspiration, a sense of passion for scholarship and an understanding of the need to gamble a little. The first thing I can inspire them to is to use their freedoms. And the first of these is to discover their own voice and style. Style—the imprinting of one's personal signature on whatever it is that one is doing—is not easily won. There is much pain in finding one's own style. Ask a pianist, a springboard diver, a ballet dancer. But, then too, there is nothing so sweet as the realisation that what others do excellently, I also do with style. Most of us are likely to experience a sense of style in something physical such as music or sport. I have had something I have said on this put into a dictionary of quotations under 'sport'. (Sports-writers, I have discovered, go often to dictionaries of quotations. So I find my words in strange places!) 'There is nothing so momentary as the sporting achievement and nothing so lasting as the memory of it', I once wrote. 'A ball sweetly hit, a catch nicely taken, a dashing movement in football, a sense of perfect rhythm on the river get branded on the mind and stay there forever.' I have tried to persuade my students over the years that it is the same with writing. I always prefer them to read their writing aloud than 'give a paper'. They discover the awkwardness of their expression in reading aloud. They catch their rhythm or their lack of it. They periodise what they have written with silences the better for hearing them. They can develop theatre in abrupt phrases and epigrammatic signings-off.

There is much fiction in your non-fiction, I tell them. The page we write on—the screen we type on—seems to be blank. But it isn't. We write nothing from scratch. Every problem we face as writers—what sort of presence should we have in our writing? what tense should it be written in? how do we give a holistic experience when every sentence is one line after another? what do we put in? what do we leave out?—there is no question that has not been resolved in some way—by a poet, a filmmaker, a novelist, a choreographer, an erudite scholar. There is no trick unavailable to a thesis writer, so long as the thesis writer is prepared to confront the disadvantages as well as the advantages of his or her approach. Actually I don't let my students call themselves 'non-fiction' writers. They shouldn't write 'non' anything. And the company they keep on the 'non-fiction' shelves in bookshops is not great—cookbooks, personality disorders, do-it-yourselves, ghost-written autobiographies of sporting stars. Maybe I don't have a word to replace 'non-fiction' But I tell them to see themselves as writers of true stories. Creative writers. Yes, they are creative writers.

The most creative thing that they have to do is to present a hundred thousand words in such a way that a reader will recognise and remember what they have said in a dozen words or so. Every one of my students will be a world expert in their topic after a few months of research. After a few months of research they will have more in their head than anyone else in the world. The trouble is that no one else in the world wants all that information in their head. The rest of the world wants them to join a conversation that they are already having. Their biggest freedom is to go out and find what that conversation is about. They won't find that conversation just in their own discipline. Discipline is their ally. Modern scholarship is built around the advantage of seeing the world through perspectives—botanically, genetically, psychologically, economically, etc. Seeing through perspectives requires discipline—a language, a sense of what is lost and what is gained by perspective, a sense of what is whole and what is part, of what is surface and what is depth. Their own discipline has a conversation which they must learn in order to join it. But that disciplinary conversation is only a part of a much broader conversation which has a much more universal character. 'Paradigm', 'episteme', 'discourse' were words that came to scholarly learning in the twentieth century. No student of mine, I hope, would not know where these words came from or could not enter a debate about them. To be creative, they need to know something more. They need to know the character of the paradigms, epistemes and discourses that affect their own thinking. They need to know their own postmodernity—their own neomodernity, as I said I prefer. And nothing joins the conversations of disciplines, of arts, of crafts, of all the representational sciences and arts more than what Ludwig Wittgenstein called 'the fictions of languaging'. Writers find their freedom in the fictions of their languaging.

Writers of true stories need a special *virtu* in their artistic science, their scientific art. They need narrative strategies. They need reflection.

At least I have been consistent over the years in my advice to these young men and women. I tell them always that they are writers, not 'doers', of theses. 'Doers' have three paid readers in mind—their examiners. Writers have to intrigue someone to read their first sentence, and their next, and the next. Writers have to be honest readers. An honest reader knows that she or he rarely reads a book in one sitting. Honest readers know when and why they skim, when and why they savour. Honest readers know that the tens of thousands of words in a book are reduced to a sentence or two by the reader. Those sentences tell what the book said. A writer wants to shape the thousands of words to control these few. Honest readers know that in their voyage through a long text they need memory stations and signposts. They need metaphors to jell the whole and to take them back from end to beginning.

Be mysterious, I tell them. Being mysterious means that there is still work to be done—not just by the storyteller, but by the reader as well. There is no closure to mysteries, only another story, another translation. Be experiential. Write with the whole body. Taste, smell, touch, hear, see. Work with the authority of you own experience as a cultural observer. Be entertaining. Victor Turner encouraged us to use the word 'entertaining' in its etymological sense of 'holding between', *enter tenere* in the Latin. Think of all the tricks we use in the theatre to hold the gaze and attention of an audience—darkened theatre, stage curtains, the triangular perspective of the stage. We have to find ways of entertaining our readers in the same way. Be compassionate. Give back to the past its own possibilities, its own ambiguities, its own incapacity to see the consequences of its actions. Don't be blinded by hindsight. Be performative. Take risks. Don't live by the formalities of the rules. Be reforming. Change the world with what you write.

Delete the 'theory chapter', I tell my students. Be reflective instead. Theory chapters are templates that don't template. Reflections are the bridge to the universal conversation we are joining. Reflections are the mirror to ourselves in our story. Reflections can be integrated into the narrative or they can be pulled out of it and stand alone. But true stories need to be reflective. That is both their science and their art.

Age itself brings many crossings and one of them is a thing called 'retirement'. A blessing of the scholarly life is that there is no such thing as retirement, only a shedding of obligations that otherwise interfered with the deepest pleasures of life, learning and professing what one learns.

Nonetheless, these past years of retirement have seen me acquire an exotic status called an Adjunct Professorship. I am not sure what 'adjuncting' is, but I do it conscientiously. I see it as a sort of academic grandparenting. Young scholars come to me for short periods of time. We enjoy one another and learn from one another. Then we all go home. I find the 'Remember me's?' in my life have grown exponentially. I exult in the talents of the young. They cross beaches I have never dared to cross. My archaeology of learning has a future. I get to see where learning is going ten years ahead.

I have my own 'Remember me's?' to ask. Most of those of whom I would ask it are gone. 'Be admiring', I have told my students many times, and I have regretted the many more times when I have kept my admiration to myself. There are moments after reading something that captivates me when I must take and put pen to paper. If I don't do it then, the moment is lost forever.

John Moore SJ I hope would not need a 'Remember me?' from me. John Moore was a 'scholastic', a Jesuit in training, at Xavier College in the 1940s. I had gone to Xavier after exciting experiences of Jesuit education at St Louis in Perth, Western Australia. I was dismayed at Xavier. There was a harshness in its environment that I had not experienced at St Louis. John Moore made it acceptable; made what was impersonal, personal; what was harsh, friendly and meaningful. I have memories of long conversations with John. On warm summer nights, leaning on a still warm parapet, the light of the Study Hall streaming down, cicadas in the trees, we would talk—of vocation to the priesthood, of ideals, of leadership, of pain and suffering in everyday life. The talks enlarged my life. They were serious stuff. They were not master and pupil. They were on the verge of adult friendship. They put life on another plane. I have never forgotten them.

Teaching was one of John Moore's strengths. He had a love for history. I learnt from him that I had special talents in history. Praise, nurturing a talent, setting ideals that you would die to achieve—a teacher's creative moulding can, I learned, change us for life. I *knew* I was good at history because John told me so.

I don't think that I would need to say 'Remember me?' to John Mulvaney either. I have the words of the first lecture he gave us at 11 a.m., Wednesday, 24 March 1955, in a lecture theatre in 'Babel', the language building at the University of Melbourne. 'Archaeology', he said, 'is the study of man, the reconstruction of how he lived in the past from material remains'. (He would probably remain gender-exclusive in language even today—but for the right reasons!) For Mulvaney a division between archaeology and history was inconceivable. They were dialogic disciplines. Each enlarged the other. He taught us then, and still claims, that the triumph of both archaeology and history was to proclaim the human spirit etched into the things of the earth. His words are etched into my mind.

Doug Oliver was the reason I went to Harvard to do anthropology. Doug is a southern gentleman with a deep reverence for learning, immensely proud to belong to an institution of learning like Harvard. He dedicated the three volumes of his *Ancient Tahitian Society*, a work of profound and exhaustive scholarship, to 'Kenneth Emory, prehistorian, Raymond Firth, ethnographer, and the late John Beaglehole [historian], who have infused new life into the study of Polynesian culture'. Meticulous carefulness for the truth would be the mark of all four. Doug gave me the opportunity to practise an historical anthropology that at the time was not possible to be done anywhere else in the world.

At Harvard I was taken into protective custody by Hallam J. Movius, who wanted to protect me from what had happened to Teilhard de Chardin, his Jesuit friend, and thought that an inch-by-inch knowledge of the terraces of the Thames River would do it. I suspect that I still know more about the Thames terraces than it is decent for any human being to know. That first year at Harvard was bleak. Doug Oliver was away and he had advised me to 'do' all that I would need to do for the General Examinations—archaeology, physical anthropology, linguistics, ethnoscience. Learning a half dozen new disciplinary languages was not easy. But I was soon to meet up with David Maybury-Lewis and Tom Beidelman. At the time Maybury-Lewis was writing his *Akwe-Shavante Society* (1967), an ethnography of a Brazilian forest people. He introduced us to a humane structuralism that let us read the works of Claude Lévi-Strauss—*Triste Tropiques* (1955), *La Pensée Sauvage* (1962)—with enthusiasm because we could moderate his extremism with Maybury-Lewis' humanism. Tom Beidelman introduced us to E. E. Evans-Pritchard with an intensity that beggars description.

I tell my students that writing is like dropping a stone into a deep well and waiting, waiting for the splash. No, said a friend. It is like dropping a rose petal into the Grand Canyon and waiting for a bang. 'Remember me's?' are the splashes and rose petal bangs in my life.

7

On the Beach

So Crook, Robarts and Kabris are off their beach, about to make their crossing. Perhaps Crook knows something of his beach, having been a little educated to it on his voyage out on the Duff. *Robarts and Kabris only know of it out of sailors' stories and the cultural dreams of the South Seas that had come out of explorers' tales and dramatic events such as the death of Cook, the mutiny on the* Bounty *and the search for La Pérouse. Only Crook has a few words of the language. The others have nothing. Everything they need and want, everything that others need and want of them, is by 'dumb shew'. It is a large step onto their beach, their first one.*

Beachcombers

The comb of a wave is its foamy crest. A comber is a long, curling, crested wave anywhere at sea. A beachcomber is a foaming wave racing up the beach and racing back again, smoothing, combing the beach. Comb, comber, beachcomber are American words of the early nineteenth century. They have a little sailors' poetry in them.

There are less poetic understandings of the word 'beachcomber'. *The Oxford Companion to Ships and the Sea* (1976), a near bible to naval types, sees 'beachcomber' this way: 'Beachcomber, originally a seaman who, not prepared to work, preferred to exist by hanging around the ports and harbours and existing on the charity of others, but now more generally accepted to describe any loafers around the waterfront, particularly in the Pacific islands, who prefer a life of *dolce far niente* to work of any description'.

Beachcombers were more threatening in home waters in the eighteenth century, as they combed the shore for flotsam and jetsam and were accused of causing the wrecks that added to the same. The 'these days' of *The Oxford Companion*, however, could be enlarged to include the many serious persons working very hard indeed, combing the beaches with their metal detectors, searching for treasure of some sort.

It was Harry Maude who alerted Pacific scholars to the importance of beachcombers on Pacific islands in encounter history. They were witnesses to island cultures in ways no other Strangers were. His 1964 paper 'Beachcombers and Castaways' (to be found in H. E. Maude, *Of Islands and Men*, 1968) has always been an inspiration to me since the day I heard it. There never has been a more modest genius in all Pacific scholarship.

Crook, Robarts and Kabris were the first beachcombers in Fenua'enata. They were not the last. More than a hundred can be named between 1796 and 1842. There would be dozens more who escape the records of whalers' logs and missionary journals. How can I say that the stories of Crook, Robarts and Kabris are typical when I know that they are not? You will need a library and archives to know the stories of the others, however. Read Harry Maude and he will show you where to go. Or you could catch up with some of them in *Islands and Beaches*.

The Beach and Brother Crook's Soul

His God is near on this, the most momentous day in his life. On the outside all is noise and stench, strange. On the inside, there is a familiar calm. When he finds that the rafters in Tainai's house are not strong enough to hold his hammock, he realises he will have to sleep on the mats with the women of Tainai's family. He is not ready for that. Tainai offers him his neighbouring *tapu* house. Women are forbidden entry there. Before he settles on the mat in the *tapu* house, his small bundle of possessions beside him, he gives himself to prayer in thanksgiving and meditation. He is not out of the gaze of a curious crowd as he prays. But they are sympathetic. They think he is practising some rite of mourning and separation.

No matter that his soul is at peace, it is difficult to pray in these circumstances. The devil, all rounded eyes, peers at him out of every housepost and *tiki*. There is no congregation for his prayer, only the chattering crowd beyond the stone wall of the *tapu* house. He reads Scripture to himself aloud, sucking strength from words that soak his person. He sings hymns. It might seem awkward to stand there singing, playing the fool for the Lord, but awkwardness has no part to play in the witnessing of extravagant sureness.

William Crook is extravagantly sure he is doing the Lord's work. He has committed himself for life to these furthest islands of the South Seas. He knows that the truth in God's word will win through over all. He does not know how the Word will do its work, but he knows that it will. He knows even on this first night ashore that he will stay here alone, and that once the *Duff* is gone he will have only the strength within him to sustain him. From the moment that the *Duff* anchored at Vaitahu—it was only yesterday—Brother Harris begins to prevaricate; he needs more time to pack; the surf is too high; he can't swim; he doesn't like the taste of the food. Crook knows he only has to say to Captain Wilson that he cannot stay on alone and Wilson will accept his decision and take him back to the other missionaries at Tahiti. Maybe the good captain will do it a little reluctantly. Wilson is a man of rule and contract and has no time for defaulters, but he is a prudent, practical man, too. He will ask of Crook questions he himself will have to answer to the Mission Directors. He has a high opinion of Crook. He presumes that he will know the right thing to do. 'Crook is a young man of twenty-two', Wilson will write,

> remarkably serious and steady, always employed in the improvement of his mind, and applied with great diligence to the attainment of the language. He also possesses a very good genius, and I have no doubt will contrive many things to benefit the poor creatures he lives with; and as the valley is capable of great improvement, I should not be surprised to hear of this and the islands adjacent becoming very plentiful places by his means. He has various kinds of garden-seeds, implements, medicines, etc.; an Encyclopaedia, and other useful books.

Nothing about loneliness. Nothing about sickness. Nothing about who will come for him and when. No word of advice. No suggestion of a missionary strategy.

Crook sleeps well that first night, well enough not to notice that someone slips into the *tapu* house and takes his bundle from his side. He is alarmed when he wakes, but it is Tainai who has crept in and taken the bundle to forestall anyone else stealing it.

These first days are full and chaotic. The surf runs high all through the three-week stay of the *Duff*. There are always problems communicating with Crook ashore and landing the many different things he needs to establish this mission—though it has to be said there is no great plan of settlement and little or no concern for his comfort. Crook must swim to the longboat to get to the *Duff*, and much of his chestful of possessions, including his 'garden-seeds', is water-damaged. Those on board the *Duff* are totally preoccupied with re-rigging and fitting out the ship for its return to Tahiti and Tonga and then on to China. None of the crew, except Captain Wilson and the Third Officer Thomas Falconer, goes ashore. Interestingly, the *Duff* has no real problem with Enata stealing. No threats with muskets. No cannon shots. This is because the ordinary sailors find a commonsense way of dealing with it. Each of them as they do their work appoints an apprentice from among Enata boys. The apprentice ties the sailor's tool around his neck and is made responsible for it for some small reward. They find the most efficient transport between ship and shore is a *va'a* they had brought from Tonga. We might wonder what Enata would have thought at a sight of a *va'a* from their Hava'iki.

Crook, ever eager to begin his new life, tills the ground the morning after his first night and plants orange seeds, corn, shaddock and Spanish pumpkin, among other things. The pumpkin strikes within a week but loses its fruit. The corn grows but the rats dispose of its heads. Enata are greatly excited when a goat and two cats are brought ashore. Tainai appropriates them immediately and begins to tour the neighbouring valleys to show them off.

At the end of the first week, Brother Harris is persuaded to come ashore with his chest of goods. He is reluctant to join Crook and Tainai and the cats on their tour. This is a mistake. The women left behind take no responsibility for feeding him, and in any case he doesn't eat *ma*, the fermented breadfruit. (Crook likes it. It is like 'Gooseberry Fool', he says. 'Fool' is a West Country stew of fruit, best eaten with Cornish cream.)

A worse mistake of Harris' is to show the contents of his chest. In it he has a red feather he has brought from Tonga. This is mythic: a red feather from Havai'iki. *Atua* made their legendary voyages in search of such red feathers. He is pestered every minute of his stay to open his chest again. The women too are curious at his apparent sexual indifference to them. They try to see if there is a physical reason for it. Frightened by it all, Harris has someone carry his chest down to the beach. But it is dusk and no one on the *Duff* can see him. He spends the first part of the night sitting on his chest. Then, terrified at the constant effort of Enata to get it, he flees to the hill on the southern side of the bay. Crook does not hear of all this till his return. Then a sudden flood in the Vaitahu stream prevents him from getting to Harris. In the end, Harris is carried through the surf and his near-empty chest is floated to the Tongan *va'a*.

Crook is not altogether alone on his beach in these first days. 'Peter the Swede' (Peter Haggerstein) and Haraiua, a Tahitian, have come ashore with him. Haggerstein had run from the *Daedalus* when it called at Tahiti on its first visit to Botany Bay. In fact, he had been to Fenua'enata twice already, once on the *Daedalus*' first visit to Vaitahu and then on a running visit to Taiohae when the *Daedalus* returned after the death of Hergest and Gooch in Hawai'i. The missionaries of the *Duff* found Haggerstein at Tahiti when they arrived. They used him to translate their first sermons, reluctantly. They don't trust him and are not sure what he is saying for them. His life-style is repugnant. Worse, he is Roman Catholic. But they take him and his Tahitian wife, Taiomau, with them to Fenua'enata to help establish Crook and Harris. Taiomau likes Crook and is kind to him, helps him greatly with his language. Crook will be surprised at how much he can hear and understand of Enata language flow. To Enata, Haggerstein is the man with the greatest authority on the *Duff*. He is the only man aboard who has a wife with him. He has great influence with them. He has bad things to say about missionaries. Haraiua, the Tahitian man meant to be interpreter, steals a compass from the *Duff* as he goes ashore. The compass's moving needle has a fascination for islanders all through the Pacific. It is his ticket to be looked after by Enata. He is frightened to return to the *Duff*. So he runs and Enata shepherd him away to the other side of the island.

These first days are filled with Crook's efforts to answer the questions Captain Wilson has put to him about Enata way of life. He knows how superficial is his knowledge but does his best to describe their religion—'a multitude of deities', 'offer hogs in sacrifice and never man'—and government—'no regular government, established law, or punishment', 'custom is the general rule'—and daily life—'no regular meals, but eat when they are hungry', 'never observed any man at work . . . idle about, and bask in the sun, telling their stories, and beguiling the time'—and marriage— 'the chief is said to have three wives'. 'Particular customs I am not yet able to describe, but I learn, the son must not touch the clothes of his father, and must walk before him on the road.' He has much to learn about those with whom he intends to spend the rest of his life.

On his first Sabbath he slips away to 'spend time alone in the Company of Heaven', he writes. The phrase 'Company of Heaven' comes from the Hymn of Praise in *The Book of Common Prayer* which he is reading to himself in this chapel of trees, the scent of flowers heavy in the early morning air. He takes comfort from chapter 10 of the Gospel of Matthew. It is Jesus' mission message to his disciples: 'Take no thought, saying What shall we eat? Or, What shall we drink? Or Wherewith shall we be clothed?' (10: 30). 'Seek ye first the Kingdom of God and his righteousness; and all these things shall be added to you. Take therefore no thought for the morrow; for the morrow shall take thought for the things of itself. Sufficient unto the day is the evil thereof' (10: 33–4).

Crook, indeed, has not much thought for the morrow. He gives himself totally to the day in his utter dependence on Tainai. There is no suggestion from the people on the *Duff* that they should help him establish his independence in some way—by building him a house, or provisioning him against tomorrow. God's work in the far ends of the earth will be fairly inexpensive. Leave one missionary, and say we will be back in two or three years. Maybe. They wouldn't be. The second voyage of the *Duff*—coming, it has to be said, with a party of men and women destined for The

Marquesas—would end disastrously when the French capture the ship in the Atlantic. The only thought we hear from Crook about the morrow is as the *Duff* lifts anchor at 4.30 a.m. on 27 June and pulls out of Vaitahu Bay. Crook sends out a canoe with a last letter to his sister, Paulina, and a request that the *Duff* send back a parcel of soap. He had forgotten the soap.

Actually, he won't have much need for soap, for washing clothes anyway. He discarded a pair of black breeches fairly quickly. Clearly Enata dress is more comfortable. But the *hami*, the men's loincloth, is too immodest for him. Instead, he takes to wearing the *ka'eu*, the women's waist-cloth or short skirt. He thus adds a certain ambivalence to his otherness. Those who wore women's dress were called *mahu*. 'Homosexual' would be one translation of the word, but *mahu* are not necessarily homosexual. They are a group of males who took on feminine roles. They are typically unthreatening both to male and female, sometimes a sort of a clown. They are not subject to some of the *tapu* that bind both genders. They find easy friendships with the elite but have no high status themselves. It is not easy to decide whether wearing women's dress makes Crook's beach more or less painful. There is a story still to be told late in his stay at Vaitahu in which Enata decide the moment of ambivalence is to be terminated.

The *Duff* is gone on 27 June. Tainai is eager to display his new assets—the goat, the two cats and Crook. And his sister is about to give birth—this is the child that will be born over his head. The path to Hanipou and then over the ridge to Hanateio and Hanatetena is too precipitous for Crook. Puaka, Tainai's brother, carries him on his back, runs with him along the narrow ridge. At Hanatetena, Haraiua the Tahitian is brought to Crook. The boy is trembling. He doesn't know what is to happen to him, but he has been long enough in this violent place to know what might. Crook, not knowing at this time what Harauia knows, lets him go free. They all then return to Vaitahu directly over the ridge.

Crook now is totally immersed in another world. He toils at his language. He knows the Word will never be heard while he has no words to speak it. He will have a vocabulary of a thousand Enata words within a few months, but he is frustrated in his efforts. Enata, especially the young, tease and mock his ignorance. 'How is it that *atua* are so ignorant?', they ask. 'What is this and this and this?', he will ask. And they will answer '*mea, mea, mea*—a thing, a thing, a thing' to whatever he points to. His hardest task is to unravel the many meanings of the same word and to fill out the domain of words that enclose any one word. He holds no great hope for his work in becoming expert in Enata language. They have an 'inconceivable barrenness of the language and their great conceit makes one despair in this point'.

Listen to him as he works on one of the simpler words. His later dictionary is a monument to his efforts. It holds more than a thousand words, many more thousands of phrases, and many more thousands of multiple meanings. He moves through the different usages of words at Tahuata and Nukuhiva.

> Páppa [*papa*], flat, level, a board or plank, a flat kind of coffin, also at Tahouatta an oval wooden dish: páppa tahé [*papa tahi*], two flat oblong boards between which the Fans are placed to keep them clean and in shape; páppa tokái [*papa taki ei*], a kind of wicker basket in which the head dress called tokái [*taki ei*] is placed and suspended from the Roof; páppa vànúa [*papa henua*], a flat hard substance or stratum of earth; páppa ána [*papa ani*], a part of the Sky, a term applied by them to iron, whence it is usually called pappá; pappá-oa [*papoa*], (at Tahouatta), a plank for a Canoe, etc, see huetána.

As he learns his vocabulary, he begins to translate his Christian beliefs—the Lord's Prayer, the Ten Commandments, a story of salvation in Jesus Christ. Enata are interested in his notions of body and soul and an afterlife. They are willing to debate the worth of their gods against his. It is a debate easily won in their eyes, when their gods give them everything they need and his patently have deserted him.

He thinks the children will hear him better if he teaches them to read and write. He has, first of all, to invent an inscribed language and an alphabet to go with it. The children are eager at first, then begin to demand rewards for learning something, then, if they belong to the socially elite, begin to send proxies if they have better things to do.

Meanwhile, it begins to dawn on him that the food shortage they had remarked on at the time of the *Duff*'s visit was really a famine. The fourth breadfruit crop of the year fails. It will be seven months—till late January 1798—before food in the valley can be said to be sufficient. He is appalled at the behaviour of the people around him. Whole families lie dying in their houses, while wealthier families have some food to spare. An old woman, reduced to nearly a skeleton, is mocked and teased and pushed to the ground. He finds now that his own wealth, his nails, tools, beads, are of no worth. They cannot buy him food. He fishes, floating in the bay, bait dangling from his neck. He has no queasiness now of eating the fish he catches raw, biting their heads off first.

In August, just two months after his arrival, horror is added to distress in his experiences. The tension in the valley is palpable. The *tau'a* is dead. He learns for the first time what that means. Tainai and his warriors are off in the night, 'fishing'. The whole valley is in ferment. He follows the crowd down to the beach in the dawn to find the catch already on their poles, the hooks in their mouths. Perhaps he had seen a 'hanging match' at Tyburn and witnessed the ugly ferment in the theatre of death before a supposedly civilised crowd. But this is naked, literally naked, savagery. The children to whom he had been teaching the alphabet are dancing around the corpses, prodding them with sticks, playing with their genitals. He is more alone than ever as he follows the crowd up the valley to the *tohua*, where already the earth ovens are open, the drums beating, the crowd frenzied in anticipation. Enata do not want him to see this last phase. They turn him away, but not before he sees two scorched heads given to the priests who have filled food vessels all around them. He has not much doubt what is to follow. Enata will always deny it, feign horror at any accusation that they eat human flesh. Whether this is a sort of cultural sophistry—*they* don't eat the flesh (only certain Enata do); they don't *eat* the flesh (not in the way they eat everyday flesh)—or whether they always see the disapproval in the question as to whether or not they eat human flesh, and refuse to be denigratory of themselves, it is difficult to know. In the years to come they will flaunt their flesh-eating reputation to titillate outsiders, thus mocking the outsiders and putting a protective boundary around themselves.

That night alone on his mat in Tainai's *tapu* house, Crook begins the dark night of his soul. His temptation—his word—begins. What these temptations are we do not know. He declines to say anything about them until he has left Vaitahu. Then his report is alarming but not specific.

> I desire to blush and be confounded before the Lord for ever temptation has been so such a strange sort that I am persuaded it would be the greatest presumption in any one knowing them to encounter ... I enjoy health and strength of body but manifest weakness of soul although I have to bear the burden of a desperately weak heart it has been for some time my time to mourn but I am not altogether without hope that I shall through the help of my God arise and say 'Rejoice not against me, O mine enemy, when I fall I shall arise, when I sit in darkness the Lord will be a Light unto me'.

This is no temptation of the flesh. He seems easily to resist the offers of both young and older women. He moves to a friend's house. It belongs to Puaka, Tainai's brother and the man who carried him over the ridges on his back. And he moves out of that house because of the 'immodest' behaviour of Puaka's wife. By now Crook is an object of contempt among Enata, useless to their every need, especially their need of warriors. He, in fact, has only one friend, Puaka. Crook is *mahu*. He is transvestite in the eyes of all who see him. Who knows but that dominant gaze makes him into something else. Perhaps his total isolation makes him cling to Puaka's friendship in ways that are profoundly mysterious to himself. But the strangeness of his temptation seems deeper than that, and more disturbing. He is in 'much spiritual exercise', he writes.

'Exercise' in this use of the word means turmoil, vexation, harassment. For a praying man like Crook this could be 'desolation', a dryness of spirit when none of the cues to his inspirational thoughts work. He would have known these sorts of ups and downs in the spiritual life before—the heights of 'consolation' when self is lost in the intensity of one's commitment to the will of God and prayer becomes almost wordless—then the lows of 'desolation', when there is nothing but the lone self struggling with weakness. He would have known these switches in the soul and would have had his own strategies—or would have been given strategies by his spiritual adviser—to deal with them. These spiritual exercises are something more. They are the Beach. Let me try to show how.

In January, the principal breadfruit crop comes good. Enata move the focus of their living from the inland parts of the valley to the seaward where the breadfruit plantations grow. Crook moves with them. Tainai lets him have Hitihiti's *paepae*. Crook's assets of nails and tools are now worth something. He uses them to build his house. He sends canoes up the coast to Ivaiva, to get coconut leaves for the thatching. He also needs a canoe to do his fishing—something better than fishing with bait dangling from his neck. He tries in vain to persuade Enata to build him a boat rather than a *va'a*. The *tuhuna*, the craftsmen, will have nothing of it.

In February, the *Alexander*, Captain Asa Dodge, out of Boston, anchors at Vaitahu. Crook makes no attempt to leave, but sends off with Dodge a copy of his journal and a vocabulary to the Mission Directors, but no letter. He has too much 'spiritual exercise to write', he says. Dodge relieves him of Harauia, the Tahitian, and lets Tama the Hawaiian leave the ship. Crook finds he has done well with the exchange. Tama asks Dodge to persuade Crook to teach him to read and write. He is not all scorn for what he has seen in foreign places. Crook tries to teach him, but Tama has an attention problem. But he befriends Crook, becomes mentor to him, reproves Enata for the way they are treating Crook. Tainai makes Tama his *toa*, warrior. Tama tells him that their battles between the Ahutini and Hema on Tahuata are small-time. Tainai must become ambitious for inter-island power. Tama leads them on the series of expeditions to Hiva Oa we have already reflected on.

These expeditions, it might be remembered, began, in March 1798, with Tainai's efforts to solidify relationships with the Pikina by marrying his eight-year-old son to the infant daughter of the *haka'iki* of Taaoa. Crook is namesake to that son, Pahivi. Tainai wants to show the Pikina what they are really marrying into with Pahivi. He persuades Crook to come with him to the marriage alliance. With Tama's advice and approval, Crook wears the scarlet regimentals that Tama had brought from the *Alexander*. So Crook arrives at the marriage carrying Pahivi's name, wearing the regimentals—and his women's dress. His arrival causes a great stir, especially among the women. They treat him with the greatest respect, but they are uneasy at his dress. They ask him to take off both the regimentals and the *ka'eu*, the woman's skirt. They take off their own *ka'eu* and headdresses, lay them on the ground, ask Crook/Pahivi to sit on them. They then ask him to wear one of their headdresses as a *hami*, a man's loincloth. Crook agrees. Presumably he stands naked and is clothed in this most *tapu* of dress. The women prostrate themselves before him, put their heads on the ground and place his feet on their heads. Crook himself says: 'These expressions of reverence and regard were the more remarkable, as the chiefs at these islands are not accustomed to receive any outward mark of homage from the people'.

It is a remarkable scene. Let us savour it. The women and Crook expose themselves to one another in their nakedness, probably a physical nakedness, certainly a symbolic one. It is not modesty that is being offended. It is an order of things being reversed. Women's *tapu* headdress becomes a man's *tapu hami*. That most sacred space of a person, the head, is invaded by the most desecrating part of the person, the feet. In other circumstances, men and women would die for that invasion. Ordinary everyday social existence is full of the casuistry that measures these spaces and the circumstances in which they are or are not broken. Missionaries in later years will use such inversion rituals to destroy the *tapu* which they think binds Enata souls.

An *atua* 'from beyond the sky' is being asked to remove the scarlet that in itself makes him as *tapu* as every part of the red-coloured landscape and binds him to a mythic present that is danced and sung at every festival. More than that, he is asked to strip himself of what makes him ambivalent, his women's clothing. At the same time, Crook is mysteriously enlarged because he is also Pahivi and is about to be allied significantly with the *haka'iki*'s daughter. It is a contract that will be sealed as all contracts are, by gifts and feast.

I cannot enter into the minds of Enata in this scene, nor say what is its full significance. I think that what is striking about it is solemnity. This is not play, nor empty ritualism. It is Enata coping with a strangeness that has entered their lives. They are ensuring that this strangeness does not change their lives too greatly. They are making solemn statements about what makes them who they are.

It is perhaps easier to say what is happening on Crook's part. Tama had given Crook a piece of advice when he saw how resigned he was to his ill-treatment. This is not how to do it, Tama was saying to him. Those with status simply demand what they need, take it. It is a matter of physical strength, yes. But more than that it is a matter of presence.

These scenes on Hiva Oa are, in fact, the first fruits of Tama's advice. Crook's 'spiritual exercise', I suspect, is his apprehension at how far the beach has entered his soul. How can he admit how far it has entered into his identity? Clothes make the man, but so does every gesture, every word, every mouthful eaten, every obedience to rules that others obey—when there is no alternative way of performing self that will be understood by the audience around—when he takes off his scarlet regimentals and his *ka'eu* and lets the women give their most *tapu* articles of clothing to make his *hami*—when he lets them put his feet on their heads, he crosses his beach in ways he had never crossed it before. It will change him forever. How and why it changes him gives him 'much spiritual exercise'.

The extravagance of violence at Vaitahu grows daily. Crook thinks he will be safer across the ridge at Hanateio and Hanatetena. Tama begs him not to go, says he will go with him if he does. Crook decides to pay a visit to Hanateio to reconnoitre its possibilities. While he is there, Tainai prepares to attack Hiva Oa. The Ahutini at Hanateio are to go with Tainai and prepare a fleet of *va'a*. They will sail around the southern tip of Tahuata to join up with Tainai at Vaitahu. Crook takes the opportunity to avoid the dangerous climb over the ridge and sails back with them. The fleets of the Ahutini and the Hema combine at Vaitahu and sail off to Hiva Oa. The high-born women of Vaitahu decide to follow the men to Hiva Oa. They would never be allowed in the *tapu* war *va'a*. They engage fishermen to take them across the straits. Vaitahu is near deserted. Crook doesn't return there but stays with the Ahutini at Hapatoni or Hanipou, a small bay south of Vaitahu.

Crook knows by now that Tainai will never let him leave the island if he can prevent it. He may know, too—for reasons soon to be given—that Tama is plotting with Tainai to cut off the next ship to come to the bay. It is what the Hawaiians had done successfully in Hawai'i. On 22 May 1798, there is a ship in the offing. It struggles to reach what its master, in a nice sailors' word, calls the 'chops' of the harbour—between the headlands of Vaitahu. Several canoes go out to it from Vaitahu and perhaps pilot it in. Crook persuades a friend, Faikiueue, the husband of Tainai's cousin Pahuatai, and Hokuhonu, her brother, to take him to the ship. Perhaps he is thinking of leaving. Maybe that too is part of his 'spiritual exercise'. Yet to leave on a ship that will take him who knows where on a whaling or trading voyage around the Pacific is a desertion of his mission. He is not prepared to do that. He is a man of the Word and of his word.

The ship is the *Betsy*, a knickerbocker barque out of New York. Its master is Edmund Fanning, a god-fearing man with a sense of the close relationship between religion and business. He is also proud to be the master of the first ship out of 'Gotham' to circumnavigate the globe. The *Betsy* has four thousand sealskins packed into its hold, fo'c'sle and cabin. They will all have a nose for their business by the time they get to China. To Fanning's surprise one of the tousle-haired, sunburnt men in a canoe, wearing a loincloth, speaks to him in English: 'Sir!', Fanning reports him as saying, 'I am an Englishman, and now call upon, as I have come to you, to preserve my life'. It is Crook, of course. Fanning is writing many years after the event. As he remembers it, there is an 'Italian renegado' trying both to kill Crook and to cut off his ship. There is no 'Italian renegado' in Crook's life, only Tama.

Crook's own story is slightly different. Prominent in his mind is his need for both a confession and an assurance to the Mission Directors. The confession is of his temptations. The assurance is that he will not desert his mission. He persuades Fanning that there are islands to the north, of which Fanning has no knowledge. If Fanning goes to Nukuhiva to replenish his supplies, he can take Crook with him. Crook will act as his interpreter and see him safe. At the same time Crook can write his letters and reports and have Fanning deliver them for him. It is at this moment that Crook leaves everything that Robarts will find at Vaitahu.

It is another remarkable step by a remarkable young man. He knows he will not go naked on the beach at Nukuhiva. Fanning has already offered him a suit of clothes and will give him what he needs to start again. Crook feels his obligations to those he is leaving. He is not leaving to go home to his own country, he tells Faikiueue and Vahaniuau, two older men left at Vaitahu. He is going to Nukuhiva and will be able to return to Tahuata. He asks them who are the principal people at Taiohae on Nukuhiva. They tell him that Kiatonui is *haka'iki* there. These two friends of Crook now must tell Tainai what has happened. One of them sails off to Hiva Oa immediately. Tainai is enraged at them for losing this asset of his. They are lucky that they are related to him in marriage. Otherwise they would be dead.

So William Pascoe Crook is about to cross another beach. His is no Pilgrim's Progress but he has certainly crossed the Slough of Despond, has climbed Hill Difficulty, and met Giant Despair. He takes with him to this new beach Tama's advice to play to his status and his own acceptance of the relativity of things. His life is about to change.

Edward Robarts

His Real and Literary Beach

The darkness of the night is almost as touchable as the sweet air that wafts off the island. A man long at sea can almost navigate by that sweet scent. It even wins over the smell of tar and hemp and burnt blubber. A glimmer of light and the sound of voices come across from where the *Butterworth* is anchored. Nearer on the deck the lantern of the fo'c'sle casts shadows on the tryworks. But that is all. There are no fires to be seen ashore and there are no torches of fishing people on the water.

He sits quietly on the foredeck waiting for the signal that Tama, the Hawaiian, will give. Tama has the small bundle of clothes he is taking and is watching for the canoe from the forestay sail net. The only break in the lonely watch comes when Captain Henry Glasspoole comes to ask why he is not eating the Christmas dinner he has just cooked. He mutters something to satisfy the captain's question about his absence and waits with a little more apprehension for being interrupted in this way.

Another of the crew, a friend and the brother of the girl he had left behind in Cheshire, comes up the fo'c'sle hatch. A babble of voices and the sound of song follow him. The grog has flowed all day. More knowing than the captain and ally to the cook because he is steward, the friend asks him what he is doing, and begs to be taken too. But he says, No! The canoe is too small, and he knows that with only one deserter Glasspoole will likely proceed without him. Two will mean trouble.

He has enough time to think in the dark of what he is doing. He knows himself as a loner and different to the wild mix of a crew on his whaler, the *New Euphrates*. The crew is restless. They have been frustrated ever since Glasspoole would not let them go privateering off the South American coast. Now they are whispering mutiny and piracy. They ask him to join them. Edward Robarts knows he would not fare well in a mutiny. He has enemies among these others. He is an officious little man, forever rescuing situations. Wherever he is, he is, by his own estimate, a poor man who has to manipulate the order of things to survive. He is not so much subservient as astute in making the systems that control his life work a little to his advantage. He is not seen by that to be a man of loyalties. He has the feisty energy of a small man. He has no privileges of birth or wealth. He lives on the margins of these privileges.

Now at midnight he has a real beach to cross. The crossing begins, if not with a leap into the dark, then with a scramble into the dark down the anchor chain. Still it is a metaphoric leap into the dark. This is the loneliest place on earth for a 'white man'—his words. He has really no idea of what is on the other side of his beach. He hasn't a word of the language spoken there. He has no gifts for those on whom he is going to impose himself. He has nothing with which to buy their charity. All his life he will remember these first days on his beach. He is a prize to these people in his person, certainly. They will finger and touch his white skin, even pinch him. He will never be out of sight. They will laugh at every false gesture, correct every false move. But in these first days, they will feed him, honour him, let him enter into their lives by sharing their names with him. He becomes brother, son, uncle, maybe even husband—he won't be sure for a while—in an instant. He will never cease to be amazed that it is they who claim to be privileged at having him.

Why does he make this leap into the dark? He says it is because of mutiny and the murder that will inevitably follow. I believe him. It is not lust. There is more romance in his heart than lust. Or so it seems. I tell you his story because fifteen years after all this is done, as we know, Edward Robarts becomes literary. Going literary can change a man. Maybe he becomes a literary romantic when he makes memory of it. Let me move as best I can between the literary and the real Edward Robarts. Let me say, however, that Robarts is more literary in the meanings he gives to his experiences than in the facticity of them. In the years that I know him, 1797–1831, I never find him out on a detail of person, place, ship or event.

In the dark of a clouded sky at about midnight, in a gusty warm wind, Robarts and Tama scramble into the canoe beneath the prow of the *New Euphrates* and paddle to the beach at Vaitahu. Tainai is waiting for them. He tells them they cannot stay at Vaitahu. He had been a hostage once before. He knows how easy it would be for Glasspoole to force Robarts' return. They must take the canoe a few miles south to Hapatoni. We never learn the name of the man whose canoe Robarts and Tama are in. He is from Hapatoni. Robarts says he is chief of Hapatoni. Perhaps chiefly is more likely. Maybe he is Tahueutafitika, father of the adopted son and the child born over Tainai's head at Hanatetena. Hapatoni, it might be remembered, is Ahutini, not Hema. By this first move to Hapatoni, Robarts' network of friends—those among whom he will move most easily—will be in a large arc which moves from the southern and eastern valleys of Tahuata, and the eastern, northern and western valleys of Hiva Oa. Atuona on Hiva Oa and Vaitahu on Tahuata are the oppositional Hema core of this arc.

Tahue, Tama and Robarts, then, paddle the canoe out of Vaitahu. As they turn the southern point, a windblast capsizes them. In the water Robarts holds onto his bundle of clothes and the canoe, while the others bail it. Robarts has an extravagant fear of sharks. He will have several experiences of capsized canoes. On some of them he thinks he feels a tough sharkskin beneath his feet. This time he is happy to get back into the canoe and continue their voyage to Hapatoni.

At 2 a.m. there is no light or life at Hapatoni. Tahue's cries bring people to the beach, and he, Tama and Robarts are led back to a cluster of buildings that makes Tahue's household. In the light of a candlenut torch they are offered the cold food available, principally coconuts. Robarts' soaked clothes are taken from him, and for the first time he wraps himself in a length of white *tapa* cloth. He meets Tahue's wife. Robarts will meet many women of high status in the years to come. All will share the feminine qualities he sees in this first meeting: a delicate lightness of skin cosmetically enhanced, flowing tresses down to the waist either in ringlets or straight, black or auburn or even flaxen in colour. Above all, the women have a composure, an air of authority, a confidence in all the qualities that bring them the respect due to them—birth, wealth, alliance, and even at times a little godliness. He'll write it many times: this, and much else, is 'not expected of savages'.

In the open sleeping house, the thatched roof slopes distinctively down to a low back wall. Rich mats cover the floor. A polished rounded log, set in from the back wall, acts as pillow. Cloth, bowls, utensils in wide variety, and weapons hang on the walls. Nets with containers of food or oils and cosmetics hang from the roof away from the rats. Leisure things—stilts, tops, surfboards, playballs, skipping ropes, string for cats' cradles—lie around. The household *tiki* with offerings sits in the corner. Coloured and sculptured houseposts, belonging to the family for generations, demand gestures of respect at every entry into the house.

Robarts, when he is finished eating, is confronted with his first cultural predicament. Tahue invites him to share the bedding under his wife's broad white wrap. Robarts thinks he is being invited to more than he is and sheepishly declines. A seventeen- or eighteen-year-old girl offers him the same. This he accepts, perhaps learning a first lesson in the relativity of things. In a society of so many freedoms, men and women naked under the same cover was no licence, just an ordinary thing.

The next day is tumultuous. The whole valley collects to poke and prod him. He is in a world with no privacy even for the most private of bodily functions. There are no niceties in Enata toiletry. A small hole dug with a stick off the side of a path will do. Maybe that is why they spend so much time in the water. Rats abound because of their carelessness. Maybe that is why cats will be so enthusiastically received.

Robarts does not follow the men, women and children to their hours of ablution and play in the sea. His fear of sharks will confine him to rock pools for his washing. *Tai*, the sea, is known to Enata as particularly as the land. Its every mood and season, its every wave and current, its every wind that shapes it has a name. Their play in the water is constant, jumping from heights, diving into caves, surfing over and under one another like dolphins. Their boards are small. They do not stand on them as they do in Hawai'i. The *Oxford English Dictionary* would have fewer words in English for fish and shellfish than Enata would have had in their vocabulary (about 367 in a rough count). Their seascape is an underwater botanical garden of grasses, kelps and algae.

Robarts has no house of his own in these first days 'on Tahuata and Hiva Oa. For all his nutritional needs, he is dependent on invitations to come and eat which cannot be pre-empted. He takes to wearing men's dress, the *hami*, a loincloth, and will suffer sunburn for that.

Early on the first day, there are shouts of *i'hepe*, 'ship'. The *New Euphrates* and *Butterworth* sail past Hapatoni and turn north towards Nukuhiva. All day they are framed between the headlands of the bay, beating north against the wind. It is a still-life that makes him wonder at what he has done.

These descriptions of his first months on his beach are overlain by his later efforts to be the literary man. Then he is writing his seven years of memories in The Land. So his slow learning and piecemeal first experience of the culture-scape and time-scape of his beach are compacted. The space and time that are the backdrop of his story are more generic than historically specific. There *is* always a first time that he experiences the closeness of the dead among the Enata living, and visits them in their canoe-coffins raised high in their enclosure. There *is* always the first time that he hears the 'prophets' (*tau'a*) cry for sacrifice, or attends a warrior's funeral and memorial feasts, or joins the socially elite on their platforms around the dancing ground at a marriage to enjoy the competitive feast. These are all happenings in the first year or so of his story. But they are suffused with details that come from later years. He will be bemused at the theatre of mourning and the ability of mourners to turn their sincerity off and on. He will be astounded at the lack of impact of religious values and belief in his own culture, and the intensity of fear, engagement and commitment of these so-called pagans. He wonders time and again how these savages have other metaphors for what he holds dear—love, compassion, loyalty, generosity, carefulness. And then at times how utterly devoid of these virtues they could seem to be in an instant. It will be the great virtue of Robarts' literary story that this generic overlay of culture- and time-scape nevertheless is suffused with a particularity that suggests how the systems that control his and Enata life actually work.

There is a liveliness in his descriptions. We who see through his eyes enter into a living moment. Let him speak for himself. (The punctuation is mine. There is not a punctuation mark or paragraph in this literary man's manuscript. Maybe he is ahead of his times. The spelling, capitals and grammar are his.) He writes:

I must beg leave to describe the dancing dress of the Ladies, something revers'd to polish'd nations. The head dress is a turban very neatly made, nearly in the shape of a trooper or light horse man's cap. In the front is placed an ornament of black feathers. Over that is tied a bunch of grey hair, the beards of old men. This, tho singular to the idea, Has a fine appearance. Their ears is decorated with sperm whales teeth cutt in two and polished. Round the neck is placed a string of porpose or black fish teeth finely polished. The next is the waist. The lady being accommodated with a fine white cloth for a petty coat, it is gatherd into large plaits. It is put on, but does not close before. Over that is placed a broad band which goes 3 or 4 times round the waist. It comes low enough to make a decent appearance. Behind is placed a broad train of two peices of fine cloth, composeing two large bows on the waist band. Behind their body is naked.

The grand day is come. The first that makes her appearance is generaly a young lady of celebrated beuaty. She is usherd on the ground with the beating of drums and the sounding of conch shells and then receives the salute of the war whoope three times. Thus commences the grand festival of ending the cerimonies of a deceased prophet, King or Chieftain. The general dance leads off. The Ladies dance on a fine matt in front of their houses. The warriers dance on the play ground in great numbers. The houses are filld with strangers who comes from all parts of the Island. During the festival, a number of marriages take place. At these times there is great plenty of food provided, such as whole hogs. Roasted fish, baked sweet plantains and prepared bread fruit. This feast is free for three days, at which time men of rank sits on the mountains at the passes to prevent any depredations being committed by the common people. By this means every one departs in peace. At these times numbers of the enemy comes. All is wellcome and free to come and go.

It is difficult to catch the inner man in these the most beachcombing moments of his beach-crossing life. He is lonely. Tama leaves him at Hapatoni, so he must struggle with the language alone. He spends days writing what he thinks are Enata words in the sand or with chalk on rocks. He has no pen or paper. He is happy to go where he is taken, even if this is on the most precipitous of paths. He knows he will be taken care of. With

Tahue he visits the most important cultural sites and personages of the Ahutini along the east coast of Tahuata to Hanateio and Hanatetena. He has no function or role in Enata society. He will have, but now he is more just an asset, an exhibit to be paraded.

There are no signs of Robarts having second thoughts about his beach, even though very early he is made aware of his precarious position. His gums have swelled, no doubt with some abscess. His face is so puffed, as he sees it in a calabash of water, that he is embarrassed to show himself. It is at this time he realises that he does have a function. The *London*, Captain Gardiner, is whaling in these waters. The *London*, it might be remembered, had met up with the *New Euphrates* and the *Butterworth* after a sudden storm had damaged them and sunk the *Liberty*. Robarts stays out of sight on the *London*'s first visit to Vaitahu, probably unsure of what Captain Gardiner would do about him. But the *London* splits its mast just a few days after the first visit and returns. Now Robarts has a role. He knows of mature wood suitable to fish, or stengthen, the mast. It is on the property of his protector, Tahue. He persuades Tahue to offer it to Gardiner and with almost a wink-wink, nudge-nudge to us his readers, says he leans on his friendship with Tahue to offer the wood to Gardiner for a trivial price. Robarts has another moment of usefulness to the *London*. One of their men is down with scurvy, its terrible bruising and scurf all over his body. Robarts buries him to his neck in soil. It is a sand-bath trick he would have learned in the African slave trade. Robarts does not tell us if it works. But now he has a rationalisation, if not a reason, for his beachcombing. He will be pilot and intermediary for the ships that come to Fenua'enata.

Perhaps it is wrong to sound sceptical about Robarts' sand-bath cure for scurvy. Surgeon Claude Roblet on Marchand's *Solide* was so convinced at the effectiveness of sand-baths that he heated dry sand in a boiler and had a scorbutic patient on the ship immerse himself to his thighs in the sand. C. P. Claret Fleurieu, the editor of the account of Marchand's voyage, tells us of it.

> After two hours rest, the good surgeon reported, the condition in which he found the patient, seemed to border on a miracle; no more swelling; no more stiffness, even in the tendons; the ecchymoses [the blotch of blood below the skin] almost dispersed, and become yellowish; the soles of the feet, before very painful, no longer causing any sensation; in short, Surgeon Roblet had the satisfaction to see his experiment greatly exceed the hopes which he had conceived from it. ... A week's sand-baths, the second of one hour, and the others of

two, were sufficient for effecting the most complete cure: all the symptoms of scurvy disappeared never to return; and the man who had been threatened with sinking, in a few days, under the attacks of the disorder, enjoyed, during the last ten months of the expedition, the most perfect health.

Roblet goes on to recommend to all seafaring people that ships carry at least one double-bottomed boiler and casks of sea-washed sand. But we have to think that the noises of the French Revolution drowned out all he had to say.

At this time Robarts makes a disturbing discovery. He happens on Hitihiti's *paepae* in the northern corner of Vaitahu, near where Josiah Roberts had his shipyard for the making of the *Resolution*. The house on the stone platform is in a run-down condition. Inside the house he finds a large sea-chest. He opens it to find:

some medicines, a bible and some other good books, an old pair of black breeches, a Keg which once had been full of nails, with several letters written in a journal. They was numberd. On peruseing them I found they had been wrote by a person of the name of Crook, one of the Missionaries that was sent out the first time the Mission Ship *Duff*—I shall make a further remark in its proper place on the *Duff*— came to the south seas. This discovery gave me a great deal of unesiness. I could not tell what to think. By the date of some of his papers he had been abscent about eight months. At times I was verry unhappy. Sometimes I thought he had died; other times I thought he had been murdered, as I found several things among the natives I supposd to have been part of the contents of the chest. Often I would weep in some secret place. How much did I regreet the loss of the company of this good young man. At least his writings was pious [and] gave me to think he would have been a very prizeable companion in my situation. However I found a very good companion in Mr Crooks bible and the other good books I found in his chest.

These were indeed William Pascoe Crook's things. He had left them at Vaitahu hurriedly, not eight months before but ten, 21 May 1798, when he went with Captain Edmund Fanning of the *Betsy*. Crook was in Nukuhiva in January 1799 when the *New Euphrates* and the *Butterworth* anchored in Taipivai. Crook went home on the *Butterworth* with Timotete, Tainai's fifteen- or sixteen-year-old cousin. We will tell their story soon.

Edward Robarts is a reader. On this beach he enjoys even serious books of the sort of *Burder's Sermons*. Crook's Bible is a comfort too. 'Lord, make them faithful. July 26, 1796' is the disturbingly equivocal inscription in it that Robarts reads. The Bible was given to Crook when he was charged and missioned at Sion Chapel, London. Then Crook had stood before a crowd of seven or eight thousand in a high pitch of religious exultation.

Robarts does not, however, have much time to enjoy either the books or the Bible. He returns to Hapatoni to find Tahue preparing a double *va'a* in which he will visit the peoples of the Pepani alliance in the eastern half of Hiva Oa. Tahue is reluctant to take Robarts with him, thinking, no doubt, that he will lose this asset if he does. And he will.

They proceed on the preferred route to Hiva Oa, first northerly in the lee of Tahuata to the northeasternmost point of the island, then across to the eastern valleys on the south coast of Hiva Oa. They land at the mouth of Hanaupe valley, which stretches back three miles inland.

They are met by a great crowd on the beach. Their double *va'a* with all aboard and their baggage is run up the beach beyond the highwater mark— the strong *temanu*-wood keels of the *va'a* are there for that purpose. Robarts is about to begin nearly a year's stay on Hiva Oa. He will visit a succession of the principal valleys of the Pepani alliance along the northeast coast of Hiva Oa, then back to the southeast coast. But first there is a ceremony on the beach that gives his whole visit to Hiva Oa a special character.

He is asked to remain on the double *va'a* until the principal woman of the valley—no doubt a *vahinetapu*—comes down from her residence deep in the valley. She arrives with her daughter, no doubt also a *vahinetapu*. They spread the white cloth of the daughter's clothing on the grass and ask Robarts to step on it. There the mother declares that Robarts is adopted in her daughter's name. It is a most unusual name exchange (*e inoa*) between genders. I hazard the guess that Robarts is being established as *pekio*. Being made *pekio* was often an incorporation into the political domain of high-born women. It could also be a feminisation and a removal of dangerous *tapu*, allowing the female establishment free access to such a prized asset as a stranger. It seems to me the more likely that Robarts is made *pekio*, an in-between person, because as he moves successively through the valleys these ceremonies of adoption by high-born women are repeated. Perhaps it is Enata's way of coping with Robarts's disordering presence.

Listen to him tell this story, too. Remember William Pascoe Crook's story of the same sort of events. Robarts has been wounded in a battle we are about to recount.

A lady—a stranger to me—came and put her mantle under me to sit on. She was a chieftain's daughter of high rank. She had several attendants with her. Other ladies of rank came and took me by the leg as I sit and put it on their head and shoulders. This was the greatest honour they could do to me. The mantle Or robe of a chiefs daughter are held as sacred, nothing to be put on them or on the head that touches the ground.

And this story. A large crowd, some thousands, has assembled on a small beach on the borderlines between the two enemies—the Nuku peoples of the west of Hiva Oa, and the Pepani of the east. I suspect the beach is Tahauku, near Atuona. There are many protocols in these meetings of enemies that allow friends and families to cross lines. There are challenges too between warriors:

In the afternoon the beach was shaded. I went to the brookside that run between the two parties. One of their warriors hove a nut. It struck me in the side. The beach was divided in a moment. Each party took to their spears. I waved with my fan. I begd my party not to close the day with blood shed on my account. Altho I was very displeasd, I was not much hurt. I only desired they call the person that hove at me and give me a fair chance to repay him the compliment. He came forward. He was a tall, raw boned, powerfull man. A bunch of nuts was brought for me. Some of them weigh about a pound. I let him heave several times before I took my aim. He was capering about. He thought that I was afraid. I heave at him twice. The second time I brought him to the ground. The nut I hove struck him on the temple. I stood some time expecting some one would second him, but no one oferd. All was composed.

Our drum beat for a dance. A great chieftains daughter came down first. One from our side in company with me went half way to receive her. She then advanced the other half. I took her hand and embraced her. I led her to my Party. She seem'd fearfull when among us. I desired my Party to leave the beach for the ladies. They obeyd and retired on to the rocks. This young lady was a fine figure. She was very fair, her hair of a flaxen color, her features very delicate. She appeard to be 19 0r 20 years of age. She was not married. After a matt was brought for her to sit on, several ladies from our party came to her. Food was brought. I helpt her to some. I fetcht her water myself. This pleasd her party. They said I now had got a wife: I must take care of her. Several Jokes was past on each side. She seemd pleasd. The ladies being seated, the cheerful song commenced. This lady had a sweet voice. She, to oblige me, sung singly, as I had heard of her fine singing a long time before. I calld two young men, sons of chieftains, to come down to dance before her. In return, two was sent from her side to dance to our ladies. Eveng drew near; the sun was retireing to its western seat. Several presents was sent to this lady. Her party in return sent presents. The warriers exchanged spears and fans.

Put aside the romantic element. Robarts cannot be literary in any other way. Think of what the stories tell us of how Enata dealt with the ineffable violence of their lives. Think of the creativity of culture as they manipulate their rules and made room for Robarts' strangeness, making it familiar.

Robarts moves from valley to valley by formal invitation. His first movement out of Hanaupe is across the narrow ridge that acts as the mountainous east–west backbone of Hiva Oa. Puamau, across the ridge from Hanaupe, is perhaps the most theatrical landscape of all Fenua'enata. Its vast amphitheatre was, at the time of Robarts' visit, the backdrop to Enata's most dramatic sculptures, the great stone *tiki*. They are ripped out now. In 1799 they still loomed over the *me'ae* and *tapu* places.

Puamau was populous and fertile, its plantations of plantains, breadfruit and coconut trees large. Robarts sees much destruction in the plantains, the result of enemy incursion. He is now clearly more confident on his beach. For the first time he gives his name to the nine-year-old son of his host. He is happy at the high status accorded him here in Hiva Oa. It is clear to Tahue that he will stay on Hiva Oa. Tahue feels betrayed. He had invested much in Robarts. It is ever thus with Strangers, he might have thought. There is no rootedness in relationships with them. Offended at it all, he leaves Robarts at Puamau.

Perhaps it is the wealth of the valley. Puamau is always in turmoil. Sixty years on it will be the scene of an awful cultural suicide as families turn on one another murderously and take vengeance on one another for a dying that none are responsible for. Not long after Robarts' arrival the *tau'a* of

Puamau calls for sacrifices. It is a well-practised performance for the *tau'a* and his assistants (*moa*), as they squeal their gibberish in a trance. They are masters of terror and use all their ventriloquists' props to do the arithmetic of how many dead will be needed.

The whole valley is immediately in a frenzy. This will not be a fishing expedition for victims, nor an ambush (*utopu*). This will be open, almost gala, war (*hetoua*). A *tapu* is on the valley. The men are segregated in their *tapu* houses. The women are out of sight. Old men carve spears and weave slings. Boys dive for smooth round stone to use as missiles. The whole of the island of Hiva Oa is alert to Puamau's stirring.

Hiva Oa's mountain spine is a road to battle. Narrowing to ten yards at its eastern end, it waves, broadens, narrows, broadens again till towards the western end becomes something of a plateau. A deserted and desolate plateau in 1799. All around are signs of former populations, abandoned *paepae* and *me'ae*, walls of plantations destroyed. The battle road has many places of ambush, inclines easily defended. At the passes, especially to the Nuku valleys at its western end, there are timber and stone fortifications.

The view along this part of the island is panoramic—of Hiva Oa itself and of nearly the whole of Fenua'enata. Valleys flow off the ridge left and right and then stretch out in broad vista to a fan of valleys at the western end of the island. These are Nuku valleys, the enemy. All the other are Pepani, in fragile alliances. To the left, if we were walking towards Nuku land, at 10 o'clock, we would have a breathtaking view of Tahuata. On the right, 120 miles away at 1 to 2 o'clock, are Ua Pou, Nukuhiva and Ua Huka. Behind on the left at 7 o'clock is Fatuiva.

In the early morning of the first day of battle, drums from the principal *me'ae* and conch shells from the warriors' *tapu* houses rouse all the valley. The *tau'a*, heads decked with a broad fan, black cocks' tails flying behind them, cloaks of coconut palm over their shoulders, skulls at their waists, dance, rock, tremble, speak in their unintelligible dialect. No army on the march here. A cluster of warriors in their regalia move in waves of bravado, confined at times by the narrowness of the ridge to a single line. The women, the old and the very young follow behind, loaded with nets of slinging stones and of calabashes of water and food. The main party grows along the first five miles of path with additions from valleys left and right. Robarts is with, but not of, the main fighting party. In fact he is glad to retreat a little when he sees how disadvantaged his party is as they meet the enemy at the top of a steep incline and are unable by reason of the narrowness of the path to face them with more than four warriors in a row.

He now becomes, by his own account, a pocket Napoleon, giving advice on tactical retreat and ambush. It is a great success. The enemy in strong pursuit is thrown into confusion by the ambush. There are wounded but no dead. In the dark, there is a long three-hour troop back to Puamau. There they rest and re-equip themselves for several days.

They begin their trek to the fighting ground this next time the day before the battle. They set up camp under shelters of plantain leaves and on beds of fern and spend the night dancing and singing. Next morning when they reach the enemy's lines at the head of their valley, their champion warrior advances alone, and an enemy warrior answers his challenge. The enemy champion is wounded and and taken prisoner as both parties scramble for his body. He is not dead at this stage, so he is taken back and strangled. Then his corpse is brought back and laid in front of the allied warriors. The women and girls dance in derision around it, probably naked. They fight for the rest of the day over the top of the body. They return home again to Puamau. The next day the body of the slain man is hung on a tree in the *me'ae*.

The third day of battle is more intense and lasts from dawn to dusk. The Pepani are hard pressed this time. They lose two of their own warriors and kill one of the enemy. Robarts claims to be playing a more tactical role in leadership. He organises a flanking movement and disrupts the enemy by rolling boulders on them. Or so he says. This time the Pepani had taken the battle deep into enemy territory but had to return in a running retreat for ten miles.

There is a fourth day. But it is 'more for mirth than war', Robarts says. There are more than four thousand on the mountain ridge, making a 'grand appearance'. There are skirmishes, but 'a very grand dance ensures; some is fighting, others danceing. At times those that was fighting would set down and talk with each other with as much composure as though they were friends and then rise again and renew the fight.'

Robarts must have been unlucky, then, in the skirmish in which he takes part. He collects a stone from a sling under his right eye. It pierces his cheek and knocks two upper teeth into his mouth. He falls down unconscious. He stands up defiantly when he regains consciousness and walks back unassisted to where his friends are encamped—'the spot of mirth' he calls it. The women of high rank take care of him, one of them binding his wound with her headdress. Robarts does not like the idea of a *tuhuna* probing his wound with a shark's tooth lance and lets the wound heal itself. The scar will add to his already rather battered appearance. He will not be able to see at night for some months afterwards.

Robarts, by his own account, spends months of idyllic days on Hiva Oa, visiting nearly every valley, enjoying the seasons of plenty and the rounds of *koina*. Perhaps he does have a reputation as a warrior. Certainly he is challenged to duels occasionally and of course wins.

On two occasions he hears of ships at Tahuata and hastens to get to them, but they are gone by the time he gets there. On one of these visits he finds Tama, the Hawaiian, 'in a dying state': 'He made several attempts to strangle himself, but I prevented him'. He finds Tahuata desperately divided by war. These are the months subsequent to the year of Tainai's life that we followed. Families are divided. His friend and protector, Tahue, now has two muskets and powder and shot. He wants Robarts to stay and be his *toa*. Robarts is unwilling to enter such an internecine war in such enclosed societies.

On Hiva Oa the principal breadfruit crop fails in January 1800. One of the friends with whom he lives now at Ha'a Mau on the south coast proposes to sail to Nukuhiva. Robarts wants to go with him. It takes several months to prepare the double *va'a* for the trip. When food is scarce in the lowlands, Enata go to the mountains. Robarts goes with them. When the double *va'a* is ready, they set off at sunset and sail all night to Ua Huka. Robarts' friend had lived there for some time and has a former wife there. They spend two weeks visiting all the places on the island.

They sail for Nukuhiva, this time in the morning, and land at Taipivai only as the sun sets. Robarts sleeps the night on the beach. He is wakened next morning by someone taking his hand. He looks up to a tattooed face leaning over him. He does not recognise the face behind the tattoo until he speaks. It is 'the French Boy', Joseph Kabris. Robarts is not happy with that.

Scene Change

We move now with Crook and Robarts to Nukuhiva. Kabris is already there. They would have experienced many changes in their move from Tahuata and Hiva Oa, mostly in the way they now will speak the language. We won't change. We will keep the language forms we have used in the southern group of islands—Hiva Oa, Tahuata, Fatuiva. Where we use *f*, as in *Fenua* (Land), the northerners (Nukuhiva, Uapou, Ua Huka) will use *h*, *Henua*. Where the southerners use *t*, *Enata* (People), northerners will use *n*, *Enana*. Where southerners use *n*, *koina* (feast), northerners will use *k*, *koika*.

The landscape will not change that greatly. The cliffs still fall dramatically into the sea without a beach. The valleys still cut deep into the mountains. The basic vegetation and foodstuffs remain the same. There will be local specialisations in food production, for which people will travel long distances.

The culture-scape remains mostly the same as well. The cultural metaphors are as permanent as the tattoos. But the workings out of the metaphors change, and with them the Beach. Our stories will tell it so.

Kiatonui, *haka'iki* of Taiohae, is no Tainai, *haka'iki* of Vaitahu. He has little of Tainai's raw violence. Power and authority among the ten thousand people of Taiohae is much negotiated. Kiatonui is more priest than warrior, more priest than prophet. He leaves his violence to his wife's *pekio*, Pieueinui, a huge man. The Russians when they come to Taiohae measure Pieueinui and find him an exact replica of the Belvedere Apollo. In battle, Pieueinui is Kiatonui's persona under Kiatonui's ornaments.

The four valleys of Taiohae are well served by *tau'a*, sorcerers and prophets possessed. Kiatonui is more *tuhuna o'ono*, craft expert in tradition. He plays with signs, mediates with the godliness around him, more socially than alarmingly. In 1798, Crook says he is between forty and fifty years old, but he is probably nearer thirty. He has about thirty years more of life. Then the kava which is beginning to white-scale his skin will kill him. He is unprepossessing in physique. He is squat, thick-necked and corpulent. He carries no badge of office—as Tainai was prone to—nor wears clothing that shows his status. Tattoos are his greatest ornament. His body is almost black with tattoos. He is variously described by strangers as rustic, not very sanguinary, slow to anger, humane and liberal, affectionate. Robarts thinks him to be the most skilful surgeon on Nukuhiva. He is wealthy, but not the wealthiest in Taiohae. At least two brothers are wealthier in land and material things than is he. With one brother he owns the sea at Taiohae and all the fish in it.

Kiatonui's greatest asset in life is his mother. Everybody in Nukuhiva knows that. She is a formidable woman. Putahaii is her name. She has the most remarkable house in all Fenua'enata. Its stone platform stretches into the bay at Taiohae. It is faced with slabs of *ke'eta*, a very expensive, light red volcanic stone, requiring much labour to dress. Putahaii has seventeen children by birth and adoption, of whom Kiatonui is the eldest. Putahaii's house is the centre of a spiderweb of networks. There is not a valley, enemy or ally that does not have some connection to Putahaii. News travels fast along that web. Knowledge is a political asset always—who is cheating on whom, who is ailing unto death, whose enmity is stirring. Putahaii's house is the nearest thing that Enata have to the assembly houses in old Hava'iki. It is a place of council, to debate and politic. Kiatonui visits his mother every day.

Putahaii's authority comes to her by birth, marriage and the accidents of life. She in her person coalesces all the lines of power and authority in Taiohae. Her own father, Moana, was *haka'iki* and a deemed *atua* of the valleys of Hoata and Meau. Her husband, Kiatonui's father, had been lost at sea soon after Kiatonui's birth. His father—so Kiatonui's grandfather—had been *haka'iki* and a deemed *atua* of the valleys of Havau and Pakui. Putahaii's elder brother and the true firstborn was of 'feeble intellect'. So Putahaii was not firstborn, but charters of social realities of this sort are, in Bronislaw Malinowski's famous phrase, 'indispensable and adjustable'. She was adjustably the firstborn to the dynasties of all four valleys, and Kiatonui actually firstborn to her. Adjustability has many dimensions. Putahaii favoured a younger son of hers more than Kiatonui and gave him much more property than to her firstborn. So wealth, status, skills, knowledge, are much crossed lines in Taiohae. That will be the politics of them.

The list of Kiatonui's siblings is long. Putahaii has ten male and seven female children. One of these Edward Robarts will marry. The marriages of these seventeen reach into the principal valleys of Nukuhiva—Aakapa, Hakaui, Hoo'umi. Kiatonui himself was married to the daughter of the *haka'iki* of Hakaui, the spectacular valley in the southwest corner of Nukuhiva. We have been there with Melville. Kiatonui's wife's sister, his sister-in-law we would say, was married to a remarkable man called Pautini. Pautini had a mind to travel. We met him parading a goat around the islands as far as Fatuiva. This might or might not have been the reason why Kiatonui fathered a child by his sister-in-law. This child was then adopted by the *pekio* of Kiatonui's own wife. That the secondary husband should adopt the primary husband's child by another man's wife should support the contention that lines are much crossed at Taiohae.

In 1798 Kiatonui's own children are mostly young. His first three children were daughters. The firstborn, Tahatapu by name, was married to

Mauateii, *haka'iki* of the Hapa'a in the valley of Muake, an inland valley famous for its baked ginger, much sought after as a cosmetic through all Fenua'enata. Mauateii was reputed to have twelve hundred warriors at his disposal. Tilesius of the Russian expedition has left us a portrait of him. Crook tells us that Tahatapu was the only woman in the *tapu* class without a *pekio* (others had as many as thirty). She was also dark-skinned, as was her firstborn, a daughter. This great-grand-daughter of Putahaii was the old lady's favourite. Putahaii puts her into a *tapu* house and has her nursed by a manservant and looked after by her own 75-year-old second husband. Blurred descent lines, blurred gender roles, blurred colour status. 'Maps' rarely work. Stories do a little better. William Pascoe Crook, Joseph Kabris and Edward Robarts blur things even more when they cross this beach.

Crook, aka Kuruka, aka Pakauoteii

Crook is in the boat sounding the bottom ahead of the *Betsy* before they warp their way into Taiohae Bay. Along the beach stands a long line of people in their best attire. Much white *tapa* cloth here. They are welcoming and apprehensive at the same time. The last strangers here in the *Daedalus* had killed one of them and wounded others when given peace offerings. There are no warriors in this line. Instead two priests come forward. Crook recognises that they are priests because of their conical caps and cloaks of coconut palm leaves. One of them is Kiatonui. He carries a branch of a *toa* tree. The other has an offering of a small pig. They walk chest-deep into the water. Crook calls out to them. They are surprised to hear him speak their language. They realise he is Kuruka. They know all about Kuruka. The two priests are happy to climb aboard the boat but baulk at going aboard the *Betsy*. They fear that they will be killed. When they are finally persuaded to come on deck and into the cabin, they are overcome with motion sickness and cannot be attentive to all the strange things about them.

Crook has been much refreshed by his few days aboard the *Betsy*. The captain, Edmund Fanning, is a religious man and appreciates Crook's idealism. There is no talk now of temptations of the soul. Crook believes that now he can make a new and better start. He has control of the language. More importantly, he now knows how to make a proper entry. He will not go ashore begging. He will play to his status and demand it be recognised. He has crossed that beach. He knows the metaphors that define power and authority.

He does not ask much of Fanning, just a Bible and some writing materials. A musket, yes. It will be the badge of his status. And a dog, a large dog, a mastiff. Enata hold it in awe. Maybe they have deep memories of the dogs that had come with them from Hava'iki but had become extinct. Pato is the dog's name. Mr Mix, Fanning's supercargo, had given him to Crook. Pato is on reprieve for having killed sheep in Newhaven, Connecticut. Mr Mix will get Pato back four years from now when Robarts returns the gift.

Crook swims ashore on his first landing at Taiohae. Kiatonui covers Crook's nakedness with white *tapa* cloth. He is Kuruka again in his woman's *ka'eu*. That will be his dress till he leaves Nukuhiva six months later. This first day of his landing is given to ceremony. Kiatonui asks Kuruka to take his own other name, Pakauoteii. Pakauoteii is also the name of Kiatonui's fifteen-month-old grandson, chosen even at this early stage to inherit his titles. Kuruka, now Pakauoteii, is bedecked with gorgets, arm and wrist bands and headdress that are the signs of his status.

Kiatonui is not inclined to talk religion with Crook. He says that if Crook cannot distinguish between this tree and that, how can he be trusted to know which god is which. But the social and cultural atmosphere of Taiohae is more conducive to reflection and friendship than the fear and tension that overhung Vaitahu. Individual conflict is more likely to be resolved by debate and negotiation than by catatonic violence. Feast more than war is a preoccupation. The culture of the four side-by-side valleys is far fuller of products of communal energy—there are five or six massive *tohua*, dancing grounds, and as many *me'ae*. There is a busyness in the bay—fishing, canoe-building, food preparation, *tapa* making, dance and song learning—that a larger population brings. Crook is an object more of respect than curiosity here at Taiohae. So he has the opportunity of more serious conversation. In these early days he lives at Taiohae in a *tapu* house in Kiatonui's compound. For prayer and peace, he still has to retire to a *fau* (hibiscus) forest. The *fau* forest is an uncomfortable chapel. It is full of mosquitoes, Crook says. Mosquitoes had not reached Vaitahu at the time. They have usually been thought to have arrived at Nukuhiva a little later, with the whalers and their water barrels. Perhaps Crook is thinking of the *noni*, a sand gnat, a curse of Nukuhiva.

Whatever it was, it induced Crook to find a property of his own. He had already begun to grow some radishes in a plot of land, but a man who had befriended him, Hiihui, suggested he should be more ambitious than that. Hiihui is between forty and fifty years old. He lives on some land of

Kiatonui. He does not seem to be of high status, more in-between *kikino* and *tapu*. He has not much to lose or much to gain from his friendship with Crook. Perhaps this sets him free to listen a little. Crook shares with him mythic stories the like of which he has never heard. He learns of his need of salvation, though we do not know what word Crook would have used for 'salvation'. He feels the need to pray. Crook gives him the words. 'To matou modua [*To matou motua*]—Our Father . . .' He translates the Lord's Prayer and the Ten Commandments among other things. Hiihui learns them by rote. It is a moment of encouragement for Crook. He sees for a second time that friendship crosses beaches. In the end Hiihui will ask to leave the island with Crook. But he is too old to be useful. So the whaler that would have given him passage will turn him away.

Hiihui persuades Crook to ask for a piece of cleared land belonging to Kiatonui. He points out a piece by a stream. It has on it a hundred breadfruit trees and coconut palms. It also has a cabin on it. A boy named Hikonaiki lives in it to give the alarm if anybody is stealing the breadfruit and coconuts. There is a *tapu* house. Hikonaiki's elderly mother—his father is dead—lives close by and looks after the *tapu* house when required. Crook sees that, with the *tapu* house at one corner, an enclosure of a high bamboo fence could be put around the property. The *tapu* house can be enlarged for himself. He knows, with Hiihui's advice, what to do. He puts on all the ornaments of his status as Pakauoteii, Kiatonui's other ego, and asks a fisherman who is living on 'his' land to provide him with a netful of fish. The fisherman obliges him with a thousand fish and more. Thirty or forty men work for the fish, and Crook's enclosure and house are finished in a day or so. With the boy Hikonaiki, his mother and Crook's friend Hiihui, they make a small agreeable community. Hikonaiki will take Hiihui's place on the whaler and go back to England with Crook. There he lives for a few months before the cold and London's foul air kill him. Crook gives his enclosure a name. 'Maria's Compound', he calls it, for his younger sister.

While Crook never has the occasion to use his musket or go into battle, his presence at Taiohae, with his musket and his mastiff Pato, seems to have frightened off any incursions of the Taipi on the Teii. From May to December, however, there were several other incursions created by the usual demand for sacrifices at the death of a *tau'a*. But these were all at the other side of the island. The counter-incursions were as destructive of the food trees as usual. Such destructiveness was payback, but it was more.

Group status on the island was dependent on the display of abundance of material wealth and of the food that could be brought to the feasts. To have none to bring because the breadfruit trees had been destroyed was a social humiliation of a high degree. It was made worse by the fact that marriage alliances and the *tapu* that went with them made a safety network across the island. Mortal enemies mingled at the great *koina* and scoffed at one another's poor showing.

In October 1798, there is to be a great *koina* at Aakapa on the north coast of Nukuhiva, across from Taiohae over and beyond the To'ovi'i, the barren inland of the island. It was a two- or three-day trek, dangerous and difficult, along mountain ridges with much luggage to be carried. Such large *koina* sometimes took years to prepare. This is a large feast. Crook later thinks that some ten thousand people are there. The reason for the *koina* is not clear. Aakapa was the ceremonial centre for the whole of the Teii group. Certainly the Teii of Taiohae are deeply involved. Kiatonui himself was under *tapu* for weeks beforehand.

Whatever the reason for the feast, one important element in it was the opportunity to see Kuruka. The first day was given over entirely to dancing. Massed, competitive and vociferous dancing played through the *tohua* in the daylight. Then quiet set dancing in the evening. Part of the daytime dancing was some sort of historical re-enactment of the double visits of the *Daedalus*, the one in 1792 when William Gooch and Richard Hergest mapped both Taiohae and Hoo'umi, and the other more disastrous visit in 1794 when Kiatonui's brother was killed in his canoe. The evening dances were held in the large pavilion of a house on the *tohua* belonging to the *haka'iki* of Aakapa. At one end of the pavilion danced the nine-year-old daughter of the *haka'iki*, a delicate wisp of a girl. At the other end danced the seventeen-year-old nephew of Kiatonui, named for Kiatonui's father, Timouteii. The youth was decked out in all Kiatonui's and his grandfather's ornaments. In-between the two dancers the crowd lay flat on the floor. At the sides two or three singers gave beat to the dancing. Behind a partition Crook entertained the two *haka'iki* with stories of Tahiti.

The gods weren't kind to the occasion. There was much rain. Kiatonui, who had paraded his *tapu* status, ended it by bathing in the sea. A woman who had expected to entertain him but was denied that privilege because of his *tapu*, sniffed at him that his *tapu* didn't keep out the rain. Godliness, we have to think, was not altogether out of this world. The rain doesn't help the return trip over muddy paths and up slippery rocks. Even Pato, who would never let anyone other than Crook touch him, was exhausted by the rain and had to be carried over the mountains.

Crook spends his energies farming his enclosure. He adds plantains, sugarcane, sweet potato, ginger and mulberry (for *tapa* cloth) to his breadfruit and coconuts. He collects a few fowls and hogs. He travels frequently to plantations in other valleys to get their roots and crops. He seems to be laying up wealth. He has always had the ambition to be the owner of a double *va'a*, or a boat if he can persuade the canoe-builders out of their conservatism to build such a thing. He will need to pay them, or he will need to trade for the tools if a ship comes by. A ship's coming is on his mind in these weeks. The thought of it even disturbs his sleep. Perhaps he is debating whether to return home and warn the Missionary Society Directors that their missionary strategies are all wrong. It would never do again to send one missionary to an island. Missionaries must create a community of example, he is thinking. He is asking Hiihui what is his best method of getting to a ship. He is not sure if he will be allowed to go.

The people of the valley know he is on the look-out for a ship. The mood towards him in the valley is changing. His usefulness is being questioned. He is no warrior. His musket and his dog will never be used in aggression. There is an imbalance perceived in their daily exchanges. They don't know what he has to give them.

In late December, on one of his travels, he thinks he sees a ship's sail to the east in what Richard Hergest called Comptroller's Bay, Hoo'umi. But Hiinui says, no. It is the double sails of a bonito deep-sea fishing canoe. But a day or so later news comes to him while he is on the far west of the island—actually overlooking the serpentine river far below him in the valley of Hakaui—that there are two ships in Hoo'umi.

Haste doesn't get him back to Taiohae till late afternoon. Kiatonui and his *toa*, Mauateii—the Belvedere Apollo—are debating whether to go to the ships by sea or by land. Mauateii is for land, but Kiatonui is for sea. Kiatonui's is the wrong decision. Only a single *va'a* is available. The seas are high. Night sets in. They come back to Taiohae. Early next morning they set off again in a double *va'a*. The sea is even wilder. They are not far along when the *va'a* is broken in two and founders. They swim to land, and take the hard walk over the ridges to Hakapuai, a beach of the Hapa'a people. They are still three or four miles from the ships. The Hapa'a are terrified to go with them in a rickety *va'a*. Not so much because of the dangers of the sea but because of the Taipi. The ships are in waters belonging to the Taipi. They are sure they will all be killed.

When they finally do approach the ships, they are even more terrified. The Taipi are swarming the decks. Crooks stands up and hails the ships in English. He is still in his woman's dress. There is a pause of disbelief before they let him aboard. He discovers that the ships are the whalers *Butterworth* (Lawrence Frazier) and the *New Euphrates* (Henry Glasspoole). They are anchored in Hoo'umi seeking supplies. They have just sailed there from Vaitahu, minus their cook, Edward Robarts.

The crews of the ships are not doing well in their trade with the Taipi. They have no interpreter. The Taipi are driving hard bargains and are stealing. Kiatonui is in a frenzy of excitement. He has seen an English sow and wants it. He had long commissioned Crook to impose an *ahui*—a secular ban on products, as distinct from a sacred ban in a *tapu*—on hundreds of coconuts and scores of hogs. Throwing aside common sense, he tells Crook that he will give four hundred hogs for the sow. And there is a Galapagos turtle that he must have.

Glasspoole, meanwhile, has begun trying to convince Crook to come with him to England. Why he should initiate this conversation we do not know. Perhaps he feels that Crook would be of some interest to the English whaling industry with his knowledge of The Marquesas. Meanwhile, Glasspoole has snatched two boys from Vaitahu without their consent. Timotete is one. Crook of course knows him. Now to all the other advantages of going home there is one more. With Timotete, the three-month voyage home would be a schooling for him in language and custom. His 'Account of the Marquesas Islands' and his 'Dictionary' will begin there.

There is still drama to be played out. Anyone might have been suspicious of Edward Robarts' given reason for deserting—his fear of mutiny on the *New Euphrates*. But his fears come true at Nukuhiva. Eight or ten able seamen of the *New Euphrates* are on shore among the Taipi. They are staying there, they say. They complain that the *New Euphrates* is leaky and won't get back to England; Glasspoole treats them badly. Now Glasspoole doesn't act in their best interests. He takes those Taipi who are aboard the *New Euphrates* as hostages. They include the daughter of the *haka'iki* of Taipivai. Get my crew back, Glasspoole demands, or something unspecified will happen to the hostages. For the Taipi it was an easy decision. They will simply dispose of the crew in their hands in a manner fitting for a warrior, man-eating tribe. Kiatonui is highly agitated. He knows the Taipi will have few qualms in doing what they say. Crook persuades Glasspoole of the same. The crew, after this closer look at life on the island, come back to their leaky ship and their unsatisfactory captain.

Crook takes a boat back to Taiohae to trade. He persuades Kiatonui that four hundred hogs for a sow is irresponsible. One of the two sows on the *New Euphrates* has now gone, probably as a sacrifice to the gods of mutinies. Kiatonui then says he will give sixty hogs for the other one. The people say that there is no way in which they will give up sixty hogs to ships trading in an enemy's bay. Twenty maybe, but then not even four. They have no time now for Crook either. He hasn't their interests at heart, they intimate. They begin to abuse him. When Glasspoole and Frazier bring their ships to Taiohae to do a trade, the scene is a debacle. The sailors are immediately off with the women. The trade goods are stolen. Kiatonui gets his sow and his turtle, but something has changed in his status. His wealth, once spent on his people, is now seeping out of the valley to strangers. The return on that trade goes not to them but to Kiatonui. His people need a share in it. They murmur. And they know Kuruka for what he is. A stranger.

Crook as he leaves his beach on this January day 1799 is disappointed too. He is affronted that the people among whom he has lived cannot discern gift from trade. There were many, too, who had promised things to him, probably the crafted bowls and tools and ornaments he sees bartered to the crew. Like as not he would have preferred to take these things home as souvenirs of his beach. Perhaps he has hopes of being a collector. The sailors do. They want women, food and artefacts, in that order.

Robarts

'Finding myself comfortable situated . . .'

To wake up to the face of 'the French Boy' is a shock to Robarts. He does not like the French Boy. Worse, the French Boy has a companion, and they both have muskets. Robarts has no desire to share his beach, and he does not have a musket. Kabris' companion is an Englishman called Walker. A whaler, possibly the *London*, Kabris' vessel, had picked him up off the wild island of Masafuero off the South American coast. He had been left at Masafuero to collect sealskins. The date now is early 1801.

Robarts is eager to be free of them both. For that matter, Kabris and Walker seem to be eager to get rid of one another. The first thing Kabris does when he gets his musket, says Walker, is try to shoot him. Robarts has old friends from Tahuata on Nukuhiva. He uses their network to tell bad stories of Kabris. He does not know the lie of the land here, so he does what he has always done. He begins to walk it. First, he treks the eastern end of Nukuhiva. This is all Taipi country, and, as it were, the domain of Kabris. He goes westward. On foot. The seas are wild. The westerlies have begun.

Robarts passes through Hapa'a country and up into the inland valley of Muake. There, for the first time on Nukuhiva, he feels comfortable. The people know all about him from Tahuata and Hiva Oa. His name is his entry point. He gives it to a three- or four-year-old boy, and the boy gives his name to Robarts, Pakauoteii. It is Kiatonui's grandson by the devious track by which these things happen in The Land. Pakauoteii is the name Crook had, and it is Kiatonui's other name. The boy at the time is part of the household of Tahatapu, Kiatonui's firstborn daughter of the highest rank. Her husband is Mauateii, *toa* of Kiatonui. Actually, Pakauoteii, the 'grandson', is the son of Kiatonui's eldest son, Tuitoua, a fourteen- or fifteen-year-old boy married to a mature woman with forty *pekio*. But Tahatapu is the perceived 'mother' of Pakauoteii. So Tahatapu becomes Robarts' 'mother' and Mauateii his 'father'. It would be a mistake to think these 'as if' relationships are unreal. Robarts certainly does not think them unreal, nor do Enata. These relationships place him very precisely on his beach. They will shape the five years of his stay. He himself, whenever he is managing the politics of living, will locate himself in them.

Tahatapu, Robarts' 'mother', is visiting her mother Putahaii in her house by and in the sea at the time Robarts visits Muake. So he goes on to see her there. He thus comes to Taiohae from an unusual direction. He sees it first not through the telescopic lens of its entrance from the sea but from its panoramic aspect high on the ridge above it. He stands on a very famous spot. Below him to his left is where David Porter in fourteen years' time will build his Madisonville and where the French in forty-two years' time will build their Saumerville. To the right, on the western shore of the bay, he can see Putahaii's house. He can discern as well all four valleys at Taiohae marked with all their public buildings. Probably on the very spot where Robarts stands, the Taipi will come and 'moon' the Americans and shout that the Americans are arses to the Teii's pricks. It is an insult that will cost the Taipi dearly. Near the spot where Robarts stands is the split in the path that Melville misses in the dark that sends him off on his awful climb down into Taipivai valley.

One panoramic view is enough for Robarts. Taiohae is the place for him. He sees it is the perfect anchorage for ships. Water is easily accessible. Food and wood supplies look abundant. He will spend the first months of his stay surveying the bay, sounding its bottom, learning the currents and the winds, noting the tidal measurements, mapping in his mind the reefs. He is a proud man and piloting becomes a professional responsibility to him. Some fourteen vessels will visit Taiohae while he is there. He counts himself responsible for their safety and for control over their relationships with the people in the bay. He believes that honesty is a two-way virtue on the beach. He will help captains get a bargain, but he will never help in duplicity. It is he who will stay on and pay the cost of their fraud. He never, to be sure, loses his own sense of superiority over 'savages', but does not think that there are very many Strangers who come to Taiohae who can say they are superior to Enata. He is outraged at the occasions when innocents are killed with unthinking violence.

Robarts comes down the ridge and proceeds immediately to Putahaii's house, where his by now large family is assembled. Putahaii's first declaration to him is that Crook was here, you should be here too. They are all comfortable that Pakauoteii has had some sort of resurrection.

Robarts knows how much the island's balance of power has been disturbed by the presence of Kabris and Walker and their possession of muskets. Robarts himself has no musket and will not have one for nearly four years. Kabris, by this time, is enthusiastically Taipi. There is not much Robarts can do about him. But Walker, without language and with no interest in crossing this beach in any intensive way, can be persuaded to leave the group that own him. His *haka'iki* keeps Walker's musket in his own house, but that can be stolen with a little ingenuity. So Robarts gets Walker to Taiohae and happily sees him shipped off in the *Minerva* of Salem, Captain M. Folger, some time late in 1801.

Even without a musket, Robarts is Kiatonui's *toa*. He is happy to reap the benefits of that role. By now he is well versed in all the protocols and etiquette of visiting and travel. He delights in the leis and dress lavished on him as he moves around the allies of the Teii on the north and west of the island. He is a good dancer—or so he tells us! He has stories to tell, the like of which Enata had never heard, and he clearly entertains them day and night with these stories. Wherever he goes the women pleasure him.

Alarums and excursions are not as frequent here as at Hiva Oa and Tahuata, but there are some. He plays general in an unsuccessful ambush deep in Taipivai valley. He is very conscious of the deep division in Enata society between the *tapu* class, of which he is part, and the commoners, the *kikino*. He knows that if he is caught alone with the *kikino* without the *tapu* elite to protect him, he is unlikely to survive. There are dangerous moments when he travels alone over the To'ovi'i, the inland desert. His 'family' is always apprehensive at these lone travels and celebrate the more at his return.

There is a deeper threat that will change life for him. The breadfruit crop failure of 1797–78 begins to repeat itself in 1801. It goes to catastrophic dimensions through three years. The memories of these terrible years hold long into the future. Later missionaries will give each of these desolate times of three, six and seven years a name—*Ivi Omo*, 'Suck Bones', *Tehi Ki'a*, 'Bite Air'. In the worst of them two-thirds of an island population dies. In this one Robarts sees three or four hundred die of hunger in one year alone at Taiohae—eleven of twelve in one household. Bodies lie around in a putrid state. Robarts pulls one young woman out of the stream to which she has crawled but from which she has not the strength to withdraw. She dies on the bank before him. People are forced to empty *ma* pits that they have held for forty years.

The famine days, as we have seen, drive the people to alternate foods and the tedious preparations that are needed to rid the toxic element in them. It is a bad time for the weak and poor. They are easy victims for sacrifice, the constant resolution of the disorder that famines represent. Slow-running, uneventful disasters—drought and crop failure—are different from eventful trauma—flood, earthquake. The long days—years—rouse suspicions and fears. Rumours and accusations are rife. Everything others do is read with damning eyes. The *tau'a* dance and read the signs more frenetically. Robarts sees it with his own eyes, when a young Taipi woman driven out into the wild parts in search of food is caught, killed, and her body brought back to the *tau'a*, who smashes her skull and scoops out the brains to eat them.

In the crisis, Robarts uses his unattached role to his own advantage. He moves along his family lines to wherever the crop failure is less stringent. So he is in Hakaui for months. Hakaui is fertile and well watered. He follows these lines of relatives in their varied generations as far as the island of Ua Pou. Ua Pou is harder hit than Nukuhiva in the famine. Whole valleys are depopulated, but the dead bring life to the survivors. As the breadfruit recovers there is superabundance because there is no one to harvest it.

Robarts is not loath to make these trips to Ua Pou, even with their hazards of sudden storms and accident-prone canoes. Returning after one visit he agrees to take a group of ten or fifteen men and women from Ua Pou to Taiohae. They have all their material wealth bundled with them—weapons domestic utensils, ornaments. They need their wealth to procure an ocean-going double *va'a*. They are determined to sail to the west, to those islands their *tau'a* tell them of. They ask Robarts to pilot them, but he tries to dissuade them from going. Even when the double *va'a* they are sailing on to Taiohae breaks up in the sea between Nukuhiva and Ua Pou, they are not deterred. Robarts bemoans what he sees as the tragedy of these voyages of emigration. He knows of many of them, but doesn't say how many. Another beachcomber, just ten years later, says he knows of eight hundred people a year setting off in this fashion. The winds from the east are a spillway into the islands of the west.

To this point in his stay in The Land, Robarts had resisted being tattooed. He is an independent man. That first tattoo is an act of dependence. He is not willing to be the 'shit' of the *haka'iki*. He sports a bushy beard that by 1801 covers his chest. The beard is his body show. At Nukuhiva and in the middle of the famine he discovers that there is a tattoo that is out of the usual order of body wrapping. It is merely the price of entry into a special club. It is an eating club. Kiatonui is its leader. Its members share meals with him in a *tapu* eating house. It has about twenty-six members. Kiatonui invites Robarts to have this six- by four-inch meal ticket imprinted on his chest. Robarts accepts. It is an insurance against hunger, to be sure. But it has other costs. In prolonged crises, the divisions between those that have and those that have not, become more and more tense. This is not so much between the utterly poor and the utterly rich. That division is always there and resolved by naked power. The division between those that have not-so-much and those that have more in the end will be destructive of the bonds of order. Privilege defended in the end by naked power will be tested by power. In a sense, Robarts' exit from the beach begins with these privileges. Inevitably they will be contested.

Owning land is the essential requirement for survival. Robarts simply occupies land he finds vacant because all are dead in the famine. But land is never really vacated. Ownership is plotted in much more complex ways. He must get to own by rights agreed on. Robarts sees that Putahaii provides for her daughters, Kiatonui's sisters, very well. He will marry into 'Blood Royal', as he will always put it. All his life this will be a source of pride. He is reduced to beggary in later years, going from one great man to another, and he is always wistful of his own days of greatness, a king's son-in-law, adopted son of every great *haka'iki* in The Land, a tribal warrior, a man whose friendship the great sought after. One day he catches a young woman coming from her bathing. She is beautiful. He asks who she is. She is the king's sister. 'Ena-o-Ae-A-Ta' is the name he transcribes for her in the only time he ever uses it. Ena is eighteen years old and she has a productive piece of land at Taiohae. He asks Kiatonui for her in marriage. Ena's property is beside a stream and has one of the many mineral springs at Taiohae nearby. He builds a new house and repairs the stone enclosure. He immediately begins to plant crops, especially turmeric for the perfume trade among Enata. A good breadfruit crop breaks the famine, and he puts it in the *ma* pits with his own hands.

> On May 27th, 1804, Just after sun rise, my royal consort was deliverd of a fine daughter. I was at the back of the house. On hearing the child, I started out of my store pitt and ran to the house. No midwife being at hand, I did the office myself. I had made rollers, etc. before. My tinder box and dry wood was ready in case of a squall in the night. I cutt the navel string and securd it, sent the child to rest, made some gruel and set of the news to my Brother in Law. The family wish me much Joy, and they a repaird to my Cottage and was much pleasd at their new relation. I was happy to see providence still favourd me thro all perils.

May 1804 is an important month in Robarts' life, and not just because of the birth of his daughter. On 5 May, news comes to him that a ship is entering the bay. He quickly collects the certificates of good repute that captains have given him and joins the fleet of canoes rushing to the ship. The ship's railing is lined with men speaking a Babel of languages— French, Dutch, Russian, German, Swedish. The captain, surprised at Robarts' English, adds English. Robarts, not to be outdone, musters his 'Rush' and starts a conversation with Ivan Fedorovich Kruzenshtern about St Petersburg. Robarts has been there, of course. Where hasn't he been? The ship is the *Nadezhda* and is ahead by a week or so of the *Neva*, Captain Yurii Fedorovich Lisyanski. The two vessels belong to Russia's first scientific, hydrographic and ethnographic circumnavigation of the globe. There will be many triumphs in this expedition—among them G. H. Langsdorff's *Voyages and Travels* (1813–14), Melville's inspiration. There is an innocent, scientific curiosity, even wonder, among these Russians. They see themselves as different to the more established authorities in these discovering ventures—the English and the French. In fact, they feel their prejudices vindicated when they find that the English–French wars were being continued on the edge of the inhabited world in The Marquesas. The French Boy comes to Taiohae and competes with Robarts to be their interpreter and informant. But that is Kabris' story. Let us leave it there.

Robarts will discover in later years that the Russians have made him famous. In July–August 1804 Kruzenshtern writes a letter from Japan about what had happened so far in their expedition. A year later *The Philosophical Magazine* publishes an extract of this letter. We have already seen Robarts, in those heady days when he is in service to the 'Immortal Dr Leydon', reading about himself and realising that he has a market for his experiences.

Meanwhile Robarts is serving the Russians well, spending wet and cold nights with the scientists among them (Drs Tilesius and Langsdorff) when they find botanising in The Land stretches their endurance too far. He is in his element, and his language picks up in courtly tones as he introduces a set of what he sees as aristocratic Russians to his royal family.

When the Russians depart, Robarts enters on the last stages of his stay in The Land. He is prosperous. He has purchased more land. He has servants to take care of it all. He is ever more entwined in the politics of the valley. Through his years at Taiohae, and especially since the famine, politics turn around ownership and occupation of property. External threats from the Taipi and their allies are a constant, but seemingly manageable, threat. At Taiohae itself the issue is the daily management of rhetorical authority and real power. Kiatonui and Putahaii have the rhetorical authority. Real power is more contingent. There are cohorts in the valley—Robarts calls them 'the warriors'. No doubt the culture of display and an ethos of ferocity throws up groups of unattached young males. They are both political resource and political threat. Some time before Robarts' arrival at Taiohae, Kiatonui had fallen out with his eldest sister. He had gone to 'war' with her. We have to think that the word 'war' includes both the physical conflict and the protocols that begin and end it. The sister had lost and had left the valley. The 'warriors' who had defeated her had occupied her land. It was an extensive and lush property straddling one of Taiohae's streams and reaching to the beach.

Through the years, this matter of land is a weeping wound in the body politic. The sister wants her land back. Putahaii wants it for her. But Kiatonui does not have the power to make it happen. Robarts, his *toa*, is asked to help. It is a ritual act Robarts must oversee. The sister must sit on her land and wait to see if someone will come with material to help her build her house. That will be a sign that she can have it back. No one does.

Some time in 1804, Robarts is asked to try again. This time he calls on his 'mother', Tahatapu, Kiatonui's firstborn daughter, and his 'father' Mauateii. Mauateii has some twelve hundred warriors at his disposal in the valley of Muake. When Robarts has Kiatonui's sister sit on her land again, Mauateii has his warriors stand threateningly on that very spot where Robarts first saw Taiohae. This time when the 'warriers' refuse to give up the land, Robarts kicks down their stone enclosure and says that there will be 'war'. The 'warriers' buckle. Robarts agrees that they have the right to their years of investment in the land and that they can take away the *ma* they have buried and all their material property. They celebrate this solution as they always do, with a *koina*.

In October 1804 a large vessel is sighted off the entrance to the bay. It is the *Leviathan*, a whaler out of London. The *Leviathan* is three times too large for whaling, in Robarts' opinion. Fifty men are too many for an industry that has so much leisure time. There will be trouble, and there is. Robarts mans a double *va'a* to meet the ship. The seas are wild and a sudden squall nearly sinks the *va'a* and puts the *Leviathan*'s sails in tatters. Robarts has to run for Ua Pou. There he is caught with a north wind for ten days. The *Leviathan*, meanwhile, has anchored off Taipivai, something Robarts does not want. He sails back to Taiohae and picks up Kiatonui and his brother. They catch up with the *Leviathan* in the dark. Clark, the captain, knows of Robarts and hears his advice: he is in danger among the Taipi.

Clark then lets Robarts pilot the *Leviathan* back to Taiohae and stay aboard to oversee the trade. Robarts senses that there is trouble among the crew. Clark is a hard man. One night six of the crew make off with a boat. They are a mixed lot, a gunner, a cooper, a bosun, cook, a landsman and a 'usefull boy'. Robarts thinks they have taken a fair wind to Ua Pou, but Clark believes they are still on Nukuhiva. He doesn't give a 'd—n' for the men, but he wants his boat back. Robarts advises him to leave for a few weeks and then return. Robarts will get the boat for him. After some serious work is done on the yards, the *Leviathan* leaves.

A little later there is news that the stolen boat had left Ua Pou and is at Taipivai. The Taipi want the boat and its three harpoons and are waiting the opportunity to take them. Robarts with Kiatonui catches up with them there. The six men are glad to see him. They had experienced a dangerous time at

Ua Pou. One of them had his arm broken by a slingshot. Robarts disposes of the Taipi *haka'iki* who is in the boat. He literally throws him overboard.

Back at Taiohae, the prospect of having a whaleboat creates great excitement. Robarts has the boat put in Putahaii's house. The six men share his old apartment there. He tells them not to approach the women in this household. Kiatonui's surgical skills are put to good use on the broken arm. He removes the swelling with oil massages and sets the two-week-old break, splints and binds it.

Six men are a problem. They fight when they are together in one house. Robarts splits them up among their namesakes. Putahaii is eager to make use of the whaleboat. It is an icon to these people, who still have their myths of the times that they were a Sea People. Soon they will be making wide *va'a* in imitation of the whaleboats. Putahaii asks Robarts if he will go on a trading voyage for her to Tahuata. She has bricks of turmeric to trade and give as gifts. Robarts agrees but needs to fix up the boat first.

He is waiting for a west wind. He sees a large bank of black cloud in the west 'with curling clouds at its top'. It is 'a shure sign of a west wind'. He sets off with the gunner and two Teii seamen. Nearly the whole valley is there to see them off, not optimistically it would seem. 'The royal family' was weeping. Some were singing Robarts' favourite song. The men finish their journey in a day and a half, paddling in calm at times, whipping along at 'sixteen miles per hour' at others. They pass around the southwest tip of Hiva Oa and land at Hapatoni, the valley where Robarts had first landed.

It is clearly a nostalgic trip for Robarts. He probably makes it for the nostalgia. But things have changed. And not changed. The Enata friend who had taken him off the *New Euphrates* on that first dark Christmas night six years before is up on the mountain pass. That is what has not changed. There is war. His friend has a new wife, younger. Robarts doesn't like her. Something has hardened in the women. He won't share her mantle as he did his friend's first wife's. He goes to visit that first wife, now returned to Vaitahu. He has a brick of turmeric for her. Old friends shower him with gifts to take home to his own wife and child. He walks up to Tainai's house and sees his own old sea clothes still hanging there as a remembrance for him. He leaves sadly after the dances and songs. He will write later:

A spark of affection and gratitude glow'd thro' my bosom; for these people had reard me, as it were, from a child. When I could not ask in their language for food, they cherish'd me unask'd for, and now I was become a powerful man where I resided. And I hope thro' all tribes and tongues to greatfully remember the Bridge that conveys me safe over.

Back at Nukuhiva, his welcome is warm. But this too is changed and not changed. The six men in the valley have changed it. Six bellies are a burden. Six overstepping marks are not easily contained. What is not changed is the underlying political malaise. The 'warriers', beaten by Robarts' invoking outsiders, now want to win by invoking outsiders too. Kiatonui is 'humane and liberal in time of need to his tribe but he is no warrier. He hadn't the least idea of forming his men to advantage in time of war.' 'Things waring such a gloomy aspect, my time hangs heavy, my nights restless.'

In February 1806, the *Lucy*, privateer from London, Captain Abe Ferguson, hoves to off his beach. It is an opportunity to leave. He takes it.

Kabris

An Unhappy Exit: Stage North

'Moi beaucoup François. Americanish ship. Uh danson la Carmagnole' were the first words the Russians heard from Joseph Kabris. They were delighted. They had come upon a civilised man who had turned so feral that he had forgotten most of his native tongue. He could not remember his own name at first, nor the names of his parents, nor where he was born. They savoured this experiment in language loss and acquisition and followed the unwinding of the tangles of his mind with pleasure. They enjoyed the fact that he exchanged a new shirt that was given him for an old red jacket. It was the redness of the jacket that he valued because only the *tapu* class can have red. There was always a hope in these early years of the Enlightenment—certainly among courtly intellectuals—that a wolf-child, a human nurtured by animals, would come into the hands of scientists. Joseph Kabris was part-way a fulfilment of this ambition.

The Russians would have plenty of time to unwind the tangles. They took Kabris, by accident they claimed, from Taiohae when they left on 17 May 1804. All the way to Hawai'i and on to Kamchatka they had him aboard the *Nadezhda*. He sang them songs that he transcribed, danced his warriors' rituals, played the *tau'a* (unsuccessfully, he said, because there was no *me'ae* on board the *Nadezhda*). They can make tracings of the design of his tattoos off his body.

Joseph Kabris comes to the *Nadezhda*, anchored in Taiohae Bay, some time after Robarts. He comes with Kiatonui. Robarts would not have liked that. The Russians think he speaks the island language more fluently than Robarts. He certainly had absorbed Enata body postures and gestures. He becomes Langsdorff's interpreter and informant more than Kruzenshtern's. Kruzenshtern is more comfortable with Robarts' 'royal family'. Langsdorff likes the crush around Kabris. The Russians do not trust him altogether. This may be Robarts' coaxing, but they suspect him of working against them on more than one occasion, but notably once when they are making a first try at exiting Taiohae Bay. They come dangerously close to grounding against the rocks in a high sea. There is a disturbing exuberance in Kabris as he gathers a large crowd on the rocks that threaten the ship. That the Russians do not like.

The Russians will later say that Kabris had been in the islands for nine years and that he had landed on Tahuata first. This last is correct, but he could not have been in the islands nine years. He deserts from the *London* at Vaitahu some time between 21 February and 7 March 1799. He doesn't stay at Vaitahu, perhaps because Robarts is there. He goes over the ridge to Hanatetena to stay with the enemies of Tainai. He seems to delight in being on the margins altogether. While Robarts is away on a visit to Hiva Oa, Kabris leaves Tahuata on some ship, probably the *London* again. He leaves that ship with Walker at Taipivai.

Among the Taipi, Kabris adopts the warrior's code with enthusiasm. He doesn't eat those he kills, he tells the Russians. He trades their bodies for pigs. He marries twice. He leaves his first wife because she resorts to eating others in her family in the famine. That's his story. His second wife is the daughter of a lesser *haka'iki* among the Taipi. By her he has two children. Later and in his loneliest days in the fairs of Brittany, it is his wife, a 'princess', and his children that he misses most. He has nothing but admiration of Enata ways. *'Beaucoup d'esprit! Beaucoup d'esprit!*—Much spirit!' he repeats over and over again when his French returns.

Kabris roves constantly around the eastern end of Nukuhiva among the Taipi and their allies. Like Robarts, he is very conscious of the webs of relationships that reach across the island. These webs bring safety. He delights in the complexities and niceties of these webs of relationships and what they affect. A son of Kiatonui, Kabris tells the Russians, is married to the daughter of the *haka'iki* of the Taipi. They came to their marriage by the sea between Taiohae and Taipivai. Their voyage makes that sea *tapu*. It is not possible for either party of the Teii or Taipi to go to war by sea. War by land is possible. By sea it is not. It is an interesting story. Certainly in the years that we know them the Teii and the Taipi move freely by sea between their valleys. It is an easy, if occasionally apprehensive, movement. The trails across the ridges are always dangerous.

Once across his beach, Kabris is never tempted to leave it. We never hear of him in contact with ships that come to Nukuhiva other than the Russians. It is a personal disaster when the Russians take him away.

Kabris was on the stage in Moscow and Brittany, singing and dancing when we first met him. He had left Fenua'enata on the stage of the deck of the *Nadezhda* dancing and singing. Perhaps we should leave him with a last performance. He has his feather headdress, his arm and ankle bands, his lei. Maybe he even has his skulls. The Russians have traded to get some. Maybe there are some drums, perhaps not the five-foot-tall drums of the *tohua*. Maybe there are conch shells. Certainly he will beat his right hand against his left elbow. Maybe if he is lucky he will lose himself in the fierce beat. For the rest of his life he will be performing before crowds who can't hear what he has heard, can't see what he has seen. The words of the song are his, even the translation is his. To really hear it, we have to imagine hundreds, even thousands of voices, living the beat in constant repetition, like 'a Romish *Kyrie Eleison*' Langsdorff says:

> Where is the light?
>> Where is the light?
> On Tahuata
>> On Tahuata.
> Wherefore the light?
>> Wherefore the light?
> To roast the enemy
>> To roast the enemy.
> Let us make fire.
>> Let us make fire.
> We have fire.
>> We have fire.
> We will roast him.
>> We will roast him.
> We have him.
>> We have him.
> He would fly.
>> He would fly.
> Now he is dead.
>> Now he is dead.

CROSSINGS

Performing

We never learn the truth by being told it. We need to experience it in some way. Theatre is the place where we experience truth. In the theatre we experience truth particularly, trivially, and then go out into the foyer and say what these trivia mean beyond themselves. Storytelling is theatre. Storytellers are performers.

Hidden in the word 'performance', Victor Turner has told us, is the Indo-European linguistic form 'per, meaning risk or gamble. There is always a gamble in performance. There is never a perfect moment for performance. The curtain call always comes before that perfect moment. A performance is always a closure of some sort. That is because a performance is never just practice. A performance is public. There is always someone else in a performance—an audience, a reader. So a performance is always artful. It is always trying to catch someone's attention, and having caught it, trying to keep it. But that also means that a performance is always self-conscious, self-critical, always contriving to do it better. Performers are always their own first reviewers.

Paradoxes in Performing

Denis Diderot, the eighteenth-century French encyclopaedist, all his life was a critic—a constructive critic—of those who represented nature and humanity in painting, who created theatre and who reported their experiences among exotic other people. He once wrote an essay on 'The Paradoxes of Acting'. The paradox of acting in Diderot's eyes was that the least sincere person was likely to be the best actor, the most sincere the worst. So to lose yourself in an art that you really were angry or loving or proud, was not to act. In acting there needs to be a distinction between the person and the persona, the mask.

There is also a paradox in performing the past in history. I best understand those I meet in the past by identifying myself with them, at least in those parts of their lives that I share with them in a reflective way. I identify myself in part with much of what Crook, Robarts, Kabris, Gauguin and Melville experienced. But I cannot clone them. There is always a difference in them that I cannot enter. Can I identify myself with Tainai and

316

Kiatonui or with Enata women such as Putahaii? In part again, yes, but much less surely.

Do I as Tainai or as Robarts have freedoms that they did not have? Did they have freedoms that they did not use, and if they did, how do I know them? Too much sincerity in an historian would seem to lead to the condoning of much evil in the world. Can an historian ever see bad faith and tell its story? Is it true that the more we understand, the less we can blame?

I am a pragmatist on these issues. In our daily lives we live with varying degrees of certainty. The only thing impossible for us is absolute certainty and absolute uncertainty. We are always in-between.

I think it is possible to discover our own bad faith. We know our freedoms. There is always someone to tell what they are. We know the cost of those freedoms. We know that the cost of some freedoms will sometimes seem unreasonable to common sense and that we will not be heroic enough to bear those costs. But common sense is not always the measure of what is right and wrong. In any case we will always know our bad faith.

I think that there are many signs of bad faith in the past. There are many calls to do things in another way. I wish I could have heard some of the songs and dances of Enata at their *tohua* and seen some of the theatre of the *hoki*. I believe they would be revelatory of what Enata bad faith might have been. I have plenty of evidence of what bad faith might have been for Crook, Robarts, Kabris and all the others in our story. We are joined in our souls much more closely.

'THE BURNT-OVER DISTRICT', it is called, though now, as we drive through it, the winter cold holds. There are no signs of conflagration. The trees are grey and bare. The pock-marked snow drifts glisten in the shadow of banks. The roadside is an ugly black and yellow icy sludge. Two hundred years ago the flames that burnt over this country were divine. The Spirit made a 'psychic highway' of souls here. Between 1815 and 1828 religious journals such as the *Panoplist and Missionary Magazine* ran annual lists of 'revivals' somewhat like football scores on a modern sports page. They score 'rushes of winds', the numbers of 'hopefully pious', the confessions of sin and hardness of heart, the unions of prayer. For decades the land shakes with the emotions of conversion and protests against infidelity, rationalism and indifference to worldly evils.

We—my wife Donna Merwick and I, she my professional equal but on this occasion my 'research assistant'—are driving to Litchfield County in Connecticut. Litchfield is the overflow of the cauldron of the Burnt-Over District. We pass towns with names such as Sodom, Canaan, Faith. Irregular hills and rocky outcrops, deep pine forests and the cold, isolated the communities here and contained the intensity of their awakenings. We are on a pilgrimage ourselves. I want to visit the only monument to an Enata that I know of for the years 1796–1814. The monument is his grave. I want to visit the grave of Thomas Hami Patu, where his mortal remains rest. And I want to visit a place where his life is partly caught in story, the archives of the Cornwall Historical Society.

The cemetery at Cornwall stands on the brow and slope of a small hill. The long summer grasses browned by winter frosts make it a field more than a graveyard. The gravestones stand like plinths against the blue sky, some straight, some leaning. We find Patu's grave in a cluster of other islanders' graves—Hawaiian, Tahitian, Maori New Zealanders. Patu rests besides two other Enata, Lewis Keah and Benjamin Toke, both from Nukuhiva. There are American first people there also—Choctaw, Cherokee, Naragansett, Oneida. The students of the Foreign Mission School died easily here in this cold place. They mostly died, like Patu, of consumption.

Moss and lichen have eaten at the inscription on his stone, but we can read it.

In memory of Thomas Hammatah Patoo,
a native of the Marquesas Islands,
and a member of the Foreign Mission School,
who died June 19, 1823, aged about 19 years.
He was hopefully pious, and had a great desire
to be qualified to become a missionary to
his ignorant countrymen. But he died here in hope
of a better country.

This stone is erected by the liberality of his
Christian friends in New Coventry, Conn., among whom
he first found the Saviour of sinners.

If I say that Patu actually died on 9 June 1823, not 19 June, it will not add greatly to our store of knowledge, but it will matter to me. I am performing, as historians are wont to do, by being very particular about detail. It is not a significant detail, but it lets me make history by remarking that Patu probably would not have wanted those extra ten days in his life. By this time, ten thousand miles from his home place of Hanaiapa on Hiva Oa, and in this cold, and in his turmoil of soul, Patu was probably ready to die.

I am performing as historians are accustomed to do in another way. I am pursuing the past wherever it takes me. The past does not come to me; I must go to it. Patu is one of those 'little people' that I must pursue doggedly to reach him. Patu has not changed the world greatly. He has affected some people as we shall see. That is why he is traceable. That small part of Patu's life that has affected others is transcribed onto paper. Paper, so fragile, is also so enduring. We historians live by it.

Importantly, Patu changes me. Who knows? Patu may change you, the reader, in some small way. I make history by performing my understanding of Patu here in the overflow of the Burnt-Over District. He is a beach crosser of another sort. He crosses *our* beach. He confronts our otherness deep in his soul. Maybe we will see something of ourselves in his crossing.

The Reverend Edwin W. Dwight of Yale University in New Haven, Connecticut, inspired the Foreign Mission School in Cornwall and was its first principal in May 1817. His ambition for the school was to educate 'heathen youth' to become missionaries, surgeons, physicians, school-masters and interpreters. There was not much doubt at the time that heathens would need to be civilised before they could be Christianised. The Word needed to be fertilised with a little greed for the material goods of civilisation that could only be got by the discipline of labour, mostly agricultural. Savages need a new definition of time—working time, praying time, useful arts time. These lost souls on the beaches of New England ports, transported there by whaling and trading captains and eager to return to their islands, could be the Lord's emissaries.

However, these islanders would need to be converted and educated first. Cornwall in the Litchfield hills was the place chosen to do it. At Cornwall there would be 'freedom from temptations in its seclusion', 'healthfulness in climate', 'kindly soil' and 'a sound moral and Christian influence'. The local community is generous. They give two buildings, one for living quarters, the other for an academy for schooling. There are four acres for tilling corn and potatoes. A hundred students will pass through

319

the school in the nine years of its existence. Twenty or thirty native Americans, Pacific islanders, West Indians and West Africans at any one time in such a small community were, however, bound to create tension and fear. The town delights in the public exhibitions when the students display their multilingual skills and the socially elite come from as far as Boston and New York to see what the lessons in Latin, Greek, rhetoric, navigation, surveying, astronomy and theology have done. But there is always a fear that these strangers will come too close. In fact, the school will be destroyed by just that. An American native marries a local young woman. Rage erupts all over the country. The pair are burned in effigy, and the school is finished.

Thomas Hami Patu comes to Cornwall in March 1823. He will be dead before the summer warms him. His long voyage from Hiva Oa to Cornwall begins in 1818. He ships on an American sandalwood trader to Hawai'i. The Hawaiian king, Liholiho (Kamehameha IV), still has delusions of a Pacific empire and Patu is welcomed to his guard. He is given the name Kahumanu—'Keeper of the Canoe-Stern'. The king is into his liquor at this time and is a hard man. He is very possessive of this young man from Hawai'i's mythic Homeland. Patu makes his escape to Canton, and from Canton to Boston.

There are probably about sixty Pacific islanders in Boston at this time. They are mostly Hawaiian. Some of the more decent captains take them into their homes as servants. A Captain J. Miles looks after Patu. One of the characteristics that would let the *Panoplist Magazine* score for a 'revival' was the establishment of 'female societies'. There is a Boston Female Society for Missionary Purposes. A pious member of that society, the daughter of the Reverend Harlan Page, one day notices Patu standing on a corner, a pail of water in his hand and a sad look on his face. She sees his 'manly form and open countenance', 'his amiable and peculiarly docile deportment'. She invites Patu to the Sabbath school where his intelligence and eagerness for self improvement are immediately noted. He learns the alphabet in a single day's class.

Patu has to earn his way in the only way he can. He joins a sealer in a trip to South Shetland Island in Antarctica. All his beaches are destined to be cold. He falls overboard in these icy waters. He is rescued, but his health is badly impaired. He returns to a sailors' hospice in Boston. There he is rescued again by his friend in the Female Society and taken to North Coventry, Connecticut. The kindly people of North Coventry are desperate for Patu's salvation. They find they have a foreign mission in their own homes. Patu easily learns all the craft skills of farming. He learns to read fairly easily, too. He arrives in North Coventry in the spring of 1822 and has learned to read the New Testament by the autumn. What the towns-people of North Coventry cannot enlighten is the 'moral darkness' of Patu's mind. It is not an evil darkness. He is a good young man. But he has no conscience. He has no words in his mind to describe his sins.

Come autumn 1822, there are 'rushes of winds' in North Coventry, much weeping for sins. A revival is in full swing. These are hard times for Patu. He wants to weep, but he does not know what to weep about. After one long night of prayer and giving witness in the meeting-house, Patu is found at sunrise weeping. But he does not have the seriousness that this sort of spiritual effort requires. For two months, he is up and down, alternating between states of cheerfulness and sadness. Then on 22 October, there is a particularly moving prayer meeting. The pastor, after more than the usual 'searching and pungent remarks', works the congregation one by one, speaking softly to each, begging them to be reconciled. Suddenly a young man—'JB'—sitting next to Patu jumps up and declares that the world has relinquished its grasp on him and he has found God.

Patu is mortified. He weeps, yes, but these are tears of jealousy and frustration. All week he puzzles with himself at what it is he has not got. He works himself into a frenzy, going out into the barn at his farm all day and night wrestling with his distress. Suddenly he finds himself praying and thinking of Christ. He goes triumphantly to the pastor to tell him that he is ready to be reconciled. The pastor, eyeing him carefully, tells him to come to a prayer meeting, not in the central church but on the margins of the parish.

There, before a small congregation, the pastor puts his questions:

'Thomas, what was the state of your mind after the commencement of the revival in Coventry?'
'Christians talk to me a great deal about my bad heart. Me think my heart good.'

'Did you endeavour to pray?'
'Mrs T. teach me to say Lord's Prayer. I think me got no mother, no father, no sister, no brother here; Mrs T. Good to me, so I do as she tell me. Then I kneel down before I go to bed, and say prayer.'

'Did you occasionally omit the duty?'
'Sometimes. The Deacon T. say you must say your prayers, Thomas, every night. Then me go prayer mad.'

'Had you any different feeling at the morning prayer meeting at which you wept?'

'Then me feel heavy, feel afraid to die, feel sorry for my sin. Me try to pray "Our Father". Me go home, think what minister say. Then I pray. Next day forget it all. Then feel light. Me never feel so before. Heavy all gone. Then me love to pray and say "Our Father" and thank great god he give "JB" a new heart. Then me think me feel to love Christ. Me go on hay to find him, pray to him. Then me think Christ everywhere. Then come down.'

'What were you feeling in the meeting in the evening?'

'Me want to shake hands with the minister, then feel to love all Christians.'

'How do you know a Christian from an unrepentant sinner?'

'Christian shake hand hard. His hand feel warm. Sinner no shake hand.'

'What do you mean by a new heart?'

'A heart that feel to love good thought.'

'How do you know your heart to be soft now?'

'Why, me no feel mad to anybody. If man strike me, no want to strike him back again.'

The good people of North Coventry cannot accept that Patu is really reconciled if he thinks that the sign of being a Christian is that a Christian shakes hands hard and warmly. They delay his admission into the church.

It is a long hard winter for Patu as he puzzles to find the evil within him. His gods in The Land had always been outsiders to him, masters of their own way, passionate, cruel. They demanded external obedience to *tapu*, but they were careless of the man within him. He did not have to love them. He could hate them, be angry at them. He knew Commandments as he knew *tapu*. Theft, fornication, adultery, worship—he knows what all these are. It is the sense that evil is within him that is hard to take: 'Me think my heart good'.

Harlan Page's daughter rescues him again. She confesses to Patu that she too has a 'rebellious heart'. With all around them in a fever of revival fervour, it must be difficult for a minister's daughter to confess that she is fighting against 'the rushes of wind'. She and Patu share their pain and pray for one another. The people of North Coventry are touched by Patu's simplicity. They arrange for him to visit the Foreign Mission School in Cornwall.

Patu—like Donna and myself—visits the graveyard at Cornwall before the school. There he sees the grave of Obookiah (Opukahaia). Obookiah was a Hawaiian 'prince'. The true hope of the Mission School for its missionary ambition was dashed by his early death. How modest Obookiah's grave was at the time Patu sees it, I cannot say. Obookiah became a mythic figure for a missionising church, and his grave was made a grander monument at least twice in the century after his death. He is now, I believe, in token of another change in his mythic status, interred in his native Hawai'i. Patu, no doubt feeling death's hand on his shoulder, declares that he would like to lie beside Obookiah. He was to do that in three short months.

Over many weeks by letter and phone from Boston, I had made an appointment to visit the Cornwall Historical Society's archives and library. For Patu's fuller story, I needed to know the spaces and times of the Foreign Mission School. I needed to know the daily routines, the diet, the powers that ruled, the freedoms, the privacies on this beach in a cold place. But local historical societies tend to be both poor and possessive. They cannot afford to be open long hours and they need to keep a watchful eye on strangers who visit them. The archives of the Cornwall Historical Society were in the basement of their small museum. Within the basement was a walk-in vault. There was no heating in this basement and vault. It was not difficult to feel empathy for the cold in Patu's soul and body as we leaned, wrapped in our heavy outdoor jackets, over the papers that told his story.

That's all right. I count it a privilege to be able to visit the past wherever it is to be found. I am everlastingly thankful for having been served by librarians, archivists and historical society secretaries in the greatest and most humble institutions all around the world. I am forever grateful to the hundreds and thousands of citizens of all countries who have laboured in their institutions and societies, in their committees and governments, so that I and so many others can touch their past so nearly.

Indeed, I had pursued Hami Patu in the most delightful as well as the most uncomfortable, the most simple and the most formal of archives and libraries. I first learned of him in the Children's Mission Library, Honolulu, Hawai'i. In the early days of my research the Children's Mission Library was small and open to the trade winds. It sits in quiet among coconut palms in the mission cemetery. When my fingers grew stiff and my mind dull, I used to walk among the gravestones. I used to visit the grave of the smallest beach crosser I had known in Fenua'enata. His name was Willie Nevins Armstrong. He was the infant son of an American missionary. He was born at Taiohae in 1834 and died at Lahaina in Hawai'i in 1835, living only one year, two months and fifteen days. Enata, for the brief time that they knew him, called him Hape ('Upside-Down'). 'Kaoha! Hape', they used to call out as they passed the thatched closed mission house where he was born. Hape, 'Upside-Down', is not a bad name for a beach crosser.

I pursued Patu in the Burnt-Over District through all the journals and papers in the Divinity School Library, Harvard, and through all the merchant papers in the same university's business archives in the Baker Library. Then there were the whaling museums in Nantucket and Falmouth. And I pursued Patu in the most formal archives of all: the American Board of Foreign Missions papers are in the Houghton Library, Harvard University. Patu is in these papers.

I've long learned the rules and practices of rare books and manuscript rooms. I know that I will need proper accreditation to work here, some testimony from my academic institution that I am bona fide, references even. There will be a declaration to sign making it clear that I know who owns this part of the past I want to visit. There will be a buzzer to press to give me entry. Heads will turn when I buzz it, just to check who it is. Manuscript rooms are privileged places immediately savoured.

Come with a pencil. No pens allowed. Come with several pencils. They break and blunt, and it is excruciating in this silent room to use the pencil sharpener. Of course, these days you can clack away on your computer. I wish I were so efficient. Log myself in. Log myself out. The papers in my hand, my notebooks and files are always in a mess. I've had to take them out of my case which I have been requested to leave in the cloakroom. Is anyone sitting in my favourite seat? At the front where I can see nobody? At the back where I can see everybody? Or wherever. The seat I had yesterday, that's mine. What's that stranger doing in it? The same seat in these rooms, like the same pew in churches, is a security blanket. I snuggle into it.

There's a slanted reading stand here. Damn! I hate them. Nowhere to write except at the side. I'll never be able to read my own handwriting in pencil.

The first approach to the librarian's desk is always nerve-wracking. I feel a cloud of suspicion. And I know how ignorant I am. I need to

balance servility with professional dignity. This young person has seen it
all before, can see right through me. There is always theatre and
performance in the archives and Rare Book and Manuscript Rooms.
Humbling self-effacing roles to be played before steely-eyed librarians.
Dissembling roles to hide one's ignorance. Brazen up-your-face roles
sharpening pencils on a noisy sharpener. Outraged 'I've come ten
thousand miles to see this' roles when denied access to critical material.
There's plenty of theatre in the archives.

Just an hour gone! I'm already exhausted. It takes me sometimes a
week, if I've got a week, to acclimatise to a new library. For each of my
projects, I have a small stenographer's notebook. I'll stand, sometimes for
days, in front of the catalogue, or seated at the computer, and fill this
booklet with titles and their place located in the library. The notebook is
my most precious asset. With it I manage the inevitable delays in one part
of the library with work in another part. I take lots of notes. They are a
yard high on a major project. And I keep them.

Even after many years manuscript rooms still make me nervous. I'm
not humble enough to ask questions. Maybe it is a male thing. If I have
any advice to give to young researchers, it would be: Don't be nervous; be
humble and ask.

There is a heavy obligation that I owe the past that I find in manuscript rooms. If I claim to represent it—if I claim to re-present it—I owe
it something, its own independence. I owe it a gift of itself, unique in time
and space. The history I write will always be mine and something more
than the past, but there is a part of it that is never mine. It is the part that
actually happened, independently of my knowing that or how it
happened. My true stories are ruled by my belief that I have always
something to learn.

Our performance in the archives is marked by two characteristics, I
think. The one is our sense of 'being there'. The other is our performance
consciousness.

The name of our game is persuasion, not domination. Our
performance is to let others perform. The extravagance of our engagement
in the archives will always give our language richness, our images colour
and sharpness, our arguments conviction, our examples pertinence, our
selection an informed boldness. 'Being there' where the past leaves itself
most particularly is our signature gesture in research performance.
Without it we are just literary critics.

There are delusions in 'being there'. Of course there are. The discipline of anthropology knows them only too well. 'Being there' can too often be a claim on an experience that can't be checked or even shared. A claim of 'being there' is blind arrogance if it is not accompanied by performance consciousness.

There is a double quality in performance. Performance is always *to* somebody, an audience, a reader, self. In the loneliness of research and writing that somebody else might only be oneself. But when there are others, it is always *also* to oneself. In performance we research and write in stereo consciousness. In performance we are theatre critics in the foyer of our minds. We are measuring the effectiveness of what we are doing against the reception in the audience. We are always measuring what we do against the ideals and ambitions we have for doing it. In performance, we know our own tricks to hide what we don't know. We know the masks (the *persona*) of our own person. That stereo consciousness is our strength. It is our realism in a postmodern world.

I'm a storyteller. A true storyteller. My students, my readers are true storytellers. That's our performance, true storytelling. Sometimes, our performance is live. And shared. An exchanged performance. The audience performs to me, the storyteller, as much as I to them. They perform with their silences and their fidgets, with their polite-but-not-yet-committed seminar faces. I read their signals in their performance. I calibrate their silences—engaged silences, disapproving silences, sleeping silences. I measure the spontaneity of their responses. I adjust my rhythms and speed to them. I'll move from my text. I'll catch their eye. I'll infuse energy into my voice to stop their attention slipping away.

This is our performance as true storytellers, as makers of history. We speak to one another, not randomly, but in disciplined discourse. We hear in company. We read for ourselves. We write for others. We travel. We lock ourselves in libraries and archives. We observe. We reflect. We claim authority, but have no other power than to persuade. We make theatre about trivial and everyday things, and about awful and cruel realities. Maybe we write to change the world in some way.

We tell our stories, but there is never any closure to them. There is always another sentence to be added to the conversation that we have joined. There is always another slant on the story that we have just told. We live by our creativity and originality. That's our pledge: 'This work is mine'. But we couldn't, if we tried, plumb the depths of our own intellectual and cultural plagiarism. Plato, Jesus Christ, Karl Marx, Sigmund Freud and so many others are in our minds somewhere.

So is our postmodernity—our neomodernity—whether we like it or not. We know—because our everyday living performances are never separated from our academic performing—how liberated we have been by the painters, dancers, composers, film directors, novelists and poets on our cultural horizon. Just by being everyday cultural performers in our own times we know that performance art engages the whole body, all the senses, all the emotions. Not just the mind, not just rationality. Performance art has given us a multitude of narrative strategies for our stories. We know that formulaic monotone won't do what we want it to do—persuade, convince, change, enter into somebody else's consciousness in a meaningful way. We have to be artful. We must take out the cliché, not just from our concepts and words, but from the very structure of our presentations. We are mouthing soundlessly, like goldfish in a bowl, unless we display our postmodernity. Not our postmodernism. Our contemporaneity to the tropes of our times.

There is art and science in delicate mix in this performance of ours. Catharsis for our readers, their enlightenment, their seeing the plot in our plays, aren't at all certain products of our performance, at least in ways that we anticipate. We've learnt enough about paradigm, episteme, discourse and language these past twenty years to know that the forms and expressions of our performances cannot be divorced from their content and logic. Our performances cannot be all style, any more than they can be all argument. We all wait in our examiner's reports and our reviews for the 'but' that follows praise for our expression and style. 'He or she writes well, but . . .'. Persuasion by our art is always linked with our science—in the exhaustiveness of our research, a display of our control over not only our discipline but also the disciplines on the edge of ours, an openness about the degrees of our certainties and uncertainties, a show of our adversarial skills.

We know some things about performing, though, don't we? That is because we are constantly observers of other performers. We know what bores us. We know what confuses us. We know when jargonistic language cuts us off from understanding. We know that the enemy of an effective performance is formalistic ritualism. Rigidity and patter will always deny the creativity of the moment. So we know when we have heard a story told well, and when we have heard a story told badly. Perhaps the most important thing that we know is that we are least persuaded by overpowering knowledge preoccupied with itself. Roland Barthes called this preoccupation a peppering of our writing with 'reality effects'—extraneous, uncontexted facts that become an end to themselves. The last things we want to know are all the reality effects that are in another performer's head. What we really want to know is how the other performer is joining a conversation we are already having in our own head.

There is always a gamble in performance. There is a commitment which cannot be taken back once the performance has begun, once we step onto the page, once we give our dissertation to the examiners, our book to the reviewers. If only we had another rehearsal, if only we had ten thousand more words, if only we had another deadline . . . No, there is never perfection in performance. We have to gamble on what we do in the conditions in which we do it. The search for perfection only strikes us dumb, only gives us stage fright.

All my academic teaching life, I taught the past by asking my students first to describe something of their present. It wasn't a surrender to presentism. It was a method of teaching my students to recognise what performances *in* the past might be. I used to ask them to 'emplot', in Aristotle's word of the theatre (*mythos*), something different in their daily living. The different could be large—across languages, across beliefs, across disabilities, across the ways people ritualise their lives. Mostly the different was ordinary—across gender, across age, across class.

Difference is always hard to see. It always requires a little giving— young to old, old to young; black to white, white to black; male to female, female to male; Seeing difference always requires entering somebody else's metaphors. It always requires catching the interconnectedness between the different parts of living. To understand difference, you have to see the system in it.

If difference is hard to see, it is even more difficult to describe. I wasn't too particular about the ways that my students described difference. They could write a poem about it, or a play. They could paint it, video it, make a tape about it. But whatever they did, they had to make theatre of it, and by prologue or epilogue, put what they thought they were doing into words.

Difference in words is usually in the silence of words, the things that words don't say. The real problem for 'ethnoggers' is a problem of translation of these silences. How do they do that? They must use their imaginations. Not their fantasies, their imaginations. Imagination is finding a word that someone will hear, a metaphor that someone will see. Imagination is taking the cliché out of something that has been said over and over again. Imagination is working the fictions in our non-fictions the better to be read.

Our description of difference must be art. There is no art in multiplying the reifications. Art is the dismantling of reifications.

In all performances we put boundaries of space and time around ourselves so that we might share each other's creativity. We entertain one another, as we entertain guests or entertain an idea. We ask ourselves to share 'an' experience. Experience is not just stream of consciousness. Experience is something reflected upon, something pulled out of the flow of things. We humans are very ingenious in creating a hedged-around space and time to have our experiences. It is an in-between space and in-between time—in-between ordinary living, in-between everyday relationships, in-between other conversations, in-between other performances. We sometimes called this hedged-around space ritual, sometimes theatre. I like to call it *limen*, threshold, beach.

I want to say that to perform the past we must cross a beach in some way. I want to say that in performing the past we need to be beachcombers to the past.

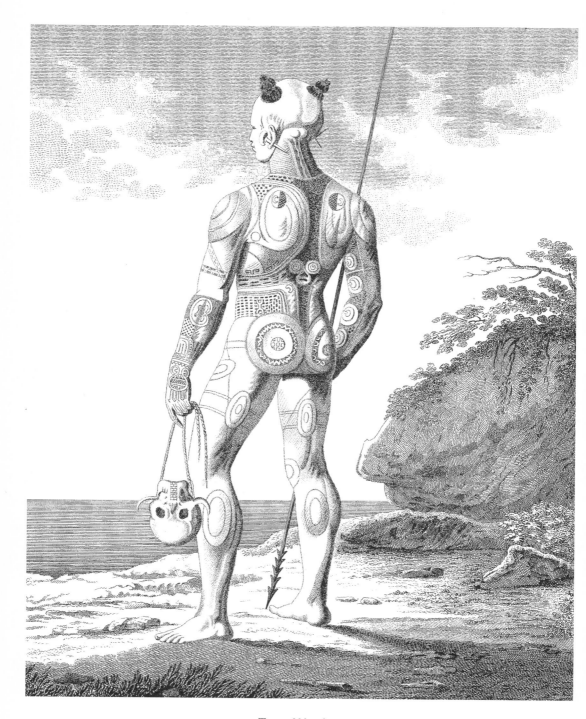

Toa—Warrior

After Beach

The beach changed the lives of Crook, Robarts and Kabris forever. None of them could resist playing it out again—in Britanny fairs, in the stories they tell of it. Kabris' After Beach is short, eighteen years. We have told his story. Robarts' is longer, twenty-six years. Crook's is longest, forty-eight years. Perhaps at this stage we do not owe them a biography. An episodic montage might satisfy our obligations, just to show the many more beaches in their After Beach.

Robarts

'An enterprizeing and unfortunate life'

Robarts doesn't hear the sniggers as he boards the privateer *Lucy*, Captain Abe Ferguson. He won't know that he is being made a fool of until the missionaries at Tahiti disabuse him of the stories the *Lucy*'s officers had told him. No, the missionaries tell him, there won't be free land at Botany Bay, nor a £150 bounty, nor four or five convicts to clear the land. And breadfruit is not in 'perfection' there. Botany Bay is a bleak, violent place—fit, as Governor Lachlan Macquarie, with his 'hawk eye' will tell Robarts when he finally gets there in 1815, 'only for rich men and thieves'.

So, a February day in 1806 is the first day of a 'change for the worst' in Edward Robarts' life. He boards the *Lucy* with Ena, seven months pregnant, and their twenty-month-old daughter. An old woman servant goes with them from Taiohae, as does his mastiff Neptune, a 'Spanish bloodhound', or 'between a mastiff and a Newfoundland breed', 'two feet four inches high in the middle of his back', Robarts tells us. Neptune is Robarts' true friend. For the rest of his life—the rest of his worsening days—men and women higher on the social scale will always look at him in a knowing way. They think they see through his mask. They see his poverty and his misfortune. They see him always on the edge of where they are. But they see him responsible for his never coming over. Robarts has many beaches in his life, but really only one crossing.

Eighteen years from now Robarts will write at the end of his journal, 'Finis Moorshedad May 3d 1824'. He muses in the journal's last words:

> I intend going up the River to purchase timber and sell again, as that will at least return 50 pr cent clear of all expenses, [by] which [in] four trips in two years or seasons [I] will realise a small trifle against a rainy day. And then I shall be able to Judge what to do in the Even^g of life as I have had a long and singular career of an enterprizeing and unfortunate life up to the Age of 53 years. And I thank God that I am now as active as when I was 20 years of age. But I am not so strong. I hope I have not intruded to long on my readers' time.

All writers have to hope that they have not intruded too long on their reader's time. These further twenty years of 'an enterprizeing and unfortunate life' of a small and ordinary man on the beaches of empire have something to say. Let me say it in six episodes.

Tahiti, March 1806

There is an ugliness on the beach at Tahiti and danger in the air. First sight and sense of it convinces Robarts that he has truly had a 'change for the worse'. Deformed, ulcerated, dropsical bodies are everywhere to be seen. The island women welcome the pregnant Ena and her daughter warmly, but the men look at Robarts sullenly and hostilely. The king, Pomare II, gives Robarts permission to stay on the island, but Robarts knows there is a new edge to his life. There is a new loneliness. He has no buffers, no 'fathers', no 'mothers', no family that comes from name exchange. He is more naked than he was on his first night on his beach at Tahuata. In this violent place, disturbed by thirty years of stranger intrusion, relationships are stripped to their opportunist essentials. All of living is realpolitik.

Robarts finds missionaries of the London Missionary Society in Tahiti, thirteen of them—five from the original *Duff* group of 1797, eight from the reinforcement that came on the *Royal Admiral* in 1801. They are about to be overwhelmed by Tahiti's realpolitik and will flee to Sydney Town in 1808. The missionaries are vital to Robarts. They monitor all comings and goings on the island. They have material supplies for which Robarts can work. He needs to have their favour, if not their approval. Robarts and a bevy of beachcombers will form an unlikely congregation for the missionaries' Sunday services. God on the beach, it would seem, is an expatriate.

Robarts is poor. Captain Ferguson of the *Lucy* reneges on his promise for pay for Robarts' services. A black American beachcomber is kind to him, lets him share a house. Robarts scrambles to barter his labour for food and material. He cuts wood, boils salt, tailors missionary trousers. He thinks he has seen enough of life to know which missionaries are solid in their calling and who are doing things on the sly. Robarts has lost his way. He is no longer the pilot for ships' captains, just another beachcomber. They have seen too many already.

One of these captains out of Sydney tells Robarts that there is a trade that he can enter. The convict settlement's dire straits bring small trading vessels to Tahiti looking for whatever food products they can muster. But there is something else. Liquor is literally the currency in the convict settlement. The captain can get Robarts a good price for any liquor he can distil. He has a makeshift still working in no time. The trouble is that Pomare and his wife get wind of it. A pint a day is their customs fee. Their capacity to swallow it surprises even Robarts. But Pomare is no pleasant drunk. The unspeakable 'filthy' things he does—sodomic rape we have to suspect—are not the worst of it. There are orgiastic killings as well. At one time, the missionaries find him with a hundred bodies of victims around him in his place of sacrifice. Robarts himself sees a stream dammed with corpses.

Ena, who had begged Robarts to stay at Tahiti so that she could have her second child, is desolate. Robarts acts again as her sole midwife to another daughter, Ellen. Ellen will survive all her five siblings. Ena slides into depression after the birth. She threatens suicide and perhaps attempts it by throwing herself off a coconut palm. Robarts says it is the Enata way. The missionaries say he is beating her.

Robarts is a drinking man. We know that. He was always over-defensive when accused of it. In Tahiti he is drinking the profits of his still. It is a dangerous practice, given the sort of liquor he is producing. It almost kills him. He goes down with near-fatal intestinal trouble. When Robarts' beachcomber partner in the still leaves the island, he sells his share to Pomare. Pomare can't work the still. He needs Robarts. Robarts knows that, one way or another, Pomare will be the death of him. He destroys the still, pretending that Pomare's enemies have done it, and looks to move on.

General Wellesley, June 1807

The *General Wellesley*, 400 tons, fourteen guns, twenty-five men, Calcutta-built, is a large ship for the Pacific trade. The *Wellesley* had brought 244 tons of much needed wheat to Port Jackson in February 1807. Now it is on a very wide circuit of the central and western Pacific to Pulo Penang on the Malayan Peninsula. It is a bricolage of a trading voyage, searching for a cargo to take home—fresh rations in Tahiti, pearls, sharkfins and bêche-de-mer in the Tuamotu, spars in New Zealand, sandalwood in Fiji, spices in the southern Philippines, guns out of wrecks on the New Guinea coast.

The company on the *Wellesley* is mixed—'chinamen, manilla men, mongrel Portuguese and escaped Jail birds' is Robarts' description. A Tahitian missionary disgraced for adultery, the Reverend James Elder, is supernumerary. There are six ex-convict women with children. David Dalrymple, the *Wellesley*'s captain, is drunk most of the time and irresponsible in the rest of it. He sees advantages in letting Robarts aboard. Robarts has experience with savages and has a native language. So Dalrymple finds space for Robarts and his family—Ena, a two-year-old daughter and an infant at the breast. They have some sort of cabin space deep in the ship.

Life on the edges in the *Wellesley* has a bizarre character. No one here owes anybody anything, certainly not life. There is not an island nor an anchorage at which one side on the beach and the other side on the ship do not try to take one another out. Robarts says that he himelf was training the cannons loaded with grape and firing them on crowds of hundreds of natives in the Tuamotu, New Zealand, New Ireland and Fiji. This is the domain of confirmed beachcombers and of captains with warrants for their arrest and the rewards that will come with it. George Bruce, convicted several times over for robbery, murder and riot, and escaping prison just as many times, helps negotiate the *Wellesley*'s cargo of spars in the Bay of Islands on New Zealand's northeast coast. Then he joins the *Wellesley*, like Robarts bringing his wife, the 'Princess' Atahoe. He is searching for gold—fool's gold, as it turns out. He is being chased by a warrant for his arrest signed by the governor of New South Wales, Captain William Bligh. Ena helps him escape by hiding him under her bed. Te Pahi, a notorious and dangerous Maori leader in the Bay of Islands, wanted for many murders, takes a liking for Ena. Robarts flushes him out of the lower depths of the *Wellesley* by firing his musket down the ladder. Dalrymple will sell Bruce's wife into slavery at the end of the voyage, and any other islander he can catch. The *dramatis personae* of this story owe society nothing for what society has done to them. In the end they will have to survive one another's cannibal instincts when they are becalmed without food for weeks.

Penang, February 1808

The *Wellesley* reaches Penang in February 1808. There is high society of the empire in Penang. Sir Thomas Stamford Raffles is in the last year of his first term as governor. The new governor, Philip Dundas, has a coterie of expatriates around him. They are in need of servants—or rather, of white persons who can manage their servants. Perhaps their need is greater than we might think. The unlikely fact is that Robarts becomes butler, storekeeper and occasional cook in the household of Quintin Dick Thompson. Mary Anne, Thompson's wife, is Raffles' sister. 'Thus', Robarts writes, 'I commenced to raise my friends on the Beach of penang. Haveing an opening before me, I patiently wated the turn of fortune. I was in good spirits.' One of his disciplinary triumphs, he tells us was to 'put a stop to smoking tobacco in the time of cooking, as I obserd the cook toasting bread with one hand and smoking with the other'.

These days are the highwater mark in Robarts' social career. He looks after his lady, Mrs Thompson, who is ill in her pregnancy and after the birth. He manages the 'festive board', writing:

> About ten o'clock the Merry Dance led off. Afterwards several songs was sung: 'The Boyne Water' was sung by Mrs Raffles in high stile. 'The Banks of the Dee', on the German Flute by Capt Phillips and sung to by Mrs Thompson. The sweetness of her voice would melt a heart of adamant. Well might the Poet say 'music has charms to sooth the ravaged breast'. The even^g was spent in the most agreeable and pleasant manner.

On 4 January 1809, Ena, with Robarts as midwife as always, 'brought forth a fine daughter'. Then followed six months 'in a state of lasting happiness'. But in June the 25-year-old Quintin Thompson takes ill of fever and is dead in three days, leaving Mary Anne with three young children. Robarts spends his last six months in Penang in the household of Sir Thomas Raffles on Mount Olivia. He has another savage bout of the intestinal trouble he'd had in Tahiti, perhaps from the same cause of the drink. Strangely, it is Ena who is begging him—he says—to go to Bengal. A gentleman friend gives the captain of an American ship Robarts' name to help load a cargo of five hundred tons of pepper. Robarts's charge is a cabin passage for himself and his family and all his livestock and other necessities to serve him in Calcutta.

In another of those seeming accidents of fortune, Robarts tells us that he leaves Penang so hurriedly that he forgets to ask for a certificate of good conduct from Sir Thomas Raffles. We have to wonder.

Calcutta, March 1810

Ena is pregnant again. On 17 April 1810, she gives birth to a son, exactly a month after their arrival in Calcutta. The boy lives only eight days. Robarts is on a downward slide in fortune. He gets temporary residence in a Sailors' Home and then takes a house in Mango Lane, just a block and a half from Government House. It is in the European quarter. He is without employment for ten months before he meets up with Sir Thomas Raffles in his palanquin in Tank Square. That is where we began Robarts's story. His moment of glory writing his journal under Dr Leyden's sponsorship and in the good doctor's house lasts only a month. Then Leyden is off to Java, where he dies. Robarts would have gone with him but Ena was pregnant with her fifth child, a boy.

Meeting up with Leyden, and through him men and women of status in Calcutta society, gives Robarts the opportunity he craves. He can now apply for positions with their support. But the world of patronage is murkily political. His reference letters and a specimen of his writing get him a position at the Lower Orphan School. It is an important step. He is now out of the ruck of the poor whites of Calcutta and is a recognisable person. The *East India Register and Directory* puts him on public record for the first time: 'On April 1st 1811, Mrs Roberts, of a son'. As teacher at the orphanage he must shift his residence to the western, unhealthy side of the river. Many people are dying there. His career as schoolmaster lasts only six months. He applies to be police constable. His referees are reluctant to see him go in this direction in his career but Robarts tells them 'half a loaf was better than no bread at all'.

Ena all this time is a sad and silent figure. There is no doubt that she is the great asset in Robarts' life. Everyone looks first at her rather than

Robarts. She has remarkable beauty. But Robarts' loyalty to her is something more than self-interest. He is always conscious that it has been Ena who has made the sacrifices to come with him. His sense of familial responsibility is strong. He knows her sadness and her desire to return home. He writes a petition to Lord Minto (Sir Gilbert Elliot), the Governor-General of India, for a grant to New Holland. Once in Sydney, he would be better able to return to The Marquesas.

The grant comes too late. *The Calcutta Morning Post*, Friday, 30 July 1813, has this death notice: 'On the 19th instant, Ena O De Atah, wife of Mr Roberts, the deceased was a native of the Friendly Islands'. Ah well! On this beach, the distance and difference between Tonga and The Marquesas is not great.

The small family is in disarray. Robarts himself is in a 'deranged state'. His children are ill with something he calls 'sleen', 'a cruel disorder'. His youngest daughter, a favourite, dies in December 1814.

In the meantime he has changed jobs again. He is now an overseer in the Botanic Garden up river. He returns each weekend to his home in Calcutta. He knows his children won't survive the Calcutta climate. He renews his efforts to get to Port Jackson. He discovers that the ship *Frederick* is ready to go. A passage will cost him 500 rupees. A gentleman friend—he does not say who—gives him 800 rupees for the voyage. The Earl of Moira, Francis Rowden Hastings, the new Governor-General of India, gives him a letter of introduction to Governor Macquarie at Port Jackson.

Robarts' 'goods and chattles' are plenty—'21 geese, 38 ducks, 36 fowl, 3 salted hogs, 2 sheep, 2 goats. 1 flitch of bacon of my own cureing'. And fifty gallons of rum. 'A drop of this was treason to drink; it was for payment for building a home and clearing of land as far as it would go.' He will discover that he has missed out again. There is a silver currency in Port Jackson now.

To Port Jackson and Back, March 1816

Robarts sets off to Port Jackson in high hopes. The capital of his life is all with him—his two daughters and two sons, aged between eleven years and fifteen months; his livestock and fifty gallons of rum; a few silver dollars in cash; a good suit of mourning and other jackets; some cloth and goods for trading. And the Earl of Moira's letter. He will be eleven months on the *Frederick*. He will be back in Calcutta where he started with all that capital eaten away, except for his children. There will be several times when all their lives are seriously in danger—in storms in southern waters on their way to Hobart Town, Van Diemen's Land, and among the shoals of Torres Straits above the northern tip of New Holland. It is a harsh world where those with little prey on those with less, where the harshness is not so much softened as blotted out with drink, where the trickster who cheats power and authority is the hero, where raising debt and evading the paying of it are the cycle of life, where the daily grind of living squeezes out any hope of making it different.

The first sight of Hobart Town for those aboard the *Frederick* is of three felons hanging in chains from the gallows opposite the wharf where they dock. Actually Robarts remarks that they are taken away the day after their arrival, and sure enough the *Hobart Town Gazette and Southern Reporter* on 8 June 1816 reports that the lieutenant-governor has ordered that gibbeting be done further away from the docks. The bodies had 'become Objects of disgust, especially for the Female sex'.

Sydney Cove is more welcoming, 'a very snug but small harbour'. The town is built on 'a soft stone rock'—The Rocks—so that 'if you stand on the door of a house you can look down the chimney of the house below', Robarts reports.

Robarts goes dressed 'in genteel suit of mourning' to put his case to Governor Macquarie for a grant of land. Macquarie has just been chastised by the Secretary of State in London, Henry the Third Earl Bathurst, for precisely making such grants to those who came privately to Port Jackson; he is in no mood to listen to Robarts. 'I have hundres of spies on my conduct, who are ready to do me any injury they can', the governor tells him. The tumultuous days of the Rum Rebellion when the previous governor, William Bligh, was thrown out of the colony are only five years past. Macquarie is not going to budge in his opinion.

So Robarts now has nothing. His fifty gallons of rum will now have to buy the provisions to get home on the *Frederick*, so long as he is willing to work his way as well. He thinks for a moment that he might go back to The Marquesas. The sandalwood trade has begun and there are at least two ships in Sydney Harbour at the time that are engaged in the sandalwood trade. On one of them is one of his 'relatives' from Taiohae. He can tell her of Ena and she can tell those back at home of them all. He gives the return to Taiohae only a moment's reflection. The Land is a very different place and he cannot go back there naked again.

The captain's wife, who was going to stay in Sydney, decides differently when he gives passage to a Mrs Elizabeth Compton. Sailors might have a wife in every port. Captains were likely to have wives on every ship. Mrs Compton is running away from debt. (The *Sydney Gazette*, 26 March 1814, had published a caution against giving credit to the same lady.) Robarts, feigning serious illness, will hide her in his bed when search parties comb the *Frederick* at Sydney Heads, looking for escapees. She is undoubtedly a frisky character, and there are dramas aplenty on the rest of the voyage as various people seek her favours. Later she shines in Calcutta's theatres for a few brief years.

The *Frederick* makes slow progress up the eastern coast of Australia. Twice it will run aground on shoals. They anchor each night off one of the many islands inside the reef. Around Cape York they make for Timor. They are not really welcome there. The Dutch have a jealous eye for any trading in these waters.

By now Robarts' relations with the captain are almost impossible. He has lost two more teeth from an already unbeautiful face in a fight with him. The captain has stolen his provisions and now would be happy to leave him in Timor. Robarts scrambles back to the *Frederick* in a canoe after selling the remnants of his clothing to the Dutch Resident—a Mr Hazaart, as we know from the series of explorer visitors at the time.

The last leg of the voyage from Timor to Calcutta is hard. Food runs low, the water is bad. Robarts arrives back in Calcutta with thirty rupees in his pocket and a half a pig's head. He has no house now in the European quarter. He now lives in the Bazaar. For the first time in his life he is in need of public charity.

Calcutta, December 1816

Robarts comes back to Calcutta to find that his patron, Dr Hare, is just leaving. He is close to despair. His children are in rags and conscious of their changed status. People who once knew him now pass him by in the street. He begins a round of begging meetings with vestry committees. He stands silent like a criminal while they read his petitions. They give him limited sums, thirty rupees per month for three months. Any time he misses out on renewing his petition because of illness, or maybe because of drink, the charity is withheld. Then it is six rupees here or a generous fifty rupees from some private benefactor. Sixteen miles out of town there is new building to be done at the Insane Hospital. He walks the sixteen miles for the interview for the position of overseer of buildings and then again to take it up. He is working the sandpits further up the river until the monsoon sets in and the building is cancelled.

In February 1819 one of Calcutta's terrible bazaar fires breaks out behind the compound where Robarts lives. 'The fires spread with astonishing rapidity and presented a truly grand and awful spectacle', the *Calcutta Journal* (9 February 1819) reported. Robarts' children run away in panic and are lost for hours. He tries to save what furniture he can, and of course his precious journal. That he does, but he loses many other papers.

The fire is an odd turn in his fortune in that it sparks some private charity and the possibility of employment in engineering works at Murshidebad. But just as he is leaving for Murshidebad, 120 miles north of Calcutta, his youngest son catches the smallpox and is gone in a few days. Within months his eldest son takes ill with an ulcerated tongue. He too is dead in a few days. Robarts himself is laid low with fever for three months. Another child is lost. Then his daughter born in Taiohae.

Then he tells us that he hopes to make some trading trips that will give him money for a rainy day and perhaps enable him to take his daughter Ellen back to England, where he hopes she 'will be found worthy of the Patronage of an Indulgeant Nobility and Gentry'.

He adds 'I have had a long and singular career of an enterprizeing and unfortuneate Life up to the age of 53 years ... I hope I have not intruded too long on my reader's time.'

Epitaph

William Pascoe Crook

In October 1803, William Pascoe Crook, refreshed in spirit, is on a beach again in the southern hemisphere. It is not as lonely a beach as his first. He has the company of 308 transported convicts and fifty-seven free settlers. It is not as lonely, but in many ways it is just as strange. And certainly it is a beach made for him by authorities as unthinking for his future and his comfort as was the London Missionary Society which left him at Vaitahu. No lush tropical vegetation here. Banksias, she-oaks, tea-trees and grass. Snakes, too, lizards, sandflies, large biting ants. There is threat. Dark figures flit among the trees.

Crook is in a tent. His wife of months, Hannah Dare, is with him. It is too dangerous to leave her aboard the ship among wild midshipmen more used to looser women. There are two ships off the sandy bay they call Sullivans. We who know it well call it Sorrento. It is the site of the first settlement of what will become the colony and then the State of Victoria.

The French had unsettled English imperial plans by looking as if they were interested in settlement along the southern coast of New Holland. They need to be forestalled, hastily.

Lieutenant David Collins, already with eight years of experience in the convict settlement of Port Jackson and author of one of the first accounts of its establishment, is made commander of the two-vessel expedition. His instructions are to establish a settlement in Port Phillip Bay. He knows virtually nothing about the place he is to settle. He has a sloppy pencil sketch of a bay ballooning back from narrow heads. He will settle just inside those heads on the eastern side. In this world turned upside-down, it is spring. They will experience the cold down to 50 degrees Fahrenheit in the night and, when the north wind blows, heat up to 96 degrees in the day. They won't stay long, just a couple of months. There is no flowing water. They have to sink casks in the sand and filter the nearly salt water.

Wathaurong and Bunwurung land is all around this bay. This first people have been in this place for forty thousand years. The first encounter with them is not promising. Marines drive some of them, who are brandishing spears and holding shields, away from their huts with shots over their heads. The marines are eager for souvenirs and take what they can from the huts, then burn them. 'What impression this first visit made on the savages I leave you to judge', writes Crook. Worse was to come. Attacked by a large group of Aborigines a few days later, Lieutenant James Tuckey reported:

> I conceived it . . . absolutely necessary, as well for own safety as for the benefit of the colony, to prove the superior effect of our arms, which they seemed to despise and, selecting . . . a violent leader as a proper example, directed three muskets to be fired at him while advancing at about 50 yards distance; two of them took effect and he fell dead on the spot.

HMS *Calcutta* transports the convicts. Most are convicted for larceny—as small a theft as a handkerchief, as large as a horse. There are forgers, embezzlers, bigamists, perjurers, mutineers as well. The youngest is nine years, the oldest fifty-seven. Most have been in the prison hulks on the Thames or in Portsmouth and are well enough socialised to prison life. Some will try to escape from Sullivans Bay. One, William Buckley, will succeed and live among the Aboriginal people for thirty-two years.

The supply ship *Ocean* accompanies HMS *Calcutta*. *Ocean* carries the free settlers, among them William and Hannah Crook. Crook has benefited by his many stays at Newport Pagnell with Samuel Greatheed, writing 'The Account of the Marquesas Islands'. He is renewed in his evangelical spirit. He attaches himself to George Whitefield's spiritual enthusiasts. He is preaching in prisons, private houses and on the streets as a member of the London Itinerant Society. He studies theology and learns the skills he will need as an educationist as well as craft skills such as printing and book-binding. He is ready to go back to the mission, and if the London Missionary Society are still a little uncertain about him, they are happy for him to proceed to Sydney and then to the mission. So he marries and gets his chance on the *Ocean*.

Crook spends his journey on the *Ocean* schooling the seven children aboard the ship, and continues with them as soon as he is ashore. The Reverend Robert Knopwood, an ordained minister, is chaplain to the expedition. Only he is licensed to preach. Crook is allowed to read and pray at the services. He can even read from books of sermons, but he cannot let the Spirit move him to preach. The Spirit moving unlicensed preachers is counted dangerous and disturbing.

It is patent to everybody that the settlement cannot stay. The *Ocean* is sent to Sydney to tell the governor that, and William and Hannah go with it. Parramatta, on the furthest edge of the colony, is their next beach. The Reverend Samuel Marsden, who is responsible for the religious welfare of the colony, has no time for Crook. But the government is happy for William and Hannah to teach the convict children who are now running wild, and gives them a house and a food allowance to do so. The better class are not going to allow their children to mix with the convict children, so Crook cannot raise an income from fees. He establishes prayer-meeting places.

Crook's chance to do something better comes with the arrest of Governor Bligh. The rebels need religion as much as does the Establishment. In fact, the rebels need to be the Establishment. The official chaplain is loyal to Bligh, so the rebels turn to Crook as the outstanding religious person in the colony. But they are not brave enough to overthrow the concept of licence. So Crook can choose prayers and readings but cannot preach.

There are those who need spiritual sustenance more than the cant of established religion. They come together under Crook and strike a covenant. They agree that in the privacy of their union they will share communion. It seems a small step, but it was to have repercussions in the colony for thirty years. If preaching is a sign of authorised voice, communion is more surely shaped by the power of the priesthood. Even though this private communion gives the sharers deep spiritual comfort, they dare not come together more than on two or three occasions, the uproar is so great.

But William's confidence as an educator is growing. He builds on what the evangelicals have learned about communication in their love-feasts, conversational meetings, Sabbath services, and what they had learned from Quaker educationalists like Joseph Lancaster and Dr Andrew Bell about monitorial education, the use of older children to tutor the younger. He opens an academy and takes in boarders. He runs an evening school between 6 and 8 p.m. for those eager in a place of so little opportunity to better themselves. Hannah opens a millinery shop. She has now given William six daughters and a son and will give him two more daughters when they return to the islands.

The Tahitian mission had been temporarily abandoned in 1808. In 1815 Crook applies to the mission to return. They are delighted to have him, and for sixteen years he has perhaps the most creative and rewarding part of his career. In January 1825, he revisits Fenua'enata and leaves three young Tahitian men there as missionaries. It is as hopeless and dangerous a mission as his own thirty years before. They barely escape with their lives after a year.

In 1830 William and Hannah are back in Sydney with their family. The fact that Crook had never been ordained still bedevils his religious career but does not douse his evangelical spirit. When he had first been in Sydney he had preached on the beach at Watsons Bay, near the heads of Sydney Harbour. Now he works to build and establish a church there.

Hannah's health has failed and she dies in 1837. William's health is also failing. He suffers from erysipelas, 'St Anthony's fire', a severe inflammation of the lymph glands of the scalp, face and neck. He needs constant care. His mind is failing too. He follows his son Samuel, now married and a furniture maker, to Melbourne. His last beach in life is the settlement on Port Phillip Bay that David Collins should have made forty-three years before. He dies on 14 June 1846, on the dissenter's edge of church life to the end.

Tana'oa—The Godliness of Sea and Wind

Exiting

In the theatre of history, there is never really an ending. There is only an exit-line that begins another conversation. The past ends in a sliding present.

I HAVE LONG PUZZLED how I would end these stories of beach crossings and voyaging across times, cultures and self. It is a hard moment for me. I must say 'goodbye' to so much that has given me pleasure through fifty years. Any historian will have sympathy with me, I think. There is not one of us who has finished a book or a study who does not feel immediately that there is another book to write, another story to tell. We have to cast our net of knowledge-seeking so widely to make one small catch in the past that we catch a myriad of other stories as well. One story told, there is another and yet another to tell. All these stories swirl in our minds, cued by the thousands of notes we have made of them. I like to take my notes in such a way that I can immediately remember the place and the occasion of my taking them. So now, as I catch sight of notes that I took fifty years ago and of notes that I took yesterday, I am a little overwhelmed by the thought that I must leave them. I have not encompassed my Sea of Islands. I never will.

I have written these pages through years of extraordinary global violence. We number not by thousands but by millions those whose lives have been snuffed out, and by many more millions those whose lives have been cruelly changed by hatred, by greed for power, by religious belief. Inevitably I wonder if my own stories of extravagant violence in Fenua'enata could ever make a difference in our world so bathed in blood. I have never counted the dead I have told about in the years 1796–1814. I would guess that eighty to a hundred men, women and children a year fell victim to be 'eaten' or sacrificed. I would never think that the life of these 'fish', lying hooked in the welter of their own blood, was worth less than mine. If I could, I would have told the story of even one of them. They are the littlest of 'little people'. They leave no mark, certainly no personal mark, on our past. I can mourn their passing. I cannot mourn the passing of cultural systems that cut their lives so short. I do not mourn the passing of the *tau'a atua*. No one has the right to live by the deaths of others. Not two hundred years ago. Not now.

Do I think my stories will change our world? Not really. Do I think our cultural systems that hide the banality of our evil under terms like 'collateral damage' and 'I just obey orders' are greatly different from cultural systems that hide the banality of their evil under terms such as 'the *atua* call for sacrifice'? No, I do not. Do I think that a marine describing the effects of his explosions as 'pink misting' very different from a warrior prancing around his kill? No, I do not.

Perhaps my ending should be pessimistic, but I am not inclined to that. There is too much immortality in a book on a shelf not to live by the hope that every idea and story has a future. I, who owe the past so much precisely because the past has a future on paper and in books, must think that having put pen on paper I will have a reader somewhere, sometime. To what words would I like the reader to reduce these thousands of words of mine? These.

Dare to voyage across times, cultures and self. Especially self. Especially self on the beaches of times and cultures. Set your global positioning system to edginess, in-between. The heroes in these stories of mine—Gauguin, Melville, Robarts, Kabris, Crook—have all put their selves in part on edge. They discovered that polarities on a beach do not work. They had to give something of their selves. In return they received a gift back. A small ray of understanding of the otherness within them. Crossing beaches will do that.

Notes on Selected Issues

My notes are an acknowledgement—not fact by fact, but by idea and inspiration—of those scholars I have been principally dependent on in this study. More importantly, my notes are meant to inspire further reading.

Prologue: A Most Remarkable Voyage

It seemed important at this time in our discourse on the encounter between Native and Stranger in the Sea of Islands to give priority to the most important historical event of the arrival of the Natives in their Land. For the data that makes my historical narrative possible, see below, Chapter 4, Finding the Land.

Beginning

The essential cross-cultural experience is to enter the metaphors of others. Perhaps it is the essential reading experience, also.

Encompass

Ornithological information on the yolla can be found in the *Handbook of Australian, New Zealand and Antarctic Birds*, Vol. I: *Ratites to Ducks*, S. Marchant and P. J. Higgins, eds (Melbourne: Oxford University Press, 1990). See '*Puffinus tenuirostris*, Short-tailed Shearwater', pp. 632–44. The yolla's story is told in Vincent Serventy, *The Flight of the Shearwater* (Kenthurst, NSW: Kangaroo Press, 1998). Matthew Flinders' count of what he called 'sooty petrels' is to be found in his *Voyage to Terra Australis* (London: G. and W. Nicholls, 1814), Vol. I, p. clxx.

Beaches

Beaches have long been a metaphor for me to voyage by; see Greg Dening, *Islands and Beaches: Discourse on a Silent Land, Marquesas, 1774–1880* (Melbourne: Melbourne University Press, 1980). Anyone interested in pursuing a different perspective on beaches should read John Stilgoe's brilliant *Alongshore* (New Haven: Yale University Press, 1994); Alain Corbin, *The Lure of the Sea: The Discovery of the Seaside in the Western World, 1750–1840* (London: Penguin, 1994), and Rachel Carson, *The Edge of the Sea* (London: Penguin, 1999).

1 Writing the Beach

History always begins there, where living is inscribed somehow. That is its first theatre.

Edward Robarts

Robarts' journal with all the information available to verify and enlarge his story is to be found in Greg Dening, ed., *The Marquesan Journal of Edward Robarts* (Canberra: ANU Press, 1974). The Pacific Manuscripts Bureau, Australian National University, Canberra, has edited in microfilm the logs and journals of whalers entering the Pacific in the nineteenth century. Harry Morton's *The Whale's Wake* (Dunedin: University of Otago Press, 1995) is as near an ethnographic study of whaling as I have encountered. Margaret Creighton's *Rites and Passages: The Experience of American Whaling, 1830–1870* (Cambridge: Cambridge University Press, 1995) would be his best challenge on that score.

Joseph Kabris

One version of Joseph Kabris, *Précis historique et véritable du séjour de Joseph Kabris, dans les îles de Mendoça* (Geneva: J. J. Luc Sestiè, 1820) is to be found in translation in Jennifer Terrell, 'Joseph Kabris and his notes on the Marquesas', *Journal of Pacific History*, 1982, 17: 101–12. My story of Kabris at Quiberon Bay is built on information from Maurice Hult, *Choannerie and Counter-Revolution* (Cambridge: Cambridge University Press, 1983); James Dugan, *The Great Mutiny* (London: Andre Deutsch, 1966); Patrick Crowhurst, *The French War on Trade: Privateering, 1793–1815* (London: Aldershot: Scolar Press, 1989). Robert Ker Porter's account of Kabris is to be found in his *Travelling Sketches in Russia and Sweden during the Years 1805 . . . 1808* (London, 1809).

William Pascoe Crook

Crook's (and Samuel Greatheed's) 'Account of the Marquesas Islands' (Ms CIII, Mitchell Library, Sydney) and 'An Essay toward a Dictionary and Grammar of the Lesser-Australian Language, According to the Dialect used at the Marquesas' (London Missionary Society Papers, London School of Oriental and African Studies Library) remain unpublished. Douglas Peacocke, a descendant of Crook, has written a biography, *William Pascoe Crook, 1775–1846* (Perth: Peacocke Press, 1995), which contains generous quotations of Crook's many letters. A sensitive understanding of the nature of Crook's experiences on his beach is to be found in Alex Calder, 'The Temptation of William Pascoe Crook: An experience of cultural difference in the Marquesas, 1796–98', *Journal of Pacific History*, 1996, 31: 144–61. Timotete's story is to be found in 'Temouteitei, or as He has been Called after the Name of the Ship which Brought Him to England, John Butterworth', *Evangelical Magazine*, 1800: 3–14. All the unpublished data of my research on the Crook manuscripts is now available in the Mitchell Library, Sydney. See Greg Dening, 'The William Pascoe Crook Papers'.

2 Being There

My story of 'being there' is no triumph of ethnographic science, and is only a little longer in time than Herman Melville's three weeks. But it is my story and the only one that I've got.

I have 'been there' in Fenua'enata in the company of many scholars— Karl von den Steinen (1899), E. S. Craighill Handy (1923) and Willowdean Handy (1963, 1973), Louis Rollin (1929) prominent among them. Their contributions can be seen in bibliographies of the Marquesas Islands such as mine in *Islands and Beaches*, pp. 310–44. Nicholas Thomas, *Marquesan Societies: Inequality and Political Transformation in Easter Polynesia* (Oxford: Clarendon Press, 1990) adds to that bibliography and contributes to a more general discussion of the place of Fenua'enata in general anthropological theory. Walter T. Herbert, *Marquesan Encounters: Melville and the Meaning of Civilization* (Cambridge, Mass.: Harvard University Press, 1980) adds a literary perspective. Perhaps the most insightful study has been the posthumous publication, Alfred Gell, *Wrapping in Images: Tattooing in Polynesia* (Oxford: Clarendon Press, 1993). I am greatly dependent on Gell's understanding of tattooing.

Any historical 'being there' is defined by archival experience. My 'being there' experience has come from The Congregation of the Sacred Hearts of Jesus and Mary Archives, Rome, and the papers there of Père Gérauld Chaulet, Père Siméon Delmas, Mgr René Ildephonse Dordillon; The Hawaiian Mission Board Papers in the Hawaiian Mission Library, Honolulu, and the papers there of Richard Armstrong, W. P. Alexander, Benjamin Parker, T. C. Lawson; The London Missionary Society Archives in the London School of Oriental and African Studies and the papers of W. P. Crook, David Darling, Thomas Haweis, George Stallworthy, Robert Thomson, John Rodgerson. The Archives d'Outre-Mer de France, Paris, 'Océanie 1842–82. Rapports et correspondences d'établissements francaises in Océanie' gave me a presence in Fenua'enata during Melville's stay there and through the destruction of Enata culture. Georges Louis Winter left his memoirs in the *Bulletin de la Société de géographie de l'est, Nancy* 1882–84, 4: 292–312, 697–702; 5: 150–9; 6: 366–74, 451–65. As did M. Collet, 'Iles Marquises, avril à juillet 1843', *Annales Maritimes et Coloniales*, 1844, 87: 336–48.

Paul Gauguin's *Avant et Après* (1903) is to be found in translation in Daniel Guérin, ed., *The Writings of a Savage* (New York: Paragon House, 1990), pp. 229–84. Bengt Danielsson's classic *Gauguin in the South Seas* (London: George Allen and Unwin, 1965) remains the best account of Gauguin's stay in Fenua'enata. Stephen Eisenman, *Gauguin's Skirt* (London: Thames and Hudson, 1997) and David Sweetman, *Paul Gauguin: A Complete Life* (London: Hodder and Stoughton, 1995) are both the most controversial and the most detailed analyses of Gauguin's art.

Hershel Parker's *Herman Melville: A Biography*, Vol. I, *1819–1851*, and Vol. II, *1851–1891* (Baltimore: The Johns Hopkins University Press, 1996, 2002) is an exhaustive study of Melville's life by a scholar whose knowledge of the writer cannot be matched. Ruth Blair, in the Oxford University Press World's Classics series, offers the most recent and comprehensive edition of Melville's *Typee* (1996).

3 By Sea to the Beach

See notes to Chapter 1, Writing the Beach.

4 Finding the Land

Epeli Hau'ofa inspired the name 'Sea of Islands' for the Pacific in *A New Oceania: Rediscovery of our Sea of Islands* (Suva: University of the South Pacific, 1993). Those who write of the Sea of Islands from outside are happy to use the name. It gives a sense of identity to those who are the descendants of the great voyages that peopled this vast ocean space.

The scholars of archaelogical, anthropological, historical and cultural studies Patrick Kirch and Roger Green have led us all in their studies of ancestral Polynesia. Their most recent contribution is *Hawaiki, Ancestral Polynesia* (Cambridge: Cambridge University Press, 2001). Patrick Vinton Kirch, *On the Roads of the Winds: An Archaeological History of the Pacific Islands before European Contact* (Berkeley: University of California Press, 2000) offers a comprehensive study of the issues advanced in Finding the Land. The studies of Andrew Pawley, Malcolm Ross and Darrell Tryon on comparative linguistics and of Adrian Horridge on the Sea People's *va'a* in *The Austronesians*, Peter Bellwood, James J. Fox and Darrell Tryon, eds (Canberra: ANU Department of Anthropology, 1995) make the foundations on which I build the voyaging story in this section. Geoffrey Irwin, *The Prehistoric Exploration and Colonisation of the Pacific* (Cambridge: Cambridge University Press, 1992) has stirred much debate with his propositions about a continuing settlement of Remote Oceania rather than paused voyaging. Philip Houghton, *People of the Great Ocean: Aspects of Human Biology of the Early Pacific* (Cambridge: Cambridge University Press, 1996) describes the environmental and biological conditions that made voyaging to Remote Oeania possible.

Ben Finney tells the story of the intellectual debate and cultural achievements of the voyaging canoes' re-enactments in *Voyage of Rediscovery: A Cultural Odyssey Through Polynesia* (Berkeley: University of California Press, 1994). Finney's most comprehensive study of traditional navigation is to be found in his 'Nautical Cartography and Traditional Navigation in Oceania' in *The History of Cartography*, Vol. II, Book Three: *Cartography in the Traditional African, American, Arctic, Australian and Pacific Societies*, David Woodward and G. Malcolm Lewis, eds (Chicago: University of Chicago Press, 1998), pp. 448–92.

I have referred in the text to my obligations to Thomas Gladwin, *East is a Big Bird: Navigation and Logic on Pulawal Atoll* (Cambridge, Mass.: Harvard University Press, 1970) and David Lewis, *We the Navigators: The*

Ancient Art of Landfalling in the Pacific (Canberra: ANU Press, 1972*)*. I should add Edward Dodd's inspiring study *Polynesian Seafaring* (New York: Dodd, Mead and Company, 1972).

My own contribution to the debate was 'The Geographical Knowledge of the Polynesians and the Nature of Inter-Island Contact' in Jack Golson, ed., *Polynesian Navigation: A Symposium on Andrew Sharp's Theory of Accidental Voyages* (Wellington: A. H. and A. W. Reed, 1972), pp. 102–58.

Will Kyselka, *An Ocean in Mind* (Honolulu: University of Hawai'i Press, 1987), gave me the story of *Hokule'a*'s voyage from Tahiti to Hawai'i and the quotations from Nainoa Thompson.

5 Encompassing the Land

Our understanding of how Enata inspirited their Land is kaleidoscopic and cumulative from the transient experience of hundreds of visitors to Fenua'enata. It is the way of things that these visitors go home and describe their experiences of the exotic to their superiors, their families and those that will come to hear them in their local academic and scientific associations. Whatever knowledge I have of Fenua'enata comes from them. Let me sample something of it.

Buisson, G. P. E., 'Les îles Marquises et les Marquisiens', *Annales d'hygiène et de médecine coloniales*, 1903, 6: 535–59.

Chaulet, *le P*. Gérauld, 'Notice géographiques ethnographiques et religieuses', 1873. Archives of The Congregation of the Sacred Hearts of Jesus and Mary [CSSJ], Rome.

—— 'Notice historique religieuse sur les îles Marquises', 1873. Archives CSSJ, Rome.

—— 'Botanique des îles Marquises', 1890. Archives CSSJ, Rome.

Collet, M., 'Îles Marquises: fête donnée à Noukahiva', *Annales maritimes et coloniales*, 1843, 83: 250–5.

Darling, David, 'Journal Dec. 8 1834 – Sept. 1835'. London Missionary Society Journals, Box 8, London School of Oriental and African Studies Library.

Dordillon, René Ildephonse, 'Notice sur la religion et le tatouage aux îles Marquises adressé au P. Omer'. Archives CSSJ, Rome.

Jardin, Edelstan, 'Essai sur l'histoire naturelle de l'archipel de Mendana ou des Marquises. Géologie et minérologie', *Mémoires de la Société impériale des sciences naturelles et mathématique de Cherbourg*, 1856, 4: 49–61.

—— 'Essai sur l'histoire naturelle de l'archipel de Mendana ou des Marquises. Botanique', *Mémoires de la Société impériale des sciences naturelles et mathématique de Cherbourg*, 1857, 5: 289–331.

—— 'Essai sur l'histoire naturelle de l'archipel de Mendana ou des Marquises. Zoologie', *Mémoires de la Société impériale des sciences naturelles et mathématique de Cherbourg*, 1858, 6: 161–200.

Lallour, Valéry, *Iles Marquises, notes sur les Marquises, 1843–1848*. 5 vols. Alexander Turnbull Library, Wellington.

Lawson, T. C., 'Notes of T. C. Lawson to Damon, Jan. 28 1866, Taiohae'. Hawaiian Mission Library, Honolulu.

—— 'Lawson Marquesan Manuscript', 1867. Bernice P. Bishop Museum, Honolulu.

Lecornu, *le P*. Jean, 'Notes sur les dieux et autres objets de religion chez les kanaks', n.d. Archives CSSJ, Taiohae, Nukuhiva.

Tautain, L. F., 'Etude sur le mariage chez les Polynésiens (Mao'i) des îles Marquises', *Anthropologie*, 1895, 6: 640–51.

—— 'Sur l'anthopophagie et les sacrifices humains aus îles Marquises', *Anthropologie*, 1896, 7: 443–52.

—— 'Sur la religion des Polynésiens', *Anthropologie*, 1896, 7: 543–52.

Virey, J. J., 'Remarques sur la flore économiques des îles Marquises et de la Société', *Journal de phamarcie et de chimie*, 1843, 4: 298–301.

I am not being falsely modest if I describe my linguistic skills as poor. Mgr Hervé Le Cleac'h has always inspired me to better them. His *Lexique Marquisien–Français: Pona Te'ao Tapaptina* (Papeete: 'Eo Enata, 1997) is an ethnographic dictionary in its cultural and linguistic detail. His translation of *Islands and Beaches*, entitled *Marquises, 1774–1880: Refléxion sure une terre muette* (Papeete: 'Eo Enata, 1999) corrected my orthographic errors and made this present study more sure.

6 *The Strangers Come*

Hope

Joseph Ingraham, ed. M. D. Kaplanoff, *Journal of the Brigantine Hope on a Voyage to the Northwest Coast of North America, 1790–2* (Barre, Mass.: Imprint Society, 1971).

Solide

Louis Infernet, 'Le voyage de vaisseau le *Solide* autour du monde', *Revue Maritime*, 1913–14, 96: 15–24, 181–90, 325–34; 97: 25–31; C. P. Claret Fleurieu, *A Voyage Round the World, 1790–1792, Performed by Etienne Marchand* (London: Longman and Rees, 1801; Da Capo Press, 1969).

Daedalus

Greg Dening, *The Death of William Gooch: A History's Anthropology* (Melbourne and Honolulu: Melbourne University Press and University of Hawai'i Press, 1995).

Jefferson

Bernard Magee, 'Journal of a Voyage on the Ship Jefferson, 1791–1792', Ms. Massachusetts Historical Society, Boston; Josiah Roberts, 'The Discovery and Description of the Islands called the Marquesas', *Collections of the Massachusetts Historical Society*, 1795, 4: 238–46.

7 On the Beach

Otherness on the beach is two-sided. How three strangers coped with the relativities imposed on them in their aloneness is more easily told than how those who were native to the beach transformed themselves in response to being positioned in a world which had little interest in them other than curiosity and exploitation. The truth is that this other, native, side of the beach lasts longer than we think, into our present and their future. Enata's story is still to be told. Deep time lasts long into the millennia. I wish I would be around to hear Enata's story told by them. But it is enough to sense its stirring.

The visit of the Russian expedition to Nukuhiva in 1804 is described in Adam J. Von Krusenstern [Kruzenshtern], *Voyage Round the World in the Years 1803, 1804, 1805, and 1806* ... (London: John Murray, 1813; Da Capo Press 1968); Georges H. Von Langsdorff, *Voyages and Travels in Various Parts of the World* ... (London: Henry Colburn, 1814; Da Capo Press 1968); Urey Lisiansky, *A Voyage Round the World* ... (London: John Booth, 1814; Da Capo Press 1968).

Edmund Fanning tells his story of rescuing Crook in *Voyages and Discoveries in the South Seas, 1792–1832* (Salem, Mass.: Marine Research Society, 1924).

Harry Maude's paper on 'Beachcombers and Castaways' is to be found in H. E. Maude, *Of Islands and Men* (Melbourne: Oxford University Press, 1968).

Crossings

Voyaging into Deep Time

That reading could be a metaphor for crossing and a dance on the beaches of the mind comes to me from Michel de Certeau, *The Practice of Everyday Life* (Berkeley: University of California Press, 1988), pp. 165–76. R. S. Khare's words on untouchable women can be found in 'The Body, Sensoria, and Self of the Powerless: Remembering/"Re-Membering" Indian Untouchable Women', *New Literary History*, 26, 1995: 147–68. My thoughts on catharsis and mythos come from Stephen Halliwell, *Aristotle's Poetics* (Chapel Hill: University of North Carolina Press, 1986). W. E. H. Stanner's report on the old man and the forces in dreaming are to be found in his *White Man Got No Dreaming: Essays, 1938-1973* (Canberra: ANU Press, 1979).

An Archaeology of Believing

François Lyotard's words on the Terror are quoted in Michel de Certeau, *The Practice of Everyday Life* (Berkeley: University of California Press, 1988), p. 165.

An Archaeology of Learning

Johan Reinhold Forster's difficulties in measuring the temperature of the sea are to be seen in his *Observations Made During a Voyage Round the World*, Nicholas Thomas, Harriet Guest and Michael Dettelbach, eds (Honolulu: University of Hawai'i Press, 1996), pp. 55ff.

Way-finding

Tupaia's paintings are to be found in Rüdiger Joppien and Bernard Smith, *The Art of Captain Cook's Voyages*, Vol. 1: *The Voyage of the Endeavour, 1768–71* (Melbourne: Oxford University Press, 1985). They are discussed by Glyndwir Williams, 'Tupaia: Polynesian Warrior, Navigator—Artist' in Felicity Nussbaum, ed., *The Global Eighteenth Century* (Baltimore: The Johns Hopkins University Press, 2003), pp. 38–51. My own description of Tupaia is to be found in Greg Dening, 'The Hegemony of Laughter:

Purea's Theatre', *Pacific Empires*, Alan Frost and Jane Samson, eds (Melbourne: Melbourne University Press, 1999), pp. 127–46, and Greg Dening, 'Possessing Tahiti' in *Performances* (Melbourne: Melbourne University Press, 1996), pp. 128–67. Ben Finney's most recent reflections on *Hokule'a*'s voyages are to be found in his *Sailing in the Wake of the Ancestors: Reviving Polynesian Voyaging* (Honolulu: Bishop Museum Press, 2003).

'Ethnogging'

John Dewey's reflections on the nature of 'an experience' are to be found in John Dewey, *The Art of Experience* (New York: Minton, 1934). I learned to think sociologically about Jean-Paul Sartre's notion of 'bad faith' through Peter Berger's *Invitation to Sociology* (Garden City, NY: Doubleday and Anchor, 1963). On matters of structure, metaphor, theatre and sacrament, I have been deeply influenced by Mary Douglas, *Implicit Meanings* (London: Routledge and Kegan, 1975); E. E. Evans-Pritchard, *The Nuer* (Oxford: Clarendon Press, 1940); Victor Turner, *The Anthropology of Performance* (New York: PAJ Publications, 1988).

'Remember me?'

See Ludwig Wittgenstein, *Philosophical Investigations*, G. E. M. Anscombe and R. Rhees, eds (Oxford: Blackwall, 1953) on language games and their fictions. My thoughts on the fictions of language and the theatre of history are more fully explained in 'The Theatricality of History-Making and the Paradoxes of Acting', *Cultural Anthropology*, 8, 1993: 73–95; 'The Theatricality of Observing and Being Observed: "Eighteenth Century" "Europe" "discovers" the "? Century" "Pacific"' in *Implicit Understandings*, Stuart B. Schwartz, ed. (Cambridge: Cambridge University Press, 1994), pp. 451–84.

Performing

Harlan Page wrote a small pamphlet on Hami Patu, *Memoir of Thomas H. Patoo of the Marquesas Islands* (New York, 1830), from which I have drawn much of my story.

EVERY MOMENT OF my voyaging across times, cultures and self through these fifty years has been in the company of others. This has been its richness and pleasure. For thirty of these years the closest of my companions has been my wife, Donna Merwick. There has not been a word that either of us has written which the other has not read and made recommendations on. Her innovative spirit in *Death of a Notary: Conquest and Change in Colonial New York* (Ithaca: Cornell University Press, 1999) and her meticulous, exhaustive research in *Possessing Albany, 1630–1710: The Dutch and English Experience* (New York: Cambridge University Press, 2002) gave me courage and energy. Those thirty years have coincided with scholarly friendships that have raised all our spirits and inspired risk-taking in our writing. Inga Clendinnen's first book, *Ambivalent Conquests: Maya and Spaniard in Yucatan, 1517–1570* (Cambridge: Cambridge University Press, 1987) and Rhys Isaac's first, *The Transformation of Virginia, 1740–1790* (Chapel Hill: University of North Carolina Press, 1982) confirmed our shared belief that whatever our individual expertise we were part of a global discourse across disciplines, genres and topics. In Roland Barthes' phrase, our pleasure was in the many texts that filled our imagination.

I cannot hope to list all these pleasures of the text. Let me acknowledge just some. Clifford Geertz (*The Interpretation of Cultures*, 1973); Marshall Sahlins (*Historical Metaphors and Mythical Realities*, 1981); Roland Barthes (*The Pleasure of the Text*, 1975); Frantz Fanon (*The Wretched of the Earth*, 1961); Paul Fussell (*The Great War and Modern Memory*, 1975); Claude Lévi-Strauss (*Tristes Tropiques*, 1961); Ronald Blythe (*Akenfield*, 1969); C. Wright Mills *(The Sociological Imagination*, 1960); W. E. H. Stanner (*White Man Got No Dreaming*, 1979); Howard Zinn (*The Politics of History*, 1970); H. E. Maude *(Of Islands and Men*, 1968); D. J. Mulvaney (*Encounters in Place: Outsiders and Aboriginal Australians, 1606–1985*, 1989); Dipesh Chakrabarty (*Rethinking Working-Class History: Bengal, 1890–1940*, 1989); Shlomo Avineri (*The Social and Political Thought of Karl Marx*, 1969); Tom Griffiths (*Hunters and Collectors: The Antiquarian Imagination in Australian History*, 1996); Chris Healy (*From the Ruins of Colonialism: History as Social Memory*, 1997); Hayden White (*Metahistory*, 1973); Oscar Lewis (*Children of Sanchez*, 1968); Richard Rorty (*Contingency, Irony and Solidarity*, 1989); Rowan Ireland (*Kingdoms Come: Religion and Politics in Brazil*, 1991); Peter Berger (*Invitation to Sociology: A Humanistic Perspective*, 1965); Edward W. Said (*Orientalism*, 1978); E. P. Thompson (*The Making of the English Working Class*, 1963); Norbert Elias (*The Civilizing Process*, 1978); Victor Turner (*From Ritual to Theater*, 1982); Richard Price (*Alabi's World*, 1990); Robert F. Berkhofer (*The White Man's Indian*, 1978); A. L. Becker (*Beyond Translation: Essays towards a Modern Philology*, 1995); Michael Taussig (*Shamanism,*

Colonialism, and the Wild Man, 1987); Bernard Smith (*European Vision and the South Pacific, 1768–1850,* 1960); Kenneth E. Boulding (*The Image: Knowledge in Life and Society,* 1966); Edmund Leach (*Culture and Communication: The Logic by which Symbols are Connected,* 1976).

There is no advancement in scholarly knowledge without the altruistic gift of time and energy that the editors of journals and the officers of associations give to their disciplines. *The Journal of Pacific History, The Journal of the Polynesian Society, The Contemporary Pacific, Pacific Studies, Ethnohistory, Rethinking History, History and Theory, Representations, Australian Historical Studies, The Pacific Manuscripts Bureau Newsletter* have given my mind and spirit sustenance over many years.

It has been my fervent hope over the years that young islander scholars would make a larger and larger contribution to our discourse on the Sea of Islands. They have honoured me and given me their respect. I thank them for that. Kaoha! I say to them. Their hopes and insights are to be seen in *The Contemporary Pacific: A Journal of Island Affairs,* Volume 13, Number 2, Fall 2001, ed. Vicente M. Diaz and J. Kehaulani Kauanui. I have learned much from the work of these editors and I honour them with Teresia and Katerina Teaiwa, Vilsoni Hereniko, and Lilikala Kame'eleihiwa.

Acknowledgements

The whole of this book in my mind has been an acknowledgement of all those who have given of their time, energy, knowledge, wisdom and love to me in my life of learning—librarians, archivists, teachers, scholars, writers, editors, lecturers, students, colleagues, friends and family. In a world so interconnected, in a life so saturated with the thoughts of others, modesty and gratitude are very proper virtues. Unacknowledged debts will no doubt pursue us to the end. A book, however, forever speaks from the grave. I like the thought of that.

I remember—oh! so many years ago—being teased by Thomas Aquinas' thesis that self touches all human love. Only divine love is selfless. There is no giving that is not also self-giving. No ideal is so pure that it is pursued only for itself. For myself, it was a privilege to live for twenty-two years, from when I was sixteen years of age to when I was thirty-eight, in the company of men who strove to live out their highest ideals, who tried to discover how their love of Jesus Christ made them 'men for others'. Just as it was a privilege to spend hours every day seeking wisdom and understanding from the sacred texts that filled our lives and measuring how we stood in relation to our ideals. There were young men whom I loved dearly and admired even more. None more than those who were tested in their vow of obedience and were sent at my age and with the same sense of bourgeois comfortableness as I had to work in India among the poorest poor. I thank them all for the laughter we shared and the inspiration they gave. Their faces and voices are frozen in my memory as they were fifty years ago. One of them, a gentle, generous man, full of scruples, has taken his own life in the most horrible circumstances as I write these last pages.

Unacknowledged debts pursue us to the end. No need for his name. Just a few of the others, though. Ken McNamara SJ, Maurie Dullard SJ, John Reilly SJ, Ferruccio Romanin SJ, Gerald Daily SJ, Barry Leonard SJ, Kevin King SJ, Antony Ruhan SJ, John Ramsay SJ, Ted Rorty SJ, John Cowburn SJ.

There is deliciousness in studying when that is all that has to be done, and when professors persuade their students of the newness of their understanding and the creativity of the students' contribution. We laughed at our professors' foibles, mimicked their voices and their habits in the theatre of our institutional life. But whether it was transcendental philosophy (Pat McEvoy SJ), scripture (Bill Dalton SJ, John Scullion SJ), canon law and moral theology (Peter Kelly SJ), sacramental theology (Peter Kenny SJ), Ignatian spirituality (Val Moran SJ), our professors persuaded us that our Australian seminary was as large as the church and our learning a living dialogue. We had companionship, too, of men whose passion for scholarship always reminded us that if we were men of faith we were also men of learning—Ted Stormon SJ, Noel Ryan SJ, Jim Flynn SJ. We were given the freedom to devote ourselves to these things of the mind and soul by a group of practical men who served us with their hands and bodies, as cooks, mechanics, carpenters, bookbinders, jacks-of-all-trades. They were the 'brothers'—Jack Stamp SJ, Maurie Joyce SJ, Ray Harris SJ, Frank Hudson SJ, John May SJ.

The politics of academic life have never been to my taste. I admire those who take on administrative responsibility but confess that teaching, researching and writing have given me the fullest satisfaction. For many years I have railed against the divisiveness of departments, faculties and disciplines that denies students the fullness of their experience of the university, but it is the altruism of my colleagues in the departments of history at LaTrobe and Melbourne universities that has enriched my academic life. We have fiercely debated teaching methods, syllabi and self-government. There has been hurt and jealousy, stubbornness and occasional nastiness and dishonesty, but I have always been edified—now there is a word that comes from my Jesuit past—by their idealism and their humane pursuit of excellence. I thank them for their inspiration, in particular Charles Zika, Graeme Davison, Barbara Falk, Pat Grimshaw, Chips Sowerwine, Stuart Macintyre, Don Miller, Alan Frost, John Salmond, Bill Breen, Jack Gregory, John Cashmere, Katy Richmond, Rowan Ireland. And of course, Rhys Isaac and Inga Clendinnen. There are those who won't see my thanks: Ian Robertson, Norman Harper, John Forster, Bill Culican, Sow Teng Leong, Laurie Gardiner and Graham Little.

If all of learning were out of books, then perhaps I have made my acknowledgements in my notes, but learning is far more mysterious than that. Loyalty, love, talk, argument, listening, play their part. I have some two thousand academic email addresses in my computer to remind me that the nature of learning has changed in recent years, but my memory takes me back to conversations, lectures, readings that shaped my thinking. Thank you: Ken Lockridge, Niel Gunson, Marshall Sahlins, David Allmendinger, Cliff Geertz, Bronwyn Douglas, Gavan Daws, Rob Borofsky, Donald Denoon, James Boon, Natalie Zemon Davis, Bill Gammage, Barry Gough, Jonathan Lamb, Akos Ostor, Klaus Neumann, Carmel Schrire, Stan Katz, Bob Langdon, John Demos. Thank you too, students of 'mine': Tom Griffiths, David Hanlon, Michael Cathcart, David Goodman, Elizabeth Wood-Ellem, Margaret Chambers, Ron Adams, David Bereson, Shane Carmody, Marie Fels, Chris Healy, John Murphy, Jan Critchett. Those issues with which this book has been much concerned—faith and knowledge, certainty and uncertainty, believing, living with the church—have also been the issues which have preoccupied a group of friends—friends? Much more than friends. We have tried to meet monthly since 1969 for reflection, discussion, and communion. These fellow pilgrims are precious to me: Virginia and Douglas Kennedy, David McKenna, Marie and Gerry Joyce, Henry and Jenny Burger, John and Kathy Funder, Val Diamond, Tony and Margaret Coady.

I have disappointed many a bookseller over the years. I have been just as happy with the reprint as I have been with the first edition. What a book says has been more important to me than its collector's value. But the aesthetics of a book matters a great deal to me as a writer. I have always told my students to exploit their computers to make their manuscripts things of beauty. Let me acknowledge Melbourne University Publishing for making *Beach Crossings* a beautiful thing through their Miegunyah Press. Louise Adler, the first director of Melbourne University Press transformed into Melbourne University Publishing paid me the compliment of being the first reader and critic of my manuscript. After dealing with a number of directors of academic presses through thirteen books, this was a novel experience for me. But Peter Agree, the Social Science Editor of the University of Pennsylvania Press, which is co-publishing *Beach Crossings*, paid me the same compliment and gave me constant support. I thank them both, and Teresa Pitt who managed

361

all my previous books with Melbourne University Press and encouraged me to take my time with *Beach Crossings*. Louise and Peter both gave me the freedom to express my ideas on design to Sybil Nolan (Managing Editor, Text), Janet Mackenzie, my diligent and gracious copy-editor, and Lauren Statham who has designed several books of mine. The work of a young designer, Emily Brissenden, had attracted my attention. It is she who has drawn all the maps, endpapers and tattoo icons. She has been very patient with me. Her work in my view is exquisite. I was inspired to ask for the interpretive drawings you see in *Beach Crossings* by Willowdean Handy's own drawings in *Thunder from the Sea* (ANU Press, Canberra, 1973), her novel about Pakoko. William Gooch's drawing of Tainai (p. 207) is reproduced with the permission of The Syndics of Cambridge University from his 'Letters, Memorials and Journal' (Ms Mm 6-48, Cambridge University Library). The illustrations of *Pahutiki*—'Wrapped in Images' (p. 10), of Joseph Kabris—*Le Tatoué* (p. 33) and of *Toa*—Warrior (p. 330 and cover) are reproduced from G. H. von Langsdorff, *Voyages and Travels in Various Parts of the World, 1803–1807*, Volume I (London: 1813–14: Da Capo Press 1968), Plates V, VI and VII. Honu (p. 184) is an engraving by J. Hall after William Hodges in James Cook, *Voyage towards the South Pole and Round the World* . . . (London: W. Strahan and T. Cadell, 1777) I, Plate XXXVI. Timotete (p. 184) is the engraving that illustrated 'Timouteitei, or as He has been called after the Name of the Ship which Brought Him to England, John Butterworth', *Evangelical Magazine*, 1800: 3-14. Tana'oa—The Godliness of Sea and Wind (p. 344) was photographed in the Mission Archives, Taiohae, Fenua'enata by Greg Dening. Geoff and Sandra Goonan walked many beaches to photograph for me that gleaming strand where the sea soaks into the sand. I thank them for that, and even more for the years of their friendship and love.

For more than thirty years now, approaching half my life, I have had the love, companionship and support of Donna Merwick. A scholar and writer of international repute in her own right, she has been extravagantly generous in the time and thought she has given to my writings. This book is dedicated to the memory of our son Jonathan whom we lost soon after his birth. In truth, all my books are written for her, my first reader. I need no other *imprimatur* than her approval.

Glossary

ahui	a prohibition	*me'ae*	sacred place
ama	candlenut tree and nut	*mana*	power
aoe	stranger	*mei*	breadfruit
ari'i nui	high chief	*moa*	temple assistant
atua	possessed with godliness	Moana	Pacific Ocean (literally, Great Ocean)
ehi	coconut	*ouoho*	ornament of hair
e ika	'fishing'	*paepae*	house platform
e inoa	name, name exchange	*pahutiki*	tattooed (literally, wrapped in images)
ena	ginger plant		
enata	native	*pekio*	secondary husband
fa'e	house	*popoi*	breadfruit food dish
fau	hibiscus	*tapa*	bark cloth
fenua	land	*tapu*	set apart, sacred
hami	man's loincloth	*tau'a*	sorcerer
haka'iki	male chief	*temanu*	tree (*Calophyllis inophyllis*)
Hava'iki	Homeland (Samoa, Tonga, Fiji)		
		tiki	image
heana	victim	*toa*	warrior
hiapo	fig, red *tapa* cloth	*tohua*	assembly place
hoki	theatrical performers	*tuhuna*	expert
ika	fish	*tuhuna o'ono*	priest
ka'eu	woman's waist-cloth	*tuhuna pu'e*	sea expert
kai'oi	dancers	*va'a*	canoe
kikino	of low status	*va'a tauna*	double-hulled canoe
koina	feast	*vahine*	woman
ma	fermented breadfruit	*vahinetapu*	sacred woman
mau	memorial feast		

Conversions

$$1 \text{ inch } = 25.4 \text{ mm}$$
$$1 \text{ foot } = 30.5 \text{ cm}$$
$$1 \text{ yard } = 0.914 \text{ m}$$
$$1 \text{ fathom } = 1.82 \text{ m}$$
$$1 \text{ mile } = 1.61 \text{ km}$$

$$1 \text{ pound } = 454 \text{ g}$$
$$1 \text{ ton } = 1.02 \text{ t}$$

$$1 \text{ pint (imperial) } = 568 \text{ mL}$$
$$1 \text{ gallon (imperial) } = 4.55 \text{ L}$$

Index

Places
Nukuhiva (Nuk), Hiva Oa (HO), Tahuata (Tah), Ua Huka (UH), Ua Pou (UP), Fatuiva (Fa)

Persons and Peoples

Subjects

aboriginality 51
'Account of the Marquesas Islands' 40, 42
Acushnet 93, 94ff
adoption 193
Adventure 250
Alexander 278
altruism 143, 229, 243
anthropology 136, 276–8
ANZAC Day 231ff
archaeology 46–7, 101, 136ff
archives 89, 323–4
atua see godliness 5, 56, 157, 160ff, 217, 236, 297
Astrea 237
Austronesians 151–3
Australian National University 104
awakenings 318ff

'bad faith' 317
battles 293–4
beachcombers 17–8, 270
beaches 13, 16ff, 19, 31, 71, 74, 186, 270, 348
'being there' 55, 187ff
beliefs 99
believing 99
Betsy 281, 298
birds: as metaphor 179; as signs of land 181; at
    Taiohae 96; bristle-thighed curlew (*Numenius
    tahitiensis*) 164; golden plover (*Pluvialis fulva*)
    164; *komako* (yellow warbler) 96; *kuku* (green
    parrot) 96; migratory 164; *pihiti* (blue lorikeets)
    96; turnstone (*Arenaria interpres*) 164; yolla
    14ff, 165, 347–8
birth 195–6
Bounty 39, 123, 171, 250, 269
Breadfruit see *mei*
'Brueghelesque' painting 186, 209ff
Bristol 127
Burke Hall 259ff
Butterworth 120, 127, 282, 288, 303

Calcutta, HMS 341ff
cannibalism 90, 205, 277
Canisius College 136
canoes (*va'a*) 153–4, 182 see also *Hokule'a,
    Makali'i, Nahelia, Rainbow, Tahiti Nui, Taki-
    tumu, Te Au o Tonga, Te Aurere, Vav'au*, as
    metaphor of identity 182; as symbols of cross-
    ing 171; materials for 3–4; 'Oro's 171; Tupaia's
    painting of 173; *va'a tauna* 154, voyaging 182
catharsis 183, 327
Charles and Henry 93
coconut (*ehi*): uses of 212
Columbia 238
colour 70
common people 193ff
contingencies 193
Cornwall Historical society 318
cosmetics 213
creativity: in scholarship 264
crews: whaling 114
crossings: as metaphor 20ff; as soliloquy 44
culture: as order 13; as talk 226; teaching 226
culture contact 46

Daedalus 122, 246ff, 273, 301
dance 286–7, 301
difference 328–9
disciplines: and scholarship 264; socialising in 229
disputation 145ff
Dolphin, HMS 172
Duff 38, 39, 131ff, 271ff
Dumouriez 123

editing 30–1
education: at new institutions 228; in writing his-
    tory 259; postgraduate 262ff
e ika (fishing for victims) 60, 277
El Ñina 153
El Ñino 3, 15, 153

373

THE MIEGUNYAH PRESS

This book was designed and typeset by Lauren Statham
The text was set in 11 point ACaslon Regular with 14 points of leading
The text is printed on 100 gsm Miegunyah Ivory

This book was edited by Janet Mackenzie

Seven hundred and fifty copies of this edition were printed in Australia by
BPA Print Group